MW
SOS
07006074

Conflicts in Environmental Regulation and the Internationalisation of the State

This book examines the global regulation of biodiversity politics through the UN Convention on Biological Diversity (CBD), the WTO and other international treaties. Using historical-materialist state and regulation theory, it assesses how the discourse and politics of sustainable development have contributed to the internationalisation of the state.

The authors argue that sustainable development, far from being a fixed concept, is a conceptual terrain on which different and conflicting symbolisations of and responses to the ecological crisis struggle for hegemony. Furthermore, they show that the multilateral environmental agreements are not at all a means to counteract neoliberal globalisation but, on the contrary, form an integral part of the ongoing transformation process. Focusing on the CBD, the FAO International Treaty on Plant Genetic Resources for Food and Agriculture and the Agreement on Trade-related Aspects of Intellectual Property Rights (TRIPS) in the World Trade Organisation, this co-authored volume addresses the following issues:

- state theory, regulation theory and International Political Economy
- biodiversity protection and valorisation of genetic resources
- access to genetic resources and sharing of benefits which arise out of its use
- enforcement of intellectual property rights and their impact on biodiversity.

This book will be of interest to students and scholars of international politics, International Political Economy, Environmental Studies, Development Studies and Political Ecology.

Ulrich Brand is Professor of International Politics at Vienna University, Austria. **Christoph Görg** is Professor of Environmental Governance at Kassel University and Senior Researcher at the Helmholtz Centre for Environmental Research-UFZ in Leipzig, Germany. **Joachim Hirsch** is Emeritus Professor in the Department of Social Sciences, University of Frankfurt, Germany. **Markus Wissen** is Assistant Professor of the Institute for Political Science at Vienna University, Austria.

RIPE Series in Global Political Economy

Series Editors: Louise Amoore (*University of Newcastle, UK*), Randall Germain (*Carleton University, Canada*) and Rorden Wilkinson (*University of Manchester, UK*) Formerly edited by Otto Holman (*University of Amsterdam*), Marianne Marchand (*Universidad de las Américas-Puebla*), Henk Overbeek (*Free University, Amsterdam*) and Marianne Franklin (*Goldsmiths, University of London, UK*)

The RIPE series editorial board are:
Mathias Albert (*Bielefeld University, Germany*), Mark Beeson (*University of Queensland, Australia*), A. Claire Cutler (*University of Victoria, Canada*), Marianne Franklin (*Goldsmiths, University of London, UK*), Stephen Gill (*York University, Canada*), Jeffrey Hart (*Indiana University, USA*), Eric Helleiner (*Trent University, Canada*), Otto Holman (*University of Amsterdam, the Netherlands*), Marianne H. Marchand (*Universidad de las Américas-Puebla, Mexico*), Craig N. Murphy (*Wellesley College, USA*), Robert O'Brien (*McMaster University, Canada*), Henk Overbeek (*Vrije Universiteit, the Netherlands*), Anthony Payne (*University of Sheffield, UK*) and V. Spike Peterson (*University of Arizona, USA*).

This series, published in association with the *Review of International Political Economy*, provides a forum for current debates in international political economy. The series aims to cover all the central topics in IPE and to present innovative analyses of emerging topics. The titles in the series seek to transcend a state-centred discourse and focus on three broad themes:

- the nature of the forces driving globalisation forward
- resistance to globalisation
- the transformation of the world order.

The series comprises two strands:
The *RIPE Series in Global Political Economy* aims to address the needs of students and teachers, and the titles will be published in hardback and paperback. Titles include:

Transnational Classes and International Relations
Kees van der Pijl

Global Political Economy
Contemporary theories
Edited by Ronen Palan

Gender and Global Restructuring
Sightings, sites and resistances
Edited by Marianne H. Marchand and Anne Sisson Runyan

Ideologies of Globalization
Contending visions of a new world order
Mark Rupert

The Clash within Civilisations
Coming to terms with cultural
conflicts
Dieter Senghaas

Global Unions?
Theory and strategies of organized
labour in the global political
economy
*Edited by Jeffrey Harrod and
Robert O'Brien*

Political Economy of a Plural
World
Critical reflections on power, morals
and civilizations
*Robert Cox with Michael
Schechter*

A Critical Rewriting of Global
Political Economy
Integrating reproductive, productive
and virtual economies
V. Spike Peterson

Contesting Globalization
Space and place in the world
economy
André C. Drainville

Global Institutions and
Development
Framing the world?
*Edited by Morten Bøås and
Desmond McNeill*

Global Institutions, Marginalization,
and Development
Craig N. Murphy

Critical Theories, International
Relations and 'the Anti-Globalisation
Movement'
The politics of global resistance
*Edited by Catherine Eschle and
Bice Maiguashca*

Globalization, Governmentality,
and Global Politics
Regulation for the rest of us?
*Ronnie D. Lipschutz, with James
K. Rowe*

Critical Perspectives on Global
Governance
Rights and regulation in governing
regimes
Jean Grugel and Nicola Piper

Routledge/RIPE Studies in Global Political Economy is a forum for innovative new research intended for a high-level specialist readership, and the titles will be available in hardback only. Titles include:

1 Globalization and Governance*
   *Edited by Aseem Prakash and
   Jeffrey A. Hart*

2 Nation-States and Money
   The past, present and future of
   national currencies
   *Edited by Emily Gilbert and Eric
   Helleiner*

3 The Global Political Economy of
   Intellectual Property Rights
   The new enclosures?
   Christopher May

4 Integrating Central Europe
   EU expansion and Poland, Hungary
   and the Czech Republic
   Otto Holman

4579708

Conflicts in Environmental Regulation and the Internationalisation of the State

Contested terrains

Ulrich Brand, Christoph Görg, Joachim Hirsch and Markus Wissen

Routledge
Taylor & Francis Group

LONDON AND NEW YORK

2 3 MAY 2008

First published 2008
by Routledge
2 Park Square, Milton Park, Abingdon, Oxon OX14 4RN

Simultaneously published in the USA and Canada
by Routledge
270 Madison Avenue, New York, NY 10016, USA

Routledge is an imprint of the Taylor & Francis Group, an informa business.

© 2008 Ulrich Brand, Christoph Görg, Joachim Hirsch and Markus Wissen

Typeset in Garamond by
Taylor & Francis Books
Printed and bound in Great Britain by
TJ International Ltd, Padstow, Cornwall

All rights reserved. No part of this book may be reprinted or reproduced or
utilised in any form or by any electronic, mechanical, or other means, now known
or hereafter invented, including photocopying and recording, or in any
information storage or retrieval system, without permission in writing from the
publishers.

British Library Cataloguing in Publication Data
A catalogue record for this book is available from the British Library

Library of Congress Cataloging in Publication Data
Conflicts in environmental regulation and the
internationalization of the state : contested terrains /
Ulrich Brand ... [et al.].
p. cm. – (Routledge/RIPE series in global political economy ; 25)
"Simultaneously published in the USA and Canada by Routledge."
Includes bibliographical references and index.
ISBN 978-0-415-45513-8 (hardback : alk. paper) – ISBN 978-0-203-92850-9
(e-book : alk. paper) 1. Environmental policy. 2. Environmental protection. 3.
Biodiversity–
Political aspects. 4. International relations–Environmental aspect. 5.
Globalization–Environmental aspects. 6. Biodiversity conservation–Law and
legislation. 7. World Trade
Organization. 8. Sustainable development. I. Brand, Ulrich, 1967-
GE170.C643 2008

ISBN13: 978-0-415-45513-8 (hbk)
ISBN13: 978-0-203-92850-9 (ebk)

Contents

Abbreviations

ABS	access and benefit sharing
AIA	Advanced Informed Agreement
ALCA/FTAA	Free Trade Agreement for the Americas (Spanish/English)
ARIC-I	Asociación Rural de Interés Colectivo Independiente (Independent Rural Association of Collective Interests)
BMU	Bundesumweltministerium (Ministry of the Environment, Germany)
BS	benefit sharing
CBD	Convention on Biological Diversity
CGIAR	Consultative Group on International Agricultural Research
CGRFA	Commission on Genetic Resources for Food and Agriculture (FAO)
CI	Conservation International (NGO)
CIBIOGEM	Comisión Intersecretarial de Bioseguridad y Organismos Genéticamente Modificados (Mexico) (Intersecretarial Commission on Biosafety and Genetically Modified Organisms)
CIEPAC	Centro de Investigaciones Económicas y Políticas de Acción Comunitaria (Centre of Economic and Policital Research for Communitarian Action)
CIMMYT	Centro Internacional para el Mejoramiento del Maíz y del Trigo (International Agricultural Research Centre in Mexico)
CITES	Convention for International Trade in Endangered Species of Wild Fauna and Flora
CNI	Congreso Nacional Indígena (National Indigenous Congress)
COCOPA	Comisión de Concordia y Pacificación (Commission for Concord and Pacification)
COMPITCH	Consejo de Organizaciones de Médicos y Parteras Indígenas Tradicionales de Chiapas (Council of Organizations of Traditional Physicians and Midwifes in Chiapas)
CONABIO	Comisión Nacional para el Conocimiento y el Uso de la Biodiversidad (National Commission for the Knowledge and Use of Biodiversity)

CONAI	Comisión Nacional de Intermediación (National Commission for Intermediation)
CONANP	Comisión Nacional de Áreas Naturales Protegidas (National Commission of Nature Protection Areas)
COP	Conference of the Parties
CPB	Carthagena Protocol on Biosafety
ECOSUR	El Colegio de la Frontera Sur (The College of the Southern Border)
EPA	Environment Protection Agency (USA)
ETC Group	Group on Erosion, Technology and Concentration (NGO, formerly RAFI)
EU	European Union
EZLN	Ejército Zapatista de Liberación Nacional (Zapatista Army of National Liberation)
FAO	Food and Agricultural Organization
FR	Farmers' Rights
GATT	General Agreement on Tariffs and Trade
GBF	Global Biodiversity Forum
GEF	Global Environmental Facility
GMO	Genetically Modified Organism
GPA	Global Plan of Action (on PGR)
GR	Genetic Resources
GRAIN	Genetic Resources Action International (NGO)
IARC	International Agricultural Research Centers
ICBG	International Cooperative Biodiversity Group
IGC	Intergovernmental Committee on Intellectual Property and Genetic Resources, Traditional Knowledge and Folklore
IIFB	International Indigenous Forum on Biodiversity
IMF	International Monetary Fund
INE	Instituto de Ecología (Institute of Ecology)
INPI	Instituto Nacional de Propiedad Intelectual (National Institute of Intellectual Property)
IP	Intellectual Property
IPGRI	International Plant Genetic Resources Institute
IPR	Intellectual Property Right
ITPGR	International Treaty on Plant Genetic Resources for Food and Agriculture
IUCN	The World Conservation Union – International Union for the Conservation of Nature (NGO and intergovernmental organisation)
IU-PGR	International Undertaking on Plant Genetic Resources
IMF	International Monetery Fund
LEGEEPA	Ley General para el Equilibrio y la Protección del Medio Ambiente (Mexican Environment Law)
MAT	Mutually Agreed Terms

MEA	Multilateral Environmental Agreement
MS	Multilateral System (for the exchange of PGRFA)
NATO	North Atlantic Treaty Organization
NC	The Nature Conservancy (NGO)
NGO	non-governmental organisation
NIH	National Institutes of Health (USA)
OAU	Organization of African Unity
OECD	Organization for Economic Cooperation and Development
PAN	Partido de Acción Nacional (Party of National Action)
PCT	Patent Cooperation Treaty
PGR	Plant Genetic Resources
PGRFA	Plant Genetic Resources for Food and Agriculture
PIC	Prior Informed Consent
PLT	Patent Law Treaty
PPP	Plan Puebla Panamá
PRD	Partido de la Revolución Democrática (Party of Democratic Revolution)
PRI	Partido Revolucionario Institucional (Party of Institutionalised Revolution)
RAFI	Rural Advancement Foundation International
RIBMA	Reserva Integral de la Biósfera Montes Azules (Integral Biosphere Reservation of Montes Azules)
SAGARPA	Secretaría de Agricultura, Ganadería Desarrollo Rural y Pesca (National Ministry of Agriculture, Stock Farming, Rural Development and Fishery)
SBSTTA	Subsidiary Body for Scientific, Technical and Technological Advice
SEDUE	Secretaría de Desarrollo Urbano y Ecología (National Ministry of Urban Development and Environment)
SEMARNAP	Secretaría de Medio Ambiente y Recursos Naturales (Ministry of Environment, Mexico; today SEMARNAT)
SPLT	Substantive Patent Law Treaty
TK	Traditional Knowledge
TLC/NAFTA	North American Free Trade Agreement (Spanish/English)
TNC	Transnational Corporation
TRIPS	Trade Related Aspects of Intellectual Property Rights
TT	Technology Transfer
TWN	Third World Network (NGO)
UNAM	Universidad Nacional Autónoma de México (National Autonomous University of Mexico in Mexico City)
UNCED	United Nations Conference on Environment and Development (1992)
UNCTAD	United Nations Conference on Trade and Development
UNEP	United Nations Environment Programme
UNO	United Nations Organization

UPOV	Union Internationale pour la Protection des Obtentions Végétales (International Union for the Protection of New Varieties of Plants)
WB	World Bank
WIPO	World Intellectual Property Organization
WRI	World Resources Institute (NGO)
WTO	World Trade Organization
WWF	World Wildlife Fund; today Worldwide Fund for Nature (NGO)

Introduction
Genetic resources and the internationalisation of the state

Since the beginning of the 1990s there have been numerous attempts to politicise and regulate crucial societal problems on an international scale. Environmental problems belong to the most important subject-matters of these efforts. This is visible not least in the fact that the series of UN conferences which took place in the 1990s was opened by the *UN Conference on Environment and Development* (UNCED) in 1992 in Rio de Janeiro, Brazil. An important result of UNCED was the *Framework Convention on Climate Change*, dealing with a subject of indisputable significance and urgency. A second and equally important result of UNCED was the *Convention on Biological Diversity* (CBD) which addresses the loss of biological diversity and its economic, social and political implications. The CBD came into force in 1993, but 15 years later the impact of this international agreement as well as of related political terrains still remains contested. After many years of further negotiations and programme formulation at the international level, designed to concretise and realise the commitments entailed in the convention, it is recognised that the implementation at the national and regional/ local levels remains crucial and that many problems of an effective "new biodiversity order" (Le Prestre 2002) are linked to weak implementation. The relationship between the international and other policy levels is subject to further considerations. Therefore, this question has been placed at the top of the agenda at the ninth Conference of the Parties (i.e. member states) in Bonn, Germany, in May 2008.

A second dimension is the highly contested relationship of the CBD and other international agreements. The CBD itself is part of a contested governance system which embraces other environmental agreements dealing with species or ecosystem conservation – such as the UN *Food and Agricultural Organization* (FAO). In particular, the relationship between the CBD and the World Trade Organization (WTO) and its treaty on Trade Related Aspects of Intellectual Property Rights (TRIPS) is one of the most controversial issues in international politics. This is not the case merely by chance. The CBD itself is not purely an environmental agreement designed for the conservation of endangered species. It addresses issues that range from the protection of ecosystems over the rights of local people, the economic value of genetic resources and the handling of technologies related to their commercialisation all the way up to intellectual property rights and the fair sharing of benefits arising from the use of biodiversity. Thus, environmental concerns are strongly connected to the regulation of economic and techno-logical processes, questions of justice as well as international and domestic power relations. Because of this broad scope and the integration of environmental and development concerns, the CBD is "perhaps the first true sustainable development convention" (Le Prestre 2002: 1). For the same reason, the fate of the CBD, its strengths and weaknesses and its impact on the new international order in general provides an ideal field of investigation to estimate the impact of the concept of sustainable development since the Rio Conference (Conca *et al.* 2007).

This book deals with one central aspect of this broad research field, that is with the conflicts concerning the appropriation of *genetic resources*. Genetic resources are one element of biological diversity, or biodiversity. This concept is actually a new one which encompasses not only the variety of species but also the diversity of ecosystems as well as the hereditary characteristics of plants and animals (cf. Chapter 2). The latter, that is the genetic properties, gain importance as a crucial resource in the context of emerging genetic technology for industrial production. Some observers call genetic resources the "oil of the information age" which indicates their enormous real and potential value. With that, a specific political dynamic has emerged around the conditions and forms of use of genetic resources.

The appropriation of biological and genetic resources is not at all a new phenomenon. Rather, for centuries it was an integral part of the colonial world order, and more recently it continues to be a key strategy in the neocolonial world order. However, during the phases of colonialism, classical imperialism and post-war neocolonialism there were rarely open conflicts around these issues, even if biological resources were central for colonial or imperial politics. This was largely the case up until the early 1980s when the issue became a subject of international concern. Three different developments are important here: the *material erosion* of genetic diversity – in particular seeds valuable for food and agriculture – which has become obvious ever since the late 1960s. Second, the *distributional* effects between Northern and Southern countries – connected with the use of genetic resources, especially in the agricultural sector – became a political issue in the early 1980s and initiated a process which was called by some observers "seed wars". This led to political struggles about the creation of a political, legal and institutional framework in order to regulate the emerging conflicts as well as rising environmental concerns regarding the erosion of biodiversity and distributional conflicts about their economic use. Third, *technological* developments, that is genetic engineering, brought a new dynamic to the conflict field. Therefore, in the 1980s, a global regulation system was created with the CBD as its central element. When analysing these regulation systems, it is important to understand that questions of how to deal with global environmental problems are inextricably linked to political and economic issues which arise from the regulation of the exchange of genetic resources as well as stemming from social conflicts regarding food supply and the potential development of "marginalised" areas.

Against the background of this historical dynamic we want to outline and analyse central elements of the *international political economy of genetic resources, that is its contested institutional and discursive terrains, in the context of the societal transformation towards post-Fordism and the internationalisation of the state.* For this, we take into account the global regulation system as an outcome, medium and presupposition of social struggles, power relations, ecological concerns and challenges for biodiversity governance.

At the centre of our inquiry are the mechanisms of the regulation of access to genetic resources and the sharing of benefits arising out of their use. *Access and benefit-sharing* (ABS), however, are not merely technical or juridical issues. Because of the specific nature of this conflict field and the strong relationships between environmental and distributional dimensions, the question of ABS constitutes the key issue of this global regulation system. Here, environmental issues such as the erosion of genetic diversity are strongly connected to the regulation of the global economy and of the most modern technologies. Moreover, ABS affects social dimensions such as the rights of marginalised local or indigenous people. Last, but not least, it encompasses a complex field of processes where the "enclosure" of formerly free available commons (Kloppenburg/Balick 1996: 177) is at stake.

This imposition is mostly vindicated via economic reasoning but is linked to the far-reaching transformation of societal practices and living conditions around the world. Decisive here is the imposition of *intellectual property rights* on genetic information which constitutes very specific and exclusive private property rights over crops and medicinal plants. Intellectual property gains importance through the extension of patents on genetic resources – including those practices which are criticised as *biopiracy*. Another important issue is the question of how those nation-states rich in biodiversity can "get their share" of the economic use of "their" resources but also of concern is how local people are involved in this benefit sharing. In this context, to some degree new forms of property titles are discussed and different models of benefit-sharing are tested.

In these highly contested processes a huge variety of different actors with diverging and sometimes opposing interests and very different power resources are involved. Indeed, the variety of actors involved includes: international and national corporations, governments, international organisations, non-governmental organisations, research institutes, epistemic communities as well as local actors such as indigenous communities and local farmers. Our investigation focuses, on the one hand, on the conflicts between these different actors and how they are inscribed institutionally and discursively at different levels and, on the other hand, on how the institutional selectivities of this complex multi-level system shape these conflicts, that is the political economy of contested terrains. Over time we became aware of the relevance of these multiple institutional levels and the complex relationships between them. A global management of genetic resources is emerging which connects supranational, international, regional (in our case NAFTA), national and local levels of policy formulation and implementation. What is at stake is, however, how these levels are produced and linked to each other: how international and supranational processes influence and are influenced by local and national structures, configurations of interest and power relations. Therefore, it is not only about the implementation of international politics as a top-down process but also how international conflict terrains and global strategies are influenced from the bottom up, that is by local problems and the interests of locally embedded actors. What is important, in other words, is the upscaling and downscaling of politics connected with the transformation of the nation-state. The global management of genetic resources is a good example, too, because the importance of the local is at least formally acknowledged. However, we need to enquire as to whether or not this formal acknowledgement is sufficient and which possibilities of shaping societal relations really exist for local actors. These questions are dealt with in a case study about Mexico.

Thus, this book focuses on the forms in which these complex conflicts are dealt with at the international, national, regional and local levels. It examines how the complex regulation system has emerged, how the conflicts are institutionalised at the various levels as well as what opportunities exist for the democratic shaping of these processes, particularly regarding the relationships between these levels.

This global regulating system is analysed as an example of the transformation of political forms of steering, participation and control, and for the shaping of global societal relations. The transformation of the state and the state system, connected with the new round of capitalist globalisation, that is the neoliberal and imperial restructuring of politics and economics, can be analysed productively and with many insights for other policy fields.

We propose an enhanced perspective on these transformations, calling this the *internationalisation of the state*. By this we mean that the nation-state does not disappear. On the contrary, our aim is to show that the formal sovereignty of states over genetic resources plays a crucial role in the creation of global markets. Nevertheless, this does not mean that nation-states – in particular those in the global South where most of these resources are located – have real control over their use and the distribution of benefits. On the contrary, it is our contention that global markets and international institutions such as the WTO impose pressure on and hence, undermine the national steering capabilities of these nation-states. Economic processes, however, are analysed in this book in the tradition of a critical (International) Political Economy which sees them as always embedded in political and socio-cultural processes. Thus, the accelerating internationalisation of the economy requires multi-level political-institutional processes and structures.

And this transformation towards the internationalisation of the state is not only about the changing capacities of control but also concerns the comprehensive transformation of relations of political and societal domination. They are linked with new forms of economic production and reproduction as well as the far-reaching transformations of societies and cultures. Our main assumption is that these developments need to be taken into account in order to adequately evaluate the possibilities of political shaping. This is the reason why the present inquiry not only analyses the possibilities and limits of political control of social and economic processes but also addresses the connected power relations and societal processes of domination. Thus, we analyse the conflicts about genetic resources against the background of broader societal changes; what we call – from the perspective of regulation theory – *the transformation from Fordism to post-Fordism*. We see the resource conflicts as an expression of new global conflict lines connected with a new phase in capitalist development. In this transformation process new technologies (such as information and communication technologies or new forms of biotechnology) are as important as *new societal relationships with nature*. This concept, developed in the tradition of the critical theory of the so-called Frankfurt School, highlights the way societies are interconnected with the biophysical conditions of their existence, while at the same time constructing nature practically (i.e. technically, economically) and discursively (e.g. culturally or scientifically). Finally, we want to analyse the opportunities that exist to realise a democratic shaping of societal relations under changing conditions.[1]

In the *first chapter* we sketch out the socio-theoretical framework and the recent transformation towards a "knowledge society" as well as the changes of the state and the state system. Moreover, we outline the concept of societal relationships with nature. In the *second chapter* we move to the concrete conflicts about genetic resources and analyse especially the Convention on Biological Diversity. We concentrate on the elaboration of a recently negotiated agreement which intends to regulate access and benefit-sharing, the so called *Bonn Guidelines on Access and Benefit Sharing*. We argue that these guidelines are not only selective towards different societal interests, they are not capable of delivering a stable compromise among the dominant groups, too. This became visible before and especially during the conference of the World Trade Organization (WTO) in Cancún in September 2003 with the first public actions of the *Like-Minded Group of Megadiverse Countries*. It is decisive that the overall tendency towards a growing commercialisation of biological diversity is lifted to a new level by this new actor.

In the *third chapter* we analyse another contested terrain: the use of biological diversity in agriculture. This area was shaped in recent years by the negotiation of a new agreement, the *International Treaty on Plant Genetic Resources for Food and Agriculture* (ITPGR). In contrast to the Bonn Guidelines this treaty deals with a partial segment of genetic resources, that is those which are decisive for the development of new agricultural products and therefore for worldwide nutrition. Unlike the Bonn Guidelines which were negotiated in a relatively short time, the ITPGR remained highly contested for many years and its adoption almost failed on several occasions. These processes clearly show the problems of the global management of genetic resources which have to do with the mentioned role of intellectual property rights (IPR) and especially the patenting of genetic materials.

Therefore, in the *fourth chapter* we focus on the international conflicts around the validity of IPR and especially the revision of the TRIPS Agreement (*Trade Related Aspects of Intellectual Property Rights*) which took place in the context of the WTO. The relationship of different agreements to each other plays an important role, especially the relationship between the CBD and the TRIPS Agreement. Moreover, what was at stake concerned how other forms of property and, more generally, other problems beyond and against "modern IPR" could be strengthened: ecological questions or those concerning worldwide nutrition. In recent times a change can be observed here: the more the neoliberal transformation of societies is criticised, the more the conflicts are shifted to other terrains such as the *World Intellectual Property Organization* (WIPO). Furthermore, bilateral pressure on weaker actors is growing.

In the *fifth chapter* we take the example of Mexico in order to better understand the relationship between different political levels or scales of conflict and to analyse the impact which international regulations have on the national and local levels. We will see that the tendency towards the commercialisation and valorisation of biological diversity which is inherent to neoliberal and imperial globalisation comes not only from "outside" Mexico but is produced by internal interest coalitions themselves. In Mexico a valorisation paradigm has become dominant and this affects those forces which are in opposition to this paradigm to perform societal relationships with nature differently. However, it would be a misleading perspective to assume that the "logic of globalisation" or global hegemony of "the" neoliberalism is dominating all other processes and actors. Indeed, certain local actors are able to influence processes on the international terrain. The indigenous rebellion of the Zapatistas in Chiapas in the Southeast of Mexico and its consequences for emerging global social movements and for a new internationalism are an example that a contested and highly contradictory shaping of societal relationships with nature does exist. This is the reason why the internationalisation of the state should be interpreted as a reconfiguration of global domination in which the resistance of social movements is incorporated, a factor which is constantly questioned by these movements. In the *final chapter* we will put these different lines of analysis together and draw some more theoretical conclusions about the International Political Economy of genetic resources and the internationalisation of the state.

The present volume is based on a research project conducted at Frankfurt University, Germany, from 2000 to 2003. The findings of this project were completely revised and actualised for the present publication in English.

Whereas originally a more general idea of the global regulation of biodiversity was the starting point of our research, very soon we became aware of the complexity of this research field. In particular, the issue of intellectual property rights and the different conflict areas connected with this highly contested and dynamic topic made it difficult to proceed as originally planned. Some very interesting aspects of the issue, for example the negotiations of the Cartagena Protocol on Biosafety (see Gupta 1999; Gupta/ Falkner 2006), had to be ignored, while others, such as the upscaling and downscaling of politics and the politics of scale, gained more space in our research than we had previously planned. In particular, this latter topic became more paradigmatic for our search to develop an appropriate theoretical approach to deal with the complex subject matter and the global conflicts connected. Even if we started with the basic theoretical assumption of an internationalisation of the state (Hirsch 2003, 2005; Poulantzas 2001) as outlined below (see Chapter 1) we realised that we had to deal very carefully with the relationships between the different political and socio-economic levels. To address this challenge we referred to the discussions in critical Geography concerning a "politics of scale" (Brenner 2004; Brenner *et al.* 2003; Keil/Mahon 2008; Smith 1995; Swyngedouw 1997) and tried to synthesise our theoretical approach on the state with these discussions. The result is an enhanced and especially internationalised version of critical state and social theory or what we could call – in order to underline a core contribution – a *neo-Poulantzian approach to International Political Economy (IPE)* which takes into account the up-scaling and down-scaling of the state. Building on Nicos Poulantzas' understanding of the state as a "material condensation of societal relationships of forces" (cf. Poulantzas 1980) and combining it with more recent theoretical developments, we deal with institutions which try to regulate economic, political and social processes on different scales (for a more theoretical foundation cf. Brand 2005, 2006). We believe that this theoretical proposal, which needs more elaboration, is helpful for any kind of IPE dealing with the political regulation of neoliberal and neoimperial globalisation. Thus, beside the empirical findings this theoretical approach is the main outcome which is built upon the material collected in our research about the global regulation of genetic resources.

We would especially like to thank Ana Esther Ceceña and Alfonso López Ramírez from the National Autonomous University in Mexico (UNAM), Silvia Ribeiro from ETC Group and all our interviewees who gave us so much information and explained to us their perspectives on highly complicated and contested topics and terrains. Karin Blank was invaluable as a research assistant and made her own contribution in the field of the organisation of interests of indigenous peoples. In updating our findings for the English publication, we strongly benefited from Gregor Kaiser's critical comments and his comprehensive knowledge on the details of a dynamically developing field. Corinna Heinecke supported us with much advice about recent developments of the CBD. Miriam Heigl delivered useful information concerning the recent developments in Mexico. Special thanks go to Irene Wilson for the translation of the German version of the research project. The anonymous referees of the Routledge/RIPE Series in Global Political Economy as well as the Series Editors, and here especially Randall German, gave us enthusiastic and extremely useful feedback in order to improve the first draft of the book. Dan Hawkins helped us in editing the final text and Simone Buckel in administering the growing list of references. Last but not least we would like to express our gratitude to the German Volkswagen Foundation which made the extensive research possible and especially Alfred Schmidt for his valuable advice and encouragement during the preparation and elaboration of the research.

We hope that this study is a useful theoretical and empirical contribution to the emerging knowledge about the contested terrains of the international political economy and the changing societal relationships with nature.

Ulrich Brand, Christoph Görg, Joachim Hirsch and Markus Wissen
Berlin, Frankfurt/Main, Kassel, Leipzig, March 2008

1 The regulation of nature in post-Fordism

There is a strongly pronounced tendency in environmental sociology and politics to discuss questions concerning how to deal with ecological problems more or less in isolation from broader societal and politico-economic changes. Even global environmental problems such as climate change or – in our example – the erosion of biological diversity are generally discussed in relative separation from the structures and processes of societal production and reproduction and the problems and conflicts involved in them. And even where such a connection is in fact made, the dominant tendency is to discuss international environmental problems in the context of the formation of cooperative mechanisms and instruments to deal with common threats. The way in which environmental problems are intertwined with global and national distributional problems, as well as with connected power relations, usually remains underestimated or even ignored.

Such an approach, however, increases the threat that the problems involved become abbreviated. This is particularly obvious in the issue areas we deal with in this book. The problem area "regulation of biodiversity" is characterised by a high degree of overlap between global environmental and distributional conflicts (Göerg 1999b). In order to make clear the manner in which these problems are intertwined, the following section shall *first*, explain the concept of *societal relationships with nature*, focusing on the constitutive interdependence of the societal process with nature. Furthermore, working within and indeed expanding upon this objective, this study centres on the emerging political-institutional terrains of international and Mexican biodiversity politics. However, this process can only be understood if the national and international *societal* developments are taken into account. Political economy and questions of hegemony are therefore decisive in order to understand the complex nature of international and national regulatory projects as well as non-intended societal regulations. Due to this fact, the *second* part of this chapter shall present and discuss the most important elements of the regulation approach. The manner in which this approach perceives the new phase of capitalist development will be outlined in order to enable us to focus, *third*, on the special meaning of knowledge and, *fourth*, on central characteristics of the emerging post-Fordist relationships with nature. In the *fifth* section, the transformation of the state and the state system will be dealt with. The aim here is to describe and further develop certain concepts of materialist state theory which will be important for the following empirical analysis. In this sense, following some general theoretical remarks on the state and political institutions, we will introduce, with key emphasis, the concept of the "internationalisation of the state" and of "second order condensations of societal power relations". Chapter 1 will end with some remarks on the methodology applied in the empirical investigations.

1.1 Societal relationships with nature

Even when, in the 1970s and 1980s, the ecological crisis began to receive ever greater public attention, it still needed quite some time before its relevance for social science research and the development of a theory of society was fully appreciated. Indeed, it was a far from easy task to conceptualise how social and non-social, "natural" processes are linked with one another. The reasons for that are manifold and sometimes contradictory, depending on the theoretical traditions involved. The history of sociology was accused of having ignored the material-substantial implications of social processes and consequently, it was considered that a new environmental paradigm was required (Catton/Dunlap 1978; for a critical discussion see Buttel *et al.* 2002; Görg 1999a). Moreover, the need for a bio- or ecocentric perception of society and nature was highlighted. By contrast, constructivist approaches to nature became prominent, at least since the 1990s, focusing more on the (discursive) construction of nature (Haraway 1991; see also Castree/Braun 1998). The underlying debates between naturalistic/realistic and constructivist/productivist approaches have yet to be adequately resolved. While in the Marxist tradition the "production of nature" became a prominent and stimulating concept (Smith 1984; Harvey 1996), the question remains as to how other aspects, such as discursive/symbolic dimensions (i.e. regarding natural sciences) could be integrated into such a concept as well as how it could possibly grasp the limits to the production of nature (Benton 1989; Castree/Braun 1998; Swyngedouw 2004).

Besides the debate about naturalism and constructivism, now widely discussed in a broad variety of approaches such as the actor-network-theory (Latour 1999), there was a further reason which was partly responsible for this delay. Different theoretical traditions, regardless of their sometimes opposing approaches to societal development, generally agreed on one point regarding the direction of progress. For the dominant version of modernisation theory of the 1970s, based on the work of Talcott Parsons, the direction of societal development was predetermined: towards the greater control of nature and the decreasing relevance of nature for the development of society (Parsons 1975; for a criticism see Görg 1999a). Even for most of the theories of the post-industrial society (see Bell 1967; Touraine 1972) it was clear that in the course of societal development, the "game against nature" would be replaced by a purely social game. Nearly the same argument occurs in the Marxist tradition. At least in the official socialistic ideology, environmental problems did not exist and natural limits to social development were not acknowledged. Social development was considered as if nature did not matter. Ecological problems were considered to be a secondary contradiction, subordinate to the development of production relations, which were considered to be of primary importance. It took until the 1980s for the relevance of environmental problems in the development of society and for the formation of social theory to be recognised (see Smith 1984; Beck 1992; Altvater 1993; O'Connor 1988). And even then it was difficult to acknowledge that the relationships between society and nature have their own logic which must be dealt with carefully. It is correct that capitalist accumulation is one central cause for the destruction of nature. In recent years, however, capitalism has demonstrated its capability of reacting to environmental problems, therein trying to manage its own conditions of production, giving rise to a new, "post-modern" regime of accumulation. Therefore, in order to analyse the relationships between society and nature in more detail, it is helpful to periodise capitalist development. In line with this objective, in the next section we refer to the concept of post-Fordism in order to indicate a new phase of capitalist development.

Some time was needed until it was recognised that the problems which were put on the political agenda by the ecological crisis were not isolated environmental problems. When this was realised, there was room for the recognition of the fact that we are dealing with a comprehensive *crisis of societal relationships with nature* (Becker/Jahn 1987). The concept of societal relationships with nature places a quite different emphasis with regard to both aspects concerning the naturalistic-constructivist debate and the concept of progress and social development. Although this concept stems from within the Marxist tradition, it was also developed in the social theory and the historical diagnosis of the "dialectic of enlightenment" in the Critical Theory of Horkheimer and Adorno (see Horkheimer/Adorno 1987; Görg 1999a, 2003a). According to that concept, society cannot be discussed independently of nature, nor does the process of history aim towards an ever more comprehensive control of nature. First, the social process is constitutively mediated through nature. The difference between nature and society, however, should not be eliminated. While naturalistic and some constructivist approaches assume that nature and society are not distinctive entities, Critical Theory emphasises that we should make a distinction between both (without falling back into a dualistic approach). In particular, this is the case with respect to the aim of liberation and social emancipation. Moreover, nature is, in one aspect, a social construction, constructed discursively through language and materially, through human labour. Nevertheless, it remains a materiality of its own which displays qualities that societies cannot really control. That leads to the second point: certainly, the process of modernity is based on an increasing domination of nature, but this domination does not lead to an increasing control over nature; rather, it rebounds in the destruction of nature and in ever greater dependency on the results and secondary effects of the domination of nature.

Thus, basically, society cannot free itself from its dependencies in relation to nature because the social process always contains material-substantial elements (e.g. "natural" resources) and this process is therefore dependent on the metabolism of nature. The mutual interdependence of nature and society is central, however, not only to one side, namely society, but also to the other, nature. At the beginning of the twenty-first century, nature untouched by human activity is virtually non-existent. Marx and Engels were completely aware of this tendency to transform nature from the state in which it was found (Marx/Engels 1978: 44). But in spite of this transformation the material-substantial conditions of human existence retain their own meaning, which can be respected or ignored by human activity – the latter with potentially destructive results for society in the form of ecological risks. Following Adorno's critical theory, this complex understanding can be designated the *non-identity of nature* (Görg 2003b).[1]

The starting-point for a critical theory of societal relationships with nature, however, is the acknowledgement of a practical, that is economic/ technical and cultural/discursive, construction of nature, and not the supposedly unchangeable laws of nature to which humanity or society has to adapt.[2] Today, scientific constructions, closely linked to the technical and economic strategies of their application, have come to the foreground, finding their expression in the diagnosis of the "knowledge society" (see below). It should be remembered, however, that there are also other practical constructions of nature, as we shall see more precisely in the following section. There is an unavoidable *pluralism of societal relationships with nature* which, however – particularly under bourgeois-capitalist conditions – is characterised by an *asymmetric relationship* and a dominance of capitalist forms, particularly in production and reproduction. However, even in the age of globalisation, cultural interpretations and, linked to them, forms of knowledge and practices, can be found which cultivate a completely different treatment of nature. These ("traditional") forms of knowledge and their agencies have been given an even greater value by the ecological crisis, for one can discover in certain practices dealing with the tropical rain forest or in certain forms of agricultural production, elements of a more respectful handling of natural resources. This poses the question as to whether these practices are today only marginal or if they have a chance of influencing the *shaping of global relationships with nature*.

After all, the dynamisms in this process are determined by actors with quite different strategies. As we have just been able to see in the example of biological diversity, the dominant strategies for the appropriation of nature increasingly aim at its commercialisation, that is at a purely economic appraisal of nature. Here, the *tendency towards the domination of nature* is continued in a new and even stronger form, even after the experience of the ecological crisis. In the tradition of the Critical Theory not every form of the appropriation of nature is defined as the domination of nature (for if it was, the development of society without the domination of nature would be inconceivable). The domination of nature tries to completely subject or subsume nature to particular objectives and ignores every "own" meaning, every non-identity of nature. This is without doubt the case in the tendencies towards the commercialisation of biological diversity, for nature is reduced here to its usability and all other elements which are not compatible with this are ignored.

As a result of more than 30 years of environmental struggles, it is now widely recognised that the increase in the domination of nature has led to a "domination of secondary effects" (Beck *et al.* 1994). Societies are confronted more and more with the consequences of the unhindered domination of nature, and that causes additional costs and a great deal of trouble. The idea of the complete control of nature has, therefore, at least partially been abandoned and the scarcely controllable risks involved in the appropriation of nature have increasingly been taken into account, that is in terms of uncertainty or the precautionary principle. The use of nature is, therefore, increasingly accompanied by attempts to mitigate its destructive effects prophylactically or to eliminate them reactively – to engage in the protection of nature and the environment. But the question is whether this means an *acknowledgement* of the non-identity of nature or whether it represents the attempt at an *accompanying mitigation* of the domination of nature because of the uncontrollable consequences. The question is, in other words, whether society acknowledges that nature cannot be totally subsumed under societally based targets, thereby allowing room within which nature's own logic can be respected; or alternatively, whether we are dealing with a *reflexive form of the domination of nature* which takes into account that although we sometimes face negative consequences, our targets will not be changed. This question can be answered via an examination of the fate of strategies which follow a different, less destructive form of the appropriation of nature, that is a handling of nature which attempts to respect its non-identity. Considerable attention will be paid to this in the following section.

This approach differs from the often analysed questions, which refer to the general chances of the protection of the environment and nature under capitalist conditions. Of course, it also deals with whether and to what extent aspects of the protection of nature can hold their own against commercialisation strategies. But precisely in the field of biological diversity, the problem cannot be grasped via a confrontation of economic and ecological dimensions, or of conservation and use strategies. On the contrary, conservation and use, as well as ecology and economy, are indissolubly intertwined. Biological diversity, or biodiversity, in the comprehensive scientific meaning of the concept, is a societal construction (which, e.g. does not exist in the same way in all cultures). In this construction, economic interests and geostrategic objectives have already been included, as we shall see more precisely in the process of the establishment of this new scientific concept (Flitner 1995a).

At the core of this are those parts of biological diversity which are of potential economic value: the *genetic resources*. By genetic resources, we mean those components which contain hereditary characteristics – that is not coffee once it has been roasted, but the seeds or its hereditary elements and generally, the genetic parts of animals and plants. These genetic resources are of particular interest because they represent an input for the newer bio-technologies and genetic technologies and the industries based on them, the so-called *life science industries*.

Because of these new scientific and technological developments there is a growing economic interest in nature. At the same time "humanity" cannot completely renounce the use of "biodiversity" as a whole. Since biological diversity also includes the diversity of the animals and plants used in agriculture and for food supply, it is of central importance in ensuring human nutrition. Thus, the conservation of nature cannot be played off abstractly against its use. The strategy of the "pure" protection of nature can only be a solution for, at most, parts of biodiverstiy, for example tropical rain forests or coral reefs. Even in tropical rain forests, however, nature supplies a habitat for many people and for greatly differing forms of human use (Hecht 1998). Thus, even there, the strategy of protection clashes with interests in the use of biodiversity – and even the setting up of a nature reservation is basically only a change in the form of use, namely use for ecotourism or as "natural capital". It is, simply put, always a question of the different forms of the socialisation of nature, of different cultures and practices in the handling of biodiversity. In this constellation the tendency towards their greater commercialisation determines the direction of the organisation of societal relationships with nature. In the process, other societal forms are marginalised and tend to be dissolved. The threat emerges that nature in the form of genetic resources is reduced to its economic value, that is subsumed under the practices of capitalist valorisation (in German: *Inwertsetzung*; see, for the specific meaning, Görg 2004). In the reflexive domination of nature, in addition, even conservation efforts are functionalised within broader strategies of valorisation. The question, however, is not use versus protection; rather, it concerns which strategies of use can the conservation of biological diversity aim for. And, as a further topic, which is central to this study: how can "the democratic content of socio-environmental construction" (Swyngedouw 2004: 24) be enhanced? This question can be translated into an inquiry about the specific meaning which is given to the strategies of the valorisation of nature, the strategies of nature protection and the practices of a different organisation of relationships with nature in the global management of nature.

The *starting-point* for our investigation, therefore, is the *specific historical conditions* in which these different strategies clash with one another. For, with regard to the objects of the conflicts – biodiversity or genetic resources – we have to ask about the new forms of their scientific description. Moreover, we can observe a new constitution of the object itself, which does not "exist" prior to its connection with new processes of its practical appropriation. The very definition of the problem – that is the numerous disputes over dominant or even hegemonic interpretation patterns – is closely connected with the economic, and beyond them the social and cultural, interests in biodiversity. Are we dealing with the loss of habitats which are supposedly *close to nature* – particularly, tropical rain forests and coral reefs? Is it a question of the "loss of the apothecary of nature" or the "treasure chest" of the tropical rain forest, that is its potential *economic* value? Or, is there a real threat of endangering culturally embedded *practices and systems of interpretation*, which have often already socialised certain elements of biological diversity for hundreds of years and have even created certain aspects of that diversity? Even the political structures and terrains are in a state of upheaval. The valorisation of genetic resources is an integral part of a new phase of capitalist development and of what we call *post-Fordist relationships with nature*. If the novelty of this phase – W. F. Haug (2001: 451) calls it "biocapitalism as a mode of production" – and its central elements are taken into account, the conflicts over the organisation of relationships with nature could be more appropriately grasped. Moreover, the chances of alternative forms can be estimated more precisely.

1.2 The formation of a post-Fordist mode of regulation

The background to the change in the economic importance of biological diversity and in particular of genetic resources is the transition to a post-Fordist accumulation regime and mode of regulation following the world economic crisis of the 1970s. We examine this development using the concepts of *regulation theory*, particularly those which have been developed in France, Britain and Germany since the 1980s (Aglietta 1979; Boyer 1986; Lipietz 1987; Robles 1994; Hübner 1989; Jessop 1990; Hirsch 1990; Esser *et al.* 1994; Grahl/Teague 2000; Brand/Raza 2003; Graz 2006).[3] It is thanks to this theory that there has been an opening up of the field for a differentiated analysis of capitalist formations which differ in space and time, and which have their own specific strategies for the valorisation of capital and their own political institutional forms and relationships of social forces. The historical development of capitalist societies does not follow an objective logic but is determined by the conflicting activities of social actors. It is characterised by a crisis-determined succession of relatively stable formations, each of which has its own forms of economic production and reproduction, its own specific configurations of institutional systems, but also, its own particular crisis dynamics. The central question dealt with by regulation theory is thus directed towards the problematic conditions of the maintenance and

reproduction of capitalist society, which is characterised by structural conflicts and antagonisms, that is towards the question of why this social relationship "reproduces itself despite and because of its conflict-driven and
contradictory character" (Lipietz 1985: 109, our translation). The institu-
tionalist approach of regulation theory proceeds from the assumption that
"the state" and "the market" as social regulation mechanisms presuppose
behavioural patterns which correspond to the dominant societal structures
(this is in contrast to the understanding of a dichotomy of the market
versus the state; see the criticism of Underhill 2000 on international
political economy). These are, as a rule, guaranteed by a complex of
socio-political institutions and norms, in which the economic and political/
administrative processes are embedded. The valorisation of capital – the
production and accumulation of surplus value – is a fundamental component and the driving force of capitalist society, but it must not be understood simply as a mechanism which objectively prevails and to which social
behaviour adapts unconditionally. In the terminology of regulation theory, a
system of regulation is necessary for this to happen. The concept of a
mode of regulation describes "the totality of institutional forms, networks,
explicit or implicit norms, which ensure the compatibility of relationships
within the framework of an accumulation regime, both corresponding to the
state of societal relationships and over and above their conflict-driven characteristics" (Lipietz 1985: 121, our translation). It circumscribes a complex
field of societal organisations and institutions: including the state apparatus,
the ideological orientations and the subjectivities which are materialised in
it, and thus, it also involves the hegemonic relationship in the sense of
generalised ideas about the order as well as the development of society.

We must therefore differentiate between "regulation" and "regulating".
This is central to the theoretical placement as well as the methodological
design of this study. The concept of regulation relates to the fact that capitalist society – based on private production guided by the market, wage
labour and competition – can have no controlling centre as a result of the
contradictions and conflicts which are contained in it. Its reproduction takes
place via permanent disputes and struggles between contending actors.
These can lead to more permanent social compromises which manifest
themselves in specific systems of institutions which thereby lend the overall
capitalist system a certain durability, albeit only temporarily. Accordingly,
the reproduction of capitalist society must be regarded as a "process without
a steering subject". Every mode of *regulation* contains a complex of institutional *regulating* dispositives, which is, in itself, heterogeneous and contradictory. It follows from this that the concept of a state which guides society
must also be rejected. The state – as an apparatus of force – is an important
point of intersection of regulative processes, but in its specific shape and
institutional configuration, it is at the same time their object and product.

The political-economic regulation approach also analyses the changes in
economic structures, using for this the concept of the *accumulation regime*.

This characterises a mode of reproduction which, for a certain time, can guarantee a relatively correlating relationship between the material conditions of production and societal consumption (Lipietz 1985: 120). In order to be relatively durable, a historically developing accumulation regime requires the establishment of a compatible mode of regulation. The accumulation regime and the mode of regulation are not to be regarded as functionally correlated, however, but underlie their own specific conditions of creation and development. They are always the contested product of social conflicts and thus, are always historically alterable.

This leads us to another aspect, which is of utmost importance for this study: every phase of development contains its own specific politico-social *axes of conflict* in which the relationships of class, gender and nature (among others) and the social antagonisms connected with them are expressed. In our example, the struggle over the (non-)commodification of societal relationships with nature is institutionalised within the framework of a mode of regulation. At the same time, this conflict is also grounded in divisions of labour and inequalities based on class, gender and "race" (especially indigenous peoples).

The *relative consistency and durability* of a historical form of capitalism depends on the formation of a mode of regulation which enables social conflicts to remain relatively compatible with the valorisation process of capital which is materialised in the accumulation regime. For this to be the case, not only must the general orientations for societal development be shared (e.g. the welfare-state class compromise, the neoliberal market and competition model), but *terrains* must also be defined and accepted by the most important actors on which political and social struggles can be fought out without resulting in fundamental interruptions to the accumulation process. A state which is in the process of internationalising itself is decisive for the creation of this terrain.

"Secular" *crises* of capitalism occur when an existing connection between accumulation and regulation breaks down as a result of the dynamism of social struggles formed by its own structure. The cause of the crisis of "Atlantic Fordism" (Aglietta 1979), which became manifest in the 1970s, must be seen, above all, in the fact that the productivity reserves which existed in this mode of development no longer sufficed to guarantee capital profitability under the conditions of the Keynesian, welfare-state mode of regulation and the corporative class compromises which characterised it (see Hirsch/Roth 1986; Altvater/Mahnkopf 1999; Hirsch 1995). This caused the forms of the international division of labour and the relationships of dominance, which had emerged after the Second World War, to fall into crisis (Hirsch 1993). Even though this interpretation is widely accepted, in more recent discussions on the existence of a post-Fordist mode of development there is disagreement about the extent to which this has already taken shape, and if so, whether its existence is relatively stable or whether it is already in a state of crisis. In the more recent theoretical discussions of regulation there is some dispute over which criteria should be used in order to be able to identify a more or less stable (post-Fordist) mode of development (see Alnasseri *et al.* 2001; Candeias/Deppe 2001; Hirsch 2001; Brand/ Raza 2003; Purcell 2002 on the economism of the – French – approach). This has led to a rather far-reaching critique of the regulationist methodology, at least with respect to the discursive connotations it has acquired. The critique refers especially to the concept of regulation. As Goodwin and Painter (1997: 23) point out, "the notion of regulation has become associated in the literature with stability, coherence, functionality, and structure." They consider it important (and possible) to rework this notion in favour of a view of regulation as a "process, unevenness, tendency, and practice" (ibid.). In this sense, but without wishing to clarify these issues here, it is of importance to the following examination that we assume the existence of a contested and still crisis-ridden, but nevertheless quite clearly outlined, post-Fordist mode of development and the corresponding relationships with nature.

The outlines which have taken shape, in a relatively clear fashion, are closely connected with the politico-economic strategies which are subsumed under the label of neoliberalism (Plehwe *et al.* 2006). The neoliberal strategy for solving the crisis – which has essentially been established by internationalised capital in cooperation with the governments of several dominant capitalist states, led by the USA – is essentially based on a far-reaching deregulation of capital and financial markets, together with the comprehensive privatisation of public enterprises, pension funds and social security systems. In this way, and based on new transport, information and communication technologies, the internationalisation of production has been given a qualitatively new impetus. Cross-border company networks have increasingly been created which make it possible to install global chains of value creation for the flexible use of socially and geographically differing processing conditions ("worldwide sourcing"). The development of transnational company networks led to the tendential dissolution of the borders of the "national economies", which under Fordist conditions of accumulation and regulation were more strongly oriented towards domestic markets. This increased the independence of multinational corporations from the regulative environments and social compromises of individual states. The Fordist connection between Taylorist mass production and mass consumption supported by the welfare state became looser, formalised wage relationships were eroded and the distribution of income generally shifted in favour of capital (Cox 1987; Marglin/Schor 1990; Altvater/Mahnkopf 1999; Jessop 2002: 80–91).

1.3 The knowledge-based economy and the "knowledge society"

This trend was accompanied by a surge in the subjugation of further sectors of society under the process of capital valorisation by way of "commodification", that is the transformation of the products of labour and natural resources into commodities. Based on new technologies – particularly information and communication technology as well as biotechnology and genetic engineering – this led to a greater capital penetration of the services sector and to the increasing importance of the so-called *life science industries* (Dolata 1999; Gibbs 2000). The key characteristic of these industries is that they are, in a particular fashion, "knowledge-based", that is founded on the systematic production and appropriation of the results of scientific research. With this development, comprehensive and systematic rationalisation processes became possible, especially in the field of immaterial labour (research and development, production preparation, production-related services). At the same time, new opportunities for investment and the creation of surplus value were opened up to capital, besides the services sector, primarily in the field of information and telecommunications, agricultural production and the pharmaceutical, cosmetic and health industries. As a whole, the post-Fordist accumulation regime combines an increase in the rate of exploitation (wage reductions, rationalisation and the intensification of labour) with a new thrust based on the "internal appropriation of land" via the subjugation of further spheres of society – not least in the extended dimensions of the human psyche and the human body – under the process of capital valorisation.

On the part of private capitalist companies, ever since the beginning of the 1990s, a dynamic process of reorganisation has taken place culminating in the development a life science industry within the central business areas of agriculture and pharmaceuticals (and in some cases veterinary medicine). This process has been accompanied by considerable fusions and take-overs. In order to show the concentration processes and the power of the large companies, we will outline some of the available statistical information.

The world market for *seeds* is about 21 billion US-Dollars (USD) and the top ten companies, after a major concentration process, today control half of the world's commercial seed sales. The world's largest seed company is, since 2005, US-based corporation Monsanto, which boasts seed sales of 2.8 billion USD per year; followed by DuPont/Pioneer, also based in the USA, with 2.6 billion; Syngenta (Switzerland) with 1.2 billion; and the French Limagrain Group (more than 1 billion.). These mega-companies are followed by: the German KWS; Land O'Lakes (USA); Sakata (Japan); Bayer Crop Science (Germany); and Taikii (Japan), all of which have seed sales ranging roughly between 360 to more than 600 million USD (ETC Group 2005a).

The top seed companies, namely Bayer, Syngenta, DuPont and Monsanto, are also leading *pesticide* producers, a market which is worth almost 30 billion USD per year; an amount which is greater than the market of commercial seed sales, and in which the concentration of companies is even stronger: ten companies control 84 per cent of the global market and further concentration processes have been predicted. Bayer and Syngenta each sell more than 6 billion USD worth of pesticides per year, followed by the German BASF (which sells more than 4 billion USD), and the three US-based companies, Dow (annual sales of almost 4.4 billion), Monsanto (almost 3.2 billion) and DuPont (2.2 billion) (ETC Group 2005b: 6, based on 2004 with data provided by Agrow World Crop Protection News).

The largest market which has to do with genetic resources is by far the one of *pharmateuticals*, with annual sales of more than 240 billion USD. The top ten companies control 59 per cent of the world market and in recent years a strong concentration process has taken place: Hoechst and Rhône-Poulenc formed Aventis in 1999 and five years later Aventis merged with Sanofi; Glaxo Wellcome and SmithKline Beecham merged in 2000 to form GlaxoSmithKline; in 2000 Pharmacia merged with Monsanto but Monsanto became an independent company again in 2002 and in 2005 bought the Mexican seed company Seminis (see Chapter 5). In 2002, too, Pfizer merged with Pharmacia. This brief list of mergers is far from exhaustive, but rather seeks to focus on the most prominent ones in the pharmaceutical industry. The US-based company Pfizer has sales of more than 46 billion USD, followed by GlaxoSmithKline (United Kingdom, 32.8 billion); Sanofi-Aventis (France–Germany, 32.2 billion); the two US firms Johnson & Johnson (22.1 billion) and Merck (21.5 billion); Astra Zeneca from Sweden and the United Kingdom (21.4 billion); and the two Swiss companies Hoffman-La Roche (19.1 billion) and Novartis, which has sales totalling 18.5 billion USD (ETC Group 2005b: 2, with data for 2004 obtained from PJB Publications and 2005 Fortune Global 500).

Compared to these figures, *biotechnological companies* which concentrate on genetically modified drugs or seeds are relatively small, with revenues ranging from 10.5 million USD per year (Amgen, which is the leader, mainly selling five genetically modified drugs) to 5.4 million (Monsanto) or 4.6 million (Genetech, majority owner Hoffman-La Roche). However, all these companies have specific interests in a great variety of genetic resources which are the basis for their research and product development and where market growth rates are considerable (ETC Group 2005b: 4, with data based on the journal *Nature Biotechnology*, without pharmaceutical companies). Nonetheless, to date most sales of genetically modified crops stem from corn, soybeans and rice (Wisner 2005: 13–14).

Despite the vast potential market that these companies hope to conquer, there has also been growing resistance to what we will term "green genetic technology" in agriculture and in the production of foodstuffs. Indeed, this technology has been confronted with considerable resistance not only for technical reasons and because of the ecological effects, but also because consumers, at least in Europe, are not (yet) willing to accept these products. As part of a survey known as Eurobarometer, it was found that in only four of the fifteen participating countries the public supported the use of biotechnology in creating food (Gaskell *et al.* 2003: 17). This also supports the argument that the establishment of new technologies should not be taken for granted but that it depends on societal conditions and that it must, therefore, be established politically. It can also be observed, however, that the life science industry did not at all regard the "wars of perception", in which it was, at first, on the losing side (see the study by Mitsch/Mitchell 1999; see also ETC Group 2005b), as being lost battles; rather, the industry had begun waging a major campaign to push for and promote the public acceptance of "green genetic technology".

Independently of how this process continues in detail, it is certain that an overlapping trend will be further strengthened. Due to the general difficulty of estimating market conditions, to the immensely high costs of research and the development of new products, and to the necessity of safeguarding the fundamental relationships of ownership during the development of new markets and branches of production, the *securing of property rights* with regard to the new products, technologies and their genetic material has meanwhile become a primary concern of industry and research – from the large corporations to small research institutes. Corresponding to this is the enormous increase in the number of patent applications, particularly in the northern industrial countries. According to data of the NGO RAFI (now the ETC Group)[4] in the year 2000 there were three million patent applications waiting to be processed by the US American Patent Office alone (the great majority of them from the sphere of biotechnology and genetic technology); this number representing half as many patents as had been granted in the past 200 years (RAFI 2000a). In Europe, patent applications, lodged at the European Patent Office, in the field of gene technology rose from approximately 1000 in 1985 to 30,000 in 2005 (Wullweber 2004). As trends in the sphere of research on the human genome or on human parent cells show, the issue at stake is increasingly that of the granting of property rights to genetic resources and thus to the "natural" basic materials themselves. The resources here are of a different type to those of the Fordist phase, however. The issue is not so much one of the availability of natural products as such, but increasingly, of the information contained within them, of the "genetic code" (see for the difficulties concerning the term "code", Kay 2000). These resources, thus, do not simply exist, but are constituted as resources (namely as economically useful and thus valuable material) via scientific descriptions and technological developments. At the same time, the basic material of the economic and technical valorisation processes is becoming an increasingly contested object, upon which exclusive and monopoly-like property rights, primarily concerning patents, are imposed.

1.3.1 *Knowledge-based industrialisation and a new economic imaginary*

The concept of post-Fordism is useful to explain what is often described as the emergence of a "knowledge society" (Stehr 1994; Wingens 1998; Krohn

2001; for a critique, Hirsch 2002b). This conceptual term is somewhat fuzzy, however, since every human society is based on "knowledge" in one form or another. Furthermore, it could suggest a technological concept of society in which the economic and political relationships of domination and exploitation are ignored. What has changed over the last decades, obviously, is the relevance of science in society. To determine exactly what this increasing relevance means, however, is not an easy task. The question of a scientific explanation about how society is constituted is necessarily connected with the question of how we, as scientists, know about it. This strong interrelationship between *the way the world is* and *how we perceive it*, is highlighted by the notion of a "co-production of science and society" (Jasanoff 2004a). According to Science and Technology Studies we have to take a symmetrical stance towards scientific knowledge about nature and social institutions (such as states) that produce and guarantee social order (Latour 1993; Jasanoff *et al.* 1995). But to say that science and knowledge are central for our understanding of both the natural and the social world does not necessarily exclude power relations and domination from the scope of investigations. Herein, of central importance are the shifting and *contested boundaries* between science and society, which are by no means given and fixed. In particular, science policy and research funding strategies (both from private and state actors) contribute to the restructuring of boundaries, blurring some of them (e.g. between basic and applied research) while creating new ones (e.g. between society and specific, constructed versions of actors, called "users" by Jacob 2005). Because in the so-called knowledge society, scientific knowledge supposedly increases its relevance, the scientific diagnosis about the character of society is even more difficult and contested. Consequently, ambiguity reigns concerning the appropriate role of scientists. Moreover, scientists as intellectuals are themselves continuously engaged in struggles for a new diagnosis of society – and their interests and revenues (e.g. funding for research) are strongly connected with this diagnosis (see Fischer 2000).

In this debate the concept of post-Fordism highlights the importance of information and scientific knowledge connected with a new mode of accumulation and new forms of societal regulation. This does not mean that we seek to explain societal development by initially looking at only one constitutive element of society – modes of production – for, if this was the case, it would only be fair to label such an approach as representing a reductionist understanding of the social (Jasanoff 2004b: 20). Instead, we ask which structural elements of society can best represent a starting point for further explanation of social change. Against this background, the "knowledge society" is less an expression of a "post-industrial" phase of capitalism; rather, it describes a new, more systematically "knowledge-based" form of industrialisation. The phrase "the end of industrial society" does not entail that the form of industrialisation – from early manufacturing to Fordist Taylorism – has continually changed in the course of history or that the dissolution of traditional factory-based forms of production, which is becoming visible in various sectors, means the complete end of industrialisation as such (Becker 2001). While Fordism – characterised by the Taylorist mass production of consumer goods – was based essentially on the commodification of the material conditions of the reproduction of labour, today, the production and appropriation of information and knowledge is becoming of central importance.

Another aspect of the role of knowledge in current transformation processes is highlighted by Bob Jessop (2003). He argues that the concept of the knowledge-based economy became, step-by-step, a hegemonic paradigm and *economic imaginary*, that is the consolidation of an accumulation regime and mode of regulation which gives the different actors a social, material and spatial-temporal frame of reference. The economy and politics as social processes and everyday actions by myriad actors are – through struggles – framed and constructed through corridors of rational and legitimate action: investment strategies, the organisation of the labour-process, laws, financial priorities of state budgets, norms of production and consumption in a broad sense, and international politics. It articulates accumulation strategies, technological innovations, cultural norms such as the learning society, perceptions of nature and political processes. Therefore, the knowledge-based economy becomes a grand narrative and a strategic vision. Certain strategies, projects and visions emerge and gain power, legitimacy, and through that continuity. The post-Fordist forms of appropriation of nature are also part of this economic imaginary and an emerging "eco-governmentality" (Goldman 2001).

In this sense, post-Fordism is, for Jessop, an imaginary of a progressively more integrated world-market which is able to orient and give coherence to accumulation strategies and to realise political and hegemonic visions of social life which put past and present narratives and experiences, and actual problems and future prospects together in a coherent framework. Jessop's main argument is that the economic imaginary of the "knowledge-based economy" is becoming, ever since the 1990s, the dominant and hegemonic discourse because it creates the framework within which struggles for political, intellectual and moral leadership as well as concrete technological-economic reforms take place. This imaginary – which is still full of tensions – orients actions throughout society: from everyday practices, via the educational and scientific system to state institutions and private firms.

Within the framework of the post-Fordist mode of accumulation and regulation, three tendencies which are basic to capitalist society are accentuated in a specific way:

(1) The capitalist production of commodities is principally dependent on being able to avail itself of *general conditions of production* which cannot be produced in the form of commodities, for example natural resources or

human labour-power. To an increasing degree, these include the necessary knowledge for societal production and reproduction. In the course of capitalist development this is less and less available to capital in the form of a "natural" factor of production or of a "free productive power". Rather, it must be produced systematically. The production of knowledge under capitalist conditions, however, remains dependent on production contexts which are outside the direct creation of surplus value. Its infrastructural foundations – for example in the form of basic research or the qualification of workers – is inadequately developed under market conditions, and complementary financial and organisational inputs, primarily on the part of the state, are necessary: schools, universities, state-financed and state-organised research institutions, as well as government subsidies for industrial research and development. With the growing importance of scientific knowledge for production, the amount of knowledge produced by the firms themselves grows, but at the same time, this increasingly requires recourse to "intellectual commons" in the form of generally available qualifications, information and understanding (Jessop 2000). In other words, in order to be successful in the competition for innovations, firms require a suitable social and infrastructural environment, for example in the form of "technology poles" or "industrial districts". This is a factor which, particularly, accounts for the competition between different locations. The relationship between private capitalist production of knowledge and the creation of knowledge as a generally available "intellectual common" takes on new and more complex forms in this process.

(2) Capitalist development is characterised by the continual process of *primitive accumulation*, that is the transfer of previously – in the form of "commons" – freely available conditions of production to private property. Marx essentially dealt with this in the context of the private appropriation of land. Today, the process of primitive accumulation relates in a particular way to knowledge, which is now being "commodified" and "enclosed" in a more robust manner than previously (May 2000). The concept of primitive accumulation must not be used as a historical category here; instead, it describes a structural relationship between capitalist and non-capitalist modes of production and of living, which in the course of history – driven by the process of the creation of surplus value – is configured in ever new forms (see Alnasseri 2003). For David Harvey (2003), the process of "dispossession" is at the core of the actual phase of imperialism. A prime example of this is the more or less legal expropriation of indigenous knowledge by the corporations of the life science industry in the form of "biopiracy" (Görg/Brand 2001; Ribeiro 2002b). In this sense, the global system of biopiracy and the establishment of a of biopatents work closely together (Delgado 2002: 103–135, 179–191).

(3) Finally, the capitalist process of development is characterised by a continuous contradiction between the growing societalisation of production

and private appropriation. The production of societal knowledge is, increasingly, less attributed to individual persons or firms, but takes place more and more in complex systems and networks. This makes it ever more difficult to identify particular owners and distribute to them the use extracted from such knowledge. Companies basically endeavour, on the one hand, to maintain as free an access to knowledge and information as possible, while simultaneously striving to reserve both elements for themselves as private property. Concurrently, the dominance of short-term profit interests which accompanies the liberalisation of the global financial markets ("shareholder value") is the reason why longer-term and difficult to calculate research and technology strategies tend not to be realised. It is left to the state to regulate the contradictions and conflicts arising from the double meaning of information and knowledge as both private and "common" property.

The thing which is special about knowledge or, to put it more precisely, about the information relevant to knowledge, is that it – in contrast to material goods and land – can be multiplied and utilised without great cost (Becker 2001; May 2000; Nuss 2006). The meaning of intellectual property rights therefore lies either in excluding others from using them, or in forcing them to pay licensing fees, either by means of technical safeguards (e.g. copy protection in the case of computer software) or by means of legal entitlements (patents, copyrights). In this way, information which is technically, freely available and utilisable is kept economically scarce. The establishment of intellectual property rights also presupposes specific relationships of power in society, for example not generally available technological competencies, organisational and financial potentials and above all, the existence of a state guarantee of the corresponding legal entitlements. The growing importance of such strategies of scarcity and exclusion leads Rifkin (2000) to claim that "property" is increasingly losing its meaning in favour of the right of "access". This argument only makes sense, however, if the concept of property is confined to material goods. It is evident that the concept of property is both being considerably extended and experiencing a considerable change in its meaning in society in the course of the growing transformation of information and knowledge into private property. At the same time, the appropriation of intellectual property rights, as we shall display in the following section, continues to be essentially tied to the disposition of material resources and the ownership of capital.

Despite the centrality of the disposition over resources and capital which is related to property, Jesse C. Ribot and Nancy Peluso introduce an important distinction between property and access. Their starting-point is the question of who actually benefits from or enjoys things, and what are the power-shaped processes and circumstances to do so (2003: 154). Property means socially acknowledged and supported enforceable claims through ownership or titles defined by law, custom or convention to use something and benefit from the use. This implies the exclusion or restriction of others from that use. Access (to natural resources), however, is a broader concept and considers the fact that some people and institutions "control resource access while others must maintain their access *through* those who have control" (ibid.: 154; italics in original). Access through those who have control does not mean only the right to benefit (like property) but the *ability* to benefit from things which can also be enabled without property rights. Struggles take place on the division of benefits between different social positions which intend to gain, control or maintain access to resources. The move from concepts of property or tenure to access "locates property as one set of factors (nuanced in many ways) in a larger array of institutions, social and political-economic relations, and discursive strategies that shape benefit flows" (ibid.: 157). Therefore, access analysis needs to identify and map the means, processes and relations by which access and the flows and distributions of particular benefits from particular resources are gained, maintained and controlled (and denied, one could add) for individuals, groups and institutions as well as the related underlying power relations within particular circumstances (ibid.: 161). The distinctions between property and access and between the right to benefit and the ability to benefit is important for this study. We intend to show how forms of access and property are specifically related in the conflicts around genetic resources.

1.3.2 Intellectual property

The process of the commodification of knowledge takes on different forms (see Jessop 2000). It refers, first, to the transformation of generally available resources of knowledge into private property, for example, when pharmaceutical firms use indigenous knowledge on the effects of medicinal plants for bioprospecting and then have the results patented. A further aspect is the production of knowledge as a commodity, for example in the form of research results, consultations, analyses, designs, concepts and so on. This field is becoming an ever more important segment of the services sector in the course of the differentiation of complex enterprise networks. And finally, all the forms of the transformation of intellectual labour into wage labour, which produces products for the market, and thus, the real subordination of intellectual labour to capital, fall into this category. The commodification of information and knowledge has two aspects: on the one hand, they themselves become a saleable commodity, and on the other hand, exclusive access to them becomes an ever more important foundation for the appropriation of material, for example genetic resources. That is, the ability to appropriate knowledge presupposes the existence of already accumulated knowledge.

One particularity of this process is the tendency to separate knowledge and machinery. Whereas in the earlier phases of industrialisation, prior to the Fordist one, knowledge relevant to production was, in principle, incorporated into the machinery and a durable part of machine systems, it is now becoming more independent of these and is taking on the form of an independently produced and tradeable commodity. What is significant in this connection is the rise of the computer software industry in relation to the producers of hardware.

The dominant form of intellectual property rights, next to copyright, is the patent. This is of course an old form of property right, primarily used by technologically advanced states and industries in order to ward off competitors, but in recent times its content and its importance have changed considerably. The meaning of this can be illustrated with an example: from 1990 to 2000 demand for patent protection for the main biotechnology subclass (micro-organisms or enzymes) "reached approximately 188,213 patent publications rising to a preliminary total of 299,163 patent publications by the end of 2003" (Oldham 2004: 3).

An important extension of patent protection lies in the possibility of patenting not only inventions but also discoveries (plants with specific properties, micro-organisms, genetic resources) – as far as they are commercially viable. In 1980 the US Supreme Court decided that the patenting of living organisms was permissible, which opened up a new era in the field of intellectual property. This means that products, processes and even forms of life – plants, animals, human cells and human DNA – are potentially "intellectual" property. The quantitative dimensions of this development are, as we have already stated, considerable. These developments continue, however, to be the subject of worldwide protest – and opposition to the patenting of living material, in particular, is at the core of this struggle. In defence of the extension of patent protection, it is argued that without it the process of technological innovation as a whole would be hindered because private companies would only devote increasing expenditures to research and development if they could realise corresponding profits in the form of innovation rents. This is because the production of knowledge – for example in the sphere of biotechnology – is very complicated, but transferring and copying it is relatively cheap (Janssen 1999). This claim should be qualified on several points, however. With the increasing speed of innovation even patent protected knowledge loses its value ever more quickly. The difference between biotechnology and the software industry is interesting here. The latter places its bets less on the securing of innovation rents via formal legal protection than on permanent (apparent) innovation, that is it operates with a planned shortening of the economic life of its products. This is probably connected with the different innovation costs, but also with the different technical and legal possibilities of establishing intellectual property rights. It is of importance for the connection between patent protection and innovation that patents can always also be used to prevent innovations. The guaranteeing of intellectual property rights can therefore, in the extreme case, lead to making research completely impossible. In every case it causes the diffusion of innovations to become slower and in some cases the exclusion of entire regions or social groups from their use.

1.3.3 Lines of conflict

While, with the appearance of a "knowledge society", among other things, the vision of an egalitarian and democratically formable "world society" as a "global village" is painted, new relationships of power and patterns of exclusion are establishing themselves precisely through this development. The post-Fordist "Infocom"-capitalism is characterised by new axes of social conflict, actors and contradictions, and at the same time, by new forms of politically regulating them. "What is to be explored, finally, is on which territory the struggles over the shaping of society and over the political, ethical and legal limits of the use of biotechnology will take place" (Haug 2001: 453, our translation).

This leads, first of all, to the paradox wherein the increasing amount of information available to the masses is accompanied by a concentration of specialised knowledge within national and international elite groups which have access to the necessary means – material resources and political power (Comor 1999: 121ff.). A universalised "culture industry" arises, centred around the internationalised media industry complexes, which commercialise information as a commodity and in so doing, proceed to market virtual realities and world views on an increasing scale. While information and knowledge are thus concentrated in an increasingly important stratum of information and communication managers, the experiences and the social relationships of the "infotainment" consumers are formed by commodities and the market (Rifkin 2000: 181ff.). Because the social conditions and the infrastructural requirements for the preparation and transformation of information into knowledge are unequally distributed, there is a tendency for society to be divided into "haves" and "have-nots" with regard to information or, rather, knowledge. The "haves" have access to the relevant knowledge complexes, and the "have-nots" are left with a mass of trite and irrelevant information. The extension of the information and communication possibilities, with their growing economisation and in view of the highly unequally distributed financial and material resources, tends to increase social inequality. The inhabitants of the "global village" have greatly varying technical and social opportunities with which to use the existing technologies. "Knowledge" thus becomes a decisive mechanism for social exclusion.

The fact that the spread of communication and information possibilities is accompanied by a clear tendency towards the privatisation of information and knowledge at the same time increases the socio-geographical inequalities on the global scale. World Bank figures show that developing countries (low and middle income countries), in 2002, had to pay 9.3 billion USD more than they received for royalties and licence fees (Bödeker *et al.* 2005). The establishment of unhindered informational freedom under these conditions becomes an instrument with the help of which the capitalist centres with their developed information and communication industry safeguard their economic, political and cultural dominance (Comor 1999: 14ff.; May 2000: 73ff.). Access to scientific and technological potentials becomes an ever more decisive factor for international relations of dominance and dependence. According to an estimate by Sachs, roughly 15 per cent of the world's population produce the essential technological innovations and about half of the world's population is able to take possession of these and use them (Sachs 2000). The rest is threatened with being cut off and marginalised – technologically, economically and culturally. This phenomenon, which within a particular society leads to new processes of exclusion, on the global level, adds a new dimension to the conflicts between "North" and "South".

These developments are the context for our empirical investigations: for the conflicts over the use and valorisation of biological diversity and especially genetic resources, it is essential that one analyses the development of the international regimes that act to safeguard intellectual property (see in more detail Correa 2000; May 2000; Drahos/Braithwaite 2003; May/Sell 2006; as well as numerous case studies on Latin America in Brand/Kalcsics 2002). At issue here is the determination of who profits from the advantages which arise from the use of genetic resources. There is a certain paradox in the fact that the most "modern" actors (research institutions and above all transnational, high-tech corporations) are dependent on access to these resources and, thus also to a certain degree, on "traditional" population groups in the global South. The core of the conflict over access, benefit-sharing and intellectual property rights basically stems from this paradox. After all, such resources are primarily to be found in Southern countries and, within them, often in the habitats of "marginalised" population groups, especially indigenous peoples. In addition, for the appropriation of genetic resources, the "traditional" knowledge of how to use these resources plays an important role, for it often serves as a "filter" in the search for economically valuable substances (Kuppe 2001: 147ff.). As a judgement of May 2000 in the case of the Indian Neem tree shows, it has not at all been finally decided how these regulations will be interpreted in the future. One of the patent claims of the US company, W.R. Grace, to the traditionally long-used genetic properties of this tree – as pesticides and medicine – was rejected by the European Patent Office. Nevertheless, it is still valid and 20 others still remain legal (www.genenet-info.org, 8 March 2005).[5] Patent law has come under discussion, which is partly due to international political pressure, but is also connected with the fact that overlapping regulations from different systems demand clarification.

1.4 Tendencies in the emergence of post-Fordist relationships with nature

The post-Fordist form of rationalisation and capitalisation implies a fundamentally altered societal meaning of nature. At the same time, the changed relevance of knowledge and science has consequences for societal relationships with nature (see in more detail, Hirsch 2002b). Simultaneously, the institutional treatment of the environmental crisis leads, together with other changes, to a new mode of regulation. One specific foundation of the Fordist mode of accumulation and regulation was the unhindered exploitation and destruction of natural resources. This formed one of its fundamental moments of crisis. The "ecological crisis", which became ever more obvious at the beginning of the 1970s, was closely bound to the crisis of Fordism. The disputes in the context of the "ecological crisis" have led, in recent decades, to a stronger consideration of ecological and socio-ecological aspects. This must not, however, be thought of as a societal learning process in which "society" as a whole begins to adjust itself to its ecological problems, but rather, as a conflict-driven process in which different actors with different interests in the conservation and use of nature conflict with each other. To some degree, even weaker actors succeed here in finding consideration within the framework of the asymmetric compromises of an emerging "ecological capitalism". Through the discussion of the "ecological crisis" the destruction of the material foundations of life has become an integral and contested component of post-Fordist restructuring (on the connection between the discussion on sustainability and that of globalisation on the fringes of the Rio+10 conference" see Conca *et al.* 2007; Brand/ Görg 2007).

New issues such as socio-ecological problems, gender issues and also North–South relations have been placed onto the political agenda since the crisis of Fordism – transmitted through the criticism of social movements, critical academics and non-governmental organisations (NGOs). That does not mean that societal relations in those areas did not develop in a crisis-driven manner previously, but that they gain increased societal relevance in the crisis of Fordism and also that they are being transmitted through new social actors. The constitution of "new" problems is itself a political process which in turn is connected with comprehensive socio-economic changes such as the new valorisation of nature.

In these disputes, "corridors" of problem-solving are created. This relates first to the political and legal terrain of the interpretation and treatment of problems. Second, a dominant understanding of problems emerges which defines the legitimacy of certain viewpoints and demands, that is that which is regarded as "reasonable" and "feasible". Thus, the dominant discussion of the ecological crisis in the "Northern" countries treats this as an environmental problem with a strongly technical solution perspective, through which privileges are granted to strategies of "ecological modernisation" (Toke 2001; Jänicke/Jacob 2004). Concern is concentrated primarily on the rationalisation of the flows of energy and materials for economic activities. Social aspects are often overlooked or de-legitimised, and questions regarding resource problems *and* distributional conflicts are *simultaneously* under-emphasised. Concurrently, the general tendency towards the control of nature and the subsumption of nature under the conditions of capitalist valorisation processes continues to be in force, although in a reflexively broken form. The appropriation of oil, with all its international economic and geopolitical implications and its consequences for the realm of nature, remains a central condition of "fossilistic" capitalism (Altvater 1993) – despite all the solemn assurances of the inevitable beginning of a "solar epoch". The disputes over "strategic resources" (Ceceña/Barreda 1995) such as oil, gas and, increasingly, fresh water, are a central component of international politics. Nonetheless, new resources are also "constituted" (Heins/Flitner 1998) by means of new technologies and socio-economic developments. This is true, particularly in regard to genetic resources in connection with genetic technology (and in the near future we can expect the reconstitution of parts of nature through nano-technology). The industries of the so-called life sciences are the most powerful driving force in the reorganisation of societal relationships with nature in this field, whereby much – from the economic and technical options available to the design of the political and legal environment – is still uncertain or disputed. This concerns important questions such as the acceptance of new patterns of production and consumption in the spheres of health and nutrition (e.g. the acceptance of genetically modified crops) and the legitimacy of specific and competing appropriation strategies of nature (e.g. private property on "life"). Alejandro Toledo speaks of a necessary "double mutation" in order to make possible the intensive capitalisation of nature: In addition to the systematic recording of potentially commercialisable resources there must be a "semiotic conquering of territory" (A.Toledo Ocampo 2000: 285). Signs and meanings are redefined, that is new forms and outputs are defined as rational and appropriate. Of decisive importance for post-Fordist relationships with nature is that nature must be newly defined in order to be able to serve as a "raw material" and as a resource for capitalist valorisation. In this context, there is a demand by capital, that individualised "private property rights" to nature should be privileged, which is a completely unacceptable demand in many cultures.

These processes, thus, are always contested and, to some degree, politically regulated. With regard to the political-institutional design of relationships with nature, an increase in international environmental politics can be observed. The UNCED conference in Rio de Janeiro in 1992 played an important role here, although national and international policies had already existed since the 1970s. The institutions of international environmental politics are, however, not at all problem-solving instruments which support one another, as is often assumed, but rather, they find themselves in an asymmetric and often contradictory relationship to one another. The following study will also focus on this aspect.

Furthermore, we can observe an increased importance of "civil society actors" in environmental politics, connected with general changes of governance structures in politics. Moreover, the enormous *knowledge-dependency* and *uncertainty* under which politics takes place here needs broader consideration. In many decisive questions it is still unclear today exactly where the problems lie and how they can be dealt with. The political terrains of socio-ecological politics, especially at the international level, are only just being structured, and in this process, in view of the intricate conflicts even "weaker" actors succeed in bringing forward their perceptions and interests. One important characteristic of post-Fordist capitalism is, therefore, that the *struggle over information and knowledge* is becoming an increasingly central sphere of social and political conflict (Drahos/Braithwaite 2003; Delgado 2002). Particularly "knowledge" – in the sense of the ability to generate and define societal problems symbolically and to bring this into political processes in the form of "expert opinion" – is becoming an ever more important power resource. Not only has the process of social production and reproduction become "knowledge-driven" in this way, but politics has as well. This has effects on the political constitution, and on the institutional and discursive treatment of problems, as well as on political strategies and forms and on constellations of alliances.

1.5 The transformation of the state and the system of states

The formation of a post-Fordist mode of development was accompanied by major changes in the institutional mode of regulation. This included not only the establishment of "neoliberal" norms and behavioural styles, but also a restructuring – completed with the breakdown of the Soviet Union – of the international relations of dominance and dependence, which is characterised by a complex arrangement of cooperation and conflict between the state groups of the capitalist "triad" (North America, Europe, South-East Asia/Japan) under the leadership of the USA. It involves an economic and political differentiation among the peripheral countries but also their far-reaching subordination. One major and still existing characteristic of the North–South relationship is that many Southern countries have become laboratories for neoliberal policies. The debt crisis, apparent ever since the beginning of the 1980s – in addition to authoritarian regimes and military dictatorships, which were a part of internal class struggles – became the central lever for achieving this.

   In spite of the – measured in monetary units – statistically declining economic importance of many regions of the capitalist periphery, they remain de facto essential sources of cheap raw materials, foodstuffs and labour for the "high-technological mode of production" (Haug 2001: 450). The Fordist as well as the – vastly more precarious – emerging post-Fordist compromises in the capitalist metropolis continue to be based, among other things, on cheap pre-products produced in the peripheral countries – whether through the relocation of sections of companies, through pre-products bought on markets or through lower environmental standards – and the cheaper reproduction of labour power – whether through unpaid work by women, foodstuffs, raw materials or cheap household employees. There is still a rising inequality in the worldwide distribution of income which is not clearly divided along North–South lines, but rather, differs among regions (Wade 2001; with respect to gender relations Wichterich 2000).

1.5.1 Global governance?

There is a certain degree of consensus within the social sciences regarding the general diagnosis of a fundamental change in the state and the system of states in the course of "globalisation". There is dissent, however, on how this can be conceptualised theoretically and what it means for the various collective actors and persons affected. What role does the nation-state play and what is the role of international politics, particularly the system of institutions that is developing there? How do the different levels of politics – from the local to the international – behave towards one another? Which actors, with what interests, play a role? What is the relationship of political/institutional and socio-economic structures and processes? To what extent do socio-ecological problems affect economic and political processes? Do they play any role at all in the social scientific and socio-political discussions?

A striking shortcoming of many political science approaches which are concerned with the internationalisation of politics is the way in which they theorise about the state (this is also true of many historical-materialist approaches; see Shaw 2000: 87). It can generally be stated that their understanding of the state usually falls into an understanding of either organisational sociology or system theory. Usually, the "modern" state as a form of political domination is presupposed without explaining its existence and theoretical functioning. This can be seen particularly clearly in the contributions of social sciences to global governance or global public policy, which claim to grasp the current upheavals analytically (see e.g. Rosenau 1995; Reinicke 1998; Held/McGrew 2002; survey and criticism in Hewson/Sinclair 1999; Brand *et al.* 2000; Saxe-Fernández 2005; Brand 2005; Behrens 2005). "Reduced to the simplest common denominator, 'global governance' means accompanying, politically, the process of globalisation" (Enquete-Kommission 2002: 415, our translation). It is about dealing with the problems arising from globalisation by means of public, cooperative policies, that is the "principal modalities of global-rule making and implementation" (Held/McGrew 2002: 11). The state is understood as an independent, sovereign and rationally behaving actor, operating in the name of a more or less unified and definable "national interest".

In a similar fashion to that found in regime theory (Krasner 1983; Rittberger 1993), the question of international cooperation between states is the core issue. International institutions are created for this purpose. Herein, from the outset, the issues are questions of political regulation, which are combined with the assumption that adequate forms would contribute to the resolution of diverse problems. The creation and the growing importance of international institutions is, as a rule, explained by the increase in international problems, which are due, not least, to the weakening of nation-state institutional systems with regard to "good governance". Global governance has, as is the case with governance approaches in general, a bias towards problem-solving theory, while neglecting, or at least under-estimating, power relations and relations of domination (Mayntz 2005). Most governance approaches suggest that there are new institutions or measures *because* there are problems; that is, they explain them in a functionalistic manner. However, this is increasingly criticised within regime theory and governance approaches themselves. Constructivist concepts which have recently gained importance within regime theory (Risse 2003; Wendt 1999; Wiener 2003) address precisely the processes of problem constitution which have been hitherto neglected by more traditional regime-based theoretical approaches. They explore the ways international regimes, once they have been established by nation-states, gain a momentum of their own and change the problem perceptions and politics of their member states.

International political economy goes beyond regime theory in many of the aspects which are important for the issues we are discussing here (Scherrer 2003). Underhill (2000: 806) identifies three common assumptions of the various IPE approaches:

> i) that the political and economic domains cannot be separated in any real sense, and even doing so for analytical purposes has its perils; ii) political interaction is one of the principal means through which the economic structures of the market are established and in turn transformed; and iii) that there is an intimate connection between the domestic and international levels of analysis, and that the two cannot meaningfully be separated from one another.

However, in IPE the state is often understood in a rather formal manner as an institution equipped with rule-setting power. It is not seen as a materialisation of contradictory social relations. Thus, IPE runs the risk of conceptualising the relationship between politics and economics as a dichotomy, thereby undermining its own claim of having developed an integrated approach (see Bieling 2003; Shaw 2000). Against this background, "global governance" is "more a site, one of many sites, in which struggles over wealth, power, and knowledge are taking place" (Murphy 2000: 799) To sum up, neither the relationships between politics and economy nor the wider societal context of political institutions, including the ecological aspects of socio-economic processes, are treated carefully.[6] To remedy the complementary deficits of regime theory and IPE, a reference to regulation theory and to materialist state theory may be helpful.

1.5.2 State and institutions: theoretical considerations

The inadequate anchoring of IR and IPE approaches in a theory of society has unmistakable consequences for the ability of the analysis to offer robust explanations, especially as far as the current transformation processes of states and the system of states are concerned. We summarise both processes under the term "changes in statehood". Therefore, this term does not only mean the transformation of the international political system. We return here to concepts of historical-materialist state theory which were developed in the 1970s by reverting to the approaches of Marx and Gramsci (see among others, Poulantzas 1978/2002; Jessop 1990; Hirsch 1997, 2002a). The state and the system of states are understood here within the framework of social theory as a specific form of the political under the conditions of capitalist socialisation. Accordingly, a fundamental structural characteristic of capitalist society is the creation of an apparatus of physical force which is formally separated from the classes in society. However, the separation of "state" from "society" and of "politics" from the "economy" does not represent a dualism because they are simultaneously constituted to each other. The state form, which was already defined by Max Weber as the central characteristic of the modern state, is based on the fact that the capitalist mode of appropriation of surplus value, that is via private production, wage labour and the exchange of commodities, both requires and accelerates the independence and centralisation of compulsory physical force. The "particularity" or "relative autonomy" of the state is the foundation of a specific mode of regulation of class and other social relations. It is this which makes possible in the first place, the formulation of a "politics of capital" which goes beyond divided, competing interests, to be able to, at the same time, enable the exploited and dominated classes to be politically integrated in both a repressive and a consensual way. The state, thus, simultaneously becomes, in this specifically determined form, a material condensation of specific relationships between social classes and groups, that is one characterised by its own institutional structures and routines (Poulantzas 1978/2002: 154ff.). It is neither an independent subject, nor simply an organisation with a rational purpose, but the expression and a component of societal relationships characterised by fundamental contradictions and conflicts. It, therefore, necessarily forms a heterogeneous complex of apparatuses with divergent societal relations which are relatively independent of one another and often operate against each other. The formal separation of state and society is at the same time the form of the presence of the political in the economy. The state – as an integral part of the capitalist relationships of production – is not outwardly in opposition to the economy. The contrasting of "state" and "market" as spheres which are separate from each other, a view which is often found in academic literature, is therefore misleading.

Although "the state" and "(civil) society" are formally separate, at the same time they form a contradictory unity. Both spheres are to be understood as complex relations of domination based simultaneously on both force and consensus (Gramsci 1991: 783ff.). "Civil society", as a part of bourgeois society, is not a sphere in which there is no domination; rather, any domination is permeated by power relations and coercion. At the same time, it is the sphere of political self-organisation, of the articulation of interests and discussion, and thus a field of struggle on which hegemony, that is legitimate concepts of societal order and development, is fought over. This implies varying, and even contradictory, practices. Since civil society is permeated by conflicts but nevertheless remains an integral part of societal power relations, it can, in the terminology of Gramsci, be regarded as a part of the "extended state". At the same time, the existence of a developed civil society is a decisive precondition for democratic processes. The latter gain their political effectiveness, however, above all, from the fact that they are based on procedures for the formation of opinion and for decision-making which are institutionalised and formalised by the state. Decisive from the point of view of the dominant actors is the extent to which they are able to present their intentions as legitimate and socially necessary or in the general interest of society, to what extent they are able, via compromises, to partially change the viewpoints and interests of other actors – but also their own – and/or to exclude groups with fundamentally opposing interests. The *discursive* and the *institutional* levels complement each other here. One central subject of dispute is the institutional safeguarding of the actors' own interests through state policies or the hindering or even prevention of the institutionalisation of contrary interests. A major indicator for the establishment of specific positions is, therefore, the extent to which they succeed in becoming "the national interest".

The concept of civil society cannot simply be applied in an analogous way to the international scale: processes of societalisation that transcend state borders do exist – although in a highly fragmented fashion – but there is no world state. The concept can be used, however, to show that there are political processes on the international scale beyond traditional state diplomacy or force. Alex Demirovic (1997: 258) emphasises the character of transnational actors such as business associations, NGOs, elites and their networks, all of whom, despite pushing for divergent interests, come to represent a civil side-stage in which a global consensus is worked out. Nevertheless, this should not be interpreted separately from the processes which take place within nation-states (see also Görg/Brand 2003; on the risks of transferring Gramscian categories to the international scale see Germain/Kenny 1998).

These characteristics are founded in the structure of capitalist societies. Their basic components consist not only of the particular form of the state but also the pluralism of (national) states (see for more detail, Hirsch 2002a: 35ff.). The system of nation-states is an expression of the contradictions and rivalries which characterise global societal relations. The pluralism of the states is itself a mode of reproduction of the capitalist political form. It divides social groups and classes along state borders and thus creates the basis both for the formation of competing "national" class formations and for "corporate" and other societal compromises. The decisive basis for this is the fact that the individual states dispose over the (legitimate) monopoly of physical force, which makes possible both the control of cross-border movements and material redistributions as the basis of social compromises. It makes possible the formation of highly differentiated conditions of production and valorisation and thus creates the inequalities which represent an essential basis for the global accumulation process. The fragmentary structure of the system of states is, thus, a decisive precondition for the stabilisation and reproduction of capitalist society within the context of the world market. It is, as is the form of the state itself, a fundamental part of the capitalist mode of production. This explains why, on the global scale, neither a coherent, comprehensive "state" nor a relatively coherent "civil society" can arise. And at the same time, it becomes clear that the political organisation of capitalist society consists of a complex intertwining of different scales: local, national and international.

Before we go into the current process of the transformation of the state and the system of states in detail, we must first deal with the relationship between the capitalist political form and political institutionalisation (on this see Esser *et al.* 1994). Social forms are, in Marxist terminology, objectivations of societal relations – resulting from the general principles of socialisation, that is private property, wage labour, the exchange of commodities and competition – which confront individuals in a reified form. This is particularly true of the commodity and money forms and of the political (state) form. The capitalist form of the state – its "relative autonomy" and the formal separation of "state" and "society" – is an expression of a social structure in which the direct and conscious creation of society, and thus the existence of radical democracy in the form of an immediate political community, is impossible. General references for consciousness and behaviour constitute and reproduce themselves in the *social forms* of bourgeois society. These become concretised in *social institutions*, or to put it the other way around, the general societal form determinations are materialised in the institutions. Institutions can be understood as consolidated modes of behavioural orientation, routinisation and coordination, which both guide social activity and make it possible, thus lending social systems a relative continuity (Giddens 1988). It is essential, however, that societal institutions cannot simply be understood as direct manifestations of social forms, fully determined by them. Rather, social forms lay the foundation for, support and limit processes of institutionalisation. A complex intermediary context must be taken into account here between the societal structure (or the social forms), the institutions and the activity which reproduces them (Görg 1994). The regulationist category of "institutional form", as introduced above, is a concept which mediates between social forms and institutions. It stands for historically and spatially specific concretisations of social forms as certain modes of state intervention, inter-state relations, monetary systems and wage relations which materialise themselves in national and international social and political institutions.

Since social activity, which is expressed in institutions, is neither "purely" objectively determined nor without conflict, it is possible for institutions and processes of institutionalisation to generate contradictions to the social forms. Societal crises and conflicts express themselves in such a process. The capitalist social forms are a fundamental and structural component of the mode of production, whereas institutional forms and institutions, as a product of social activity and societal struggles, are changeable within this mode. This means that the capitalist social forms do not determine a specific system of institutions and the political form therefore does not determine a particular form of the state. Each concrete form of the state is a historically determined expression of the capitalist political form. The "particularity" or the "relative autonomy" of the state, the specific characteristics of the monopoly of physical force and the institutions and institutional forms which are taken by the material condensation of class and other societal relations are historically and spatially variable, according to the specific economic conditions of reproduction and societal power relations. The strong condensation of political processes at the level of the nation-state, with all its "extensions" in civil society, is only one possible form of the institutionalisation of the political. It was expressed in the north-western part of the world under the conditions of class compromise which characterised "Atlantic Fordism" until the second third of the twentieth century. It follows from this that the question as to the possible "end" of the "(nation-) state" is wrongly formulated. Instead, it must be examined whether, and if so how, the capitalist political form is institutionalising itself in a new way, and what conflicts and what possible societal processes of crisis are implied in this.

However, there are some limits to this form of theorising when we consider the state in countries of the capitalist periphery. Here we can find a variety of state forms that differ in many aspects from those in the advanced capitalist countries, ranging from South-East Asian developmentalist states to the "failing states" in large parts of Africa. This variety results from the specific articulation of capitalist and non-capitalist sectors within these countries and the respective modes of integration into the world market. Because of the very different socio-economic conditions and colonial heritages in the capitalist periphery, it is not possible to formulate a coherent theory of "the" peripherial state.

Materialist state theory as outlined above refers to developed capitalist societies with their specific economic and class structures. In the capitalist periphery, these conditions exist, at best, only partially (Castro Escudero *et al.* 2005; Olivier Costilla 2005; Burchardt 2004: 131–146; Schedler *et al.*

1999; Heigl 2007; see the current transformations in Latin America, Velinga 1998). In the capitalist periphery, we often find highly segmented class structures, important sectors of non-capitalist production, economies with a high degree of structural heterogeneity, a minor degree of wage labour and, therefore, a civil society which is "less" developed. Independent social actors, self organised societal associations and a free public often exist only in a rudimentary form, non-governmental organisations very often are organised and financed from abroad. In many cases, the "modern", centralised state apparatus is – due to the colonial heritage – set upon societies which do not have corresponding economic and social structures. For these reasons, the relative autonomy of the state with respect to the dominant classes or class fractions often does not really exist. That means that a central characteristic of the capitalist state is missing. Likewise, there generally does not exist an "extended state" in the Gramscian sense, as a complex unity of state and civil society. One decisive factor for state structures in the periphery is the presence of land reform, that is the abolishment of quasi feudal or oligarchic agrarian structures, which is important for industrial development with its consequences for class structures, the establishment of comprehensive market relations and the existence of a state apparatus equipped with relative autonomy. This, for example, makes an important difference between Latin American and South-East Asian states. In general, peripheral states are, therefore, more repressive ones. The regulation of class relations and economic exploitation is, to a higher degree, based on physical force. Compared with more developed capitalist countries, the relation of "consensus" and "repression" appears to be significantly one-sided. However, some features have been changing, particularly in the last two decades, with democratisation processes and neoliberal transformations in many countries (Schedler *et al.* 1999).

Especially in African countries, we can observe a special weakness or even absence of a centralised state apparatus and the increasing importance of economic activities based on the violent exploitation of large parts of the population by warlords. As a result, governments lose control over parts of their territory; the monopoly of force erodes in favour of clan-based warlords fighting each other; and new and extremely violent modes of societalisation, beyond the capitalist state and market, emerge, which are nevertheless integrated in the capitalist world market (see Seibert 2003). But also in Latin American and South-East Asian countries, whose state forms are more similar to those in the capitalist core, we have to introduce some differentiations. The state in these countries must be conceptualised against the background of their subaltern status in the world economy. Especially due to the debt crisis, supranational and Northern dominated institutions such as the International Monetary Fund (IMF) exert a much greater influence on the societal power relations and the state politics than in Northern countries, often preventing a national or even an internal bourgeoisie from developing itself (Poulantzas 2001; see Alnasseri 2004).

1.5.3 The internationalisation of the state

The neoliberal globalisation strategy, which has been established since the 1980s as a reaction to the crisis of Fordism, has aimed at a comprehensive restructuring of global class relations. Central to it was the destruction of the class compromises which characterised the Fordist state of the post-war era. The structure of the states and of the state system was profoundly altered – a process which was further accelerated by the collapse of the Soviet Union and the accompanying unilateral political dominance of the capitalist triad centres under the leadership of the USA. The background for this was the growth of the internationalisation of capital during the Fordist epoch (Poulantzas 2001), which had led to a fundamentally altered relationship between capital and the states of the now relatively unified capitalist world system. The new thrust of capitalist globalisation is based on the increasing internationalisation of production which, at the same time, works to accelerate the it. This means that state–society relations as well as the relations of states to one another have been considerably modified; a process which we describe as the *internationalisation of the state* (Jessop 1997; Hirsch *et al.* 2001; Robinson 2001; Hirsch 2002a). This process has several dimensions which are important for understanding our empirical research. Although an internationalisation of the economy already took place during Fordism, the processes of deregulation and privatisation since the 1980s have led to an increased dependency of the nation-state apparatuses on the international capital and financial markets. The actors of these processes – particularly multinational corporations and international financial institutions, but also international networks of managers, politicians and members of international institutions – determine in a quasi "de-politicised" way, that is relatively independently of formalised democratic political institutions and decision-making processes, essential contents of individual state politics. This is a contested process and implies the shifting of relationships of social forces. This development is expressed in the type of the *competition state*, which is centrally aligned towards ensuring the optimal conditions for the valorisation of capital (Hirsch 1995). It involves a considerable shift in the state's capacities for economic and socio-political intervention. The transformation towards a competition state has also involved changes in both the configuration of the state apparatuses and in the modes of political decision-making and decision enforcement. The position of the finance ministries and of the central banks, which are largely autonomous in relation to the democratic political institutions, was strengthened and the political parties transformed themselves in this process from "mass integrating" organisations for the mediation of interests to medial agents for the procuring of legitimacy. This is not the result of a historical law in whatever form – whether that of the logic of capital or of the modernisation and differentiation of societies – but of a political strategy which has been partially enforced through hard struggles. We can also call a state whose apparatuses are increasingly dependent on international capital and finance markets and which interiorise these dependencies and the related relationships of forces, "internationalised competition states" (Hirsch 2005: 145–51).

As a consequence, the opportunities of the states for the coherent and integrative regulation of society within national boundaries have been diminished. The result is increasing economic and social fragmentation. As we have shown above, the geographically fragmented system of nation-states, which both politically and economically integrates its component parts in various ways and which is mediated by competition, is a general structural characteristic of the capitalist world system. Nevertheless, the competition among different capitals, between socio-political areas ("locations") and wage-earners (migration plays an important role here) has a greater importance now than during Fordism. Material and ideological integration paths and macro-economic coherencies are less stable than under Fordism and are less tied to the nation-state. The apparatuses of the competition states, particularly those of the impoverished parts of the periphery, are given the role of handling the consequences of the neoliberal transformation with their restricted regulatory possibilities and of creating a minimal amount of social cohesion. In the following section, we will sketch out some central features of the transformation of statehood. The process in which "civil society" actors gain in importance beyond that of the Fordist corporate institutions can be described as the *relative privatisation of politics*. Decision-making and decision enforcement by the central bureaucracy changes to "governance" in the form of the "cooperative" or "negotiating" state, that is the state integrated into a complex network of state and private actors. The private actors, who are increasingly gaining in political importance, are not only multinational corporations but also the so-called non-governmental organisations (NGOs). At the international level, too, structures of the "negotiating state" are developing. This creates room for activities involving the definition of problems and the representation of interests which are conducted by NGOs (see Görg/Brand 2003; Demirovic 2003; Hirsch 2003; McCormick 2005). One change is decisive here: in periods of neoliberal hegemony, conditions to which political activity has to adapt – or is perceived to require adaptation – are claimed, ever more, to be determined by the "market" and the political processes are, to a certain extent, economised, that is relatively, directly subordinated to economic rationality. NGOs are thus, particularly as organisations which carry out, for instance, development projects, among other things "a consequence of neoliberal marketization" (Murphy 2000: 795; on private financial regulation Palan 2003; Malcher 2006).

A further process can be described as the *denationalisation of state politics*. As a result of the transformation towards a competition state, of the limited possibilities for a coherent regulation of the national economy and the increasing cross-border economic interlinking, an *increased importance of sub-national and local regulating contexts* can be observed (Brenner 2004; Wissen

2000). Regulating institutions and social compromises of forces manifest a move from the level of the central state to towns, communities, semi-states and – often crossing national borders – economic regions, which strive for their own paths to development and policies of locational competition.

The denationalisation of state politics comprises a further aspect. The process of globalising accumulation is accompanied by the *internationalisation of political regulating complexes*, which can comprise formal institutions, regimes, treaties or networks. In the discussion among political scientists, the process of the denationalisation of state politics and the newly emerging political institutions and their interrelationships are examined using the concept of multilevel analysis. This is done particularly with regard to the European Community or Union and the supranational political processes and institutions emerging from them (Scharpf 1999; Hooghe/Marks 1999; Bache/Flinders 2004). Attention is directed primarily towards the cooperation of the supranational and the national levels. The dominant perception in political science is that this is a process for dealing with the economic globalisation process, a process which generates crises and problems that need to be addressed by politics. But this explains only a part of the dynamism. First of all, it is a case of a "new constitutionalism" (Gill 2000), which is advanced by the capitalist triad centres in order to institutionally safeguard their global dominance, in general or with respect to specific actors – for example in the form of the North Atlantic Treaty Organization (NATO), which has been reshaped into an instrument of global military intervention, of the International Monetary Fund (IMF), the World Bank (WB), the Organization for Economic Cooperation and Development (OECD) or the World Trade Organization (WTO). Shaw understands international politics as the generalisation of the "global-Western-state-conglomerate" which grew out of the increasing international cooperation among the capitalist core after World War II (2000: 199ff.). At the same time, regional integration processes serve to strengthen the position of individual groups of states in the relationship between competition states (European Union, North American Free Trade Area). The growing weight of international organisations and regimes means that state apparatuses that are based on a large number of national societies gain in relevance. International political institutions are supported by the states and their autonomy is limited: "they usually remain the creatures of the most powerful of their state members" (Murphy 2000: 793). Nevertheless, they develop their own political dynamism, which even the most powerful actors cannot completely escape. John G. Ruggie (1982), with respect to the "embedded liberalism" of the post-war constellation, elaborated that although there were generally accepted compromises, their specific institutional, international and national implementation was contested. This is probably even truer with regards to the post-Fordist mode of development and its "disciplinary neoliberalism" (Gill 2000). The following study concentrates on the detailed analysis of this process.

One particular aspect of this development is the *internationalisaton of law.* The development and enforcement of law tend to separate themselves – although in very different ways – from the states. Examples of this are the setting up of international courts: the European Court, the International Criminal Court, but also the dispute settlement body within the WTO, which is concerned not only with jurisdiction but also, de facto, with the creation of law. The international enforcement of private property relation-ships – not least those concerning intellectual property rights, for example within the framework of the WTO-TRIPS Agreement – is especially gain-ing in relevance. Of particular importance is the development known as *lex mercatoria* of a private civil law, supported chiefly by international companies and lawyers' firms. This is not necessarily new: state legislation was always strongly based on the formalisation and codification of socially developed legal norms. But the generation of law relatively independently of the states has increased in importance and has begun to, ever more clearly, transcend individual state borders (Günther/Randeria 2001; for a critical voice, see Buckel 2003). Here the difference between the creation of law and the enforcement of law is important, however – a difference which is not always clearly made in political science. The enforcement of the law in the case of conflict remains tied to the monopoly of force in the individual states and is dependent on its relative effectiveness. "Strong" states can evade interna-tional jurisdiction more easily than "weak" ones, if indeed, they submit to it at all – as can be seen in the case of the behaviour of the USA towards the International Criminal Court. Generally speaking, however, it can be assumed that there is a stronger separation of the creation of law from the enforcement of law.

The internationalisation of capital, which was further advanced by the transition to post-Fordism, and the transformation of the system of states have changed the *conditions for the formation of hegemony at the international level.* The pattern of the present world order shows a contradictory picture in this regard, where a strong tendency towards transnationalisation is coun-terbalanced by a global world order still fragmented through nation-states. On the one hand, there is a system of international organisations and regimes – from the CBD to the WTO – in which the interests of interna-tional capital and of the dominating states in the safeguarding of the capi-talist market economy and private property as well as the policy of neoliberal deregulation are solidly institutionalised – even if they remain contested. In the course of increasing cultural and communicative interac-tion, there are also indications of tendencies towards the creation of inter-state "civil society" structures. And last but not least, in the wake of the internationalisation of the state and of capital, an "international managerial class" is growing, consisting of company and state functionaries, members of international organisations, scientists and think tanks, and representatives of NGOs, which is in a position to formulate concepts of world order and development, cutting through political conflicts, and over and beyond national borders. Kees van der Pijl (1999: 138) names this group a *cadre class* which is in a position to conduct "planning and the propagation and monitoring of social norms". This group tends to represent the long-term interests of the reproduction of capitalist societies and can therefore take a position which might be in contradiction to company managers. This is particularly clear in the current discussion on the negative implications of the transformation processes. Michael Goldman (1998) uses, for the specific sphere of environmental and resource politics, the term "global resources managers", who do not per se have an interest in the short-term valorisation of nature. On the other hand, not only is this "international civil society" characterised by considerable inequalities of power and asymmetries but it is still fragmented along state and regional borders.

The present international order basically possesses the *characteristic of hegemonic instability*. The post-Fordist accumulation regime is more prone to crisis than the Fordist one and we cannot speak of coherent modes of regulation. The terrains of international political conflict are still emerging. With regard to the dimension of international leadership, the USA finds itself in a dominant position, above all in a military sense but also with certain qualifications economically, but it is at the same time unable to develop the political leadership which is crucial for hegemony. This, in turn, is connected essentially with the enforcement of the neoliberal mode of politics, which places its stakes on economic privatisation, deregulation and the liberalisation of market forces, and which largely does so without a materially supported integrative organisation of societal relations, both in a national and in an international framework (Hirsch 2002a: 145ff.) This is the basis for the complex relations of cooperation and conflict among the "strong" states. They are forced to cooperate out of their common interest in the safeguarding of the existing economic and political order or its transformation in their interest, and this expresses itself in the development of comprehensive international organisations and regimes. Simultaneously, this relationship of cooperation is in tension with the diverging interests of specific states and groups of states, not least in the relationships between the USA/NAFTA and the European Union, and due to the increasing unilateralism of US politics in some important areas, which are expressed in repeated policies of refusal and blockade. Capitalist competition continues to be determined essentially by the existence of reproduction complexes which are regulated by individual states.

Following the collapse of the Soviet Union and the end of system confrontation, the capitalist periphery is – despite dynamic socio-economic developments in some regions, especially in Asia – in a greater position of dependency, which expresses itself in reduced political and economic room for manoeuvre. In view of failed "development" strategies and uncertain societal and economic perspectives, we can hardly speak of a stable hegemonic relationship. Instead, we could speak of a *fragmented hegemony*, in which worldwide, the compulsory elements of a permanent crisis management move, ever more strongly, into the foreground (Brand 2004).

The issue is to grant these processes within the metropolitan countries legitimacy and to safeguard them with political institutions. This constitutes a large part of present-day international politics. Regarding North–South relations we could, modifying Gramsci, speak today of hegemony in the sense of "coercion with selective elements of consensus".

The process of the "internationalisation of the state" leads, as a whole, to the fact that the *liberal democratic institutions* at the level of the individual state *threaten to run idle*. Relevant political processes of discussion, consensus formation and decision-making shift to levels on which those affected have only very limited influence. The more political alternatives and decisions are formulated at the international level, the more strongly they will, in view of the heterogeneous complex of regulating systems which is to be found there, become the subject of non-transparent and hardly democratically controllable negotiation processes between powerful state and private actors. It is, therefore, not completely wrong to speak in this context of a process of the "refeudalising" of politics (Maus 1991; Anderson/Goodman 1995). It is not least these problems which feed the debates on an "international civil society". The hoped-for democratic quality of the latter breaks down, however, due to the complex fragmentation and power structures which characterise the international political system just as much as global societal relations.

Nevertheless, *nation-states retain a central importance* (see e.g. Panitch 1994; Murphy 2000: 797; Jessop 2003) and, as we will see, even gain importance because in international biodiversity politics *national sovereignty* over biological diversity and especially genetic resources is granted as a precondition for conservation and use. This is based on the fact that their "monopoly of legitimate physical force" despite some differences and qualifications – and despite developments since September 11, 2001 – remains, at the core, unchallenged. Moreover, the core nation-states, in particular, still have, within their complex apparatus, an enormous amount of material resources as well as knowledge and experiences. The states thus remain the decisive institutional configurations in which the capitalist form of the political is manifested. They continue to be the decisive guarantors of the social order – particularly of property relations – and of societal cohesion. The states, therefore, continue to be the centre of the regulation of class and other societal relations and it is essentially up to them to provide the general conditions of production (infrastructure, research, technology) and reproduction. Even though the "state–capital" relations are being formed anew under the conditions of globalisation and internationalisation, this does not mean that corporations become "stateless" or independent of the state. Although they can relate more flexibly to the states – by establishing and utilising different locational conditions – and can, up to a certain point, play them off against one another, they remain dependent on them for the enforcement of their interests, whether through their reliance on the potential force of the state or for reasons of political legitimacy. It is, therefore, no coincidence that the most important multinational corporations, as a rule, have their headquarters or their operative centre in the dominating states of the capitalist triad.

1.5.4 Internationalisation and the problem of "scale"

As we have seen, the internationalisation of the state means that state–society relations are being newly configured on a global scale. The institutional shaping of the state apparatus, thus, takes on a more complex spatial form. Political-administrative regulating and controlling functions increasingly shift from the nation-state to the subnational, regional and international levels. A system of more or less strongly institutionalised bodies of regulations arises which differ, but also intersect and overlap, in their range of activity and which are related to materials and problem areas which are different from, although not independent of, one another, and in which different societal relationships of power are concentrated. This is essentially a problem of scale.[7] Scale is not simply given; rather, it is a social construction resulting from conflict-driven processes of socialisation and dispute. Scale should therefore, in principle, also be regarded as a dispositive of power, which both symbolises and defines processes of politico-social inclusion and exclusion. It can be regarded as the result of institutionalised social compromises and power relations, with which – not least via the externalising of costs and the imposition of relationships of exploitation – the cohesion between different conflicting actors is produced. As such it is "the *spatial* resolution of contradictory social forces" (Smith 1995: 61). For example, the historical constitution of the nation-state level required sustained (class) struggles over the centralisation of political power in the course of the transition to capitalism (Poulantzas 1978/2002: 123ff.).

It follows that politico-social struggles are always, among other things, about the dominance of a certain scale within the geographical-institutional asymmetric setting or about the reconfiguration of that constellation ("rescaling"). The transition from Fordism to post-Fordism can be understood as a process in which the global capital and financial markets, with their dominant actors, gained in importance over the nationally institutionalised social compromises and relationships of power. At the same time, there was a growth in the importance of subnational and regional levels, together with the social relationships that were institutionalised there. In view of the lack of a centralised apparatus of force at the global level, the different regulating complexes form, in a certain sense, a relatively incoherent *network of international regulation*. However, this network is characterised by the fact that in its individual components highly unequal ranges of activity and relationships of power and dominance are manifested. It is marked by asymmetries and, thus, highly selective possibilities for the definition of problems and the consideration of interests. In connection with the present study, we are concerned, above all, with the conflict-driven relationship between the Convention on Biological Diversity (CBD), the Food and

Agriculture Organization of the United Nations (FAO) and the World Trade Organization (WTO) with its Trade-Related Aspects of Intellectual Property Rights (TRIPS) Agreement. We will also examine how the scales of regulation, constituted by these agreements, behave towards the national, local and regional scales. The incoherence and contradictory nature of the international system of regulating and the connected complex asymmetry of scales is reflected in the fragmentation of a "world society".

1.5.5 Hegemony and the second order condensation of power relations

In recent years there has been an ever stronger awareness that the regulating potential of international regimes can only really be estimated when the complex relations of tension between overlapping areas of regulation and their interplay are taken into account (Young 2002; Rosendal 2001; Thomas 2002; Oberthür/Gehring 2006; Raustiala/Victor 2004). This is particularly true of the relationship between environmental regimes and regimes for the liberalisation of world trade.

In order to understand this conflict-driven interplay of international regulating processes, we revert to the concept of *international hegemony*. In order to explain the way in which we use this term, we must first discuss the different meanings of the concept of hegemony, which is usually not very precisely defined in academic literature. Hegemony should not be equated, as it often is, with the dominance of one or several states. Such dominance is important, but the historical-materialist concept of hegemony goes beyond this (see Cox 1993; Scherrer 1998; Gill 2000, 2003; Borg 2001; Bieler/ Morton 2004). International hegemony, in the sense of a transnational and consensus-based societalisation, has two dimensions: namely, (1) the establishment of certain living conditions and concepts of value in societies, and (2) the ability, through governments and other societal groups, to formulate projects, follow strategies and work out compromises on the international scale.

(1) International hegemony first comprises norms of material production and consumption which are established in the core societies or regions and penetrate dependent societies in a "capillary" and broken fashion, that is they are translated into a multitude of strategies and activities. This is accompanied by the generalisation of certain concepts of social order and development and, thus, the consolidation of expectations and planning horizons. It is not about the relationships of dominance between states in the narrow sense (i.e. the opportunity to wield relational power) but about complex processes in which greatly differing economic, political and cultural actors are involved. Of particular importance is the "inter-iorisation" of production and consumption norms and of societal concepts of development by groups *in* the dependent societies or regions. An integral part of international hegemony is political leadership in the sense of the ability to ensure that subordinate societies recognise the existing

      international relations of dominance by means of economic and political compromises.

(2) International hegemony is expressed, politically and institutionally, either in the clear dominance of one state or one region (such as England in the nineteenth century) and/or in a system of international institutions and "regimes" within which the definition of problems and suggestions for dealing with them are struggled over and in which generally effective decisions can be taken and binding compromises negotiated. The system of international institutions can, under these conditions, be understood as the institutionalisation of hegemonic relations which, especially in the political terrain, define rules of negotiation, and participation and access rights. In contrast to the nation-state the power relations are, however, much more complex because you have the operation of, first, nation-states, in the form of governments, as well as, second, "private" international actors. Cox (1993: 62), therefore, speaks of relations between states and classes. Hegemonic relations and their institutionalisation always remain contested under the conditions of social antagonisms and competitive relationships and the complex condensation of power relations based on them.

The international system of institutions is not a coherent unit – not even in the sense of still-to-be-created. The apparatuses, which are, partially, in a contradictory relationship to one another, are terrains on which very specific and differing social power relations are concentrated. In addition, resources and the legal possibilities of sanction play a large role in the effectiveness of specific institutions (Shaw 2000: 215ff.). This perspective differs from regime theory, which usually simply diagnoses the existence of overlapping regimes or network-like institutions without explaining the phenomenon. In our approach, by contrast, international institutions are embedded theoretically in the more comprehensive process of the transformation of the state.

    Our central argument is to understand the international state, its international political institutions and its discourses as "second order condensations of societal power relations". Drawing on and further developing the analysis of the nation-state as given by Poulantzas, the term "second order condensations" refers to the complex process of institutionalising societal power relations on various geographical scales in the course of the internationalisation of the state. This process is driven by "social strategies and struggles for control and empowerment" (Swyngedouw 1997: 141) and can result in new relations of dominance. These power relations are inscribed into the structure of the international state apparatuses. Those forces are, most of all, national-governmental actors which are themselves asymmetric material condensations at the level of the respective nation-states and which, through time, come to form a condensation of competing domestic forces that is given cohesion via formulating "a national interest". Besides the nation-states, there are class actors and other representatives of societal interests such as feminist, environmental or indigenous groups. This varies from field to field. Moreover, international political institutions are both material condensations – as in the case of the European Union – and at the same time actors on other terrains.

The concept of "second order condensation" does not mean a priori existing asymmetries between different scales. If there is any hierarchy, for example between the national and the international levels, it is a question of historical developments. Material condensations of second order might – not must, as crises are always possible – express hegemonic projects in the sense that the dominant forces are able to universalise their interests and that there are poorly contested orientations of the relevant political and social actors.

The materiality of the internationalised state exists besides the national (and even local) states of the international institutions. These spheres, although not being centralised, are organised, as well as being formally separated from economic power, stabilised over a certain time period, as well as disposing over expertise, knowledge, legal means and financial resources. The legal means usually need to be implemented by nation-states and the resources come from them. More generally speaking, the international institutions do not dispose over their own state power to stabilise capitalist relations and to give hegemonic projects continuity, but this power is "lent" by the (powerful) nation-states. However, there might evolve a certain density and resistance against the will of dominant states.

Our approach has one important implication for the present study: this concerns the question of coherence among different international political terrains. As we said, a major debate in international politics as well as in International Relations and especially in regime theory relates to the problems of creating coherence among international political institutions. Incoherence in international politics is, from the outlined perspective, less the inability of nation-states or international political institutions to control political processes than of contradictions and tensions among the dominant forces and the inability to create consensus among the dominated. From our perspective, the lack of coherence has to do both with the contradictions and tensions among different policy fields and with the material condensations of the balances of forces in specific political institutions and with the asymmetries among them (see Görg/Brand 2006).

Moreover, incoherence is a mode of international politics in the sense that among political institutions we can observe a strong asymmetry even if they were to regulate the same issues. The fact that in many cases several political institutions claim responsibility for the same issue area is not only a consequence of incoherence but can be interpreted as a power strategy of dominant forces. Because, if a terrain is too politicised and weaker actors become stronger the more powerful actors have the possibility to re-evaluate other terrains (or to act in a bilateral mode). We can borrow, from John Braithwaite and Peter Drahos (2000, ch. 24), the concept of *forum-shifting* which means that a political actor, especially the USA, can shift strategies from one organisation to another, leave an organisation or pursue strategies towards several ones. But beyond Braithwaite and Drahos we can understand forum-shifting not only as a strategy of actors towards existing terrains but also as a strategy to change power relations and to structure the terrain itself.

1.6 Questions of method

The theoretical framework presented and the outlining of the problem should have made clear the complexity of the subject at the centre of the study. Not all of the aspects mentioned here will be pursued to the same degree of detail in the following sections. In the foreground are two questions: first, the relationships between the different political negotiation terrains and international agreements; and second, the connections among the various political scales and their production. Two further things must also be taken into account. First, the field is characterised by an enormous historical dynamism. New actors, who had scarcely been in evidence previously, appear continually, and new terrains and fields of conflict receive new meanings which could not previously have been foreseen. The danger is, therefore, great that important factors can be either lost from view or over- or underestimated. We are not dealing with solid *ceteris paribus* conditions but with a developing conflict terrain. Second, the descriptions by the social and natural sciences in these conflicts are not neutral instances but themselves form an element of the developing conflicts. Whether or not tensions exist between the CBD and the TRIPS Agreement is not at all a neutral description but a part of the subject matter. Since, last but not least, actors participating in the conflict try to substantiate their positions and weaken those of their opponents with the assistance of these descriptions, there can be no neutral observer positions in the strict sense of the word, but only a permanent self-reflection of one's own experiences.

In view of the historical dynamism, being too strict regarding the subject-matter to be examined, and its temporal classification, always entails the risk of losing sight of important processes and new developments. An additional problem is the consideration of the materiality of the problem subject-matter. If we take our introductory remarks on the concept of relationships with nature seriously, we have to take into account the biological-technical characteristics of the subject-matter concerned, namely biodiversity or genetic resources. This is true both for the definition of the problem and the solution options referring to it. Where exactly the problem lies or what an adequate treatment of the problem would be, is not simply predetermined; rather, corresponding descriptions develop as components of the development of the conflict. An interdisciplinary approach which critically examines the corresponding bioscientific descriptions would, strictly speaking, be indispensable here. For example, for many years the economic interest in genetic resources was simply regarded as given in view of the options for applying genetic technology, which gave impetus to the talk of a "green gold of the genes". Recently, by contrast, the signs have been increasing that in industry, very varying economic/technical strategies are being applied and that the economic value of biodiversity cannot simply be assumed (see Macilwain 1998). The possible misunderstandings are also serious if certain attributions with regard to the ecological importance of biological diversity are simply used uncritically (e.g. regarding the relevance of biodiversity for the stability of ecosystems).

We have attempted to methodically limit the barriers and possible dead-ends in both directions. To start with the second problem: we do not present an interdisciplinary examination of the access and benefit-sharing problem here, which would include natural or technical sciences. However, since before beginning this investigation we already had at least a few years of familiarity with the particularities of this field (including the natural science and technical dimensions; see Görg *et al.* 1999), we believe that we have been able to avoid the larger traps.

On the other hand, the temporal dynamism presented us with some difficulties. In the course of the study, terrains (such as the WIPO; see Chapter 4) and actors (for example the Like-Minded Group of Megadiverse Countries; see Chapter 2) appeared, the importance of which was not to be foreseen or which, at the time of the planning of the project, did not even exist. Other developments, by contrast, have taken much longer than was to be expected (e.g. the revision of the TRIPS Agreement; see Chapter 4), while others in turn fortunately found themselves in an important phase precisely in the time-period of the study (the adoption of the Bonn Guidelines within the framework of the CBD; see Chapter 2; and the process within the framework of the FAO; see Chapter 3).

The kernel of this study is represented by open questionnaire interviews which were conducted on the different negotiation terrains between May 2000 and July 2001 (see the list of interviews at the end of the book). Our interview partners were experts and representatives of the various conflict parties or actor groups participating in the process. The objective was not to receive representative answers to the subject-matter but to gain a deeper insight into the negotiation processes and their difficulties from the viewpoints of the different parties to the conflict. The interviews were analysed in different phases and according to various criteria. In particular, we tried to figure out the interests of groups involved and their positions regarding the subject matter, as well as trying to understand the conflict dynamic and, particularly, changes in the perception of the problem and the formulation of interests. Last but not least, we tried to estimate the relevance of the different terrains, their relationships with each other and their impact on different political scales, in particular the national and the local scale.

Participant observation at conferences – at least one for every terrain – was also essential. Without direct observations it is very difficult to estimate the exact meaning of specific purposes and the environment, the mood and the political tensions where negotiations took place. We participated as observers at COP 3 in Buenos Aires (1996), COP 4 in Bratislava (1998), COP 5 of the CBD in May 2000 in Nairobi and COP 6 in The Hague in 2002; the negotiations of the Bonn Guidelines in October 2001 in Bonn; the Sixth Extraordinary Session of the CGRFA in June 2001 in Rome; and some other national and international conferences (expert and NGO meetings). The evaluation of the TRIPS revision process was more complicated. Access to the negotiation process in this case was extraordinarily difficult. While we attended a conference designed as an invitation to the global civil society at the WTO's headquarters in Geneva in July 2001, to discuss the topic of intellectual property rights, we were not allowed to participate in formal negotiations and relied upon the negotiation documents and published reports of the negotiations. A further terrain, which was not at the centre of the *access and benefit-sharing* problem but which comprised an important theme in this context, could also only be dealt with by us to a limited degree: the question of indigenous knowledge. Here, we observed some meetings of the International Indigenous Forum on Biodiversity (IIFB) which took place in connection with the formal meetings of the CBD in Bonn and The Hague.

2 On the value of nature

The Convention on Biological Diversity and the commercialisation of genetic resources

At first sight, the Convention on Biological Diversity (CBD) appears to be an important contribution to the conservation of biological diversity. Moreover, it could be perceived as offering a new direction for conservation strategies because, compared to earlier agreements, a variety of ecological, social and economic aspects are taken into account, creating one of the most comprehensive environmental agreements of the past century. In recent years, however, the ambivalent character of the Convention has become ever more evident. Indeed, some of the most important challenges (i.e. the integration of different aims, national implementation and its relationship to other agreements) are still far from being resolved. Above all, it becomes obvious that the CBD, in general, expresses a tendency towards a view of biodiversity which is primarily concerned with its economic utility and (exchange) value. The frequent accusation is that the CBD has even accelerated the commercialisation of biological diversity and thus contributes less to its conservation and more to its marketing.

The problem cannot be grasped, however, with an isolated appraisal of the Convention, for it concerns the entire context of different international agreements and negotiation processes. Only if their interplay and the multitude of their mutual tensions are examined, can an assessment of the actual regulating effects be possible. Only then can it be understood in what way post-Fordist relationships with nature in the field of biological diversity are regulated by a political institutional framework and what this framework actually means. Furthermore, it must be clarified that post-Fordist relationships with nature are created and formed in a specific way with the support of just such a framework (and not with economic-technological strategies alone).

The CBD was signed, in a complex and difficult negotiation situation, in the run-up to the UN Conference on the Environment and Development (UNCED) in Rio de Janeiro in 1992 (on the negotiation process see Sánchez/Juma 1994; Swanson 1997; Arts 1998; McGraw 2002). It was originally conceived as an "umbrella convention" which was to align the many already existing agreements on the protection of species (e.g. the Convention on International Trade with Endangered Species of Wild Fauna and

Flora) and make them more efficient. But in the course of the negotiations up to 1992 and in its further development after the first conference of the convention parties, the CBD increasingly changed its appearance. While in the first drafts for a framework agreement, which had been submitted by the International Union for the Conservation of Nature (IUCN) in the late 1980s, distribution conflicts and their regulation (i.e. the regulation of technology transfer, of benefit-sharing etc.) did not yet play any great role (IUCN 1989; Arts 1998), this changed increasingly in the negotiations on the CBD in the run-up to the Rio conference in 1992. The text of the CBD, which was passed at that conference, can only be understood adequately if economic aspects and the distribution conflict over the use of genetic resources are taken into account. The reasons for this are complex. Certainly, of central importance is the CBD's specific character of compromise as well as the economic interest in genetic resources which had significantly increased during the late 1980s. The idea of the "reconciliation" of "North" and "South" and of "ecology" and "economy", which characterises the concept of sustainable development, shapes the CBD to a particularly high degree. It is precisely for this reason that the Convention makes evident the pitfalls contained in this concept. In analysing these shortcomings both the limits of this double "reconciliation" and the definite effects of the international institutions which try to translate this model into action are unveiled (see also the contributions in Görg/Brand 2002; Brand/Görg 2007 and Conca *et al.* 2007).

In the following the assumption advocated by many observers will be closely scrutinised, according to which the CBD is naturally opposed to processes of the economisation of social relationships and the institutions which support this – particularly the agreements within the framework of the World Trade Organization (WTO) and the neoliberal restructuring of social relationships as a whole (IIED 2001; Ling/Khor 2001; and the assessment in many of our interviews). According to this position, in the CBD and in the other agreements signed in the Rio process (particularly Agenda 21), interests in the protection of nature and of weaker actors are taken into consideration. This is without any doubt the case. However, questions remain as to how the different processes are articulated, with each other as well as regarding the actual relevance of these international agreements for local actors.

If the CBD is to be examined in the following as an example of the internationalisation of the state, it will be done by means of a detailed examination of interests and political strategies which are condensed in those aforementioned institutions. In other words, it is not only considered as an instrument for solving problems or for guaranteeing global relationships of power and dominance, but also as a terrain on which different actors struggle for their interests. By taking the double position of international institutions as regulating authorities and as an expression of global relationships of power into account, the role of the CBD can be appraised in a more precise manner. The central issue concerns the specific relationship between conservation and use. As we shall see, very specific ideas and practices exist, each representing different mixtures of protection and utilisation and each partially interconnecting – at times surprisingly – but at the same time, also standing in a relationship of tension to one another.

Our argument is that the CBD itself tends, under post-Fordist neoliberal conditions, to create a framework for the commercialisation of nature. Not even the CBD can escape from the valorisation paradigm which is central to post-Fordist relationships with nature. On the contrary, this paradigm is institutionalised in the CBD, although in a different way to that of the WTO agreements. At the same time, the commercialisation of nature is not a unilinear process but one which is characterised by social struggles and contradictions. This may allow weaker actors (e.g. Southern governments, NGOs or indigenous peoples) to bring their interests to bear in the negotiations and to be at least partially considered in the compromises. However, it must be examined exactly *how* this occurs as well as how this process allows a degree of manoeuvrability for certain interests. In doing so, it must be taken into consideration that in part, the interests of the different actors are first constituted, or further developed, during the negotiations and the implementation processes of the CBD as well as in light of the experiences in the different countries. This becomes especially clear in the questions as to how access and benefit-sharing are to be ensured and what strategies are used by different actors as a reaction to this.

At the centre of the study are the processes connected with the regulation of access to biological diversity and the fair sharing of the benefits from its utilisation. The negotiations on the *Bonn Guidelines on Access to Genetic Resources and Fair and Equitable Sharing of the Benefits Arising out of its Utilization*, which began in Bonn in October 2001 and were signed in April 2002 at the sixth conference of the signatory states in The Hague, as well as the following negotiations of an *International Regime on Access and Benefit-sharing* right after the approval of the Bonn Guidelines, are interesting examples of the process of the constitution of interests and their condensation in an international agreement. A further example is the Like-Minded Group of Megadiverse Countries, which was formed at the beginning of 2002 and whose appearance on the international stage was perceived as jeopardising the solutions achieved in the Bonn Guidelines. Closely connected with the questions of access and benefit-sharing are issues such as the safeguarding of intellectual property, the rights of indigenous peoples and local communities and finally, of course, the issue of nature protection. It is important to us, first, to follow and understand more precisely the international processes within the CBD: what interests are articulated there and how are they condensed? In addition, the CBD should be placed in relationship to other international agreements; particularly the *Food and Agriculture Organization of the United Nations* (FAO) and the Agreement on *Trade-Related Aspects of Intellectual Property Rights* (TRIPS) within the WTO. Both will be briefly discussed here and will be dealt with in their own right in the following chapters.

The following section will present a brief summary of the issue of biodiversity and the problems connected to it. This will be done by looking at the development of the CBD and the most important regulations associated with it. Following this, important interest groups and their positions will be outlined and some central lines of conflict presented. It is remarkable in the context of the CBD that central concepts and measures based upon them are still characterised by considerable uncertainty and are part of the political disputes. This is reflected in the major role of experts but also in the fact that the argument of uncertainty is itself repeatedly brought forward in order to strengthen certain policies. Neither the exact extent of the erosion of biological diversity nor its ecological, economic or social consequences can be determined precisely. Moreover, the character of the problem – in terms of what the issue actually is; what is central and what is arbitrary? – is anything but clear. This is directly connected with the central concept of biological diversity or biodiversity, which does not in any way represent a precisely defined scientific foundation for the entire process.

2.1 Biodiversity as a political concept

The concept of biological diversity was, for a long time, used synonymously with the concept of the diversity of species. Today, by contrast, it describes a much more comprehensive *synthesis of three elements*: the diversity of species, genetic diversity and the diversity of habitats and ecosystems. This new meaning of biodiversity is relatively recent – and it involves far-reaching political and economic implications. The new concept first established itself in the second half of the 1980s. However, even as early as the late 1970s, the report "Global 2000" to the US President outlined an interesting shifting of weights, as a prelude to later developments, in which *ecological* threat scenarios are connected with the strong emphasis on the *economic* value of biodiversity and its *geostrategic* importance (Flitner 1999). Of decisive significance for the presently established meaning of the concept was the *National Forum on BioDiversity*, a conference of the *National Academy of Sciences* and the *Smithsonian Institution* in the USA in 1986, at which the abbreviation was introduced (Wilson 1988). Nonetheless, another aspect can be found at this conference which characterises the new concept to this day: the partially metaphorical elevation of biodiversity to the "diversity of the living" – a metaphor which eludes scientific description because it means everything and therefore nothing in particular (see, as an example: Wilson 1992; for a critique: Hertler 1999). The synthesis of the three main elements of biodiversity – as problematic as their scientific foundation may be – led to the restructuring of the corresponding spheres of politics. This becomes evident, not least, in the negotiations on the CBD, which began in the late 1980s.

In contrast to popular notions, it is not obvious what exactly the central problem is and what the "loss of biological diversity" is actually all about. Both in the public discussion and in scientific research a whole number of arguments are brought forward which are not congruent but rather, accentuate the very different and partly contradictory aspects of this subject-matter. Most common is the listing of data on the *extinction of species*, that is estimates of the rate of extinction of the species which exist world-wide. In the red list of the species threatened with extinction in the year 2000, The World Conservation Union – IUCN, for example, points out that worldwide, of 4763 mammal species 24 per cent are threatened with extinction, as are 12 per cent of 9946 bird species (according to the first Global Biodiversity Outlook in 2001). But this does not really represent the whole threat associated with the diagnosis "loss of biodiversity". The esti-mates have a high uncertainty factor, since all the figures are imprecise and provisional. It is not without reason that the extensively studied and "famous" mammals, birds, fish, reptiles and amphibians form the core of the IUCN's "red lists", as little is known about other species (in particular insects and microbes) and therefore, specific figures can hardly be pre-sented. All other data are good estimates at best, because not only the rate of extinction but also the total number of the species is unknown and therefore must be extrapolated. Indeed, the *Millennium Ecosystem Assessment* claims that there are 1.7 to 2 million identified species and realistically estimates the number of species existing today at between 5 and 30 million (BSR 2005: 19).

According to this interpretation of the problem, which is geared towards the diversity of species and its erosion, at present we are experiencing the sixth wave of extinction in the course of the Earth's history. In contrast to earlier phases of the mass extinction of species this phase is unequivocally caused by anthropogenic changes in the environment (e.g. WBGU 1999). Putting aside existing uncertainties, the threat is obvious. The "Global Biodiversity Outlook 2", published in 2006, points out: "a common mes-sage emerges: biodiversity is in decline at all levels and geographical scales" (Secretariat of the CBD 2006a: 5). This trend can be reversed only when immediate measures, such as the creation of protected areas or pollution prevention programmes, are taken seriously. The so-called 2010 Biodiversity Target – to reduce significantly the erosion of biodiversity as a contribution to poverty alleviation – may only be reached when "unprecedented addi-tional efforts" are provided (BSR 2005: 14; Secretariat of the CBD 2006a: 5). In these notions, other descriptions of the problem arise, thereby pointing out the ecological or economic usefulness of "biodiversity" at very differing levels. From an *ecological* point of view, it is argued that biodi-versity offers inestimably valuable functions or services for the conservation and stability of ecosystems; something which also impacts upon the exis-tence and causes of other environmental problems (from climate change to soil degradation and desertification), and the possibilities of treatment. In particular, the Millennium Ecosystem Assessment, which up to now is the most comprehensive study about the connections between ecosystem services and human well-being, focuses on such services and highlights the important value of biodiversity (or "Life on Earth", see Figure A in MASR 2005: vi) for all the services nature provides. As a main message, the Millennium Ecosystem Assessment argues that 15 of 24 ecosystem services are in decline with unforeseeable consequences both for nature and global society (BSR 2005: 22–41).

Seen from the perspective of the Millennium Ecosystem Assessment, the value of biodiversity is not restricted purely to the wealth of species diversity; it also refers to the contribution biodiversity provides for social use and human well-being in a wide range of areas: from nutrition and shelter, moving on to clean water and flood control as well as to basic conditions for social relations (security, social cohesion etc., see Figure A in MASR 2005: vi). Nonetheless, this redirection of conservation issues is not at all unproblematic. While the Millennium Ecosystem Assessment itself is not framed within a purely utilitarian perspective – it focuses merely on trade-offs between different kinds of use and also on limits of human utilisation – it does offer ground for such a reductionist perspective (see McCauley 2006; and the comments in *Nature* vol. 443, 19, October 2006: 749–750). Nevertheless, in recent years, the *economic* value of biodiversity has become even more important, representing itself in a broad variety of socio-economic fields of application. The reason why this concern has grown cannot only be seen in this broad variety of ecosystem services that biodiversity provides. Of more importance are recent technological changes due to the development of new bio- and genetic technologies. The issue at stake is primarily that of the loss of "natural capital". The leading metaphor here is that of the tropical rain forest as "nature's pharmacy" or more simply as a "capital asset". The main interests in the use of genetic resources are represented by pharmaceutical and agricultural companies. Due to the fact that throughout the world, biodiversity provides a wide range of ecosystem services, in many places quite different forms of utilisation are affected, from nutrition and leisure activities in developed countries to farming communities in developing countries and the population of the tropical rain forest regions. Ultimately, the protection of biological diversity, thus, is interconnected with economic interests and global social relationships of power and dominance.

The different arguments illuminate not only reasons which complement one another, for instance, why the erosion of biodiversity represents a problem. They also give quite different and sometimes contradictory answers to the questions: *What* exactly is the problem? *How* and *for whom* did it become a problem? *Why* and *with what means* should this problem be tackled? In international biodiversity policy it is therefore not a question of the solution to a given, more or less objectively existing problem, which must only be more or less well grasped and treated. On the contrary, the problems connected with the scientific definition of concepts show that there exists a struggle, with global dimensions, fought out over the regulation of relationships with nature – with locally and nationally different characteristics. Despite the widely recognised agreement that erosion of biodiversity is a major problem, an important question remains: What exactly is the problem and how should it be described and defined?

In view of the indicated perspectives on different aspects of the problems involved, the assumption that the concept of biodiversity is based on an immanent progress of knowledge in biology or its individual sub-disciplines is misleading. It is evident that in view of the problems concerning the subject-matter, an *external* reason must be sought based on the fact that very differing disciplines have agreed on a new definition of their field of study and on the overlapping and intersecting nature of, partly competing, disciplines such as taxonomy and molecular biology. The key to understanding the problem's constitution lies in external societal conditions and in the history of the establishment of the concept. This gives reason to argue that the unification of heterogeneous research fields is not based on reasons of content but is *strategically motivated* (Hertler 1999: 49).

The difficulties mentioned above are closely connected with the expansion of the meaning of the concept and particularly with the increased emphasis on the economic value of biodiversity. With genetic diversity, in addition to the diversity of species, growing attention was paid to the potentially economically valuable elements of biological diversity, that is: the genetic resources. This dimension was not completely new (on this cf. the following chapter on the conflicts at the fringes of the FAO). But as a new creation, the concept of biodiversity was particularly suitable for taking up the different interests which come together in this field of conflict and to reflect on the societal fronts of the conflict (for more detail see Flitner *et al.* 1998; Brand/Kalcsics 2002; Takacs 1996; Swanson 1997). Its width and its lack of focus predestined it to absorb these different conflicts, on the one hand, but also to conceal them again, on the other. Finally, in the subject-matter of biodiversity, traditional themes concerning the protection of nature are combined with newer attempts at environmental protection going under the title of *sustainable utilisation*. Here, questions of the *utilisation of resources* are related to *access* and more or less exclusive *rights of utilisation*, and thus with questions of the *sharing of benefits* and *intellectual property rights*. The latter is indicated through the widely accepted concept of "genetic resources" instead of "genetic goods" (in our study we use both concepts interchangeably, having in mind that the concept of genetic resources is biased towards utilitarianism, cf. Kaiser 2003). The transition from a pure "umbrella convention" on the protection of species and nature to a convention which attempts to regulate not only the ecological dimensions of the problem but also the economic and social dimensions, is neither trivial not accidental – and neither can it be simply reversed at will.

2.2 Functioning and provisions of the CBD

The conservation of biodiversity is quite a complex cross-sectional task, encompassing the classical protection of nature and the organisation of agriculture as much as related questions, connected with the regulation of global trade and the transfer of the modern biotechnologies. The text of the CBD was completed in Nairobi on 22 May 1992, and it was then laid out for governments to sign as of June at the UNCED after which it finally had to be ratified by national parliaments. On 29 December 1993, the CBD entered into force, exactly 90 days after the thirtieth member state had ratified the Convention. As of June 2006, there were 188 member states which had ratified the CBD (counting the states of the European Union individually, even though it appears as one signatory). One important exception is the USA, which signed the CBD, after having hesitated for some time, but has not yet ratified it (which gives it, as a signatory, the right to take part in proceedings without being bound by any obligations, see section 2.2.1). The CBD is a case of *soft law*, which is signed by governments and ratified by national parliaments but which does not possess any sanction mechanisms (as for example, does the WTO with its Dispute Settlement Mechanism) but which first has to be implemented nationally. This latter aspect often opens up dispute over interpretations. The same is obvious at the international level: By the time of the eighth Conference of the Parties – which took place in Curitiba, Brazil, in March 2006 – all governments had to have submitted a report about the national status of biodiversity, especially protected areas. But only around 25 per cent of the parties, that is governments, did so.

Even if it, in contrast to the Framework Convention on Climate Change (FCCC), is not so-named explicitly, the CBD is, in fact, a framework convention which not only has to be translated into national law but whose provisions are also the subject of further negotiation at the international level. This occurs at the *Conference of the Parties* (COP) which takes place every two years, in the *Subsidiary Body for Scientific, Technical and Technological Advice* (SBSTTA) and via a relatively small secretariat in Montreal (cf. Le Prestre 2002).

Broad participation of non-state actors in the process is permissible and it has been welcomed in quite an impressive manner.[1] However, it is important to note that the active personnel involved in the CBD is fairly limited in number. It is always the same important delegation members, experts and NGO activists who meet at the conferences. The permeability of delegations and NGO activists is quite large in some countries (which only seldom means that NGO activists have a great deal of influence). This is obviously sensible in view of the great complexity with regard to both content and procedures. But there seems to be a recent shift which might have to do with the growing importance of the CBD: while the participation of NGOs was discussed for the first time in such an open and critical way, at the same time the CBD seems to have opened it more to private companies and their associations (ENB 2006a: 23).

One important element of the material implementation of the CBD is the funding mechanism, the *Global Environmental Facility* (GEF), which – against the decreasing resistance of the Southern countries – is established at the World Bank and still retains only a temporary status. Funding mechanisms not only shape the implementation process of the CBD, through concrete projects, but they also influence the development of the CBD as a political terrain itself. For example, before the COP in 2006, held in Curitiba, 2 million USD (United States Dollars) were considered necessary by the CBD secretariat in order to allow a comprehensive participation of delegates from Southern countries. But only 25 per cent of this amount was provided by Northern countries, which eventually meant that there were not enough delegates from Southern countries present at the COP.

In general the CBD follows three equally important objectives:

> The *conservation* of biological diversity, the *sustainable use* of its components and the *fair and equitable sharing* of the *benefits* arising out of the utilisation of genetic resources, including by appropriate access to genetic resources and by appropriate transfer of relevant technologies, taking into account all rights over those resources and to technologies, and by appropriate funding.
>
> (CBD 1992, Art. 1; emphasis added)

In other words, the CBD already lays down in Article 1 that the expected (economic) benefits which are to be shared will be created by guaranteed *access* to biological diversity. However, the concept of access includes three very different forms: access to natural resources, access to knowledge and – closely connected with the latter – access to technology (ibid.: Art. 16). Access must, however, be accompanied by fair benefit-sharing, namely of those benefits which arise from economic utilisation. Seiler and Dutfield (2001: 15) call this "a cornerstone of the CBD philosophy of convergence between the interests of the North and the South". In addition, the *prior informed consent* (PIC, CBD: Art. 15.5) of the "providers" to access must be attained and access should take place on *mutually agreed terms* (MAT, ibid.: Art. 15.4). This should be the case not only for access to genetic resources but for all forms of access. A decisive innovation in international law is also the prescribing of *national sovereignty* over natural (not only genetic) resources in the CBD (ibid.: Preamble, Art. 3 and 15). It is described in Article 3 as the central "principle" of the CBD. The previously existing principle of the *common heritage of humankind* to plant genetic resources is thus replaced by the *common concern* named in the preamble. This does not mean that nation-states are therefore also the owners of genetic or biological goods (cf. the critique of Harry/Kanehe 2005). National sovereignty here means only that states have the right to lay down national rules and laws governing the treatment of biological diversity. Thus national sovereignty is a central element in the international system of property rights in dealing with genetic resources.

The CBD also encourages technology transfer, that is it is concerned with access to technologies as a part of benefit-sharing. Article 1 states, however, that the objectives of the CBD are to be achieved by "taking into account all rights over those resources and to technologies". The second half of this regulation is an important formulation and represents a limitation to the technology transfer Southern countries had hoped for because it restricted this transfer according to the existing intellectual property rights laws (see below).

The rights of the local population and particularly of the indigenous population are mentioned in Articles 8(j) and 10(c), but they are relatively vaguely formulated. The rights are not listed in the preamble or independently, but are subpoints of the regulations for *in situ* conservation and thus are subjected to an instrumental approach (Stoll 1999). The role played by indigenous peoples (although the concept of peoples is not used in the official political process but that of communities) and locally based practices in the conservation of biological diversity are thus recognised, but their rights are only explicitly strengthened as far as they serve conservation and sustainable utilisation. Furthermore, they are subjected to national laws. Article 8(j) lays down that each party to the contract (i.e. the national government) *shall*:

> subject to its national legislation, respect, preserve and maintain knowledge, innovations and practices of indigenous and local communities embodying traditional lifestyles relevant for the conservation and sustainable use of biological diversity and promote their wider application with the approval and involvement of the holders of such knowledge, innovations and practices and encourage the equitable sharing of the benefits arising from the utilization of such knowledge, innovations and practices.
>
> (CBD 1992, Art. 8(j))

The fact is also significant that the Convention only covers those *ex situ* genetic resources which fall under the regulations of the Convention *after* the coming into force of the Convention in December 1993 or after the individual countries have signed the Convention (ibid.: Art. 15.3). Thus, neither the *ex situ* collections which have been set up over the centuries, nor botanical and zoological gardens, nor scientific collections and genetic bases in the field of agriculture, fall under the regulations of the CBD. This not only means that collections of inestimable economic value are excluded. It also changes the field of conflict, since, particularly in the field of the biodiversity utilised in agriculture, it is unclear whether the research institutes and biotechnology firms in the Northern countries are actually dependent on access to *in situ* material or whether the *ex situ* collections in the North are adequate for their purposes (see the following chapter on this). Similarly, the botanical and zoological gardens are confronted with an increased demand from companies, as the latter believe they will be able, in this way, to achieve faster and more secure access to genetic material. It is also important that the regulations of the CBD are not of equal standing but are related to one another in a hierarchical fashion. National sovereignty is binding. The facilitating of access (ibid.: Art. 15.2), the principles of mutually agreed terms and prior informed consent are, by contrast, "shall be" clauses; this means that governments are urged to take appropriate measures. Altogether, the formula "subject to national legislation" is central, and regulations – particularly concerning intellectual property rights – are limited in the sense that they are not allowed to contradict other international norms.

At the various conferences of the parties to the Convention, the regulations of the CBD have been developed further by a number of decisions, whereby with regard to access and benefit-sharing, questions of national legislation, the precise definition of concepts and the assessing of various experiences are in the foreground (see Siebenhüner and Suplie 2005 who describe this development as a process of institutional learning).

2.3 Positions of the most important actors

Due to the complexity of interests, a clear classification is not easy to make. The argument is continually brought forward that all the countries of the world are in one way or another providers and users of genetic resources. Nevertheless, this fact is of little importance for political momentum. As the home of "wild" and *in situ* biodiversity is primarily in the countries of the geographical South, but their commercial valorisation until now has primarily taken place in the countries of the North, this leads to a North–South conflict, which is largely the reason for the existence of the CBD in its basic structure (Svarstad 1994). The actual front lines of the conflict are much more complex, however, for neither "the South" nor "the North" are uniform entities, but are divided in themselves by a multitude of differences of interest between individual countries – not all Southern countries are rich in biodiversity; only a few Northern countries are capable of commercial valorisation – as well as within both Southern and Northern countries (between governments, the rural population and different sectors of industry).

In the following – with no claim to completeness: for example botanical gardens are not considered – the positions of the most important political actors and groups of actors in international negotiations are outlined. Essentially, this is an attempt to present a first picture of the most important interest groups and their view of the terrain of conflict, in order to be better able to appraise the individual conflicts and the approaches to the regulation of access and benefit-sharing.[2] International institutions, which also sometimes appear as actors in the questions which are at the centre here, particularly the FAO and the World Intellectual Property Organization (WIPO), are not listed separately. Their representatives are above all actively interested in the clarification of certain facts or in the thematic boundaries to other processes (the FAO wishes to remain responsible for agro-biological diversity and WIPO wishes to take over a guiding function for intellectual property rights). Therefore, as actors, they are more or less directly involved in the design of the CBD.

2.3.1 Governments of the Northern countries

In countries where a strong domestic pharmaceutical, agricultural and cosmetics industry exists, the governments quite clearly represent the interests of "their" agricultural or pharmaceutical companies or research institutes in access, planning and legal security (see the interviews at CBD/19, CBD/22). Despite all their differences they are united on one point: there must be no softening of "hard" rules on the security of intellectual property. Especially, the TRIPS Agreement must not be questioned, which is why the CBD is not a suitable place for the legally binding regulation of intellectual property rights. In addition, the great uncertainty and the high costs of biotechnological developments are emphasised, as it takes several years before new products can be developed. Different forms of benefit-sharing are therefore proposed: from, for example, short-term sample fees and advance payments to participation in possible profits from marketable products (see below).

In the concrete access agreements, the Northern actors see the Southern governments in a moderating, supervisory position rather than as direct partners to the agreement (the stakeholders at this level are not the governments; for a typology of access agreements see Trommetter 2005: 758–781). The governments or national authorities are regarded as necessary, however, in order to create trust for the users in the direct providers (CBD/4). On the question of the rights of indigenous peoples and local communities, the Northern governments tend to point out that at the international level at best, guidelines and awareness of the problems could be created, but that these are "internal" concerns of the Southern countries. With regard to important concepts such as benefit-sharing, prior informed consent or the participation of indigenous peoples and the importance of "traditional knowledge", they point to the great conceptual uncertainties. In part, the work of the WIPO is registered positively, which has, in recent years, taken up the subject of traditional knowledge. The change in the attitude of those involved and the creation of trust are regarded as central concerns of the international negotiations (CBD/4). With regard to the national implementation of the CBD, the Northern governments see no need for action. This view clearly exists on the part of the provider countries. The Northern governments warn here of "over-regulation", that is the inflexible and time-consuming legal and administrative regulations for the preparation of bioprospecting. The Northern governments argue very ahistorically because the previous appropriation of genetic resources plays no role in their position. There are clear differences among the Northern countries, however. There are governments which are more ready to compromise, such as the Swiss (Novartis in particular plays an important role here) and the Norwegian (Novo Nordisk plays an independent role), which are concerned with establishing a stable legal framework in which the providers should share in the economic benefits. The hard-liners, on the other hand, are Japan, the USA, Canada, Australia and New Zealand, which have formed the *JUS-CANZ Group* (the abbreviation is formed from the initial letters of the countries' names). As was previously mentioned: the US government plays a special role as a signatory state which did not ratify the CBD but acts as a "party" of it. It is one of the architects of the global rules for the appropriation and protection of biodiversity in other countries without the duties to implement the results in its own territory (and without the duty to finance the CBD secretariat and its activities). The particular interest of the JUSCANZ Group is that the developments within the CBD should not contradict WTO regulations. These governments tend to play the role of "brakesman", but they are also very influential in the formation of compromises due to their importance.

2.3.2 Governments of the Southern countries

The most important difference between the individual countries is whether or not they in fact "possess" considerable biological diversity – and if so, to what degree? Thus, for example, Brazilian governments (liberal and leftist ones) tend to represent the interests of commercialisation with regard to "wild" diversity, while with regard to agro-biological diversity, it tends towards free exchange which should not be restricted by commercial interests (something which has been institutionally laid down in the multilateral exchange system in the FAO, see below). This is connected with the fact that in Brazil an immense "wild" diversity exists, while the country is dependent on other countries for seeds from genetic resources. However, the leftist government under President Lula da Silva – surprisingly, for many observers – has been an even stronger advocate of the interests of agro-business and especially the introduction of genetically modified soy bean seeds. Argentina, by contrast, which is not a country of great biological diversity in either area, but which is one of the most important cultivation areas for genetically modified plants, usually votes with the USA and Canada.

Since the end of 2001 there has been an interesting development among the provider countries, in which the position of the Megadiversity Countries has played a special role. The governments of Bolivia, Brazil, China, Colombia, Costa Rica, Ecuador, India, Indonesia, Kenya, Malaysia, Mexico, Peru, the Philippines, South Africa and Venezuela (later on Madagascar and the Democratic Republic of Congo joined the group), represented by environmental ministers or their delegates, signed the *Cancún Declaration* of the Like-Minded Group of Megadiverse Countries in mid-February 2002, following a meeting in Cancún, Mexico (where at the end of 2003 the WTO ministerial meeting was going to take place) and prior to the World Summit on Sustainable Development in Johannesburg in June 2002 where the group intervened in the debates. The aim of this group is, or was, to create a common agenda for sustainable development and to strengthen cooperation. Sixty to seventy per cent of the world's biodiversity and 45 per cent of the world's population live in these countries. The responsibilities for biological and cultural diversity and the great potentials for development are emphasised. The protection and the sustainable use of biological diversity, access to genetic resources, benefit-sharing and the protection of traditional knowledge are the core issues. A central point is national sovereignty over natural resources. Cooperation is to consist above all on a common position at international conferences and the exchange of experiences with regard to national implementation. The national legislation has a clear objective, namely "that the adoption of an appropriate legislation can become a highly useful tool in participating efficiently in international markets and in taking full advantage of their own comparative advantages" (SEMARNAT 2002a: 116). The fact that this group has coordinated itself alone can be understood as an answer to the situation of competition of Southern countries with regard to Northern actors, which is felt to be disadvantageous. Its formation is also part of a several-year process during which the interests of the megadiverse countries have been given a more distinct contour by the negotiations. Their perception of the present situation is: "The megadiverse countries have not yet obtained the considerable benefits that should come with their privileged position, in large part due to the absence of political will and long-term strategies" (Caillaux/Ruíz 2002: 161; cf. a critical account in Ribeiro 2005: 73–74). Responsible for this are also the asymmetrical international relationships of power. The perception of two structural problems in the exercise of national sovereignty is also interesting:

> On the one hand, it is difficult to enforce this right over genetic resources due to their reproduction capacity and natural dispersion, as well as the fact that these are scattered over several countries – none of which can claim exclusive rights over them. On the other hand, defining sovereign rights is complicated even further by the existence of vast ex-situ collections that often contain genetic resources originating in other countries.
>
> (SEMARNAT 2002a: 115)[3]

Until 2005 the group was very active. The last known document is dated January 2005, when experts and governments met in Delhi to discuss how an international regime on access and benefit-sharing might be arranged. The Delhi declaration stated that the proposed international regime on access and benefit-sharing should include mandatory disclosure of the country of origin of biological material and associated traditional knowledge in the IPR (Intellectual Property Rights) application, along with an undertaking that the prevalent laws and practices of the country of origin have been respected and mandatory specific consequences in the event of failure to disclose the country of origin in the IPR application.

(New Delhi Ministerial Declaration of Like-Minded Megadiverse Countries on Access and Benefit-Sharing 2005)

This group's subsequent disappearance is at first glance quite surprising. On the one hand, at COP 8 in March 2006, the Like-Minded Group of Megadiverse Countries acted as such (see the final report: Secretariat of the CBD 2006b: 22) and on the other hand, the Group and other developing countries, especially the "Group of 77 and China", made joint statements and proposed a common position on access and benefit-sharing.

Two interpretations are possible. One could argue that the small group of megadiverse countries was able to build a consensus among the larger Group of 77 and China. In this case the so-called provider countries clarified their interests and strengthened their positions in negotiations which are now represented politically by the Group of 77 and China. The other interpretation is that the Southern countries were again divided by their heterogeneous interests and strategies as well as their situation of competition (see below) and their relative political weakness compared to Northern countries. One indicator of this could be the WTO ministerial conference in Hong Kong at the end of 2005 where the governments of India and Brazil accepted the invitation of special treatment from certain Northern governments. Future developments of this issue depend on negotiations, alliances, conflicts and compromises.

The governments of the so-called provider countries find themselves in a dilemma. On the one hand, they want their countries to share in the valorisation of genetic resources, and on the other hand, they fear that potential investors may be discouraged by regulations which may appear to be too strong. They are part of a *supply competition* which is exploited by the Northern governments in the CBD negotiations and by firms in the search for suitable locations for bioprospecting. Even if they sometimes still act as one in the Group of 77 and China – an NGO representative described that as a bargaining tool (CBD/15) – there are differences among the provider countries. These can be explained primarily by inner-societal relationships. In the Philippines and in India, for example, issues pertaining to biodiversity are highly politicised and interlinked with the disputes over the rights of indigenous peoples and small farmers. The African Group, led by government representatives of Ethiopia and Cameroon, plays an important role in the questioning of patents based on traditional knowledge.[4] Finally, concerning the delicate subject of the rights of indigenous peoples and local communities, it is not at all clear if Southern governments represent those interests internationally and promote strong international regulations.

2.3.3 Biotechnological companies and business associations

Heterogeneous positions are also to be found on the part of the biotechnological companies of the Northern countries. There are firms which continue to place their bets on a weak legal framework for access and benefit-sharing and a correspondingly stronger one for intellectual property rights, and which are present at the negotiations via government positions or as lobbyists (see the representative of the Japan Bioindustry Association, CBD/10). Basically, for the hard-liner position, the entire process is cumbersome, because what is at stake is the creation of good conditions for the companies (CBD/10). The representative of the already mentioned Japan Bioindustry Association made fun of the – from his point of view – not very helpful CBD: it was obvious that neither economists nor natural scientists had been asked for their advice (CBD/10).

Other companies place more emphasis on juridical security, particularly in questions of access and intellectual property rights. These companies, which take the CBD process seriously, also see, in the creation of a common understanding of the problem, in negotiations over guidelines and the building of trust, the central value of the international agreements (CBD/13). Explicitly, they are concerned with the lowering of transaction costs via a worldwide harmonisation of requirements, which would facilitate the exchange of genetic material (CBD/13; CBD/6). Despite their aim of legal certainty, they are sceptical with regard to legal rigidities and "over-regulation". The question of whether or not companies were present at the conferences was answered by a representative of Novartis, who said that the Swiss Government delegation was in permanent email communication with this company (CBD/13). By contrast, on the part of the Federal Government of Germany it was claimed that industry did not show much interest (CBD/27).

The activities of business associations, some of which describe themselves as NGOs or are described as such in the United Nations system, were less visible, for many years, in the CBD process (in contrast to the negotiations of the Biosafety Protocol where they were quite active). This was the case because they exerted their influence on national strategies in the run-up to the conferences or because representatives of the associations or of individual businesses were part of "Northern" delegations (on the classification and the different positions see Brand 2000: 203ff.; on the business associations see CEAS 2000: 27ff.; on business lobbying see Finston 2005). But since 2005, the visibility of the associations of biotechnological companies has increased; especially in relation to access and benefit-sharing as well as technological issues.

Indicators of the growing awareness are that the International Finance Corporation Group, a member of the World Bank Group, highlights in an internet based "Guide to Biodiversity for the Private Sector" the growing importance of biodiversity for business, especially in those countries with emerging markets (IFC 2006). The Organization for Economic Cooperation and Development (OECD) published, in 2004, a "Handbook of Market Creation for Biodiversity" and the International Chamber of Commerce (ICC) recently established a Task Force on the Convention (see Secretariat of the CBD 2006b: 25). But more important for the negotiation process is that in 2005, the American biotechnology industry founded the American BioIndustry Alliance (ABIA, www.abiallience.com). One of its aims is to ensure that its foot is already in the door when negotiations on access and benefit-sharing become more effective. Its members advocate the "full patentability of biotechnology inventions and the maintenance of the current minimum standards for the protection of intellectual property" (quoted in IP-Watch, Nos 10/11, 2005/6: 5). The president of ABIA, Jacques Gorlin, as well as the executive director, Susan Finston, are well-known experts in trade and intellectual property rights issues and have strong roots in governmental politics and experience as lobbyists for pharmaceutical and other industries. Members of the group include Bristol Myers-Sqibb, Eli Lilly, Pfizer, Procter & Gamble and Tethsy Research. At the last CBD meetings in Granada (Spain) and Curitiba (Brazil), Susan Finston played an influential role.[5] It seems that the CBD has become more important for business because it is here that progress is made (i.e. its interests in securing access and property rights) and the CBD might be used by Southern governments as a means of enhancing the legitimacy of its demands in the TRIPS negotiations. Therefore, biotech companies and business associations might consider the CBD as a more important agreement than they had previously thought.

One of the central obscurities in the further negotiation process is the question of to what extent the (transnationally acting) biotechnological companies do in fact have a strong interest in access to new resources. There is first, as we have already mentioned, the existing *ex situ* collections in the North (which might be adequate for agricultural aspects, for example; cf. the next chapter). In addition, varying technologies and production methods exist within the industry, which make themselves noticed in diverging appraisals. A "renaissance of the classical search for natural substances" (Heins 2001) confronts the approach of combinative chemistry, which believes that new products can be designed without inputs from nature. Again and again it is stated that the high expectations of the "green gold of the genes" have not yet been fulfilled – not *yet*, it must be emphasised.

2.3.4 Non-governmental organisations and social movements

Precisely because of the fact that policies, in the highly complex field of biodiversity politics, are conducted "under conditions of uncertainty" and that considerable contradictions exist – particularly between the different institutions such as the CBD and the WTO – there is considerable room within which different (types of) NGOs can manoeuvre. Indeed, they can contribute, as experts or as part of epistemic communities, to the clarification of complex issues. With a huge number of informal meetings, conferences, consultations, reports and publications, and direct lobbying and campaigns, the NGOs and other non-state actors, and also individual scientists, have contributed to the definitions of the problems, even if these were not at all uniform. Individual NGOs often develop their political positions and effectiveness in cooperation with other NGOs. An important example for such networks and forums is the *Global Biodiversity Forum*, founded in 1993, which usually takes place before major international conferences such as the COPs or other CBD meetings or at the regional level (as well as in conjunction with the Climate Convention FCCC). The Forum – and alongside it, organisations such as the IUCN, WWF and WRI, see below – are important in developing policy proposals, supporting implementation and getting private companies and business associations involved in the political process. Specific campaigns such as "No patents on life" or "Ban Terminator" are also important.

NGOs and social movements – the latter play an important role particularly in Southern countries – have considerable differences among themselves (cf. the separate section on indigenous NGOs and peoples).[6] This is an expression of a complex conflict field in which very different interests organise and articulate themselves. There are not only differences with regard to the political proposals, the setting of priorities or specific attitudes. Even the problems to be regulated are perceived differently. The conservationist NGOs such as the World Wide Fund for Nature (WWF), the World Resources Institute (WRI) or the "semi-NGO" The World Conservation Union (IUCN) regard themselves primarily as representing the interest of the "protection of nature", although social questions are becoming more widely discussed (see Delgado Ramos 2004: 33–42). They play a major role in the formulation of expertise, particularly legal expertise, and in the implementation of specific projects. Their political style is cooperative and is concerned with integrating all the stakeholders, particularly companies. The clearest expression of this was the Global Biodiversity Forum which was organised in the run-up to the sixth COP, and which was dominated by these NGOs. The annoyance at the very industry-friendly position of the Global Biodiversity Forum (see for example, GBF 2002) apparently led to the fact that at the COPs an *NGO Caucus* has recently spoken out as an NGO alliance. The two major conservationist NGOs – beside the WWF which is the largest in the world – Conservation International (CI) and The Nature Conservancy (TNC) are very important in the implementation of protection policies. Despite the fact that they are not very present in the context of international biodiversity politics, they play a major role in the implementation process. One important example which shows the differences among NGOs is their consideration of indigenous and local peoples: the "Big Three" which receive most funds and dominate the world's conservation agenda – WWF, CI, TNC – are "increasingly excluding, from full involvement of their program, the indigenous and traditional

peoples living in territories the conservationists were trying to protect"
(Chapin 2004: 17).

Other NGOs, by contrast, set about agitating, particularly on the fringes
of the FAO, in order to draw attention to the problem of the erosion of
genetic resources, but also to the problem of distribution in the utilisation
of genetic resources. They did not participate in the CBD process until the
mid-1990s, and have far fewer resources than the protection of nature
NGOs. Of particular importance are the relatively small but politically very
efficient NGOs, Genetic Resources Action International (GRAIN), Erosion,
Technology and Concentration Group (ETC Group, previously Rural
Advancement Foundation International - RAFI) and the Intermediate
Technology Development Group (ITDG). These NGOs perceive themselves
as trying to articulate the social interests particularly of small farmers in
Southern countries. The dominant process of biodiversity policy is seen as
the privatisation of genetic resources and the expropriation of the previous
owners, namely indigenous peoples and rural communities. Scepticism with
regard to Southern governments has recently been expressed, for example as
criticism of the Like-Minded Group of Megadiverse Countries, which is
accused of forming a cartel and "a front for selling their biological diversity
to the highest bidder" (Ribeiro 2002a: 40).

Following Rio and the coming into force of the CBD in the 1990s a large
number of NGOs appeared in the biodiversity debate, such as the US
American BioNet (Biodiversity Action Network; now dissolved), the Afri-
can Centre for Technology Studies (ACTS, founded by the later General
Secretary of the CBD, Calestous Juma) or the Third World Network
(TWN). The latter represents similar positions to the above-mentioned
GRAIN or ETC Group.[7]

Despite all their differences, the NGO types named have in common that
from their point of view the CBD can only achieve effectiveness via the
broad involvement of different groups of actors as well as ensuring that
their involvement is bound by legal safeguards. The NGOs that are active
on the fringes of the CBD (and the FAO) also have a critical position
regarding the TRIPS Agreement and generally on the free trade logic
institutionalised in the WTO. They believe that the CBD must be
strengthened in opposition to these. Positions vary with regard to private
industrial companies and research institutes directed towards commercialisation. As a whole, the participation of those companies which are open to
the process is regarded as positive while their minimal participation is
viewed as regrettable (CBD/6; CBD/18). Many NGOs see new opportunities
for political manoeuvring being opened up by the CBD which allows them
to formulate critical questions.

But quite different "NGOs" have also become active, although less publicly than the "political" NGOs, namely consulting firms and business
associations (for the latter see above). Consulting firms offer their expertise
as private-sector actors, for example in producing reports for national

implementation. They use the international conferences as a market where they can offer their services. They do not involve themselves directly in the political disputes, but are important actors through their knowledge of technical or organisational questions. They play a major role in the implementation of the CBD at the national level.

Our own research (see also Arts 1998; Brühl 2001) has shown that the influence of NGOs is greater when their proposals move relatively closely to the dominant perception of the problem and to political interests and proposals. Specific expertise and information for suitable interventions, cooperation and contacts between NGOs, lobbying and negotiating capabilities are those aspects which are regarded by the NGOs themselves as central (Arts 1998: 258ff.). Particularly apparent is the idea of "political neutrality" which becomes a strong selection mechanism, integrating certain actors and subject-matters into this process and ignoring others, or at least diminishing the possibilities they have for clear articulation. NGOs and other actors compete with one another with their articulated interests and strategies, something which is often overlooked in the official view of the "NGO community".

2.3.5 Indigenous peoples

The representatives of indigenous peoples repeatedly point out that the question of biological diversity is not about its economic value but about a complex connection between humans or peoples and their cultural practices regarding nature. They demand their rights in self-determination and rights over land as well as referring to human rights (Harry/Kanehe 2005). Therefore, they sometimes question benefit-sharing procedures (for example, in the Hoodia case, see below), because basic needs such as education, health care and so on must be guaranteed without being coupled with the exchange of genetic resources or traditional knowledge (ibid.: 100–101). The issue of access from their point of view is not one of effective and legal appropriation but an invasion of their societal practices (most strongly when it is a case of sacred plants or knowledge). The protection and use of bio-diversity and other natural goods is put into a comprehensive framework by indigenous peoples, that is neoliberal globalisation, militarisation, development aggression, migration, political misrepresentation, as well as all other forms of discrimination (see for example, the Baguio Declaration 2004). A document written by indigenous women highlights that the central principles of the CBD should be expanded to other spheres of life and politics. "Free and prior informed consent should include the full and effective participation of indigenous women in the decision-making process" (ibid.).

Moreover, questions of indigenous knowledge cannot be separated from those of the control of these practices, which includes the control of territories (which is more than just land) and resources. Resources are regarded from the perspective of the safeguarding of food. Especially important is their fundamentally different understanding of questions of property. Property for indigenous peoples is often collective property, and private property of elements of nature is usually ruled out completely (Posey 1999). Their ideas are therefore incompatible with "modern" forms of property (least of all with patents). The indigenous representatives draw attention to the same demands again and again: their rights should be recognised internationally, including the rights to their territories and resources as well as their effective control. At the bottom of this is the demand for self-determination (CBD/24, CBD/26). They have an attitude of scepticism towards their own governments (see Chapter 5). In the countries in which there is national legislation, indigenous rights usually find no consideration (CBD/25). One important problem here is that the existing legal systems in these countries are dominated by modern, Western-based concepts. The idea that different forms of development should be given a political voice within the framework of the CBD is of central importance to those groups that see themselves as representatives of indigenous peoples.

The international level is regarded as a possible supportive sphere, particularly in very specific disputes at the national and local levels (relating to Article 8(j), protection, sustainable utilisation, benefit-sharing and the role of knowledge). Nevertheless, the main criticism of the CBD process is that the Convention itself – and its further development – were, and are being, developed without the participation of indigenous peoples. Especially in the case of the regulation which affirms a national government's sovereignty over natural resources, it is clear that the rights of indigenous peoples do not play any significant role: "The CBD is an agreement to take our resources from us." And the WTO is considered as having more influence on the CBD than do the indigenous peoples (CBD/26). Furthermore, their rudimentary and belated participation primarily serves to legitimise government policies. The momentum of development embedded in neoliberal policies – the biotechnologically motivated interest in genetic resources and in the spreading of genetically modified organisms (GMOs) and correspondingly in biosafety regulations – is emphasised (CBD/25): "The system does not allow any discussion and overrides all those who wish to question it" (CBD/26). With regard to the relationships of power existing at the international level, which are to the disadvantage of indigenous peoples, there are no illusions; it "is a foreign terrain" (CBD/26) on which they must operate diplomatically. Room for manoeuvring is seen more in the process of implementation and concretely in the individual regions where in some cases alliances can be made with environmental ministers, for example on the administration of national parks. Tactical references to the CBD are made here. The question of a moratorium on bioprospecting has been in discussion ever since the mid-1990s. This concerns the recognition of "the right to say no" to bioprospecting – not in order to refuse the utilisation of resources in general, but in order to criticise its dominant form (CBD/26). At the same time the ambivalent role played by the governments of the Southern countries is questioned (CBD/25).

A major debate on the part of the indigenous peoples or their representatives at the international level is whether they should get involved in the international processes at all (CBD/24). However, despite many calls to boycott participation in the international forums, the need to participate in the CBD process, in order to exploit the existing space for contestation, remains the dominant position.

The indigenous peoples have developed networks in recent years as a way of giving voice to their concerns at international negotiations. The official forum in international negotiations is the *International Indigenous Forum on Biodiversity* (IIFB).[8] In recent years the Indigenous Forum has successfully developed a platform for entering into international politics. The COP and the signatory states can no longer ignore the representatives of the indigenous peoples and the IIFB, although appropriate recognition of their concerns is still lacking. The problem of expertise is central, for example in order to be able to adequately appraise juridical issues. Benefit-sharing could start here, for instead of monetary compensation benefit-sharing could take place in the form of capacity building of technical knowledge in the different areas. However, in the opinion of the IIFB, the precondition for access and benefit-sharing is the mutual respect of the sovereignty of all the negotiation partners – and in its opinion, this is still missing (Blank 2002). The IIFB demands from the signatory states of the CBD the recognition of its existence as a forum of legitimate self-representation and of the rights of indigenous peoples (in the sense of the ILO 169), as well as the chance of real prior-informed consent or of the granting of an effective right of veto in access and benefit-sharing questions ("the right to say no": CBD/24; CBD/25; CBD/26).

There are also other networks. Prominent is the Indigenous Peoples' Biodiversity Network (IPBN), which is especially oriented towards the CBD. Since 1998 the Indigenous Women's Biodiversity Network (IWBN) has been formed, which emphasises the specific way in which women handle biological diversity (particularly in nutrition), the poverty of women and their under-representation in the negotiations, and which demands greater participation and education for women (IWBN 2006). An important strategy is also to get female indigenous representatives into the government delegations.

2.3.6 The importance of gender relations

Inequalities based on gender and gender specific conflicts over the use of genetic resources, that is the gendered division of labour, are central in the appropriation of biological diversity. Recent studies show that mainly women gather wild plants and manage them, that they are homegardeners and plant domesticators as well as herbalists and healers and also, that women generally keep the seeds. And it has also been discovered that in many regions women act as the principal farmers, often breeding plants informally (cf. the case studies in Howard 2003). However, these contributions are seldom recognised in research or in political processes.

> In those areas where women have traditionally held control, because of modern technologies and perceptions, women have lost substantial influence and control over production and access to genetic resources to men who benefit from extension services and have the ability to buy seeds, fertilizers and the required technologies. In this way women have also lost their status and self-determination and are not compensated in any way.
>
> (FAO Focus 2006: 2)

This has to do with dominant gender relations which make the contributions of women invisible, thereby obscuring gender relations. Patricia Howard argues that, first, it is necessary to open up the "black box" of the household which includes the societal relationships with nature in the domestic sphere, that is gendered knowledge and the transmission of knowledge, the social division of labour, the relationship between subsistence and market-oriented production, concepts of masculinity and femininity and the systems of indigenous rights to and knowledge about plants (Howard 2003: xviii, 2; GTZ 2002: 10–11). This is an expression of the "cult of domesticity" which is the dominant and mainly Western idea that the (domestic) sphere of reproduction and subsistence is less important than the sphere of production. This, in fact, privileges men and patriarchal norms and obscures the fact that the domestic realm is enormously productive and crucial for the development, conservation and sustainable use of plant genetic resources.

Therefore, it is of utmost importance that women participate beyond concrete conservation and sustainable use activities as well as in political processes. The CBD does not develop a legal framework for this but, at least, states in its Preamble that women play a "vital role ... in the conservation and sustainable use of biological diversity" and considers the "need for the full participation of women at all levels of policy-making and implementation for biodiversity conservation" (CBD 1992, Preamble) as important. Nonetheless, this remains a rather instrumental understanding of the role of women in biodiversity politics.

In international biodiversity policy, however, women continue to play hardly any role. The German GTZ (2002) did organise a lunch-time workshop at COP 5 in Nairobi, and at COP 6 in The Hague, isolated voices were raised that the role of women needed to be given more importance in the discussion and policy process. There are also recommendations to integrate gender issues into the CBD process through capacity building and the raising of public awareness, gender-sensitive programmes, the creation of gender focal points and a gender monitoring and evaluation system, as well as gender balance in expert panels, among other proposals (GTZ 2002: 29–32). But in the political institutions and on the part of the NGOs the subject is non-existent. And despite the formation of the IWBN, even at the meetings of the indigenous peoples, it is not at all easy to get the subject of gender relationships onto the agenda. This indicates a very hard structural selectivity which makes the discussion of gender-specific aspects extremely difficult. There appears to be a consensus among the actors – including the critical NGOs and indigenous peoples – that discussion at the international level should be about so-called hard issues, namely about politico-economic questions, whose gender implications are neglected.

However, the provisions of the CBD have a strong gendered impact. Because of the gendered structure of decision-making processes in state politics and at the local level they tend to strengthen a patriarchal system when mechanisms of benefit-sharing, prior-informed consent or mutually agreed terms are implemented or when protection areas are created. Who is going to benefit and who obtains which rights? Whose food-security is in danger? These are not gender-neutral questions since socio-economic processes as well as those of political decisions are notoriously patriarchal (see BUKO-Kampagne 2005: 117–124).

Not by chance, women and their collective organisations tended, until now, to articulate themselves outside the established political terrains. Thus, internationally there are a number of social movements which expound the problem of control over genetic resources from the perspective of women (see e.g. Akhter 2001; Ayales *et al.* 2002; Baguio Declaration 2004).

2.3.7 *Preliminary summary*

We can see that the conflict lines are much more complex than suggested by the notion of a North–South divide between biodiversity-rich countries in the South and Northern high-tech countries. Even if a broad variety of actors with complex interests are involved, central characteristics of the conflict field can be figured out. The dominant groups of actors – Northern and Southern governments, private companies and research institutes – assume a potential win–win constellation because benefits which can be shared arise in the first place from the access to biological diversity and its valorisation. It is only the forms of appropriation and the distribution of the potential benefits which remain controversial. The governments of most countries – and thus the protagonists of the CBD – also agree in their opinion that insisting on national sovereignty over biological or genetic resources by the CBD is important. The considerations behind this vary, nevertheless. It was through the criticism by the Southern countries of the centuries-old practice of utilisation by Northern actors without benefit-sharing that this gene robbery came under pressure to legitimise itself, and this led to the formulation of national sovereignty regarding biogenetic resources. The interest of Southern governments, companies and research institutes was strengthened by the commencing "biotechnological revolution". With the provision of national sovereignty, an important condition for the valorisation of biological diversity was created.

The debate on environmental politics, which placed the erosion of biological diversity at the centre of attention, contributed considerably to the politicising of North–South relations and to creating a new terrain for compromises. Nonetheless, during the CBD negotiations in 1992 and the continued shaping of the CBD as of 1994, questions concerning the structural inequalities in North–South relations disappeared into the background. Within the framework of the ecological perspective it is usually argued that the national sovereignty of states should be limited and a global management programme set up in order to take action against the exploitation of natural resources. Countries such as Brazil, nevertheless, have always resisted such an external influence. However, the situation today seems to have changed, to the extent that biodiversity-rich countries now recognise the value of their natural resources and attempt to use but also to conserve them. Therefore, the protection of nature becomes interesting for these countries. Discussions on military and ecological security can even overlap and mix here (for Brazil, see Acselrad 2002). External experts on nature protection are in some cases consulted for the corresponding supervision and control.

Disposal of resources concerns not only their protection, however, but has more to do with their valorisation and with planning security. This is the case because on the one hand, the Northern businesses and research institutes require clear legal relationships for the case that marketable products result from bioprospecting. This legal security can be granted best by the nation-state with its monopoly of legitimate force. National sovereignty is the necessary condition for the distribution of rights of disposal and the state's guarantee of these rights: state-political activity is not opposed to the interests of the economic actors here, but it is the precondition for valorisation. On the other hand, the issues at stake are much broader than suggested by the conventional view on ABS (access and benefit sharing). As the Millennium Ecosystem Assessment (MASR 2005) pointed out, the decline of ecosystem services is a major obstacle to reaching the Millennium Development Goals of the United Nations. In this context, the commercialisation of biodiversity and its monetary evaluation, in general, is considered as putting at risk, or even ignoring, important contributions of biodiversity for development purposes.

In the context of the CBD, however, only a few actors, particularly the representatives of indigenous peoples and some NGOs, focus on the issue of the erosion of biological diversity from a perspective which does not primarily centre on its potential economic value. Protection and utilisation are closely connected here, too, but from the perspective of local living conditions. This leads to a critical appraisal of international biodiversity policy and its dominant development.

2.4 Problems and fields of conflict

The CBD is recognised by most actors as a fundamental compromise. More was not to be expected in the negotiations up until 1992, a fact admitted by some NGO activists who are well acquainted with the process (CBD/11, CBD/15). There is a far-reaching consensus among the participants that the design of the Convention is still in the making. The further shaping of the contents of the CBD and their effects are also highly controversial and even a representative of the CBD secretariat has come to the conclusion that the immense inequalities of power between the countries and other actors is a major problem (CBD/18). The conflicts are condensed in a certain way, in that the central concepts of the CBD are unclear and in the opinion of various actors still require concretisation. In this section, therefore, the controversies surrounding the central aspects will be examined more precisely.

2.4.1 Access to genetic resources and benefit-sharing as the central conflict

As we have already stated, by "access" the CBD means different things: access to natural resources, access to knowledge and, closely connected with the latter, access to technologies (see below). With regard to access to genetic resources, the governments of the individual signatory states have the right to regulate access (CBD 1992: Art. 15.1). According to the CBD access should generally be "facilitated" (ibid.: Art. 15.2). The idea behind this is that the potential utility of genetic resources should be made available to everybody. In fact, however, the economic value of biodiversity is strongly pushed into the foreground. This leads to a different appraisal of natural goods as resources and of knowledge. Certain forms of knowledge are, however, not market-compatible per se (traditional healers and forms of exchange in agriculture; cf. the next chapter on this). In order to facilitate access they first have to be made into market-compatible forms of knowledge and thus they must be comprehensively modified in their social foundations. Not only are questions of property rights, in the narrow sense of the word, at stake here, but also of key importance are comprehensive societal practices.

There is a great potential for conflict with regard to the concrete application of the prior-informed consent (PIC) and mutually agreed terms (MAT) regulations. While the Northern governments are clearly in favour of flexible and voluntary conditions, some Southern governments (i.e. the members of the Like-Minded Group of Megadiverse Countries) push for binding regulations. They consider the CBD to be inadequate on access and benefit-sharing because it simply formulates general principles but does not lay down a uniform terminology or procedures (CBD/23). But among the (so-called) provider countries, the concretising of the regulations is controversial. The CBD, in Article 15.5, lays down that prior-informed consent is to be granted by the providing signatory state, if the latter does not decide otherwise.

In the negotiations on the formulation of the access and benefit-sharing mechanisms it has, furthermore, become clear that prior-informed consent and mutually agreed terms require comprehensive knowledge on the part of the national and local actors if there is a real desire to reach an "informed consent". Since this requires technical, economic and juridical knowledge in order to comprehend the complex regulations and to be able to weigh their consequences, and since this knowledge does not simply exist, these mechanisms require the setting up of corresponding structures. One important instrument which is recognised by all actors as such is the construction of corresponding competencies: *capacity building*. However, it is still an open issue as to what is specifically understood by this term (see below). In addition, although the need for necessary flexibility is often emphasised, many Southern representatives see a danger in this in that it tends to favour the stronger actors.

Indigenous peoples and critical NGOs increasingly politicise the problem of access by making accusations of *biopiracy*. This stance is intended to criticise the historical and current process of the appropriation of genetic resources, which is regarded as being illegitimate. This does not become more legitimate through the formal agreement of state authorities, as indigenous peoples and local communities are not involved in the process in which the legal framework is developed (see Ribeiro 2005; Egziabher 2005; Shiva 2005; cf. the detailed study of Central American countries in Delgado Ramos 2004: 107–182).

> For ETC Group, biopiracy is the privatization through intellectual property systems of biological resources and/or related knowledge, regardless if this is legalized by a national law or a bioprospecting agreement, and even if a so called "benefit-sharing" agreement is included. As Alejandro Argumedo, a Quechua activist describes it, benefit-sharing in bioprospecting contracts is like waking up while your house is being robbed, and the thieves try to calm you down by offering to share the benefits derived from the commercialization of your stolen goods.
> (Ribeiro 2002a: 37; cf. BUKO-Kampagne 2005, http://en.wikipedia.org/wiki/Biopiracy)

One consequence of this for the above position is that potential local beneficiaries of benefit-sharing must also have the right to refuse access. However, Southern governments have also claimed the term as their own, although they have a rather different understanding of it (SEMARNAT 2002a: 124). By biopiracy they do not mean a fundamentally illegitimate process of the privatisation of nature; rather, they use the term when the legal conditions (particularly prior-informed consent and mutually agreed terms and thus their participation in benefit-sharing) are not met (cf. section 2.2). And even companies use the term when their intellectual property rights are abused.

Altogether, the question of access illustrates that the decisive actors – Northern governments and biotechnology firms – determine the momentum of the CBD. Since it is unclear, however, how strong the interest in genetic resources for pharmaceutical research actually is, and the fact that often these firms prefer bilateral access via bioprospecting agreements, these dominant actors are not necessarily interested in internationally binding rules on access. This is why the negotiations on rules for access and benefit-sharing started relatively late, knowing the controversial character of the regulations. However, the lines of conflict have become clearer due to the negotiations of the past years. The question concerning *how* appropriation takes place in a specific case is determined less by formal legal regulations and more by their interpretation. And that is ultimately dependent on the corresponding power resources.

Just like access, benefit-sharing can also take very different forms. Within the CBD and its further development, it remains closely interlinked to access to genetic resources. However, this ignores a perspective, which for ecological reasons would certainly be worth considering, namely to fairly distribute the utility which arises from access *forborne*, that is from the fact that certain parts of nature are not put to any economic use. This is indeed often demanded of the rural population near to nature conservation areas without any compensation taking place, particularly in the Southern countries. Furthermore, access also includes non-monetary benefit-sharing in addition to monetary benefit-sharing – which arises primarily from the commercialisation of genetic resources. In addition to participation in research results and capacity building, non-monetary benefit-sharing can include technology transfer, although this can lead to conflicts with regard to intellectual property rights and patents (Seiler/Dutfield 2001: 24f.) Benefit-sharing is therefore not only a question of monetary payment. The provider countries hope for technology and knowledge transfer from benefit-sharing, while the so-called user countries or the private biotechnology companies hope for an improvement in the conditions for further bioprospecting and the further processing of the samples – for technology transfer can also be used for that purpose. Benefit-sharing thus plays a central role in the Convention but, surprisingly, it plays a very subordinate one in the further negotiations. On the part of the receivers and valorisers of genetic resources, it is repeatedly emphasised that in the negotiations on the CBD high expectations have been awakened with regard to the potentially sharable economic benefits. This could lead to disappointments and conflicts (e.g. CBD/2; CBD/4; CBD/9; CBD/10; CBD/15). A representative of a research institute active in the area of seeds described benefit-sharing linked to the actual development of products as a "lottery" (CBD/1).

Benefit-sharing involves a double distributional conflict. At the *international* level it is highly politicised because the motivation of the Southern governments is essentially determined by their interest in sharing in the biotechnological developments which are driven forth by companies or research institutes located in other countries. At the same time, it remains a decisive accusation on the part of the provider countries that the benefits are monopolised by the receivers of genetic resources (e.g. CBD/11). The other level of conflict, namely that of the *national* distribution of the potential benefits within the provider countries themselves, is discussed much less in the international negotiations. A representative of Novartis openly speaks of an inner-societal conflict with regard to benefit-sharing: the indigenous peoples in most cases prefer to achieve respect and an improvement in their living conditions (schools, roads, hospitals), while money as a medium of benefit-sharing is as a rule demanded by the governments (CBD/13). The interests of the Northern actors, however, go beyond simply paying money to the governments and in return receiving legal access and the safeguarding of intellectual property rights. Their practices and proposals show that they are primarily concerned via benefit-sharing to improve the conditions for valorisation, for example by equipping local research institutes with technical apparatus and know-how. The interest in non-monetary benefit-sharing is supported by NGOs and indigenous organisations. The governments also increasingly agree to non-monetary benefit-sharing because in their estimation this comes closer to the interests of the users as well as favouring technology transfer. This continues to be accompanied by the demand for monetary participation in the development of marketable products, however.

Finally, it is important that, as mentioned before, the genetic resources acquired before the coming into force of the CBD do not fall under the Convention (CBD 1992: Art. 15.3). This means that the material collected until 1993 now continues to be freely available for commercial purposes. This fact has hardly been politicised until now, however.

To summarise, benefit-sharing has a rather weak legal status in the CBD. This is an expression of the international relationships of power regarding this question. The Northern actors wish to secure legal access for themselves and cannot therefore completely withdraw from the discussion on benefit-sharing. On the other hand, in this area no initiative on their part is to be expected. In addition, the large quantities of genetic resources with immense economic potential which were already available in the Northern countries before December 1993 are excluded. Initiatives, for example by botanical gardens to introduce a voluntary retrospective benefit-sharing, have been greeted benevolently, but they only cover a small fraction of the material which flowed from the South to the North over the last centuries.

One danger for weaker interest groups is that the specific meaning of "fair and equal benefit-sharing" is left to bilateral negotiations. Power resources play a decisive role here, but so does knowledge on the part of the providers about potential benefits and their sharing. Furthermore, benefit-sharing is seen here exclusively in the context of the valorisation of genetic resources, so that other perspectives – such as benefit-sharing for the conservation of biodiversity without at the same time having the perspective of its marketing – are devalued. This commodifying perspective is strengthened by the competition of the "suppliers" among themselves. A study by the NGOs GAIA and GRAIN (2000) points out that in spite of an immeasurable quantity of literature on benefit-sharing,

> the scope of the benefit-sharing debate is actually very narrow. Almost without exception, benefit-sharing examples focus on bilateral and contractual agreements, generally between some company or institute from an industrialised country interested in a resource or knowledge, and some country or community from the South that can provide it. *Benefit-sharing is defined from the perspective of the bioprospector: how much money is paid, and whether other non-monetary benefits flow to the provider.*
> (GAIA/GRAIN 2000: 2, our emphasis)

A very limited and commercial interpretation of the use arising from genetic resources is dominant, mainly because the use for local communities, for the direct securing of their means of living, for health and food security, is ignored, as is the protection of nature and public research. Only marketable exchange values are of interest. In future it will have to be shown whether benefit-sharing is a clear right with which certain standards are set or, rather, whether it is a symbolic act in order to do justice to the regulations of the CBD and to legalise the appropriation of biological diversity. The starting-point should be the interests of the local communities and farmers. It will be decisive to what extent access and benefit-sharing are seen as inseparable and in what way this inseparability is specifically created. Second, with regard to access and benefit-sharing, the question of control over knowledge and resources, but also over land and social processes, is central. Thus, *ex situ* collections have largely been removed from the control of the Southern countries, which is why they are not a major issue in the international negotiations. In contrast to this, intellectual property rights are the central lever for the control of genetic resources and their further development.

2.4.2 Indigenous rights

There is no doubt that the CBD is an international institution within which the concerns of indigenous peoples are heard relatively strongly. Article 8(j) of the CBD lays down regulations for national implementation, but without clearly defining the demands and legal consequences. A special role is played here by the different legal opinions on the relationship of indigenous knowledge and the scientific knowledge used in the industrial context (see Agrawal 1995; Brush 1993; Posey 1999; on the role of indigenous peoples in the CBD see Potvin *et al.* 2002). But even if the indigenous peoples have succeeded, in recent years, in procuring more weight for their demands, their interests nevertheless continue to play a subordinate role in the specific momentum of the negotiations.

At the international level, the area most fraught with conflict is that of intellectual property rights. The pressure placed on the governments by private companies with regard to the strict safeguarding of intellectual property rights is diametrically opposed to the interests of indigenous peoples. The degree of manoeuvrability is regarded as being very minute here: "its (patents are) the only game in town" (CBD/24). The recognition of already existing and inalienable indigenous rights has not happened, never mind the notion of respecting the fact that "traditional" knowledge is not only knowledge of different things but also a "different institutional treatment of knowledge by human societies" (Kuppe 2002: 117, our translation). Nor do the attempts to strengthen alternative concepts such as community rights or traditional resource rights find any support. Even regarding benefit-sharing, ambiguity predominates.

> That's gonna be a difficult thing. Where do the benefits come from? What kinds of benefits are they? Are they monetary, capacity building or what? What exactly is the range of benefits? How are they identified and made broadly known to the community?
>
> (CBD/8)

In general the governments of the provider countries fear that by granting the indigenous peoples a legal position that is too strong, they would be effectively discouraging potential bioprospectors (CBD/15). The strengthening of the rights of indigenous peoples is avoided in the CBD in two ways: their voluntary character is emphasised, and they are made "subject to national legislation and policy" (e.g. the governments of Australia and Malaysia at COP 6 in 2002; ENB 2002: 2). Furthermore, the broadly interpretable regulations of Article 8(j) involve the problem that indigenous peoples would have to be educated for effective participation. Nevertheless, indigenous peoples, supported for example by the governments of Norway and India, were able to enforce one important aspect. At COP 5 (2000 in Nairobi) in Decision V/16, the provision of prior-informed consent was extended to indigenous peoples. Since then the representatives of the indigenous peoples have the status of official consultants and no longer simply that of observers.

In order to show some of the complex dimensions of bioprospecting, access and benefit-sharing, it is pertinent to offer a brief outline of the case of the San people and the Hoodia cactus in Southern Africa (see Harry/Kanehe 2005: 97–103; Hoering 2004; Frein/Meyer 2005: 140–153). To use this cactus in modern medicine a benefit-sharing agreement was negotiated which is often perceived as being a success story as an instrument to alleviate poverty. But it still remains quite unclear whether this objective can really be reached, as well as, generally, how this agreement should be judged.

The plant was used for hundreds of years by the most ancient people of Southern Africa, who live mainly in the Kalahari, in order to suppress hunger while hunting. In 2001 it became known – by chance – that the Council for Scientific and Industrial Research in South Africa (CSIR) had undertaken bioprospecting and found that the substances of the Hoodia plant can be used for a drug against obesity, that is to suppress appetite and aid slimming, which is, in the Northern countries, a billion dollar market. CSIR obtained a patent and gave the pharmaceutical company Phytopharm a license. (For a time, the transnational company Pfizer owned the licence, after having bought it for 21 million USD, but later this company withdrew from this branch and the licence went back to Phytopharm.) Among other things, it was agreed that CSIR had the right to cultivate and produce Hoodia for the South African market while Phytopharm had market rights for the rest of the world. When Phytofarm's Richard Dixey said in 2001 that the San people had died out and, because of this, could not be part of a benefit-sharing agreement, a lot of concern rose up and San from four countries raised their voices. The criticism of Phytofarm and CSIR by the San people and international NGOs led to the negotiation of a benefit-sharing agreement which was signed between the San people and CSIR in March 2003. As part of this agreement, the San people were to receive 8 per cent of the royalties that CSIR receives from Phytofarm; Phytopharm is not part of the agreement. At the same time, the San people are not permitted to use their knowledge for commercial ends. A Hoodia Trust was created (also with members of CSIR and the South African Government) and benefit flow to the San people was expected to reach one million USD. A small amount of money has been paid already, but held back until the San have established a legal entity. The Working Group in Indigenous Minorities in Southern Africa (WIMSA) played an important role here in promoting the interests of the San people in the negotiations.[9] The ambiguity lies in the fact that the benefit-sharing agreement was negotiated after the appropriation of the Hoodia substances through CSIR and that "prior informed consent" – a crucial requirement of the CBD, see below – was not given.

> It is important to note that the San were compensated for their traditional knowledge and not for any right they might have in the genetic resource itself. It was the CSIR, and not the San who consented to access to the genetic resource itself.
>
> (Harry/Kanehe 2005: 99)

Some say that at best, the agreement is "very lenient punishment. Imagine if a thief could get away with his crime as long as he gave his victim a few percent of whatever the receiver paid him for stolen goods" (Hoering 2004: 18). It is questionable whether the patenting was in line with the commitments of the CBD. Moreover, there is criticism that not only prior-informed consent was not given but that the San people could not decide about the patent registration. With the agreement, Phytopharm has the right to monopolise the knowledge of the San people concerning Hoodia for commercial ends (Harry/Kanehe 2005: 99). Even in the case of a prior-informed consent, the San people could only wait if the pharmaceutical company was able to develop and market a product with Hoodia which might be the "first African blockbuster drug" (Rachel Wynberg, quoted in Hoering 2004: 19). The Hoodia case is also important in demonstrating the fact that indigenous peoples "are seen only as traditional knowledge holders and not as territorial rights holders whose consent must be sought before accessing resources within their territories" (Harry/Kanehe 2005: 97). Another criticism is that the flow of benefits is not related to another provision of the CBD, that is the acknowledgement and protection of traditional knowledge and peoples. And finally, the major interests for CSIR and especially the South African Government are less related to the San people than they are to other lucrative ideas related to the seed production, cultivation, processing and eventual exportation of Hoodia and many other plants (Hoering 2004: 23).

However, WIMSA and many San people are glad that at least today they have the agreement and that they did not file a suit against the patent, which they saw as having little prospect of success. And throughout the process of the last years, there has been a recognition of their knowledge which has helped to raise their consciousness. In many other cases the traditional developers of the plants have not received anything. For example, the cancer drug Vincristine embodies the knowledge of indigenous peoples from Madagascar and genetic resources from a periwinkle and is marketed by the US-based corporation, Eli Lilly, to the tune of 100 million USD annually (see other examples in Sharma 2005).

There is another ambiguity in the San case which can reveal some challenges of the existing ABS regulations. Even if there are doubts as to whether the patenting was legal and whether some other provisions were respected or not, in pure legal terms the negotiation of the CSIR was not in contradiction of the CBD. The consent of indigenous peoples is only required when it is subject to domestic law.

> Therefore, what transpired with the Hoodia was totally consistent with the Bonn Guidelines [see below, the authors]; that is, the CSIR acted as the South African national authority granting access to the Hoodia. The indigenous San peoples had no established legal right vis-à-vis Hoodia under South African law and so their consent was not required.
> (Harry/Kanehe 2005: 99–100).

The lesser meaning of indigenous rights in the context of access and benefit-sharing can be clearly seen in the fact that the negotiations on access and benefit-sharing and on Article 8(j) are conducted separately and the indigenous perspective is very seldom integrated into other processes. The major institutionalised forum in the CBD is without any doubt the *Ad Hoc Open-ended Inter-Sessional Working Group on Article 8(j) and Related Provisions* of the CBD (established in 1998). It works on elements of a *sui generis* system for "the protection of the traditional knowledge, innovations and practices of indigenous and local communities" (Secretariat of the CBD 2006b: 38, 154) and intends to collaborate with the Working Group on Access and Benefit-sharing. But the latter seems to be hesitant. The Working Group on 8(j) is an important but weak form of institutionalised interests.

As a whole, indigenous peoples are threatened with being made into a "negotiation mass" by the Southern governments. At the international level, the governments speak prominently of the protection of their "own" indigenous peoples, but they are criticised that this takes place only from the perspective of valorisation. One proof of this is that the much quoted indigenous peoples were not consulted in the initiative for the Like-Minded Group of Megadiverse Countries (Ribeiro 2002a). An indication of the rather symbolic meaning of indigenous rights could also be that the governments often do not speak of indigenous peoples but of indigenous communities or groups. This implies a weaker status in the sense that "communities" cannot claim rights, or traditional and indigenous knowledge (CBD/24), which more or less suggests a resource.

For Article 8(j) the issue will be decisive whether the rights of indigenous peoples (and of local farmers) are instrumentalised for facilitated access, or whether in the case of conflict the rights of these weaker actors can be protected. Here, the question of information is certainly a central one, as is the concrete design of prior-informed consent and mutually agreed terms. Even though conflicts over the rights of the indigenous peoples, like those of other local users of biodiversity, have been repeatedly discussed at international conferences, ultimately, they are fought out in the countries themselves as well as at specific locations. Concrete strategies and the successful organisation of interests play an important role here. Competition between subordinate actors is, by contrast, supportive of the exercise of rule. For one thing, it legitimises regulating intervention by states; and at the same time it places the users in a position of advantage, because they have a weaker "negotiation partner". In the case study on Mexico (see Chapter 5) this will become even clearer.

2.4.3 Intellectual property rights

The safeguarding of intellectual property rights is the central concern for the industrial utilisation of genetic resources and in particular for gene technical utilisation, and it is taken into consideration in various places in the CBD. Taken from within the question as to whether and to what extent this is permissible or what consequences it has from an ecological, economic and social point of view, one of the most important and controversial fields of conflict between different international regulations systems is unearthed. Intellectual property rights are discussed primarily in connection with the rights of indigenous peoples and in access and benefit-sharing questions. The representatives of the Southern governments (CBD/23) and most NGO representatives (CBD/7; CBD/11) see a central weakness of the CBD with regard to the low value of intellectual property rights in the sense of the protection of indigenous peoples and the provider countries. Nevertheless, the CBD is regarded as the only international forum in which weaker actors can assert their interests with regard to intellectual property at all. An adequate legislation on access must contain regulations on intellectual property rights. "It's going to be the make or break situation" (CBD/11). However, this poses the question as to what power the Southern governments and NGOs have to cause a break. Hardly anyone is thinking of withdrawing from existing international agreements; instead, of concern is the question of to what extent other forms of intellectual property will be accepted. These discussions are taking place on the fringes of the World Trade Organization's TRIPS Agreement and have more recently been strongly reinforced in the World Intellectual Property Organization (WIPO). The debate is centred on whether, in addition to "hard" intellectual property rights protection (particularly by patents), other protection standards should be accepted.

2.4.4 *Protection and conservation*

With the CBD, the economic value of biodiversity has shifted to the centre of the problem, while ecological and socio-ecological problems threaten to be displaced to the background. Thus, representatives of the German Federal Ministry of the Environment, for example, complained that protection interests were neglected in the CBD (CBD/20, CBD/22). This is connected with the fact that the economic value of biodiversity was, and is to some degree, largely regarded as an unproblematical lever or incentive for the greater protection of biological diversity. The dominant line of argument concerning the treatment of biological diversity on the fringes of the CBD is that the economic value of genetic resources is suitable to open up new sources of finance for nature protection and to increase the public appeal of biological diversity. The consequence of this perspective is that the aims of the CBD are to be achieved *via facilitated access*. This argumentation and practice is surprising at least in that the original point of nature protection areas was *to limit access*. Whether it was a case of pure protection areas or biosphere reservations with graduated forms of use, the practice was always aimed at conserving threatened species or ecosystems by regulating and limiting human access. The classical concept of protection, however, which aimed at the waiving of utilisation altogether, had already come under criticism at the beginning of the 1980s and was replaced by the concept of sustainable use.

Two arguments are used here, each of which is based on the other. First, the setting up of protection areas should not take place against the will of the affected population, which must be allowed to continue to follow its sustainable forms of use, or an acceptable compensatory income must be created. In addition, a second argument says that an incentive to ensure that protection areas are respected, for example in the form of income sources from ecotourism or even bioprospecting, must be promised. If the first argument places the economic use in the service of conservation, the second argument places conservation in the service of economic use – for only if nature is conserved can it be profited from, whether this is through tourism or in the form of bioprospecting. The two demands thus not only complement each other but there is a threat that they turn the relationship between protection and use upside down. To put it more pointedly, the tendency towards the commercialisation of biodiversity itself works to promote the conservation of nature (see e.g. Escobar 1996; Heineke/Wolff 2004: 30). This means in fact that the protection of nature itself becomes profitable, and protection interests are no longer, per se, in contradiction to commercial interests in the exploitation of nature. It cannot be ignored, however, that in many parts of the world the exploitation of minerals or biological resources such as tropical wood by far exceeds the use and conservation of genetic resources. For this reason alone, it is doubtful whether the economic value of biodiversity does in fact represent a central lever for its conservation. Moreover, there are many doubts that economic benefits for the valorisation of genetic resources will fund conservation (Siebenhüner *et al.* 2005: 40–41).

Doubts are also appropriate because the described practice of bioprospecting does not at all make the long-term conservation of the ecosystems necessary. Once the information has been gained, that is the genetic characteristics discovered, interest in the conservation of the organism studied is exhausted, at least from an economic perspective (cf. articles in Burrows 2005).

The conservation issue reveals once again the missing enforcement mechanism of the CBD. Because there is no sanction mechanism, the parties, that is the governments, cannot be forced to evaluate the impact of their policies and to initiate actions that protect and conserve biodiversity. The aim of creating a funding mechanism for a global protection area system by 2008, and then establishing it as a system by 2010 and thereafter working towards the creation of a network of biotopes by 2015, seems at present to be a completely unfathomable task. Moreover, at COP 8 in March 2006 the activities of the large conservation NGOs – especially Conservation International, The Nature Conservancy and the WWF – with respect to protection and conservation were praised, despite the fact that they involve hardly any indigenous peoples and local communities within their organisations or campaigns.

More recently the relationship between the conservation and utilisation of biodiversity was newly framed by emphasising its relevance for the functioning of ecosystems and for ecosystem services. In particular, the Millennium

Ecosystem Assessment highlights the interconnections between ecosystem services and human well-being in a broad variety of societal sectors and fields of social actions: from nutrition and shelter up to recreation and tourism (MASR 2005). Compared with earlier assessments, the Millennium Ecosystem Assessment focuses more on the trade-offs between different ecosystem services and reveals that some – in particular regulating and cultural services – are degraded because of substantial net gains in provisioning services (in particular agriculture and fishing). Thus, the Millennium Ecosystem Assessment requires that gains and losses regarding the use of ecosystems must be assessed more carefully and taken into account in decision-making processes. Moreover, it states that some ecosystem services could be under-valued and therefore they could risk being destroyed if the focus is only on market values (MASR 2005: 98). Even if in the Millennium Ecosystem Assessment economic and other flexible governance instruments are recommended, it also identifies the limits of pure economic approaches and requires at least the incorporation of non-economic considerations.

2.4.5 Participation and capacity building

The imposition of national sovereignty over biological diversity raises the question of to what extent local population groups can articulate themselves under the principle of national sovereignty and what rights they have – particularly if their interests are contradictory to those of nation-state actors or dominant interest groups. There seems to be at least an implicit consensus between the governments here that the rights of local communities are internationally recognised but that this recognition is of a primarily symbolic nature. One catchword in the CBD is *participation*. Four levels play a role here: participation in the international negotiations, in the formulation of national legislation, in the negotiating of access agreements and finally, in the process of the appropriation of resources and knowledge. Participation in the appropriation of resources and knowledge is the most important for the prospectors because this can increase effectiveness. At the other levels, however, there is a danger that participation may serve to cultivate legitimacy for a process which is basically without an alternative. It is therefore essential to determine what exactly is meant by participation, not only at the level of the consultations but also with regard to the decision-making processes; above all in order to be able to influence decisions in the case of deviating appraisals. This is made considerably more difficult by the fact that it is a case of political processes with many preconditions in which the implications of certain developments and decisions are not at all obvious.

At first glance, there is no politically explosive material behind the formula of capacity building. However, different forms of application of the CBD are expressed in the ideas of what capacity building should look like concretely, that is which strategies and material resources should be applied. Capacity building not only means educating people or making the CBD publicly known, it also means the development of comprehensive organisational, institutional and knowledge capacities. It is exactly this subject which has been placed at the centre of examination in the so-called Bonn Guidelines on Access and Benefit-sharing, which are outlined below. A critical examination of their suggestions illustrates that the corporate and governmental side is principally concerned with improving the conditions for valorisation. By contrast, NGOs and indigenous peoples see, in capacity building, the opportunity to strengthen the rights of weaker actors.

The current proposals for capacity building at the local level have been criticised for leading in the wrong direction. Instead of training even more access and benefit-sharing experts who can negotiate bilaterally with corporations, the aim should be to create strong, legally binding, multilaterally consensual and internationally sanctioned rules of the game in order to protect communities and to define the extent of corporate manoeuvrability (GAIA/GRAIN 2000).

2.4.6 Problems of national implementation

The implementation of the CBD regulations at the national and local levels should take place on two planes: first, through national policies (national reports, legislation, nature conservation projects etc.) and second, through specific access agreements. The interests of the Southern countries, and especially the megadiverse countries, are relatively clear here, namely "that the adoption of an appropriate legislation can become a highly useful tool in participating efficiently in international markets and in taking full advantage of their own comparative advantages" (SEMARNAT 2002a: 116).

In the estimation of many participants, the national implementation and legislation processes have been accorded the highest priority at present. Nevertheless, they are tackled, if at all, only on the part of the so-called provider countries – and even here it tends to be slow.

The implementation of the CBD is considered to be part of a third phase of the convention, after the negotiation of the convention text and, after 1993, the policy development within the CBD (Zedan 2005: 2–4). However, in recent years, national implementation has been considered one of the central weaknesses of international biodiversity politics (see Executive Secretary of the CBD 2005). The implementation process is considered too slow (Secretariat of the CBD 2006b: 184, i.e. Decision VIII/8). Therefore, national biodiversity strategies and action plans should be discussed in detail at COP 9 in 2008.

Although it is seen as problematic that no access legislation for appropriate user measures has been enacted in the user countries, this issue has not been brought forward in the negotiations. A few years ago, a survey of the legislation in more than ten Southern countries, which at the time had either been passed or was under review, clearly showed that in the majority of cases there was no independent legislation; the state had almost exclusive property rights over genetic resources (there were exceptions in the countries of the Andes Pact: *Comunidad Andina de Naciones*, CAN); and finally, that PIC had to be negotiated and approved by the state (Caillaux/Ruiz 2002: 162–166). The statement by a member of the Brazilian government is probably expressive of the general opinion held by those countries, namely that the provider countries "should provide a very robust legal enabling environment" (CBD/23). The inadequacy of the legislation is connected with the fact that it is not clear what content the national regulations should have and to what extent they should be binding. Different demands are formulated by different actors.

Another aspect of the protracted implementation of the CBD is based in the competition among the national state apparatuses. The leading environmental ministries usually carry little weight with regard to such issues, something that will become even clearer in the case study of Mexico (see Chapter 5). A further aspect named by an interviewee is the lack of sanction mechanisms in the CBD in the case of non-implementation (CBD/12). The national implementation of the CBD not only means the provision of an adequate legal framework but also requires that the nation-state is able to finance and to apply it (as a part of public policies). Here too, there is a great deal of potential for conflicts to develop, as different interests are expressed in individual policies. At the international level, the monitoring of the implementation, via reports among other things, is prescribed, but this obligation does not seem to be taken particularly seriously.

The fact that room for manoeuvre does exist in the process of the national implementation of the CBD is demonstrated, for instance, by the Philippine legislation or by the corresponding regulations of the Andes Pact. They both go beyond the CBD and insist that existing local communities or indigenous peoples must agree before national implementation can go ahead (ten Kate/Laird 1999: 28f.; on the Philippines see also Liebig *et al.* 2002). From the perspective of the Northern governments, the Philippine legislation is considered to be "over-regulated" (CBD/1; CBD/4; CBD/9; CBD/10), while from the point of view of NGOs, it tends to be seen as a positive example (CBD/3; CBD/7; CBD/24). The representative of a Philippine NGO which contributed to the formulation also defends it (CBD/2). The problem here is seen in the fact that the legislation is not implemented. Moreover, the problem remains very obvious that the national regulations also have to be implemented institutionally.

2.4.7 A multilateral system of rules for bilateral policies?

As shown above, with regard to the regulation of access and benefit-sharing, the CBD has created legal security in that, with national sovereignty, the regulating authority of the nation-state became internationally recognised. This recognition was demanded and enforced by the governments of the Southern countries in the CBD negotiations with reference to the centuries-old practice of the unregulated (and indeed, free-of-charge) appropriation of genetic goods. Behind such actions was the practice which today is condemned as *biopiracy*. There are, however, different understandings of what biopiracy exactly is. Two positions are important. The first is advocated primarily by governments of the South and most NGOs, which understand biopiracy as the gratuitous and legally unregulated appropriation of genetic resources. According to this view, the practice of biopiracy would be ended if appropriate legal regulations existed, particularly the fulfilment of prior-informed consent and benefit-sharing in access agreements (legalistic view). A second, alternative position can be outlined, which places stronger emphasis on the inequalities of power among the different actors and problematises the function of legal regulations in the practice of biopiracy itself (particularly intellectual property rights and patents, but also rules in the CBD). According to this point of view, legal regulations as such are not at all adequate as long as they do not remove the inequalities of power. Rather, it is decisive whether or not the weaker actors (above all rural and indigenous actors) are really able to defend their rights against stronger interests (this could therefore be described as the "realist" view).

In a strictly legalistic sense the CBD and the further negotiations on access and benefit-sharing can be seen as attempts to remove the practice of biopiracy by creating a legally binding framework for the appropriation of genetic material. However, in doing so the CBD at first favours a bilateral approach. Agreements between providers and users are to take the place of unregulated and gratuitous appropriation. Access agreements are not bindingly required in the CBD but it is highly likely that they will become the central instrument for regulating concrete access and benefit-sharing in the existing international and national framework. It is remarkable that, until now, access and benefit-sharing agreements have predominantly been made, above all, in the field of pharmaceuticals in contrast to their general omission in the fields of agricultural and cosmetic products. The agreements should regulate, among other things: who the partners to the agreement are (state agencies, research institutes, companies etc.); to whom the samples of genetic resources belong and whether the samples are to remain in the provider countries; which authorities are responsible; whether and how trust is to be safeguarded; how, for whom and by whom intellectual property rights are to be safeguarded (patents, licenses etc.); whether there is to be joint research; and finally, whether research results are to be returned and to what extent prior-informed consent, mutually agreed terms and benefit-sharing are to be safeguarded. Although it is not explicitly foreseen in the CBD, research institutes and companies such as Novo Nordisk and Glaxo Wellcome, as well as botanical gardens and research institutions such as the US National Cancer Institute or the CGIAR (Consultative Group on International Agricultural Research), have been developing their own guidelines for the conclusion of access and benefit-sharing agreements (Caillaux/Ruiz 2002: 167–170). Until now the accusation has been raised with regard to the access agreements that these not only focus on bilateral agreements, which already favour stronger actors, but also that the specific models for benefit-sharing represent an "exclusively economic approach" (GAIA/ GRAIN 2000: 1).

It is not enough simply to contrast bilateral and multilateral approaches to the regulation of access and benefit-sharing. Although the CBD clearly favours bilateral access models and is therefore considerably different from the multilateral system for the exchange of genetic resources as now established within the framework of the FAO (cf. the next chapter on this), it nonetheless is also, in fact, a multilaterally recognised framework in which these agreements and thus global markets for genetic resources are to be safeguarded. The differences thus refer primarily to what exactly is to be regulated multilaterally, what strength these regulations have over bilateral agreements and in what form they organise global exchange: what interests are taken into consideration and in what form? It is decisive as to whether or not, beyond national sovereignty, recognised minimum standards and enforceable rules continue to exist (see below).

2.5 The Bonn Guidelines on Access and Benefit-sharing

After a long consultation and a short negotiation process, at COP 6 in The Hague in April 2002, the Bonn Guidelines on Access and Benefit-sharing were officially adopted.[10] The Guidelines express the great importance which has been attached in recent years to the development of national strategies and policies. In different parts it is outlined, in very great detail, how national strategies should be developed, what roles they should attribute to providers and users, what prior-informed consent and mutually agreed terms and concrete material transfer agreements could look like (the latter in Appendix I), and finally, what benefits are possible (Appendix II). In a formal legal sense these are not a part of the Bonn Guidelines but they are closely connected with them. The Guidelines are regarded as "a useful step of an evolutionary process in the implementation of relevant provisions" (Decision VI/24, point 6, www.biodiv.org/decisions/), and it is regarded that there should also be a review process. Even in the Guidelines themselves, careful and less binding formulations dominate. They should be voluntary, simple, acceptable, complementary to other international instruments, flexible, transparent and subject to changes. Furthermore, the subject of capacity building is given an important position through the detailed listing of what is understood by it, and through the decision of the COP (VI/24 B) to set up an *Open-Ended Expert Workshop on Capacity-building* within the framework of access and benefit-sharing (which met for the first time in December 2002; report under UNEP/CBD/ABS/EW-CB/1/3). With this, this subject has gained an important position in the CBD process. At the end of the Bonn Guidelines there are regulations on intellectual property rights, in which on the one hand, countries are encouraged to integrate designations of origin for genetic resources with the registration of intellectual property rights, and on the other hand, the WIPO is granted an important function in the generation of proposals as to how the former can be implemented.

How should the Bonn Guidelines and the process of their creation be judged? At first glance, it is surprising that, in view of the difficult problems involved, the negotiations within the framework of the CBD could be brought to a close in an astoundingly short time. This quick success was not expected, particularly because of the dispute over the importance of intellectual property rights. Whereas this dispute dominated the first expert panel, the arguments in the second panel, in the working group and at the COP itself were more "objective" (CBD/27), that is interests were increasingly defined as objective issues. What is of decisive importance is that within the Bonn Guidelines a specific compromise was found and institutionalised which is strongly directed towards the commercialisation of biodiversity and which also has the special characteristic of being voluntary. The real meaning of the Guidelines probably lies in the way that they provide an orientation. They contain an enormous collection of knowledge which can be referred to in concrete legislation, strategy-building and negotiation processes.

At the same time the compromise which was found with the voluntary Guidelines did not lead to a real clarification of the points of dispute behind it. By contrast, in the same year in which they were adopted, the demand for legally binding regulations was once again put on the agenda. The group of megadiverse countries, in particular, had obviously come to the conclusion that under the Guidelines, benefit-sharing had not been dealt with in a satisfactory manner. In the final instance the compromise was not strong enough to be able to include the interests of all the leading actors. Even in this weak form it shows a very selective consideration of the different interest groups, as it essentially serves the need for clear rules for the commercialisation of genetic resources, while the interest groups that are less interested in commercialisation (indigenous peoples, nature protection organisations) do not expect much from the Guidelines. In addition, in the Guidelines, there is no questioning of the fact that the implementation of the CBD is only to take place within those countries that contain most of the world's biodiversity ("provider countries").

Nonetheless, the problem of the voluntary character of the Guidelines should not be misconstrued as meaning that the global market for genetic resources could indeed regulate itself. Rather, at this point it becomes apparent that binding state agencies are of central importance in constituting markets. In line with this notion, the most pertinent aspect concerns the explicit manner in which the interests of the different actors are included in the regulating institutions. Herein, the interests of the companies are expressed in the Guidelines with the statement that international law is to have a guiding rather than a binding effect (CBD/13). At the same time, regarding capacity building, the issue is whether and to what extent local actors have the opportunity to help design the conditions for the marketing of genetic resources. The proposal to set up a working group on this and to take into account, in a stronger manner, the role of intellectual property rights in the implementation of access and benefit-sharing agreements can be interpreted as a type of concession to critical voices by the supporters of the Guidelines.

Basically, the initiative of the countries of megadiversity does not go beyond the horizon of valorisation; rather, it simply refers to the conditions of benefit-sharing and the role of intellectual property rights in this. Indeed, the essential demands of the Bonn Guidelines from the Like-Minded Group of Megadiverse Countries' perspective refer to their unbinding character and the question of intellectual property rights – and precisely concerning the question of intellectual property rights, it is not to be expected that there will be any great concessions. In addition to the Philippines, Ethiopia, which does not belong to the like-minded group, is also pressing for a legally binding international access and benefit-sharing instrument (Caillaux/Ruiz 2002: 170–174). The initiative of the mega-diverse countries is thus first of all directed towards an improvement of the marketing conditions in the sense of the "providers". However, in this respect it is also about building up political pressure on this terrain in the direction of a revision of the TRIPS Agreement. With this, the concrete appraisal of the access and benefit-sharing regulation within the CBD shifts towards the question of the relationship between the CBD and other international agreements. We shall deal with this question in more detail in Chapter 4.

Finally, it can be stated that the problems of the concrete appropriation of biodiversity are condensed most strongly in the concept of capacity building. Capacity building can therefore be understood as the terrain on which the concrete form of the implementation of the Bonn Guidelines is negotiated. Thus, it is not a neutral, technical problem, but a deeply politically determined terrain. Ultimately, here it is decisive whether it will be designed as technical, scientific knowledge for better valorisation, or whether capacity building offers a chance for weaker actors to be able to receive training in accordance with their interests and thereafter, to follow these interests. The "key areas requiring capacity building" (Appendix to Decision VI/24 B, www.biodiv.org) clearly place the emphasis on an improvement of the valorisation of biological diversity. For example, traditional knowledge appears when the issue – apart from the protection of that knowledge – is that of the stock-taking of biological resources in the framework of the Global Taxonomy Initiative. Indigenous peoples and local communities play a role only in the points concerning "development and strengthening capacities … for participation in decision making and implementation" and "contract negotiation skills" (Appendix to Decision VI/24).

2.6 The emerging International Regime on Access and Benefit-sharing

Since COP 7 (2004 in Kuala Lumpur, Malaysia), an International Regime on Access and Benefit-sharing has been an official part of the work programme of the CBD (Decision VII/19). However, ever since the deliberations regarding the terms of reference for the negotiation of a regime, the main object of contention has remained the same: there is no agreement as to whether the agreement should be legally binding or non-binding. It is particularly the JUSCANZ Group, that is the governments of Japan, USA, Canada, Australia and New Zealand, that opposes a legally binding regime. This was one of the reasons for the relative failure of the Third Meeting of the Ad Hoc Open-ended Working Group on Access and Benefit-Sharing that was held in Bangkok in 2005. The JUSCANZ Group and the European Union insisted on further analysis of the gaps in already existing legal instruments dealing with access and benefit-sharing – resulting in an open list of legal elements to be considered at the next meeting. However, given the enormous expectations, the chair at the Fourth Meeting of the Working Group, held in Granada, Spain, at the beginning of 2006, surprisingly presented a draft version for an international regime (the so-called Granada Paper, CBD 2006). The Northern governments did not succeed in rejecting it but, as a compromise, most provisions were put into brackets. This can be seen as a success for the Group of 77 and China. Northern governments consider the Granada Paper more as a useful overview of positions and intend to slow down the process with the argument that more knowledge is needed about what should be done.

After long deliberations at COP 8 in Curitiba in 2006, it was agreed that negotiations for a regime should be completed by 2010. By the time the Working Group convenes its next meeting, it is expected that an international group of experts will have evaluated the feasibility of a "certificate of origin" which means that a patent can be applied for only when it is documented that the material was acquired legally. The negotiated compromise of the Bonn Guidelines should serve as a central orientation. However, the draft version for an international regime indicates that negotiations have hardly begun and that at least until 2010 there will be considerable conflict (regarding its final make-up?) (Secretariat of the CBD 2006b: 129–136).

At least three different positions became obvious: first, those wishing to complete negotiations as soon as possible; second, those keen on negotiations but still undecided as to their key components; and finally, those more interested in exchanging information and experience than in developing an international regime (ENB 2006: 22).

Of course, we are not able to predict either the results of the future negotiations or the concrete bioprospecting practices. But our analyses of the CBD process over the last 15 years, of the characteristics and importance of environmental and biodiversity politics at the international level, of the actual state of the CBD, and of power relations and political dynamics, suggest some conclusions.

Like the Bonn Guidelines, the regime will perform a number of duties: it will reiterate the importance of access and benefit-sharing issues; enhance the knowledge of the enormous complexity of the issues at stake; and help to understand and articulate the concrete interests in the negotiation process, particularly regarding the protection and use of biodiversity. Furthermore, at the concrete level, capacity building might be improved and there may be more money put into subjects related to it. However, as we argued above, capacity building is not a technical issue; rather, its concrete forms shape the way biodiversity is dealt with.

The major conflicts arising during the formulation of a regime are:

- Comprehensive rules in order to secure intellectual property rights for the so-called provider countries. Strict intellectual property rights are only foreseen for the marketable products of biotechnological "innovations". There will be a conflict if the "disclosure of origin" of genetic goods, that is a required certificate of origin when a patent is applied for, is negotiated, either in the CBD or in WIPO and TRIPS (an expert group on that has been established: cf. IP-Watch, 4 April 2006; Heineke/Wolff 2004: 29–30).

- In line with this, the effective forms of fair and equitable benefit-sharing will be contested as well. Here, derivatives of developments of genetic goods attain importance since the so-called provider countries want to see them included in the benefit-sharing mechanisms. "The issue concerning these materials is to what degree they are based on the original natural genetic material, and to what degree scientific knowledge has added value to the development of theses materials" (Chambers 2004: 63). But this is decisive for the question of benefit-sharing.

- The modalities of a regime: this regards the concrete meaning of the "binding" character of an international agreement as Northern actors will invariably favour a voluntary one in the sense that the multilateral voluntary principles form a guideline for bilateral agreements.

> [I]f the nations want the regime to regulate the trade of genetic material with customs regulations, control the use of foreign genetic material under domestic jurisdictions, create a certification scheme, require disclosure of origin in patent applications, and create a system of legal redress and dispute settlement, then the regime will need to impose changes on domestic laws and therefore will need to be legally binding and ratified by national legislators.
>
> (Chambers 2004: 63f.; Frein/Meyer 2005: 154)

- An exemplary illustration of the strong position of the US biotech industry is given by the following quotation: "A mandatory patent disclosure obligation of any kind would radically increase uncertainty for industry and make it very difficult to invest in bioprospecting needed to develop and commercialize genetic resources inventions" (Finston 2005: 4). The draft version of an international regime is still full of brackets, something which does not mean that all issues are really controversial but rather, that some will serve as bargaining tokens. Among other things, the draft version still leaves open a number of issues: whether or not a regime should "facilitate" or "regulate" access to genetic resources; if alongside genetic resources their "derivatives and products" should also be included; and which provisions remain subject to national legislation (Secretariat of the CBD 2006b: 129–136).

● Additionally, the participation of indigenous peoples and local communities seems to be a problem for some actors in the negotiation of the international regime. The question of whether or not indigenous participation in the future negotiations on the regime should be enhanced was discussed exclusively by governmental representatives in closed groups, something which does not indicate an open attitude of the negotiators (see report of COP 8 in Secretariat of the CBD 2006b: 35).

● And finally, it is not clear how fast the regime will be negotiated. The negotiations about the regime should be finished in 2010. But, it is still not clear if the parallel "gap analysis" will slow down the process or promote it.

Despite the fact that through the Like-Minded Group of Megadiverse Countries the Group of 77 and China managed to create an internal compromise – the "G-77/China, speaking with a single voice for the first time in the ABS process" (ENB 2006: 22) – thereby gaining some power in the CBD process, this is not likely to shift the overall tendency of the CBD towards the valorisation of biodiversity in general and genetic goods in particular. The conflicts within the CBD remain most of all distributional among the dominant actors, including the governments of the provider countries. All of them are interested in global rules for the commercialisation of genetic goods and therefore they all generally accept the overall setting.

2.7 Summary: the importance of the CBD in the international process

Without doubt the most important achievement of the CBD process has been "to have developed an integral approach in the treatment of biodiversity" (Krebs *et al.* 2002: 25, our translation). The CBD is neither a pure nature protection convention nor one exclusively oriented towards valorisation. This is also the reason why the CBD is confronted with such multifarious claims (which is often seen as a problem, e.g. CBD/17). In contrast to other international conventions – such as the WTO – the CBD allows widely different actors with divergent views to bring in their perspectives and interests. In addition, the CBD – in contrast to the ILO Convention 169 on indigenous rights, for example – has weight in international law and "new" political questions can apparently be more easily raised and dealt with on a terrain which is structuring itself anew – which is one difference to the FAO. Its strong compromise character obviously represents the great attractiveness of the CBD.

The CBD has this compromise character primarily, however, because major Northern and Southern actors have an interest in the valorisation of genetic resources. The CBD has become a central terrain for negotiating modes of valorisation (particularly the conditions of access and the accompanying benefit-sharing). The compromises achieved here are not at all symmetrical even between the governments, and in addition the Northern and more powerful actors attempt to secure specific interests, namely those which safeguard their intellectual property rights, on quite another terrain: the TRIPS Agreement. The concrete forms of compromise formation in the individual fields of negotiation are therefore decisive, as is the relationship of the agreements to one another. Furthermore, it can be observed that the over-riding importance of access and intellectual property rights is emphasised by the Northern governments.

In many interviews it was pointed out that the CBD is not primarily or exclusively concerned with legal, institutional regulations, but above all with moral, symbolic and political questions in the broader sense. International regulations "can focus desire and attention" and can stimulate reflection (CBD/3). The Guidelines should supply a framework which acts more as an orientation for the concrete negotiation of access. This guiding and problem-focusing effect of the CBD is without doubt an important element of the entire field of conflict, because it includes the chance of a politicisation of new problem dimensions (traditional knowledge and indigenous peoples, biopiracy etc.) It only represents the *chance* of a politicisation, however, because the concrete institutionalisation of these problem perspectives is closely connected to the interests of the different actors and the chances of compromise formation. If regulations of the CBD and the Guidelines gain in importance in individual disputes, they become part of a *power bargaining*, that is of a negotiation process which depends on concrete power relations. This is true both for the Bonn Guidelines and the actual negotiations of an international regime as a whole (e.g. for the compromise with regard to voluntary guidelines) and for individual elements (e.g. what are recognised benefit-sharing mechanisms?) and of course, to a particular extent, for the working out of individual access agreements. In the specific negotiation situations over a bioprospecting agreement questions of power will remain central against the background of the Guidelines or a regime – whereby here, power ranges from discursive power to the establishment of an "own" view of the problem via the institutional capacities for the enforcement of own interests to become a sanctioning force in the nation-state. The compromise recognised by the parties to the conflict thus represents a type of *guiding corridor*, in the designing and further concretisation of which power potentials play a decisive role.

The recognition of power relations and the search for room for manoeuvre on the part of Southern governments can be seen particularly clearly in one thing: the CBD, which came into force at the end of 1993, imposes national sovereignty over genetic resources. The discussion which followed focused on the *in situ* resources to be found in the Southern countries. As we have discussed above, this ignores the immense resources which are already to be found in Northern institutions (private companies, research institutes, botanical gardens).

One important aspect of the global conflicts over genetic resources is the *structural supply competition* of the countries in which biological diversity exists. Because the majority of biodiversity-rich countries are confronted by a relatively small number of biotechnology firms, all of which have the technical know-how and the financial capacity for research using genetic resources, these countries find themselves in a difficult situation. Thus, the biodiversity-rich nation-states of the "South" find themselves trapped in a competitive relationship, one against the other, over the scarce demand on the part of the life sciences industries. This strengthens, above all, "Northern" interests in the appropriation of biological diversity because they can insist on "good conditions". By founding the Like-Minded Group of Megadiverse Countries an effort was made to achieve a uniform position on this question. However, even despite this cooperation, the competition mechanism has not been annulled. The situation is aggravated by the fact that genetic resources – in contrast to oil and therein, the strategy of OPEC – are not resources which are required in large quantities, but rather, as a rule, all that is required is the genetic information they contain.[11] The supply competition also contains an uncertainty factor in that governments may possibly invest in good conditions for valorisation (e.g. by establishing research capacities) and then perhaps go short in the bioprospecting agreements.

With regard to the prescribing of the rights of weaker actors, their representatives or allied NGOs have been able to see to it that these remain on the agenda in the negotiation process. This is connected with practical problems regarding the legitimate appropriation of genetic resources. The importance of local actors lies in the fact that they may have useful knowledge for the valorisation of resources. In addition, NGOs are an important element of the negotiation process at the international level with their knowledge and experience. Against this double background, critical NGOs and indigenous organisations have succeeded in politicising the process. They were helped by the fact that on the part of firms and governments there is great uncertainty as to how the appropriation of genetic resources can take place effectively and legitimately. This process remains controversial.

For without denying completely the interests of weaker actors, governments use three mechanisms to weaken them. For one thing, the voluntary character of regulations is emphasised (using the argument of the danger of "over-regulation"); this is followed, second, by reference to the national level; and third, reference to the complicated and to a degree, completely new situation. This is the case for questions of benefit-sharing, for prior-informed consent or for indigenous and local rights. Altogether, it has become clear up to this point that criticism of the valorisation paradigm is more difficult at the international level than at the national or local one.

Finally, there is one thing which should not be forgotten. The appropriation of biological diversity and in particular of genetic resources takes place permanently with or without a legal framework. It can take on legal forms if a national legal framework based on the CBD has been created. The individual access agreements can also be guided by international law, without the latter already being transposed into national law. In many cases the appropriation takes place largely without a legal framework or with one which does not satisfy the CBD. This is the reason why in addition to some NGOs and experts, increasingly, Southern governments also speak of bio-piracy. It remains an open question here as to whether or not – at the material level of the ecological crisis, which consists in the continued and dramatic loss of biological diversity – the CBD can be an effective instrument, or whether perhaps the work of stock-taking will be "the scientific accompanying music to the burial of biological diversity" (CBD/17, our translation).

3 Limits to commercialisation?

Genetic resources in agriculture and the conflict over a multilateral exchange system

The field of agriculturally utilised biodiversity has some particular characteristics, each of which can both help to illustrate the breadth and complexity of the problems involved and bring to light some of the central lines of conflict in a compromised and explicit form. These particular characteristics are manifold. On the one hand, the structure of the problems in the field of agro-biodiversity is characterised by the fact that genetic diversity is the product of human activities over centuries. Therefore, this genetic diversity must be examined from the perspective of the utilisation of nature. Moreover, genetic resources are – apart from their economic importance for capitalist industries – of central relevance for worldwide nutrition and even more for food security in certain regions. On the other hand, the quest for the conservation of Plant Genetic Resources for Food and Agriculture (PGRFA) is no less pressing due to the dramatic erosion of this genetic diversity. But this search becomes acute under different general conditions and throws up different lines of conflict and actor constellations.

The conflicts over the appropriation of genetic resources in this field already have a much longer history and their principal features can be traced back to the beginning of European expansion and colonialism (Crosby 1972, 1986). However, these conflicts have been given a new momentum by the technological and political shifts in the 1980s. The institutional attempts to deal with these conflicts also go back further and they had already produced important regulating procedures before the CBD. At the same time, the changes which are connected with the coming into force of the CBD, and later with the TRIPS Agreement, are also central for later developments and allow insights into some central dimensions of the problem. Finally, the characteristics of this problem field are reflected in an agreement which has some distinct features compared to the CBD and is characterised above all by an alternative approach to access and benefit-sharing: a Multilateral System for the exchange of genetic resources.

At the centre of the following presentation is the genesis and the enhancements of the *International Treaty on Plant Genetic Resources for Food and Agriculture* (ITPGR). This agreement, which is based within the framework of the FAO, was concluded in November 2001 following lengthy negotiations and thus belongs to the more recent agreements in this field. It regulates international exchange for the subsection of genetic resources which play a particular role for world nutrition. In this part of the PGRFA a multilateral exchange system was developed in the International Treaty, mentioned above, which is intended to take into account the specific characteristics of these resources. The negotiations, however, were extremely difficult and were repeatedly threatened with failure. Even after their conclusion in 2001, some important issues had not been appropriately resolved and it took another five years until the specific regulations concerning the multilateral system of exchange could be finished – and their actual effectiveness is still difficult to judge. Thus, in these negotiations, the question of the relationships of the different international agreements to one another as well as that of their relationship to the sovereignty of nation-states became highly divisive. The options of regulating the use of genetic technology remained controversial, as did the applicability of intellectual property rights and patents and the chances local actors and farming communities had of having their interests in these international agreements adequately considered (here, primarily in reference to the embodiment of the principle of *Farmers' Rights*, see below).

These controversial issues, however, are not expressions of the contradictions between ecology and economy or between conservation and utilisation. Rather, they represent a *conflict between different forms of human utilisation of nature*. These conflicts can be described as conflicts between traditional and industrial forms of agriculture (whereby the traditional forms can vary quite considerably). At first glance, this produces a North–South conflict. But this line is shaped in various ways, since in Southern countries the conflicts of interest reproduce themselves internally in face of a variety of agricultural production systems. In the field of PGRFA in general, it is particularly difficult for nation-states both in the South and in the North to formulate a policy which is consistent within itself. At the level of nation-states a whole number of different ministries and authorities are involved (from the usually responsible agricultural ministries through environmental, trade and justice ministries to the foreign ministry) and the complexity of the problems requires particular expert knowledge (Petit *et al.* 2000). Even the interests of the most important actors, that is the governments of the nation-states, can be internally clarified and harmonised only with difficulty and in lengthy negotiations as part of a state project. In addition, the interests of the biotechnology industry and those of traditional, non-capitalist forms of agriculture conflict with each other here, although usually not by way of direct confrontation between the actors but rather in the form of different interpretations of the problem and the corresponding strategies. Representatives of indigenous or rural groups are personally present at the negotiations only in exceptional cases, for example at the conference "In Safe Hands" on the occasion of the FAO Conference in June 1996 in Leipzig. In the course of the negotiations, their interests were often represented by certain NGOs (primarily seeds NGOs; see Brand 2000: 209ff.). The NGOs in this sector usually proceed from a decidedly political standpoint and understand themselves explicitly as the representatives of these interests. They are concerned above all with the respect of particular characteristics of agriculturally utilised biodiversity and, related to that, with the propagation of Farmers' Rights and the limiting and prevention of intellectual property rights. The conflict is also partly interpreted as one between the private and the public spheres, between genetic resources as private property or as a public or common good (e.g. Petit *et al.* 2000). It remains quite unclear here what exactly is meant by a public good and in what relationship it stands both to private property and to Farmers' Rights. In any case, the strategy of capitalist valorisation, including its ecological effects, is at the centre of the conflict. On closer examination, however, this strategy is supported by a broad spectrum of actors with quite varying interests: from middle-class seed growers to biotechnological TNCs. Since in this area a considerable process of concentration and displacement is taking place, an identity of capital interests cannot be assumed, particularly between small, specialised firms and the large monopolies. Nevertheless, they ultimately work together in the privatisation of genetic resources. The industry is permanently represented at international negotiations by relatively powerful associations – such as, for example, the lobby association Bio or the international association of plant producers, ASSINEL. However, it is not clear whether they in fact have an interest in obtaining access to genetic resources in the Southern countries or whether the material which already exists in the *ex situ* collections or in the large gene data bases in the North is sufficient for them (RAFI 2001a; see Le Buanec 2005).

The cooperation of the actors and their interests in this field is therefore complex. In the following section we shall elaborate on how a valorisation paradigm was established in this area even though it met with considerable opposition from a number of actors, much of which stemmed from the highly explosive conflict over the exclusion of the patentability of PGRFA. The different interpretations of the problem and their interplay in the genesis of the ITPGR play a decisive role here. We shall deal in particular with the important function of experts and the constitution of a dominant interpretation of the problem and the options relating to its resolution. In addition, we shall examine the fundamental question of the coherence of state and inter-state politics. Are the tensions and contradictions between different fields of politics (agriculture, environment, trade, property rights, to name only the most important) decisive for the fact that "governments can't make a policy" (Petit *et al.* 2000)? Or are these contradictions between different parts of the state apparatus (and the connected international state apparatuses) the expression of antagonistic social relationships at the national and international level – and is the search for coherence in fact an attempt to establish a power-shaped stabilisation of these relationships? What does the search for a coherent policy in this area actually mean? To

what extent can suitable answers to the problem structure in fact be formulated? And how do national and international lines of conflict overlap here?
We shall have to deal here above all with the questions of whether and to what
extent the "multilateral system of exchange" with regard to the regulation
of access and benefit-sharing and compared to the CBD is in fact as differently designed and constituted as sometimes claimed. What is the function
of the ITPGR and the Multilateral System with regard to the problem and
to the interests of locally situated actors? Can it in fact consolidate their
interests and does it increase their chances of gaining influence? In order to
be able to answer these questions it is first necessary to take a closer look at
the complex problem, the history of this conflict and the genesis of the
ITPGR before the agreement itself can be examined in more detail.

3.1 Structures of problem and conflicts

Although critical voices have pointed out that "wild biodiversity" in many –
and often in the really important – cases is not really so "wild", instead
being interlinked to greatly differing forms of human intervention (Hecht
1998) – this is particularly pertinent with regard to the very beginnings of
the field of agricultural biodiversity. The diversity of the hereditary characteristics of useful plants, in which we are interested here, is closely connected with the practices of humans. Without human cultivation of nature
this diversity would not exist in its present form and in no way should this
practice be abandoned. The waiving of the agricultural use of PGRFA by
concentrating solely on the protection of these varieties is neither mean-
ingful nor possible. Rather, and decisively, the conservation of this threatened diversity can only be achieved in the long term by the further use of
such varieties (Oetmann-Mennen 1999). The conflict in this field is therefore interlinked with specific societal practices related to the production and
reproduction of genetic diversity. This has in fact been recognised in the
international conflicts and negotiation processes – at least in principle – in
the form of Farmers' Rights (see below).

With the provision of Farmers' Rights it is recognised that the present
diversity of PGRFA has arisen over the centuries, and is conserved today, by
means of farming practices. What is controversial, however, is whether and
if so which rights actually derive from this and how the tension between
collective rights and private intellectual property rights should be dealt
with. The particular characteristics of this field are condensed in the distinctions between the bilateral model of the CBD and the multilateral
approach of the International Treaty, as well as going far beyond them. At
the same time, it appears to be completely unclear whether the present
politico-legal developments will be of benefit to the socio-economic practices and the living conditions of social groups which have created this
diversity – or if they will result in their weakening. This in turn would not only
have far-reaching consequences with regard to the direct living conditions of

these people but also with regard to food security and the development opportunities of entire regions (Egziabher 2002). In order to be able to estimate the relevance of international regulation processes for the local and regional levels more precisely, first the problem as well as the interests and action capacity of the different actors need to be examined more closely.

3.1.1 *Plant genetic resources as a cultural product: the concept of Farmers' Rights*

The introduction of the concept of biodiversity was accompanied in the public debate by a considerable mystification of the subject to the all-encompassing unity of every living thing (typical of this: Wilson 1992). In this process, not only were the bio-scientific problems forgotten which were linked to the introduction of the new concept (Hertler 1999), but what was also ignored was that biodiversity comprises not only tropical rain forests and coral reefs – and beyond that perhaps specific varieties of threatened mammals and bird species – but also the species of cereals and vegetables used by humans. Pat Mooney (1998: 14) remarked derisively of this short-sighted view of the problem, in which rice, potatoes and wheat do not exist: "In general, nothing requiring spoons or chopsticks is biodiversity." In spite of the fact, however, that the introduction of the concept was linked to economic motives from the very beginning (Flitner 1999; see Chapter 2), the bracketing of the biodiversity used and produced by humans seems to be very helpful. It contributes to the obscuring of the real interests in genetic resources and therefore to the reframing of the field.

In contrast to the conservation of species diversity, in this case the diversity within species, in particular the diversity of genetic characteristics which is embodied in different varieties and subspecies, plays a decisive role.[1] This genetic diversity is not something naturally given, but rather, is the product of cultivating practices of seed selection over thousands of years. This selection created the varieties with the desired characteristics – yield, length of stalk, resistance to dryness or dampness and so on. Due to non-intended mixture with related wild varieties it also produced a broad range of certain varieties that were not directly used (so-called traditional varieties and land races). The technique of selection, which is not dependent on knowledge about the laws of heredity, determined farming and breeding practice for a long period of time beginning with the Neolithic "revolution" – which itself was not so much a historical rupture, but a long passage of transition. It was not replaced until the end of the nineteenth century by the technique of cross-breeding according to Mendel's laws of heredity. However, in large parts of the earth it still determines the practice of rural agriculture today (de Boef *et al.* 1993). In addition, it is accompanied by certain forms of a gender-specific division of labour, culturally based patterns of interpretation and traditional norms and rules for the treatment of plants and animals. Of central importance here is the practice of the *free exchange* of seeds. This form of use can only continue to function within the farming communities if suitable varieties are freely available and knowledge freely circulates as to which varieties fare best under which conditions or which varieties are particularly resistant to certain types of damage. Without these social practices the diversity of useful plants and animals would not have developed and it is very much a question whether these practices are in the process of disappearing along with the disappearance of biodiversity. One further specific feature of agricultural biodiversity is the fact that due to the free exchange of the last 12,000 to 15,000 years it has spread over almost the entire earth and is seldom restricted to individual areas. At the same time, there continue to be centres of diversity in which even today we can find a particularly large number of varieties of wheat, corn or potatoes, with all the inherent conflicts arising from this.

The fact that the agriculturally used genetic diversity of today is the product of previous generations was explicitly recognised on the international stage in the 1980s with the introduction of the concept of Farmers' Rights. "Farmers' Rights means rights arising from the past, present and future contributions of farmers in conserving, improving and making available plant genetic resources, particularly in the centres of origin/diversity" (Resolution 5/89 on the International Undertaking of the FAO). This recognition was preceded by fierce political struggles, however, and until the coming into force of the International Treaty in 2001 it was not a legally binding commitment. Even today it is still not clear what this recognition really means and whether it is of any practical relevance.

In order to be able to more fully understand these conflicts a brief glance at their history is necessary. The interest in genetic resources was formed at the latest with European expansion and the conquering of America, which in view of the more strongly noted interest in gold and precious metals is often forgotten. As Alfred W. Crosby (1972, 1986) has shown, the conquering of the "New World" was a dividing-line in the history of evolution, since continents which had been almost completely separated for millions of years were now brought into cultural contact (the "Columbian exchange" according to Crosby 1972). Even the conquest itself was, from the beginning, accompanied by interest in genetic resources: it was intended to ensure control of the trade in spices and specialities with East Asia.[2] New varieties were introduced to Europe which led to a decisive change in living conditions there. The planting and exploitation of certain biological resources such as sugar cane, tobacco and bananas have, in the longer run, had perhaps an even more decisive and at least as fateful a role in colonisation as the exploitation of mineral resources. The influence on living conditions is due not only to the introduction of luxury goods such as tobacco or chocolate, but even more so to the potato, without availability of which, as a cheap staple food, the development of European capitalism would have taken a different course. Therefore, globalisation is also in this respect of the same origin as the establishment of capitalist relationships on a world scale.

Already, in this first phase of capitalist globalisation the availability of bio-logical and genetic resources played an important role in the division and subjugation of the world. As in a "botanical chess game" (Brockway 1988), the European colonial powers handled entire countries and regions as stakes in their geopolitical strategies and thus constituted the globe as the object of their imperial interests.

The practice of collecting genetic material for aesthetic or research pur-poses and the establishment of botanical or zoological gardens is also grounded in this early phase. As we have seen in the previous chapter, these collections and the genetic resources contained in them are of increasing importance today. However, grave changes in the treatment of genetic diversity and of PGRFA in particular can be observed in the last 100 years (on the phases see Heins/Flitner 1998). The first change concerns the application, already mentioned, of Mendel's laws of heredity and the accompanying emergence of a breeding practice based on scientific methods. With the technique of cross-breeding the possibility arose of deliberately introducing genetic characteristics into a new product in the course of breeding. This technique was introduced long before the introduction of the concept of DNA as a theoretical basis for the understanding of genes was developed. With this, the commercial and political interests in genetic resources received a decisive impetus. The concept itself was defined at that time by the Soviet geneticist Nicolai Ivanovic Vavilov. He was the first to point out the *geographically unequal distribution* of the diversity of useful plants and combined this with the reference to their *economic importance* – bringing into discursive existence the concept of *genetic resources* (Flitner 1995b).

Since the beginning of the twentieth century the collection of seeds has become a goal of national politics. Driven by scientific advances in breeding and accompanied by commercial interest in their marketing, the central goal is at first still food security, that is national autarchy in the supply of food (for a more comprehensive outline of this, see Flitner 1995a). Already at that time lengthy collection journeys were put together in order to pro-vide more supplies of genetic resources for breeding. At the Fifth Interna-tional Congress for Hereditary Sciences in Berlin in 1927, Vavilov presented for the first time a map with the centres of diversity, accompanied by the theory that the present-day centres of diversity are also the areas of origin in which certain plants were first domesticated (see Flitner 1995a: 53ff.). Even if this theory has since been refuted, at the time, the search for genetic resources was given an additional impetus after this presentation. Looking back, this phase has been described as the phase of "the primitive accu-mulation of genetic resources" (Kloppenburg 1988: 153–156). However, this – just like the primitive accumulation of capital itself – was not a purely technical or economic process involving the collection of material but was instead more expansive, being accompanied by far-reaching socio-economic changes in production and the social division of labour. And it was accompanied by the state-secured establishment and enforcement of property rights which were necessary to enable capitalist valorisation of this diversity as an industrially utilisable resource (Kloppenburg 1988; Fowler 1995).

This process is also not a historically completed phase, instead being a tendency that permanently accompanies the development of capitalism, just as the primitive accumulation of capital itself continually subjects itself to new social relationships. That means, capitalism imposes its relationships of production and property on other social relations and secures itself against these (Alnasseri 2003). It is only the way in which this is done which changes in the course of time. During the colonial epoch it was based more on the military and security through violent forms (despite being complemented by legal measures such as, for example, prohibitions of exports). In the late and post-colonial eras, security by means of legal and political measures is of increasing importance. The enforcing and securing of capitalist relationships of production, however, the valorisation and primitive accumulation in a Marxist sense (the separation of the producers from the means of production, see Görg 1998), is accompanied by violent social transformation. This remains evident even today. Indeed, in contemporary times, this violent form of capitalist accumulation and its social and ecological consequences stand out ever more clearly.

3.1.2 The "green revolution" and the erosion of diversity

Following the Second World War (WWII) the appropriation of PGRFA entered a new phase. Overlapped by bloc confrontation and accompanied by a strong tendency towards the industrialisation of agriculture, plant genetic resources became an element in the Fordist appropriation of biodiversity (Brand 2000: 179ff.). Starting out from the industrialised agriculture of the countries of the North, the model of the intensification of agriculture was exported to the global South. Methods of production directed towards increasing yields and the planting of large-scale monocultures were introduced there during the phase of the "green revolution". Although not all regions of the South were affected by this to the same degree – while it has been put into practice massively in some countries in South East Asia, such as India and the Philippines, the African Continent has largely been spared – the effects were and remain serious. The introduction of high-yield varieties, so-called hybrid varieties, at the beginning increases the yield per acre in many areas, but soon the far-reaching social and ecological effects become visible. Since the expensive high-yield varieties can only meaningfully be introduced if they are planted on a large scale and with a considerable amount of capital deployment (the deployment of labour and chemical products) there is a strong tendency towards cash-crop products for export, which results in a considerable process of concentration and social polarisation and contradicts the declared goal of increasing food security. In the process, the gender-specific division of labour also changes and there is a displacement of the practices which were responsible for the genesis of the diversity of useful plants.

Above all, however, the green revolution was accompanied by a considerable shift in international power relations. Thus, countries such as the Philippines became strongly dependent on the seed companies of the North, primarily from the USA. This, too, contradicted the goal of securing the food supply (Pelegrina 2001). But this shift was based on the strategic decision to use the "green" preventatively against the threatened "red revolution" – not only against the growing influence of the Soviet Union and China but also against a social transformation and a change in property relationships. Therefore, the green revolution was introduced without social reforms, especially without land reform for a fair distribution of the ownership of land. During this phase, in addition, certain actors appeared for the first time which, to this day, remain of great importance in the area of plant genetic resources: the International Agricultural Research Centres (IARC) such as the International Rice Research Institute (IRRI) in Manila or the International Maize and Wheat Improvement Centre (CIMMYT) in Mexico. Originally founded with the support of the Ford and Rockefeller Foundations as central institutes of the green revolution in which the high-yield varieties were developed (see Fowler 1995: 182ff.) their function has now changed considerably. With the fusion of these institutes into the Consultative Group on International Agricultural Research (CGIAR) with its seat at the World Bank, one of the most important international organisations has been created which today still retains influence in this sphere.[3]

Yet another development is important for our discussion. Already in the early 1960s it became clear that the green revolution had considerable ecological effects: first, because of the increased use of fertilizers and pesticides with regard to the ecological context (soil, waters etc.), and second, from the erosion of genetic diversity itself. It is no longer a contested point that the intensification of agriculture and the introduction of high-yield varieties is the main cause of the loss of agricultural diversity. Experts from the FAO such as Otto Frankel and Erna Bennet pointed out this development very early on and alarmed the expert public (Frankel/Bennet 1970). As a result, *gene erosion* became an important topic at the FAO, although at the beginning in a rather conventional way. At first, the International Agricultural Research Centres were given the task, together with already existing and yet to be founded national gene databases, of conserving the agriculturally used diversity in the form of *ex situ* collections. This is problematic not only from an ecological point of view, because *ex situ* cannot secure the further evolution of seed and its co-evolution with possible pests. Even more important are the socio-economic effects, because the setting up of large *ex situ* collections favours commercial breeding and strengthens the trends towards concentration and monopolisation as well as international dependencies and the unequal exchange of genetic material (Mooney 1981).

3.1.3 The "seed wars" and the International Undertaking

The last point led to the so-called "seed wars" of the 1980s. While the high-yield varieties and the fertilizers, herbicides and pesticides necessary for their cultivation had to be bought for money from private companies of the North, the *germplasma*, which was stored in the seed banks and made available from there to the commercial breeders and to the state or semi-state breeding programmes, flowed gratuitously into the North. This unequal exchange, even at that time secured by intellectual property rights, was denounced by the countries of the South at a conference of the FAO in Mexico in 1981, and a threat was made to stop the gene transfers. Heated disputes followed which inspired the *Washington Post* to make a comparison with the "Star Wars" programme of the then US President Reagan. These conflicts ended, although only temporarily, with the founding of the Commission on Plant Genetic Resources (CPGR, now CGRFA) and the conclusion of the International Undertaking on Plant Genetic Resources of 1983. The former was, and still is, the place at which further official inter-governmental negotiations take place, accompanied however by several informal negotiation circles. The International Undertaking, however, as a set of agreements which are not binding in international law, forms only the starting-point for the regulation of access and benefit-sharing in the treatment of genetic resources. It was in fact not at all able to resolve the conflicts via mutual agreement. Although it contains (in the amendment of 1989) a recognition of Farmers' Rights, the question of benefit-sharing could not be resolved. A corresponding international fund remained de facto without finances. Nevertheless, with the International Undertaking, Farmers' Rights were formally recognised as a counterweight to the rights of commercial plant breeders.

The reason for the very limited regulation capacity of the International Undertaking goes beyond its non-binding character in international law. Ultimately in the International Undertaking the central question of access was not really clarified. In contrast to the CBD, the International Undertaking is based on the principle of the *common heritage of humankind*. This principle, which was developed in the UN Convention on the Law of the Sea, is referred to in order to subject certain regions (the sea bed, the Antarctic, outer space) and the resources to be found there to international management. Thus, these regions are removed from the states' desire to exploit the resources or at least they must subject this exploitation to international standards (among other things in the consideration of ecological perspectives). At first glance this principle also appears appropriate for subjecting the diversity in the sphere of PGRFA, on which further breeding and thus the development of ecologically adjusted seed depends, to an international regulation mechanism. There is a trap involved, however. As a "common heritage of humankind" not all plant genetic resources are freely available to the same extent. The products of commercial breeding are subject to specific property rights which couple access to the payment of fees or licenses, while the traditional varieties are passed on freely and gratuitously. The area of application of the common heritage principle therefore only extends to a part of the PGRFA – and therefore this principle cannot function here either.

As Jack R. Kloppenburg and Daniel L. Kleinman (1988) analysed very early on, the contradictory interests of Northern agriculture and the Southern countries were not adequately taken into consideration in the International Undertaking. Therefore, it was not really suitable as a regulating authority for access and benefit-sharing. Present attempts to establish a "global commons" mirror the same problem, as does the Multilateral System within the framework of the International Treaty. How should they deal with intellectual property rights and the interests of commercial plant breeders and the biotech industry? Since the commercial breeders do not agree to subject their varieties, which are protected by special forms of property rights, to free exchange, the countries of the South were on their part also no longer prepared to do so. Instead, Kloppenburg and Kleinman suggested another mechanism which in their opinion could prove more suitable for conciliating contradictory interests: the principle of *national sovereignty* over genetic resources. In a certain way, they anticipated the principle which was in fact to become the foundation of the CBD several years later. They did *not* do this, however, in the attempt to establish a bilateral regulation mechanism aimed at individual contracts. On the contrary, their idea was that national sovereignty should do justice to the international interdependencies which decisively characterised the sphere of PGRFA (in contrast to "wild biodiversity"). Their proposal shows that the nation-state level of regulation offers itself as a compromise model for the global conflicts over plant genetic resources. In this model, however, the interests of the different groups of actors are taken into account very selectively.

The main part of their central paper deals with the derivation of the international interdependencies. They attempt to prove that no region and no country on this earth is autarchic in respect to the question of the availability of plant genetic resources. All regions are more or less dependent on the flow of genetic resources in order to be able to adjust crops and industrially used biological resources to changed ecological conditions or to be able to incorporate new characteristics into seeds. The thesis of the *international interdependencies of plant genetic resources* forms the theoretical background for regulation models such as the multilateral exchange system within the negotiations on the International Treaty. Its details are, however, far from being uncontroversial. This model does not in any way take into account the dependencies between modern, industrialised and traditional agriculture. These dependencies concerning plant genetic resources, however, are absolutely central, since one sector requires (and uses or destroys) the diversity while the other produces it (Flitner 1995a: 207). Between these groups of actors the model of national sovereignty does not create any conciliation, and it does not even attempt to do so. Also, in regard to different regions of the world and different varieties of plants, the differences are in part considerable, and this has also influenced the strategy of the actors in the negotiation process (RAFI 2001a). Nevertheless, the model of international interdependence has remained the dominant description of the problem to which the different actors refer, although with very differing accentuation: some, in order to define plant genetic resources as "public goods" and to propagate the free exchange of genetic material, and others to legitimate free access to genetic material for commercial purposes and thus implicitly or explicitly play into the hands of the valorisation paradigm.

3.1.4 The situation following the conclusion of the CBD: "environmentalisation"?

The International Undertaking was therefore not a suitable model for the regulation of access and benefit-sharing for a number of reasons. It was neither legally binding nor capable of being enforced, nor could one speak of an acceptable compromise between the different groups of actors. Altogether, therefore, appraisals of it have varied quite considerably. While its weaknesses were obvious, on the other hand the anchoring of Farmers' Rights was positively emphasised. In addition, as a whole, it was regarded as being the expression of a worldwide distributional conflict. Considering the relationships of power not much more was to be expected. Thus, the countries of the South had achieved some smaller victories and even the existence of the International Undertaking was, according to Pat Mooney (1998: 22), regarded by the countries of the North as an attack on intellectual property rights for plant genetic resources. Just as with regard to the Commission on Genetic Resources for Food and Agriculture (CGRFA), the very existence of an international regulation system was already judged to be a success in view of the conflict structure and the relationships of forces involved.

At the same time, there were a number of other processes in which it was attempted to deepen the international consensus with regard to the treatment of plant genetic resources. Of particular importance here are the *Keystone Dialogue* (Keystone 1991) and the *Crucible Group* (1994, 2000, 2001). Both are quite different. The Keystone Dialogue was oriented towards the model of consensus-oriented negotiation systems (see Fowler 1994: 196ff.; for a critique: Görg 2003a: 175ff.). Representatives of the different conflict parties (governments both from North and South, international organisations, industry, universities and NGOs) attempted, in a long-winded negotiation, to find consensus on the central issues of dispute.

Although such a consensus – or at least a compromise – was finally found, its practical meaning was rather trivial. Nonetheless, Pat Mooney (1998: 24f.), one of the participants and a central figure in the NGO camp, considers it successful in clarifying the central conflict lines. Moreover, governments and experts from the North tempered their previous view on plant genetic resources. But even if in this sense NGO activists and the countries of the South had achieved partial success here, this dialogue forum had practically no influence on the political regulation process, and particularly not on the GATT negotiations (Fowler 1994: 203f.; on the Crucible Group see below).

The conflict structure changed considerably at the beginning of the 1990s with the conclusion of the CBD and the negotiations on the GATT. In spite of all the remaining contradictory interests within the framework of the FAO, slow progress, or at least a serious negotiation process, could be observed. With the conclusion of the CBD, however, it was feared that in view of its more ecological orientation, the distributional conflicts and the accompanying politicising of the issue could once again be overshadowed. Frederic Buttel (1992) coined the expression "environmentalisation" for this threat. And there were good reasons for such fear. During the negotiations on the CBD, national sovereignty was anchored as the central principle of access. Moreover, in the appendix, in Resolution 3 of the Nairobi Final Act, the final document of the CBD negotiations before being passed to the UNCED Conference in 1992 in Rio de Janeiro, the particular role of the plant genetic resources was recognised. However, at least two dimensions had been excluded which were of central importance for the genesis of the seed wars in the 1980s: the issue of Farmers' Rights and the status of the collections which had been set up before the coming into force of the CBD. Both topics could not be clarified and had to be left to further negotiations (CBD Handbook 2001: 287f.). While the first was judged to be an enormous step backwards in view of the conflicts and negotiations of the 1980s, the latter is highly explosive in view of the economic importance of the collected material. It is clear in international law that contractual regulations cannot be applied retrospectively. But at the same time, it was precisely these collections that had provided a decisive impulse for the seed wars.

Particularly in the countries of the North and among the public there, the CBD had contributed considerably to mystifying the socio-economic and political explosiveness of the subject by focusing more on the conservation of species and nature. Nevertheless, the fear that the subject would be depoliticised was not justified. With the CBD and the recognition of the principle of national sovereignty, the conflicts were lifted onto a new terrain and in turn had an effect in this form on the continuing negotiations within the framework of the FAO. Thus, the second negotiation body, the Crucible Group, which had been assembled after the coming into force of the CBD, attempted to sound out the new situation. This situation was overshadowed in addition by the preliminary negotiations on the GATT and the TRIPS

Agreement. Thus, the first report of the Crucible Group (1994) was particularly important because the conflict lines which characterised the international discussion in the 1990s were already contained in it in a condensed form. In contrast to the Keystone Dialogue, the Crucible Group was not geared towards consensus. In its final reports (both in its first round in 1994 and in its second round in 2000/01) the different positions on which no agreement could be reached were placed side by side. With regard to the CBD there was agreement that the role of agro-biodiversity had not been well understood in the CBD and that the unsolved problem of the collections could grow to become the greatest gene robbery since Columbus (Crucible Group 1994: 31f.).

Ultimately, the topics intellectual property rights and Farmers' Rights/ traditional knowledge became central within the Crucible Group. At that time, the discussions still stood in the shadow of the GATT negotiations and the formulation of the TRIPS Agreement. Although at this point the countries of the South had not yet taken a decidedly antagonistic position to the TRIPS Agreement (see Chapter 4 on this), for a part of the Crucible Group the consequences were foreseeable. The expansion of intellectual property rights would not only put pressure on the Southern countries; it would particularly undermine Farmers' Rights and the practice of the free exchange of seeds: "Farmers have the absolute right to save seed, to experiment with exotic germplasm, and to exchange seed with neighbouring communities. To deny these rights is to cut the heart out of conservation and enhancement of plant biodiversity" (ibid.: 87). As this only expresses one of the positions represented in the Crucible Group, the core of the conflict was clearly named. While industry insisted on the necessity of intellectual property rights for the protection of its innovations, the opponents see in intellectual property rights the main danger with regard to farming practice. In between there is a third, more mixed position, which emphasises the national room for manoeuvre (above all with a view to the *sui generis* clause in the TRIPS Agreement) and rejects the resistance to intellectual property rights, patents and the TRIPS Agreement as an unrealistic maximalist position.

In these debates ecological, socio-cultural and socio-economic dimensions are closely interlinked. Ecological questions concerning the conservation of the diversity of plant genetic resources are related to the different material (agricultural) practices and connected life-styles, which in turn are overlapped by global distribution problems and economic valorisation strategies. This complex set of problems is expressed in the tensions between different international agreements and the problems of their national implementation – and also in their local effects on specific places (see Chapter 5). In the International Undertaking, local practices are recognised as important with the concept of Farmers' Rights and it is also attempted in other ways to consider the particular material characteristics of this field (which to this extent represents a complement to Article 8(j) of the CBD, see above). Seen from the perspective of the International Undertaking, both the CBD and the TRIPS Agreement bear the threat of neglecting these particular characteristics by way of commercialisation: the former by means of privileging bilateral access agreements, the latter in addition by the international securing of minimum standards for intellectual property rights. In this dispute no agreement could be achieved, either within the framework of the Crucible Group – or even later – or on the question of an appropriate regulation of plant genetic resources or in the understanding and the role of the different agreements. With the conclusion of the GATT/WTO Agreement and the TRIPS Agreement a new political momentum became apparent in the negotiations. To this extent the fear of a de-politicisation of the issue has not come to fruition.

3.2 The genesis of a multilateral exchange system

Before the conclusion of the CBD it was already becoming apparent that the previous foundations of the International Undertaking were in need of revision. Already in 1991 the principle of the common heritage of humankind had been replaced in Resolution 3/91 of the Commission on Genetic Resources by the principle of national sovereignty and thus the most important difference between the (then not yet existent) CBD and the International Undertaking was settled. Nevertheless, the problem of the harmonisation of the two treaties was far from being resolved. In 1993, the official negotiations on the revision of the International Undertaking began in order to bring this into harmony with the regulations of the CBD, according to the official line of reasoning. It took until November 2001 before the revised version, the International Treaty on Plant Genetic Resources for Food and Agriculture (ITPGR) could finally be concluded. Between those two dates lay more than seven years of extremely hard international negotiations, which were more than once on the brink of failure. The reasons for these extremely tough negotiations, which at the same time were the main barrier to an earlier conclusion of the agreement, were questions of intellectual property rights, the particular treatment of biological diversity in agriculture and the principle of Farmers' Rights, as well as the – closely connected – national interests of major states and blocs of states (see on the regulations of the International Treaty: Mekouar 2001; Seiler 2003). Therefore, the very existence of this agreement can be booked as a success, since with it an important international problem area – with consequences for the development strategies of the poorer countries and their food security as well as for the further development of "green gene technology" – is regulated by an international agreement. Yet even now, some of the most important issues of dispute have not been clarified, nor is it foreseeable what actual effects the International Treaty will have, especially on farming communities in poorer countries and the global structure of agriculture. In spite of the apparent success of the negotiations in the final round, a delegate made a sarcastic remark on the outcome, saying: "We do not only not know whether the glass is half full or half empty – we don't even know what liquid is in it" (personal communication to the authors).

3.2.1 Negotiations on the harmonisation of the CBD and the International Undertaking

In the following section, we describe in detail a complicated and long-winded negotiation marathon as it encapsulates very well the difficulties of the entire process. The replacement of the principle of common heritage by that of national sovereignty before the conclusion of the CBD demonstrates two things. First, at the end of the 1980s and the beginning of the 1990s there was generally a strong tendency to give preference to national interests at the expense of global commons. This took place in parallel to the often evoked upswing of multilateralism following the end of bloc confrontation, which reached its zenith in the "spirit of Rio". Therefore, it illustrates clearly the differences that ruled at that time between rhetoric and reality. However, we should not simply complain about this incongruity. Instead, what is needed is an attempt to provide a closer examination of the effects the multilateral institutions actually have and in what relationship they stand to national interests. If the safe-guarding of national interests took priority even at the zenith of multilateralism, then this is a clear indication of the increasing economic appreciation of genetic resources, because for their commercial use, national sovereignty and state-political regulation are both necessary. Second, it becomes apparent, in contrast to the official statements, that the negotiations on the harmonisation of the two agreements were not necessarily hampered by the two different central principles – here common heritage, there national sovereignty. Rather, the question of intellectual property rights (FAO/1; FAO/4) and, closely connected with them, hopes of bilateral benefit-sharing and the dimension of the multilateral system of exchange (FAO/1; FAO/2; FAO/5; FAO/7) must first be named, along with the special treatment of agro-biodiversity, including the question of Farmers' Rights (FAO/2; FAO/5). Up until the end it was not clear whether, in view of the opposing points of view on these issues, it would be possible to find a compromise or whether pure power politics would prevail (FAO/1; FAO/7). A further point of continuing controversy, which must be resolved in the ongoing process of the International Treaty negotiations, is the treatment of the *ex situ* collections. Thus, some of the most important issues in the whole process have not yet been entirely resolved. This gives rise to the question of what meaning such vague provisions actually have in the eyes of the actors which enter into them as well as in their regulatory content.

The official negotiations within the framework of the Commission on Genetic Resources for Food and Agriculture (including the extraordinary sessions of the CGRFA), an Inter-session Contact Group and the FAO

Council, comprised almost 20 meetings (see the overview in the ENB 2001). In addition, there were both smaller and larger conferences which dealt with related subjects, such as the FAO Conference in Leipzig in 1996, at which with the acceptance of the Report on the State of the World's Plant Genetic Resources and the passing of the Global Plan of Action (GPA), the two most important elements of the Global System on Plant Genetic Resources, next to the International Undertaking, were established. The World Food Conference of the FAO in 1997 and the follow-up conference in 2002 should also be mentioned. The International Undertaking is only one part of a global system for the conservation and utilisation of plant genetic resources. To be sure, even the negotiations in this sub-area of biodiversity are extremely complex and in their multitude of scientific, technical, economic and legal dimensions, are only really understandable by a small circle of experts. In this area, which is concerned with the special role of plant genetic resources for international politics, the global economy and the interests of national governments and other actors (TNCs, local communities etc.), expert and specialist knowledge plays a very special role (Görg/Brand 2003). Interests of different actor groups do not exist per se; instead, they become interpreted and formulated by this expert knowledge. Nevertheless, the often contradictory or even antagonistic structural conditions of the major actors are not even remotely transcended by this knowledge, as the protagonists of this knowledge or post-industrial societies like to claim. The history to date of the conflicts over plant genetic resources shows that in spite of, and even because of, dominant and generally accepted interpretations of the problems and interests involved (e.g. the international interdependencies in the plant genetic resources), the conflicts have not at all been brought closer to a solution, and it has not even become easier to attain compromises. The genesis of a multilateral exchange system can illustrate that something different occurred: interests are reinterpreted with reference to expert knowledge and this knowledge therefore becomes part of the power struggle.

The model of international interdependencies in the area of plant genetic resources has in principle established itself as the description of the problem since the 1980s. However, despite this, there was still a long way to go from that description to the development of a multilateral system of exchange. One decisive step in this direction was taken by the International Plant Genetic Resources Institute (IPGRI, a research centre based in Rome in the vicinity of the FAO). Via various preparatory documents since 1994, the idea of a Multilateral System was gradually established (Cooper *et al.* 1994; IPGRI 1996), until in about 1997 the core idea was accepted by the majority of the parties to the conflict (see ENB 1997). Up to that time, the negotiations had been repeatedly described as preliminary. Only with this idea of a multilateral system of exchange, developed by scientific and legal experts, was it possible for the parties in conflict to aim for a compromise regarding their interests. This demonstrates the great importance of scientific expertise in such a complex negotiation process. Its role should not be misunderstood as neutral, however, nor should it be perceived as being synonymous with a transitory mode of negotiation, beginning with hard bargaining and argument and ending with constructive discussion and dialogue. The Rome-based IPGRI suggested the need for a compromise between partially opposing interests. But these interests were rooted in structural conditions which were not in any way undermined by this suggestion and consequently, the distributional conflict was not overcome, but simply reproduced at a new level. Moreover, when the idea of a multilateral system of exchange was established in the negotiations, the distribution conflict really began. Therefore, the far-reaching consensus with regard to the interpretation of the problem (international interdependencies) and the approach to a solution (Multilateral System), did not at all lead to a real consensus; instead, it brought about the reformulation of the opposing interests at this new level. Experts thus played an important role in the formulation of a "general interest" to which all the conflict parties could agree. But, they were included precisely as a part of the more far-reaching bargaining processes. It can be contended that the supposed general interest ultimately remains a "generalised" particular interest. This remains true despite the fact that it exists within the framework of a compromise between several interest groups, as we will see in the following.

From the perspective of one of our interview partners, in the negotiations following the formal agreement on a Multilateral System, at first nothing really changed. Rather, the different positions were upheld and ensured that they would mutually block one another until in 1999 the chairman of the Commission on Genetic Resources, Ambassador Gerbasi from Venezuela, presented a new draft. This draft was the starting-point for further negotiations, which took place primarily in a smaller contact group of representatives from 41 countries (FAO/7; see ENB 2001: 2). However, not only was there a dire need that the relevance of the Multilateral System for the global regulation of plant genetic resources be made clear, but also, the national delegates had to understand the system to the extent that they were able to formulate the interests of their countries, or what they perceived these to be, with regard to this proposal. In the context of these clarifications it may well be concluded that in the opinion of observers, the international negotiations almost resembled a university seminar – although this was only the case for a brief period – before the conflict over the specific regulation of access and benefit-sharing, and with it hard bargaining, exerted itself once more.

Despite the fact that ever since 1999 the most important core ideas of the agreement had been on the table, the negotiations were repeatedly threatened with failure. The core part of the revised International Undertaking was to be the Multilateral System, although both the question of benefit-sharing (and closely connected with it the problem of intellectual property rights) and the dimension of the Multilateral System were controversial. The regulation of benefit-sharing proved to be particularly difficult. Here, most of the actors recognised that the main benefit of the International Treaty was the Multilateral System itself. Facilitated access to plant genetic resources, because of the international interdependencies, constitutes a benefit for all participants – but how can this benefit be "fairly and equitably" distributed as the International Treaty demands (ITPGR 2001: Art. 13.1)? In the International Treaty itself, first, non-monetary forms of benefit-sharing are dealt with such as the exchange of information and technology (Art. 13.2(a) and (b)), as well as capacity building, as mentioned in the last chapter (Art. 13.2(c)). With all these provisions, the question arises as to whether and to what extent the different groups of actors really benefit and whether the whole process can, in fact, be described as "fair". These questions are ultimately not clarified within the framework of the CBD. Furthermore, in the International Treaty there are two additional problems: do the practices which are responsible for the production and conservation of the genetic diversity of plant genetic resources actually benefit from these regulations? This question points above all to the problem of whether Farmers' Rights are strengthened or not. The second problem is directly linked to the form in which benefits are granted: what are the expectations, first, in the special case of *monetary* benefit-sharing and, related to this, with regards to the commercialisation of genetic resources?

In reference to this second question, during the negotiations an interesting turn took place. While the Southern governments had long insisted on monetary compensation, by the end of the negotiations even the lobby associations of industry had agreed to the payment of such compensation. In line with this, a corresponding model was formulated by the breeders association, ASSINEL, and a corresponding proposal was then brought into the negotiations at the third meeting of the contact group in August 2000 by the Norwegian Government (FAO/2; FAO/7; ENB 2000a). However, the formulation proved to be a stumbling block in a double, contradictory fashion. It said that a payment to an international fund would be due if intellectual property rights were claimed based on material from the Multilateral System, and it was therefore branded a door-opener for intellectual property rights. Nevertheless, on the basis of this proposal, at the third meeting of the contact group, it was possible to formulate a compromise which at the beginning all participants (although some with reservations) could agree to. At the fourth meeting of the contact group in Neuchatel, in November 2000, a severe set-back took place, which in the opinion of observers from NGO circles brought the negotiations to the brink of failure (RAFI 2000b; Mulvany/Redding 2000; see ENB 2000a, 2000e). However, it was not the reservations of the opponents of intellectual property rights which took effect here, but very surprisingly, those of the USA and other industrial countries.

Although the proposal for a monetary benefit-sharing, compensatory system had already been accepted by the commercial plant breeders and the biotechnological industry (see FAO/2; FAO/4), it was brought into question once again at Neuchatel by a group of four countries which delegated their group's leadership to the USA. According to observers (Mulvany/Redding 2000) it was more or less the same group which had previously almost blocked the negotiations on the biosafety protocol, namely the USA, Canada, Australia and New Zealand (Gupta 1999). These "foolish four" (RAFI 2000b) not only overlooked the fact that industry was prepared to pay monetary benefit-sharing, but they also took the position that without a principle willingness to pay a monetary compensation it would hardly be possible to achieve a compromise with the Southern countries. This event is of general importance beyond the individual case. At first it may seem surprising that the USA, which is usually seen as an outspoken representative of the interests of industry in such negotiations, ignored their agreement here and in doing so risked being declared the bogey-man of any further negotiations.[4]

The reasons responsible for such a seemingly contradictory position had to do with the supposed fears this country had with regard to the general importance of this regulation on monetary benefit-sharing. The USA and the other four countries were alarmed, as they had been during many other negotiations, that certain regulations of the TRIPS Agreement would be infringed (ENB 2000e: 5). Although the US delegation had at first agreed to the compromise on this issue in Teheran, it had placed this agreement in reserve, awaiting final assent by the government. But the delegation was apparently unable to definitively impose its position in the face of the opposing interests of the trade policy-makers. Or, as other observers who were in contact with one delegate expressed it: The "Biocrats" (meaning the bureaucrats in the field of biodiversity) could not convince the "high priests of patents" (from the trade ministries) of the meaningfulness of the regulations on plant genetic resources for food and agriculture. "They couldn't get their trade people in Washington to pay attention. Those people think a plant is some kind of industrial manufacturing facility" (quoted according to RAFI 2000b). This means that the international negotiations were endangered by the internal contradictions of a central actor: the divergent strategies of the agricultural and the trade ministries were an expression of the contradictions within the US government.

We can assume that behind these contradictions are diverging appraisals of the problem and the conflict situation, above all with regard to international agreements and the representation of national interests by these agreements. While it appeared obvious that the agricultural ministries would reluctantly agree to the proposed compromise on monetary benefit-sharing if a compromise could not be reached any other way, the trade ministries feared that with a commitment to benefit-sharing, the TRIPS Agreement would be violated and a dangerous precedent would appear, threatening the case for patent laws. What we can observe in this case, therefore, are complex relationships in this multilevel system, characterised by a multitude of overlapping concerns between the national and international levels. The national level does not disappear, but is present even in a fragmented and contradictory way at the international level. This is what we mean when we refer to the concept of a "second order condensation of power relations". Moreover, at least implicitly, most actors have the expectation that the government of a country should advocate a coherent policy and behave as an undivided, single actor. Even critical NGOs often refer to this fiction, even if they know that in different ministries very different interests and relationships of power are condensed. Accordingly these power relations, condensed in national ministries, often cause tensions in international negotiations.

The uncertainties of the USA (and a few other states) were dealt with at Neuchatel when a representative of the WTO explained the regulations of the TRIPS Agreement and the dispute settlement body (DSB) of the WTO. This explanation made explicit that the on-going negotiations on an agreement between sovereign states would depend on the expertise of another international organisation. It is interesting that the latter's representative had to disappoint the expectations of her, however. She pointed out that she could not supply a legal interpretation of the International Undertaking regulations in question and that fundamentally, the competence to examine violations of the TRIPS Agreement lay with the member countries of the WTO (ENB 2000c). With regard to the relationship between the International Undertaking and WTO/TRIPS this means that it can only be explained in advance by legal expertise to a limited degree. Since here different views of the law clash, it ultimately depends on whether a member country ascertains that there has been a violation of the TRIPS Agreement and whether its view of things is confirmed by the dispute settlement body. This cannot be clarified completely in advance and the question of consistency between the two agreements continues to be unanswered (ENB 2000e: 11). Apart from this procedural problem, the WTO and its representatives are put in a political position in which they accrue a high degree of interpretational competence. There is at least a threat that in the end, the WTO's dispute settlement body will become the decisive authority in which decisions on conflicts are made.

The above description of this negotiation process illustrates that even behind the commonly shared interpretations of the problems, the distributional conflicts remained firmly entrenched. Moreover, we can observe the manner in which national and international actor constellations overlap each other, both horizontally (e.g. the relationship between the International Treaty and the dispute settlement body or TRIPS) and vertically (e.g. different US ministries and their impact on the International Treaty negotiations). One further interesting aspect is that the expectations regarding monetary benefit-sharing have always accompanied the formulation of the

Multilateral System and have been used as a door-opener for intellectual property rights. So, it appears clear that the functionality of the international fund which is to administer the monetary benefit-sharing and to transfer the money should be coupled to the granting of intellectual property rights. Even if this coupling ultimately remained without enforcement in the International Treaty,[5] the close connection between monetary payments and private property rights as an element of the valorisation of genetic resources becomes quite lucid. By contrast, the omission of intellectual property rights as part of the material to come under the Multilateral System was one of the central elements of the negotiations, as we will see in the following. They were condensed in the last round of negotiations in spring 2001 to the four words "in the form received". In order to understand their meaning, it is helpful to take a look at the Multilateral System which was finally passed at the International Treaty. It must be examined whether and to what extent this in fact represents – as is often claimed – a counterweight to the commercialisation and monopolisation of seeds.

3.2.2 The international seed treaty: strengths and shortcomings

The Multilateral System and the problem of intellectual property rights

The Multilateral System of access and benefit-sharing to plant genetic resources as the central element of the International Treaty articulates the particular characteristics of the area of regulation and its subject-matter. The necessity of a system of its own on plant genetic resources for food and agriculture is formulated in the preamble to the International Treaty with a view to the particular nature of those resources, the erosion of genes, international dependencies and the general importance of these resources for world food security (ITPGR 2001: Preamble). With regard to these particular characteristics, in Part IV of the Agreement, the constitution of a Multilateral System for access and benefit-sharing is approached. However, the Multilateral System covers only certain plants, which are listed in Appendix I. This contains only 35 food crops particularly important for worldwide nutrition and 29 forages. In addition, the range is limited even further. It automatically includes only those varieties which are under the control of the signatory states (i.e. the states which have joined the International Treaty) and which are to be found in the public sphere. All others (e.g. private collections and commercial breeders) are only "invited" to include their varieties too (Art. 11.2); or governments should "encourage" them to do so (Art. 11.3). Within the framework of the Multilateral System a facilitated access is granted, which is explained in more detail in Article 12 and particularly in point 12.3. Facilitated access here means that access, free of charge or for minimal cost (12.3(b)), is to be granted exclusively for the purposes of research, breeding and training and explicitly not for other industrial purposes (12.3(a)). In contrast to Article 15 of the CBD, facilitated access here does not include marketing for profit but is, on the contrary, directed towards the establishment of a *public* sphere in which certain material is not to be subjected to commercial aims. The exchange in this public sphere is to be regulated by Material Transfer Agreements (MTA), finalised during the first meeting of the Governing Body of the Treaty in June 2006 (ENB 2006b).

The aim of the Multilateral System is to provide access to genetic material for public and private breeders under particularly favourable conditions. In the case of the commercialisation of plant genetic resources the International Treaty requires a monetary benefit-sharing regulated by an international fund, from which the measures of the FAO Global Plan of Action from 1996, that is for the conservation of plant genetic resources, are to be financed (Arts 13.3 and 13.4). For material from the Multilateral System the monetary benefit-sharing scheme does not serve the parties but the system itself. A monetary benefit-sharing falls due above all when the material is later no longer available without limitations, and in all other cases the recipients are only to be "encouraged" to pay. Nevertheless, the principle drawback of the Multilateral System is apparent here, namely, that such a multilateral system of exchange can only function if the most important plant varieties are included in it and if the material also continues to be freely available, that is when it is not removed from the public sphere and privatised. In both points, the Multilateral System shows considerable deficits. For one thing, the list of plants is kept to a bare minimum; indeed, even such important varieties for food security as soy beans cannot be found listed. Behind this tactic rest the interests of some developing countries, which wished to keep out of the Multilateral System those species of which they possess a considerable diversity of rural types and traditional varieties, as they hoped to attain considerably more advantages from bilateral trade. For example, in the case of the soy bean, which is among the most genetically modified plants, this strategy was adopted by China, which prevented the inclusion of soy beans in the Multilateral System due to the diversity of this species in China and the commercial interest in soy beans in the USA.[6] Brazil has repeatedly been accused of similar strategies (FAO/6; FAO/7). Despite the general criticism of developing countries against such a trend, even NGO representatives admit that the Southern countries are thus reacting in their own way to the general tendency towards commercialisation.

Another problem is connected with the already discussed question of intellectual property rights. If the commercially important varieties were to be placed under strong property protection and thus removed from the public sphere of the Multilateral System, this would in the long term undermine the substance of the Multilateral System. This danger was articulated publicly early on by NGOs with the term "grain drain". At its core this danger is also recognised in the International Treaty and subsequently, there were attempts to outline some precautions against it. The four words "in the form received" play the decisive role here. In Article 12.3(d) it is stated, "Recipients shall not claim any intellectual property rights that limit the facilitated access to the plant genetic resources for food and agriculture, or their genetic parts and components, *in the form received* from the Multilateral System" (emphasis added). What sounds good at the beginning – namely the prohibition of claiming intellectual property rights over plant genetic resources from the Multilateral System – is in the end decisively weakened. For "in the form" in which genetic resources are taken from the Multilateral System, namely as seeds, they are not capable of being patented in any case. Patentability requires as a minimal criterion novelty and invention – and both are clearly not given in the case of seeds.[7] For this reason the insertion was also controversial. It causes the clear exclusion of intellectual property rights, that is patents, to be turned unnoticed into an inclusion. As seed, in the form in which it is received, the material cannot be patented, but its genetic characteristics can. In order to counter this threat, a second insertion is made, which at first glance also excludes "their genetic parts and components" from patentability, in addition to the seeds themselves. In the process of negotiation, the two passages were highly controversial. After the US government, at the sixth meeting of the contact group in Spoleto in April 2001, insisted that the passage "or their genetic parts and components" should be placed in brackets (i.e. it is not consensual and must be further negotiated), the Group of 77 and China reacted by putting the other passage "in the form received" in brackets (see the NGO report on this at www.ukabc.org/iu4htm#3, of 3 May 2001).

In this example we can observe very clearly the contradictory interests of the developing and major industrial countries on the subject of patents on plant genetic resources. The formulation which was finally passed represents a compromise between the two positions, which ultimately really clarifies nothing and whose effectiveness is controversial. Both perspectives were incorporated within the compromise, at least formally, but the real challenge was avoided. From the point of view of the biotechnology industry it is not parts or components of plants which should be protected by patents anyway, but a technical procedure for isolating individual genetic characteristics and transferring these characteristics to other organisms (FAO/2; see also the statements of the lobby association BIO). In the opinion of representatives from this industry the new insertion to Article 12.3(d) does not change this. Perhaps they are right and it does not help in any way to combat "grain drain", nor does it work against the privatisation of genetic material from the Multilateral System.

The relation to other agreements

As a result of the final compromise, the International Treaty does not present any clear conditions on this issue. Therefore, it will be finally interpreted in patent law. Additionally, of even more importance is the fact that the International Treaty is decisively weakened in relation to the TRIPS Agreement. The International Treaty would only have had a chance as an instrument against the patenting of plants if it had contained clear regulations on the exclusion of intellectual property rights. In the opinion of those actors who pushed for the exclusion of intellectual property rights, however, this ultimately political statement of the International Treaty is not as clear as they would have wished (FAO/6). At least the final adjustment has been postponed to the further negotiations and the implementation of the International Treaty (FAO/1). The relationship between the International Treaty and other agreements, in addition to the TRIPS Agreement and above all its relationship to the CBD, is not only a question of legal interpretation but also of the political weight of each agreement. Furthermore, these relationships are subject to continual change and re-interpretation. Whereas at the beginning of the negotiation process on the harmonisation of the International Undertaking the relationship to the CBD was the central focus, in the course of the following negotiations the problem of the relationship to the TRIPS Agreement moved more and more into the foreground.

Tensions in the relationship between the CBD and the International Undertaking and the International Treaty, respectively, continue to exist. This has to do, primarily, with the contradiction between bilateral and multilateral access and benefit-sharing (FAO/1; FAO/5; FAO/6), even if this tension is questioned by the industry (FAO/2). But now in the foreground of this relationship are the material differences between "wild biodiversity", on the one hand, and plant genetic resources and the particular characteristics of agriculture, on the other. Here, almost all our interview partners pointed out that the CBD – despite all the progress of recent years – does not have the necessary competences. In the CBD, among other things, the environmental ministries, which often regard agriculture in general as an enemy (FAO/5), lead the negotiations and not the agricultural ministries. This appraisal of the peculiarities of this field combines a judgement of international institutions with the responsibilities and competencies of nation-state apparatuses. With regard to the international level, this scepticism, which appears to be the expression of a general tendency, has an effect on the legal relationship of the two international agreements. Indeed, by the end of the negotiations, two alternative models for the international regulation on plant genetic resources for food and agriculture stood facing one another: a protocol to the CBD, similar to the biosafety protocol, and an agreement and an institution within the framework of the FAO. Concerning the variation of making the International Undertaking into a protocol to the CBD, the apprehension is articulated: "If it is a protocol of the CBD environment would take over agriculture" (FAO/7). Most of our interview partners therefore preferred the annexation to the FAO, which was in fact chosen (via Art. 14 of the FAO statute; see FAO/2; FAO/5; FAO/7). Nevertheless, almost all of the interviewees expressed a desire that *both* international institutions be closely related. This includes the obligation for the International Treaty to report to the Conference of the Parties of the CBD. This reference to the CBD is explained by the NGO side with the argument that the CBD is *more political* and less bureaucratic than the FAO (FAO/1; FAO/7). Interestingly enough, this viewpoint is confirmed by industry, although it comes to the opposite conclusion: the International Undertaking or the International Treaty should remain at the FAO precisely for this reason (FAO/4).

Problems of bilateralism and the use value of genetic resources

While at the beginning of the 1990s the fear of depoliticisation via "environmentalisation" was prominent, ten years later the tide has turned: the conflicts within the framework of the CBD are now regarded as more political and more explosive by both sides (NGOs and industry). The dangers of bilateral mechanisms in the exchange of genetic resources, privileged by the CBD, continue to be pointed out, however (FAO/1; FAO/6). Particularly, threats towards commercialisation and privatisation and the completely different power resources of those TNCs and indigenous communities connected to bilateral negotiations are mentioned. Altogether, it was clearly recognisable that in the sphere of plant genetic resources, a monetary benefit-sharing scheme was regarded with considerably more scepticism than in the context of the CBD. Just as on the NGO side the "hype about benefit-sharing" has been publicly denounced (GAIA/GRAIN 2000), in the interviews, too, there was clear criticism of the fixation on monetary benefit-sharing schemes and the accompanying commercialisation of genetic resources (FAO/1; FAO/5; FAO/7). Unrealistic expectations with regard to bilateral benefit-sharing are, according to this view, in addition to intellectual property rights, one of the main obstacles in the negotiation process (FAO/1). One representative of an international organisation declared the confusion of "usefulness" and "value", that is of use value and exchange value, to be one of the main problems (FAO/5; similarly FAO/7; a literal differentiation between *use value* and *market value* is to be found in FAO/1). While plant genetic resources have a high use value for agriculture, for breeding and for food, it is argued that their economic exchange value is often overestimated, particularly with regard to bilateral access agreements. This has negatively influenced the tactics of the Northern countries as well as some of the Southern ones, for the latter now expect more advantages from selling their resources than from implementing the Global Plan of Action (FAO/5; FAO/6). In contrast to this, representatives of industry have no problems with a monetary benefit-sharing scheme. As we have seen, this is also true of payments to an international fund in the case of the commercialisation of genetic resources. Representatives of the biotechnological industry propagate a win–win situation if intellectual property rights are also accepted (FAO/4).

From the point of view of the actors in the seeds area, the relationship to the CBD is therefore not free of tensions. They refer to the fact that the

CBD favours a particular model, namely that of bilateral access agreements with their orientation towards a monetary benefit-sharing scheme. This model has also gained importance within the framework of the plant genetic resources and the International Undertaking with consequences for the negotiation procedures and for the agreement itself (among other things with regard to the limited range of the Multilateral System). By contrast, with regard to national sovereignty, in principle no problem is seen, since it can be used by states in different ways. National sovereignty can be a door-opener for privatisation (as in the CBD), but it is not necessarily so, because it could also be used in order to create a Multilateral System (FAO/1; FAO/5). Therefore, their effects are judged as being very ambivalent, particularly on the part of the seed NGOs. A legal framework at the national level could protect the actors who are most vulnerable, that is the rural communities (FAO/1). Nevertheless, no plea is made for all controls to be left in the hands of national governments. A "privatisation" in favour of local communities is even demanded in order not to endanger the use value of bio-diversity (FAO/1). In this case, privatisation is not understood as commercialisation or in the sense of private property rights, but in the sense of a local common. In addition, the difference between sovereignty and property is pointed out (FAO/5) and it is emphasised that national sovereignty does not mean real independence. A national agricultural system today is simply seen as nonsense (FAO/7), since no-one can escape the international interdependencies.

It is therefore too simple just to contrast the bilateral CBD model with the multilateral model of the International Treaty. There is no clear dichotomy between the two because the latter is permeated completely by the bilateral model in its genesis, its structure and its problems. The extent of the Multilateral System and some of the most important regulations of the International Treaty can only be understood if the practice of bilateral access agreements, privileged by the CBD, is kept in mind. The hope of bilateral benefit-sharing was the reason why only a small share of plant genetic resources was in fact covered by the Multilateral System. Furthermore, it is also held responsible for the fact that the real benefits of a Multilateral System and the responsibility regarding the conservation of the diversity of plant genetic resources (which is laid down primarily in the Global Plan of Action) is not really recognised by the governments (FAO/5). The functioning of the Multilateral System, established by the International Treaty, is not at all so clearly defined that it is really able to fulfil even this limited task of securing facilitated access and the free exchange of plant genetic resources in a public sector. Representatives from the NGO sector see the main problem as being whether or not it will be able to establish itself as an alternative model or whether the tendency towards commercialisation will in fact win through. Here – because of the central role of intellectual property rights – ultimately, the relationship to the TRIPS Agreement and to the WIPO will be decisive.

Negotiations in the "shadow of hierarchy"

As we have seen, the relation of the International Treaty to the TRIPS/ WTO Agreement was an immanent problem in the negotiation process. We can state, therefore, that the relations between environmental and trade agreements are not only external in character, following their coming into force. At least in these cases the relationship between the new agreements and the TRIPS/WTO formed part of the discussions during the negotiation process, thus becoming part of the formulation of the agreements. Corresponding regulations even belonged to the most controversial elements in the genesis of the International Treaty. As we have seen, this concerned the question whether a binding monetary benefit-sharing scheme could be linked to the granting of intellectual property rights or whether this was an infringement of TRIPS. The answer in this case was made dependent on the interpretation of the parties to the agreement and here, it was the dispute settlement body of the WTO that was granted autonomy in making a final decision. The second point of controversy remained unsolved, literally until the last minute, and concerned the questions as to whether patents on plant genetic resources should be prevented, and if so, whether they could be prevented, with the aid of the International Treaty.

The interpretation of the TRIPS Agreement plays a central role here, particularly the *sui generis* clause of Article 27.3(b). It allows exceptions to the obligations imposed by the TRIPS Agreement on the national formulation of strict intellectual property rights standards, if a system of IPR protection "of its own kind" exists. Nonetheless, the exact nature of a *sui generis* system of intellectual property rights remains to be clarified, as does the still prevalent controversy surrounding whether or not existing or yet to be developed legal systems could actually do such a system justice. Particularly relevant here is the International Union for the Protection of New Plant Varieties (UPOV), which is recognised as a *sui generis* law but is rejected by its critics as being too similar to patent law (Leskien/Flitner 1997). By contrast, a draft law of the Organisation for African Unity (the OAU model law; see Ekpere 2000) is intended to do justice to the particular characteristics of agriculture in Southern countries (Egziabher 2002). However, from the point of view of the World Intellectual Property Organization (WIPO) it contradicts the requirements of the protection of intellectual property rights precisely for this reason. In the next chapter we shall examine the question in more detail as to the latitude which follows from the TRIPS Agreement and the developments within the framework of the WIPO, and what momentum can be observed there.

There is another dimension concerning the relationship of different agreements. Usually it is stated in the legal text that the agreement should be "mutually supportive" of other agreements, that they should not contradict any rights or obligations from other agreements, and that neither should they establish any hierarchy to other agreements – in other words, they should not be subordinate to the WTO Agreement (ITPGR, Preamble). What this means in practice is something which remains to be seen.[8] At the moment there are diverging appraisals of the relationship between the International Treaty, on the one hand, and the TRIPS Agreement, on the other. There are optimistic expectations that the International Treaty could establish itself as a technical explanation of the concrete problem area, in this case the treatment of plant genetic resources in food and agriculture (as is hoped for the Biosafety Protocol with regard to the treatment of GMO; see ENB 2000a: 12). In the final analysis, this expresses the hope that the International Treaty could be referred to as an authority for a binding definition in controversial cases. However, there are fears that the International Treaty will be subordinated to the TRIPS Agreement in the important issue of intellectual property rights: because of the link between a monetary benefit-sharing scheme and intellectual property rights, it is seen as being a door-opener for patents on seeds and plants in general (FAO/6).

Ultimately, much will depend on how the Governing Body, the controlling organ of the International Treaty, works and what decisions it will take after its constitution. The issue will above all concern what stocks are in fact designated to the Multilateral System and how the system treats those private actors, in other words, the commercial breeders and the biotech industry, which do not bring their stocks into the Multilateral System (Seiler 2003). Even if NGOs welcome the existence of this agreement as a whole and have put considerable effort into lobbying for its realisation, most of them remain sceptical with regard to the question of whether their main objective – to counteract the commercialisation and privatisation of plant genetic resources – could in fact be achieved. An important point in this context is the question: to what extent will it be able to exert itself against the TRIPS Agreement? The danger exists that the weak and imprecise text could result in an insidious transformation of the agreement (unnoticed) into a "crop genetic trade fair" (GRAIN 2001b).

3.2.3 *The strategies of actors and the relevance of the international regulation system*

The central conflict during the negotiations on the International Treaty concerned the limitation of commercialisation in this partial area of biodiversity. Whether this agreement, in view of the bilateral framework of the CBD which is directed towards commercialisation and of the strengthening of the valorisation of genetic resources by the TRIPS Agreement, can in fact set such limits is highly questionable. A further weakness of the International Treaty stems from a rather sceptical viewpoint: the very weak anchoring of Farmers' Rights. The legal dimensions of Farmers' Rights have never been clearly stated or, indeed, defined before. Therefore, the International Treaty represents the first time in which Farmers' Rights have been formally endorsed by a legally binding instrument at the global level.

Moreover, with international recognition and the national anchoring at least an important step towards legal recognition has been made (Mekouar 2001; Correa 2003). According to these provisions, the rights of informal innovators (traditional farmers), should be equated with the rights already granted to formal innovators (plant breeders, Mekouar 2001: 21). Article 9 recognises the contributions of local and indigenous communities to the conservation and development of the diversity of plant genetic resources (Art. 9.1) and advocates the protection of traditional knowledge, fair benefit-sharing and participation in the political decision-making process (Art. 9.2 (a)–(c)). Nonetheless, these regulations do not go beyond general principles. The responsibility for Farmers' Rights is generally seen as lying with the national governments (Art. 9.2) and in their practical meaning they are explicitly subordinated to national legislation (Art. 9.3). This limits the relevance of Farmers' Rights in a double fashion: they can scarcely be used as a lever in conflicts with national governments; and they are not an adequate counterweight to the advancement of intellectual property rights, particularly in the area of the International Union for the Protection of New Plant Varieties (UPOV).

The weakening of the concept of Farmers' Rights has been appearing in the negotiation process for a long time. Even critical NGOs neglected to take up the issue again in order not to further endanger the negotiations (FAO/1; FAO/7). This is the expression of a fundamental problem: because of the general importance of plant genetic resources for food and agriculture, both NGOs and some of the contracting parties were primarily interested in successfully negotiating an agreement in this field. When the negotiations were threatened with failure at a certain point, on several occasions, the internationally active NGOs began campaigns in order to prevent this failure (see Mulvany/Meienberg 2000; Buntzel-Cano 2000; Berne Declaration 2001). Therefore, a compromise even with the hardest opponents seemed to be the top priority. Without the JUSCANZ Group an agreement would not have made much sense, because this group contains the most important producers and the largest exporters of agricultural products. In view of their massive strategies of obstruction the question arose whether the USA, Australia and several other countries were prepared at all to join the International Treaty (FAO/1). After the USA at first did in fact abstain from the International Treaty, in November 2002 it signed the treaty, much to everybody's surprise. It is less clear what the motives for this change of mind were. The US ambassador to the FAO declared that the USA had meanwhile recognised "the wisdom of the treaty" (according to Associated Press, 6 November 2002). Apparently, the US government considers the International Treaty to be less dangerous than it had at first thought, or it preferred to be on board, as in the case of the CBD, in order to be able to pursue a more effective strategy of hindrance from that standpoint.

A further problem is closely connected with this: the divergent appraisal of vague and unequivocal phraseology, which is also criticised by industry

(FAO/2; FAO/4). The issue here is primarily that of binding and clear, that is calculable, regulations concerning benefit-sharing, in which differing interests within industry also play a role (FAO/2). Thus, the conventionally working, smaller breeders appear to assume that they will not have to fall back on new material to a great extent, but will be able to work with the existing collections. For them benefit-sharing is therefore relatively unimportant. For some industrial countries the wish for more specification is, by contrast, an important instrument to raise the negotiations to a more technical level at which only the consistency of legal details is negotiated and no longer the differences of interests which are behind them. This strategy was applied by the industrial countries particularly in the negotiations on intellectual property rights (see the next chapter on this).

For the representatives of the NGOs, by contrast, it is, in principle, clear that the lack of clarity in the regulations of the agreement shifts the problem onto other terrains and can thus be used as a tactical element – sometimes to their advantage – if provisions, which they consider better, could not be integrated into the Treaty (FAO/1; FAO/7). Individual regulations and even the International Treaty as a whole are regarded as important in an instrumental way: in order to slow down the process of privatisation and to strengthen the interests of small farmers. In this sense, obligations should of course be as specific as possible in order to open up clear negotiation options against these dominant processes. But, since in the final analysis all regulations represent compromises which evolve according to the respective relationships of power and situational constellations of strength, many actors have no illusions about the results which can be achieved or their practical consequences. To a certain degree, the individual regulations themselves are not necessarily the real goal. They are, rather, more or less partial results which can be used as instruments in further negotiations, and even on other terrains and in other processes.

At least some NGO representatives show an awareness of the international regulating system and its momentum, which can be described as exceptionally realistic, realistic in terms of Poulantzas' theory of politics and law. According to this, international regulations are important for opening-up the strategic opportunities of different actors and in particular, the rights of weaker interest groups. They are not, however, an expression of a real general interest, because the contradictory individual interests and the corresponding relationships of power are not abolished. Other NGOs, particularly from the field of the environment, and interestingly, even representatives of industry, fabricate a contrasting hope of gratifying a real general interest, although with differing strategic intentions. Thus, a representative of industry articulated the continuing hope of a win–win solution for the regulation on benefit-sharing which would do justice to all interest groups – if both intellectual property rights and patents were accepted (FAO/4). In contrast to the position of many NGOs in the field of the environment, this position is not at all naïve, as the representative of industry is quite clear about the fact that intellectual property rights represent the most controversial and still most contested aspect of the entire negotiation process. But he assumes that in the struggle for hegemony, in spite of the individual interest involved, his position has a good chance of establishing itself as the general interest. The representatives of environmental NGOs, by contrast, are in many cases integrated into such a compromise as subordinate actors.

3.3 Structural selectivities and the limits to the multilateral exchange system

How little international treaties really have to do with the establishment of a global general interest can be seen in the negotiations on the International Treaty. As some observers confirmed, the negotiations have, for a long time, been moving away from a point of common orientation to problem solutions (conservation of genetic diversity on plant genetic resources, food security) towards the direction of a distributional conflict over valuable economic resources (ENB 2000e: 12). As figured out, a widely shared view of the problems has crystallised as the background to the negotiations. The further design of the institutional system and the development of the strategies referring to it are more the outcome of hard bargaining than of the argumentative clarification of the problems involved. Against the common background, diverging interests emerge all the more clearly. Such continuing contradictions of interest are usually accepted in the negotiations if they are about the interpretation of legal questions and it emerges "that there will be as many interpretations as there are lawyers" (ibid.: 11). But the fact that they touch the interpretation of the problem as a whole and affect all the individual problems in one way or another is quickly forgotten. Closely connected to this is the fiction of a general interest created by international institutions in a similar way in which it is supposed to be created by the nation-state. Through this fiction, or what could be termed the state fetish, both the continuing existence of contradictory, partly antagonistic interests and the structural selectivities of the institutional system are obscured. This is precisely what forms the character of domination of political institutions in the process of the internationalisation of the state. Political institutions secure the reproduction of contradictory interests and the connected relationships of power. In two closely connected fields it can be demonstrated which structural selectivities are in fact included in international treaties and how the International Treaty functions in the sense of the valorisation paradigm: in the fate of the existing *ex situ* collections and in the question of how and to what extent plant genetic resources are to be treated as a global common.

Since the conclusion of the negotiations on the CBD, it has become clear that the fate of the existing collections, above all those stored in the International Agricultural Research Centres, represents one of the most difficult problems for the further treatment of plant genetic resources. In 1994 these collections were placed under the auspices of the FAO and given to the Research Centres in the form of a trusteeship. A decisive issue is whether and to what extent these collections will in fact remain in the public sector. In addition, there is the question of compensation or of benefit-sharing with the original countries of origin. In the opinion of critics, these questions are not satisfactorily regulated in the new International Treaty (ITPGR 2001: Art. 15). With regard to the first point, there is the same problem as with the International Treaty as a whole: protection against intellectual property rights is only offered for material "in the form received", even if these four words are not explicitly mentioned in the article on the International Research Centres collections. What makes the issue even more burning is the suspicion that some International Research Centres are themselves prepared, in the future, to claim intellectual property rights over their own research results (GRAIN 2002a). This is probably understandable as a reaction to the advance of patents on genetic resources – why should public research institutes not attempt to protect their own results? But in this case it could cause the entire system to collapse, or to make a 180 degree about-face on its original objectives. The erosion of the Multilateral System would then only be a question of time, and in particular, the most economically valuable material would gradually disappear into the private sector. In addition, the International Treaty would even cushion this process by lending it legitimacy.

This becomes even clearer when we ask the question to what extent the International Research Centres belong to the public domain and what are the actual characteristics of this domain. To merely promise that they will exclusively serve general welfare, the conservation and further development of plant genetic resources and therein, the securing of world food, is not enough, particularly when the rights of the areas of origin and the problem of Farmers' Rights are simply excluded. As the NGO GRAIN has stated: "By unilaterally declaring all 500 000 designated accessions as 'public domain', the CGIAR [Consultative Group on International Agricultural Research, the authors] in particular has severed whatever relationship farmers and indigenous peoples may consider that they have towards those materials" (ibid.).

Here a certain interpretation of the problem – we need the *ex situ* collections of the International Research Centres in order to be able to confront the problem of food security – is subtly re-functionalised into the construction of a general interest. If this is examined more closely, however, it is plain to see that doubts are growing with regard to the generality of this interest. Moreover, the claim to generality even works in the opposite sense by privileging commercialisation and private interests, that is it represents a structural selectivity towards specific interests. While the official interpretation of the public domain emphasises that no exclusive property rights to the material may be claimed (Correa 2003), the contradictions between different legal systems and in particular the difference to collective property rights is not taken into consideration (GRAIN 2002a). In this way, under the problematic definition, "We have to protect the public domain for the security of world food", in a de facto process, a reverse tendency gains the upper hand, leading to the replacement of collective property rights systems by a public domain and the construction of a global commons, which in fact favours the privatisation of research results with the aid of intellectual property rights. Even if the International Agricultural Research Centres do not claim these private property rights themselves, this tendency could win through, because the Research Centres, according to the International Treaty, are not obliged to control the further use of material from their collections. What the receiver does with it remains outside their authority. In the final analysis, we cannot therefore speak of a satisfactory solution. Rather, GRAIN appears to hit the nail on the head with its question: is the FAO-CGIAR system "biopiracy by another name?" (ibid.)

Beyond the treatment of the collections, the question arises of what in fact is to be understood by the public domain and to what extent this represents an answer to the problems in the treatment of plant genetic resources for food and agriculture. In the run-up to the Rio+10 summit in Johannesburg in 2002 an initiative for a "treaty to share the genetic commons" was formed (RAFI 2001b). This initiative, in contrast to others, is completely awake to the fact that global common goods can only be meaningfully established if intellectual property rights are explicitly excluded to parts of the commons. That is basically a tautology since it only repeats the definition of a common good, according to which no-one can be excluded from the use of the good. Indeed, precisely for this reason it would seem that this demand has a contra-factual status in view of the present situation: the demand for plant genetic resources as a global common is identical to the demand for the prohibition of intellectual property rights on plant genetic resources. In view of the real relationships of forces, however, this demand will not be realisable, at least not in the foreseeable future. Therefore, the threat exists that via the de facto definition of a general interest, the powers for the privatisation of genetic resources will be legitimised or even be strengthened, because the underlying processes are concealed and the necessary demand for a prohibition of intellectual property rights is ignored due to power relations.

The actual effects of the International Treaty cannot yet be completely estimated. The Treaty is still too recent. Many important elements will, in addition, depend on the further design of the Governing Body. Therefore, in conclusion, only the fundamental problem of nation-state and inter-state regulation processes will be elucidated. On the one hand, there is official recognition of the fundamental problem that the conservation of agro-biodiversity is of decisive importance for the security of world nutrition. On the other hand, we can observe a tendency away from the common heritage principle and towards national sovereignty and intellectual property rights.

The solution to the problem is defined as the general interest and delegated to state authorities. It is precisely this solution, however, which plays into the hands of the valorisation paradigm. It is therefore not at all adequate to contrast the Multilateral System of the international treaty with the bilateral system of the CBD. The precise formulation of the Treaty cannot be understood without the system of the CBD – including its central elements: nation-state sovereignty and bilateral access agreements. The provisions of access and benefit-sharing of the CBD, therefore, form the framework in which not only by far the largest part of plant genetic resources are traded (only a relatively small share are subject to the Multilateral System), but which also contains the decisive conditions for the Multilateral System, that is the tendency towards the commercialisation and privatisation of genetic resources, connected with intellectual property rights. Even the apparently global general interest which is anchored in the Multilateral System of the International Treaty does not represent, as we have seen, a really binding instrument against the privatisation and commercialisation of plant genetic resources, but can even support them. This logic can easily be recognised in the latest publications of the Crucible Group (Crucible Group 2000 and 2001). Despite the scepticism of several members of the group (and against the judgements of mainstream political science) they accord the national laws and the latitude for action of nation-states a decisive role in the shaping of this field. But expectations regarding the creative power of the state are not at all free from contention. Doubts are articulated as to whether the complex socio-political questions can be dealt with by purely legislative measures (Crucible Group 2000: ix). Moreover, the problem is mentioned of whether or not the nation-state options for the regulation of bilateral negotiations, which are in the foreground here, are actually the problem: "In fact, many members of the Crucible Group argue that bilaterally oriented national access and intellectual property laws will ultimately have a negative impact on the resolution of these very issues" (Crucible Group 2001: xiii).

Apparently, even in this field bilateral negotiations are not at all marginal or even excluded, but form the centre of the problem. In addition, recourse to the (nation-)state as a regulating instance prevails, even where its inadequacy has long been obvious. This can be taken as a clear indication that even in complex international problem areas the state form continues to be relevant. First, the nation-state remains in power as a fetish from which a regulating effect and the construction of a general interest is expected. Furthermore, national and international regulations are not only a condensation of relationships of forces. Rather, these regulations can only develop their real strength vis-à-vis the contradictory interests which continue to reproduce themselves if they take on a specific *form*, namely the state form. Only when they take on this specific materiality or a relatively independent political form vis-à-vis the individual actors, can they develop their effectiveness in the regulation and reproduction of antagonistic relationships.

4 Politicising intellectual property rights

The conflicts around the TRIPS Agreement and the World Intellectual Property Organization

In the previous chapters, the importance of the agreement on *Trade-Related Aspects of Intellectual Property Rights* (TRIPS) was frequently mentioned. Without exaggeration, this sub-agreement of the WTO can be described as the most controversial international agreement of the second half of the 1990s. While it was hardly known when it was signed within the framework of the GATT negotiations and its effects could only be estimated by a few experts, it quickly advanced to become one of the main points of criticism of the mechanisms and the effects of neoliberal globalisation. The TRIPS Agreement is so important not only because of the subject-matter which it regulates or because of its own objectives, but also because of its effects on other international treaties. This chapter explores the contested character of intellectual property rights (IPRs) and their institutionalisation on the international scale. It begins with an outline of the creation of the TRIPS Agreement and of the tensions and contradictions which are inherent in it (4.1). Second, we analyse the ways in which Southern governments, NGOs, social movements and indigenous organisations have politicised these contradictions since the late 1990s (4.2). This is followed by an examination of the growing importance of "scale jumping" strategies, which for example take on the form of bilateral trade agreements (4.3). Fourth, we explore the "forum-shifting" from the TRIPS Agreement to the World Intellectual Property Organization (WIPO) (4.4), before, in a fifth step, turning to the conflicts which have recently emerged within the WIPO itself (4.5). The chapter ends with some more general observations on multilateralism and hegemony (4.6).

4.1 Shaping an international regime of intellectual property protection: evolution and contradictions of the TRIPS Agreement

The TRIPS Agreement was negotiated during the Uruguay Round of the GATT which started in 1986 in Punta del Este (Uruguay), and concluded, along with the latter, in 1994. It contains internationally valid minimum standards for the protection of intellectual property. Besides the GATT and the GATS, which regulate international trade in goods or services respectively, it is one of the three central multilateral agreements that fall under the umbrella of the WTO. The socio-economic background of the TRIPS Agreement stems from the fact that, during the last decades of the twentieth century, the production and appropriation of immaterial goods has significantly gained importance in the process of the valorisation of capital. This increasing "knowledge intensity" of the economy has strong implications for the issue of property rights: whereas the generation and initial industrial application of new knowledge is a complex and costly process, the imitation of knowledge-intensive goods can be quite easy. Examples include the production of generics in the pharmaceutical sector or the copying of computer software. Hence, the rise of the "knowledge society" has also given rise to demands for a stronger protection of intellectual property:

> Due to the tendential de-materialisation of production and the increasing share of immaterial contributions to new products, from the point of view of industry and the political actors representing its interests, there is an imperative necessity to protect the knowledge and technological parts of these products via intellectual property rights, in order, in this way to once again lengthen the time-period necessary for product imitation, which is permanently becoming shorter, and to amortise the increasing expenditure on R&D.
> (Seiler 1999, our translation; cf. Chapter 1; Jessop 2003; Nuss 2002).

In most industrialised countries, intellectual property had already been extensively protected before the coming into force of the TRIPS Agreement in 1995. Patents, copyrights and rights on trademarks, industrial designs or geographical indications (e.g. "Champagne") guaranteed a high level of intellectual property protection. On the international scale, the protection of intellectual property was organised by the WIPO, an organisation which had been founded in 1970 and which acted under the umbrella of the UN since 1974. However, the agreements administered by the WIPO, among others, the Paris Convention on the protection of industrial property and the Berne Convention on the protection of literary and artistic works, were of a sectoral nature. Furthermore, they were not generally binding, but covered different groups of participants.[1] Above all, the WIPO had no sanctioning mechanism which would have made it possible to prosecute a claim for intellectual property protection internationally. From the point of view of Northern business, this became a problem the more the knowledge-intensity of production, as well as its internationalisation, progressed. In the course of these developments, the markets and genetic resources of developing and threshold countries gained importance, where the protection of intellectual property was far less extensive than in northern countries:

> In most developing countries, IP regimes were geared towards supporting national economic development, and therefore offered low levels

of IP protection with weak enforcement mechanisms. Western-based MNEs [Multinational Enterprises, the authors] began complaining about the loss of hundreds of billions of dollars every year to piracy in developing countries.

(El-Said/El-Said 2005)

It was against this background that the interest of powerful economic forces in establishing internationally enforceable IPRs increased.

However, the institutionalisation of strong IPRs on the international scale did not simply follow the demands of Northern business. On the contrary, it was a contested process, whose result was in no way predetermined. Even in the 1970s, it had been an open question who would gain the power of definition over the subject-matter of IPRs: the Group of 77 had succeeded in placing intellectual property rights on the international political agenda and discussing them in the context of the problems of development. The existing IP protection was criticised as a tool of protectionism which prevented the developing countries from closing the technological gap between themselves and the industrial countries, and which, therefore, reinforced the unequal development of North and South. With the support of the UNCTAD (United Nations Conference on Trade and Development), the Southern countries initiated a process for the revision of the Paris Convention on the protection of industrial property. This failed, however, due to the irreconcilability of the positions of the developing and the industrial countries (see May 2000: 83ff.). Against the background of this failure and the rising demands for stronger international IPRs in the course of the post-Fordist transformation, the perception of the problem shifted: the development policy dimensions of the protection of intellectual property moved into the background behind the question of legal security for knowledge-intensive enterprises, and the protection of intellectual property was increasingly regarded as a decisive condition for the valorisation of capital. In other words, the discursive claims were staked anew: a "universalising discourse of knowledge as property" evolved, which delegitimised the competing forms of the conceptualisation of knowledge as they had been pushed forward, for example by the governments of developing countries in the 1970s (ibid.: 85). The issue of intellectual property protection which Southern governments had tried to subordinate under development goals was (again) framed by "mercantilist policy ends" (May/Sell 2006: 204).

During the first half of the 1980s, Northern governments succeeded in establishing the protection of intellectual property as a subject of the GATT negotiations. In doing so, they acted in the interest of their influential information technology, pharmaceutical and seed industries. If there was resistance on the part of the developing countries, this was broken with bilateral negotiations and the threat of imposing penal duties or of withdrawing trade facilities. From the beginning of the 1990s then, the issue was no longer that of whether an agreement on the protection of intellectual property would be reached in the negotiations under the Uruguay Round of the GATT, but only, as Drahos puts it, of

> how far an agreement on intellectual property would deviate from the blueprint that had been provided to negotiators in 1988 by Pfizer, IBM, DuPont and other members of the international business community in the form of a draft proposal entitled *Basic Framework of GATT Provisions on Intellectual Property: Statement of Views of the European, Japanese and United States Business Communities*.
> (Drahos 2001: 9; cf. Drahos/Braithwaite 2003; May/Sell 2006: 161ff.)

The institutionalisation of the protection of intellectual property within the WTO can be judged as being quite paradoxical: "It is an aberration that TRIPS is located in a trade organisation whose main functions are supposed to be the promotion of trade liberalisation and conditions of market competition, whilst TRIPS is protectionist and curbs competition" (Khor 2001: 8).[2] However – and this was decisive for the "forum-shifting" (Drahos 2001: 5) from the WIPO to the WTO – the latter has the advantage over the former from the point of view of the dominant forces in that it not only widens the geographical scope of IPRs but also possesses the means to control their implementation and, in the form of the dispute settlement body, to enforce their compliance. In addition, it offers the opportunity to use trade issues as leverage to establish high IPR standards where they have not existed before. May and Sell summarise the features of the TRIPS Agreement compared with the weaker regime of the WIPO as follows:

> (1) to bring all members of the WTO under the same set of principles and minimum standards for the recognition and protection of IPRs; (2) to give this governance regime "teeth" by applying the WTO's dispute settlement mechanism to any international disputes regarding the undertakings within TRIPs; and (3) by linking IPRs to the wider issues of international trade at the WTO, to make significant inroads into the hitherto sovereign ability of countries to establish, govern, and regulate intellectual property in response to perceived national political economic priorities.
> (May/Sell 2006: 175; cf. Byström/Einarsson 2001; Correa 2000; Seiler 2000)

The TRIPS Agreement was a victory of dominant economic and political forces from Northern countries. However, with its establishment, conflicts over the international standards of the protection of intellectual property did not come to an end. This is largely due to four tensions and contradictions which are inherent in the concept of "intellectual property" in general and in the TRIPS Agreement in particular. The *first* contradiction affects the producers of technological knowledge themselves. The more rigid the protection of intellectual property, the more difficult it is for research to build on patented discoveries: private or public research institutions which attempt to develop new knowledge or products are forced to first try to obtain licenses from firms which possess the patents for the products and processes needed for research. This is not infrequently beyond the financial capacities of the institutions involved and therefore can block the research plans or cause high transaction costs. Of course, the disadvantages which result from this contradiction do not affect all producers of technological knowledge equally, but are divided unequally along several conflict lines: South vs North, public vs private, small enterprises vs big corporations and so on. Thus, IPRs may support knowledge monopolies and actually act to hinder precisely that which they are said to promote: socially useful innovations.

> Patents on genes, for instance, restrict their use as tools to identify possible therapeutic molecules and therapies. Access to these tools, and hence progress of science, may be slowed down, particularly in developing countries and in public research institutions, due to the need to obtain multiple licences and the escalation of research costs from license fees.
>
> (Correa/Musungu 2002: 19f.)[3]

A *second* contradiction lies in the fact that, through the strengthening of intellectual property rights, the advantages of achievements which more than in other spheres are the result of social processes are privatised. The private appropriation of the means and results of a socialised production is one of the constitutive characteristics of capitalism, but in the latter's "knowledge society" phase it becomes of particular importance. As we saw in Chapter 1, the production of knowledge is a highly socialised process, which makes it difficult to allocate the parts of an intellectual achievement to particular actors. "The increasing socialisation of knowledge production in networked economies makes it hard to distinguish legally between the intellectual property of different firms – let alone the individual knowledge workers – as a basis for allocating the returns to innovation" (Jessop 2003: 105). Within the context of biodiversity, this problem is illustrated particularly in the issue of "traditional knowledge": for generations, local and indigenous communities have contributed to the conservation and further development of biological diversity. The knowledge they have accumulated in this process is essentially collective and thus cannot simply be subordinated to a regime of private IPRs. The TRIPS Agreement ignores this fact. It strengthens the protection of private property which is "scientifically" achieved by individual actors and does not have a concept of "traditional" collective forms of generating and using knowledge or, to put it more generally, of the social character of knowledge generation. Consequently, it does not recognise, let alone protect these forms. There is an "inherent mismatch between the protection that was created for finite, inanimate objects coming out of industrial activity, and the flowing, mutable and variable properties of biological materials and associated indigenous knowledge" (Sahai, cited in May/Sell 2006: 196f.; cf. Hoering 2002). The universalisation of individualised private IPRs under the TRIPS Agreement increasingly jeopardises collective practices of knowledge generation. It strengthens the rights of private firms which use traditional knowledge as a key with which to access genetic resources and their commercial valorisation. As a result, indigenous communities may find themselves in a situation where their own practices of using genetic resources are restricted because private firms are granted property titles for an "invention" which is essentially based on the very knowledge and practices of these communities (see May/Sell 2006: 194ff.). Thus, the global regime of individualised private IPRs, as it is institutionalised in the TRIPS Agreement, largely builds upon collective practices and at the same time threatens them in their existence. In this way, it is in danger of undermining, in the long term, the conservation of biological diversity and thus its own foundations (see Delgado Ramos 2001: 482).

Third, besides strengthening the asymmetric relationships between different groups of *producers*, a rigid protection of IPRs as institutionalised in the TRIPS Agreement also disadvantages certain groups of *users* of knowledge and technology. On a global scale, these are the developing countries. Because of their often less-developed infrastructure for research and development compared to the industrial countries – all developing countries together account for only 4 per cent of world expenditure for research and development (Correa 2001) – they are dependent on technology transfer from the North. Strong IPRs make this transfer difficult and expensive, especially from the point of view of the least-developed countries (May/Sell 2006: 170). Furthermore, they threaten to undermine their access to medicine, their opportunities for the production of generica or their food security.

A *fourth* area of tension is marked by the relationship between the TRIPS Agreement and other institutions which regulate access to genetic resources, above all between the TRIPS Agreement and the CBD. The latter propagates the protection of biodiversity through its commercial use[4] and proves, in this respect, its compatibility to the former. However, there are a number of regulations in both agreements which, at least in their implementation, could come into conflict with one another: whereas the TRIPS provisions on patents, as well as on plant and animal variety protection, strengthen the ownership rights of individuals, the CBD provides for the protection of (collective) traditional knowledge and practices, for the protection and the sustainable use of genetic resources, for the "national sovereignty" over these, as well as for a sharing of benefits which arise from their commercialisation and for a technology transfer to Southern countries (cf. Chapter 2; CIEL/WWF 2001; Plahe/Nyland 2003: 33f.; Thomas 2002).

These inherent tensions and contradictions of the intellectual property issue in general and the TRIPS Agreement in particular have become more manifest since the late 1990s when Southern governments as well as NGOs, social movements and indigenous communities began to articulate their interests more emphatically. The result is a politicisation of the TRIPS Agreement. This is what we shall turn to now.[5]

4.2 Intellectual property rights and development: politicising the TRIPS Agreement

There are several factors which have contributed to the politicisation of the TRIPS Agreement. The *first* one is the review process of the controversial paragraph 3(b) of Article 27 of the Agreement which began in 1999. Article 27 requires countries to make patents available for any product or process which meets the criteria of novelty, inventiveness and industrial applicability. Exceptions to this rule which concern living material are stipulated in 27.3(b). They can be made for "plants and animals other than micro-organisms, and essentially biological processes for the production of plants or animals other than non-biological and microbiological processes". According to this, micro-organisms and non-biological and microbiological processes must be patented. Furthermore, plant varieties must be protected "either by patents or by an effective *sui generis* system or by any combination thereof".

At first sight, the provisions of Article 27.3(b) offer national governments significant leeway. They lack, for example, a clear definition of the term "micro-organism" (see Dutfield 2001) and thus seem to allow more than just one interpretation of it. They also leave open what is to be understood by an "effective" *sui generis* system for the protection of plant varieties so that national governments seem to have the possibility of shaping such a system according to their own needs. This has led even critical academics like Carlos Correa to argue that "How WTO members use the flexibility they have to implement the Agreement's obligations is a matter of policy decision" (Correa 2000: 97). With reference to the patenting of living material, Correa writes, "Nothing in the Agreement obliges Members to consider that substances existing in nature, biological or not, are patentable, even if isolated and claimed in a purified form" (ibid.: 228). This interpretation is in danger, however, of detracting from the really existing power asymmetries which counteract the formally existing room to manoeuvre. It cannot be denied that the TRIPS Agreement does not oblige its members to patent living material, but as long as it also does not oblige them to *exempt* living material from patenting, weaker actors from developing countries lack an effective means of resisting the demand for patents on life forms in bilateral negotiations with more powerful actors from Northern countries. And as far as the *sui generis* protection of plant varieties is concerned, representatives of the industrial countries have emphasised that they see such a system in the Convention for the Protection of New Varieties of Plants (UPOV) in the version of 1991.[6] This strengthens the rights of plant

breeders – that is in fact, the Northern seed corporations – vis-à-vis those of
the farmers. The latter are not allowed to exchange among themselves seed,
retained at the time of harvest, which belongs to a protected plant variety,
for the purpose of breeding and sowing. That this is a significant restriction
becomes clear if one takes into account that the exchange of seed in many
developing countries is an essential basis for food security and for the conservation and further development of biological diversity.

Its economic, social and environmental implications have made Article
27.3(b) "arguably the single most contentious element of the WTO agreements" (Thomas 2002: 187). Therefore, in the course of its review, government representatives from the South have insisted on clarifications and
amendments which would enable them to, in actual fact, take advantage of
the exceptions offered by it. They consider such substantial revisions also
necessary in order to harmonise the TRIPS Agreement with other international systems of regulations, above all with the CBD. Thus, they demand,
for example, the inclusion in the TRIPS Agreement regulations of the disclosure of the origin of genetic resources used in an invention, of prior
informed consent and of benefit-sharing. Such regulations would enable
them to monitor whether or not a patent was granted in a legally correct
manner or if the invention the patent was granted for is based on biopiracy.
The furthest-reaching and most substantial proposal stems from the "African Group", a group of African developing countries, which favours a general prohibition on the patenting of life.[7] Even if such a demand has no
chance of being anchored in the TRIPS Agreement, it does not remain
without effect. According to Hepburn, it not only influenced the debate in
the TRIPS Council, "but also resonated with the concerns of campaign
groups and the media, and helped raise awareness amongst a wider public"
(Hepburn 2002; cf. GRAIN 2000: 8).

The *second* reason for the politicisation of the TRIPS Agreement is the fact
that the period within which many developing countries should have
implemented the TRIPS Agreement ended on 31 December 1999.[8] Implementation can be accompanied by domestic political conflicts which give
rise to processes of interest formation and articulation. When the TRIPS
Agreement was negotiated internationally, the national constellation of
interests in many developing countries was less clear than in the advanced
capitalist countries, where strong scientific and economic forces, stemming
mainly from the seed, software and life sciences industries, were in favour of
a tightening of the protection of intellectual property on an international
scale (even if there were also economic groups and sectors from whose point
of view this was less beneficial or even detrimental). By contrast, many
developing countries lacked experience in the protection of private intellectual property rights which the industrial countries had had for a long time,
a fact which was not least due to "very different traditions of thought about
the possibility of property in knowledge" (May/Sell 2006: 209; cf. El-Said/
El-Said 2005). Furthermore, knowledge on the complex IPR issue and on

the possible consequences of an intensified protection of intellectual property was often missing. Finally, there were no societal forces that possessed anything like the power resources of the corporations from the North and that could correspondingly have influenced the negotiation positions of their governments. The necessity of enforcing the TRIPS Agreement domestically might have changed this situation. Now became more obvious the ways in which the Agreement and its dominant interpretation actually strengthened Northern capital's freedom to act and at the same time restricted the practices not only of indigenous communities but also of Southern research institutions, state apparatuses and enterprises which were interested in developing a national knowledge-based industry. Thus, together with the review of Article 27.3(b), the approaching end of the implementation period might have had the effect of strengthening protest against tight IPRs and developing alternative knowledge within Southern countries and, consequently, speeding up the formation of interests and the positioning of the Southern governments in the international negotiations.

Third, international NGOs, such as the Third World Network, the Canadian ETC Group (Action Group on Erosion, Technology and Concentration) or the Spanish group GRAIN (Genetic Resources Action International), as well as critical political intellectuals such as Vandana Shiva, persistently pointed out the threats contained in the TRIPS Agreement in relation to food security and health provision, especially for the people of the South. Furthermore, they contributed to developing and disseminating alternative knowledge on biological diversity and the protection of traditional practices. As far as the Third World Network is concerned, it also participated in the elaboration of the "African model law" of the Organisation for African Unity (OAU) of 1998, together with African scientific institutes under the leadership of the Scientific, Technical and Research Commission of the OAU (Ekpere 2000; Oh 2000; Kongolo 2001; Egziabher 2002; see also Chapter 3). This law contains provisions on the regulation of access to genetic resources, which are intended to put an end to biopiracy. It takes account of the decisive role of farmers (including the gender-specific aspects of their role) for food security and for the conservation and further development of biological diversity, and it protects their knowledge and strengthens their rights vis-à-vis the breeders' rights. Furthermore, it provides for benefit-sharing and prior informed consent, which must be obtained both from the state and from indigenous and local groups. The model law stays within the framework of the TRIPS Agreement. At the same time, however, it confronts it with a different accentuation: it protects local and indigenous groups against unlawful access to their resources, their knowledge and their technologies – a danger to which they are increasingly subjected due to the internationalisation of Northern IPR standards through the TRIPS Agreement. The law can therefore be used as a basis for national and supranational *sui generis* systems for the protection of plant varieties which in contrast to the UPOV also take into account the interests of subaltern actors. As such, it is an important Southern contribution to the Northern-dominated debate on the protection of intellectual property.[9]

Fourth, the criticism of and resistance to crucial stipulations of the TRIPS Agreement are (implicitly) supported by the developments in other international forums which also deal with conservation and the use of bio-diversity. Among these are the adoption of the International Treaty on Plant Genetic Resources by the FAO in November 2001 (cf. Chapter 3), the passing of the Bonn Guidelines within the framework of the CBD in April 2002 and, most importantly, the negotiations about an international regime on access and benefit-sharing, to be finalised before 2010 (cf. Chapter 2). These developments lend additional legitimacy to many of the claims articulated by Southern governments in the TRIPS Council. Furthermore, Southern countries try to strengthen their position vis-à-vis the North by intensifying their cooperation. This is expressed, for example, in the constitution of the "Like-Minded Group of Megadiverse Countries" (cf. Chapter 2).

However, one has to avoid conceptualising the politicisation of the TRIPS Agreement only as a North–South issue. The constellation of conflicts is far more complex than that. Thus, the cooperation between Southern countries is always superimposed by a structural supply competition: every mega-diverse country is principally interested in the exploitation of its biological diversity, provided that an appropriate share of the profits is guaranteed via benefit-sharing arrangements. Therefore, the megadiverse countries always compete over the issue of who offers the most favourable supply conditions to (Northern) corporations. Besides this contradictory constellation of interests *between* Southern countries, there are conflicts *within* every country, with the result that the "national interests" government representatives articulate in international negotiations are essentially an expression of domestic relationships of power. For example, indigenous communities and small farmers, whose rights are often disregarded by the states they live in, are represented in a very selective manner by their governments at the international level. Their traditional knowledge, which is referred to in nearly every Southern submission to the TRIPS Council in order to under-mine the necessity of a revision of Article 27.3(b), is often perceived under the aspect of "national" development.[10] Furthermore, it seems to be used in an instrumental manner:

> Indigenous peoples' organisations and TK [traditional knowledge, the authors] holders sometimes suspect that the subject is being used by their governments to secure trade advantages that will be of no benefit for them. They see particular irony in a situation in which governments of countries where indigenous peoples are victims of human rights abuses are among those calling for protection of TK as a matter of justice in international trade.
>
> (Bridges Trade BioRes 2002)

The politicisation of the tensions and contradictions which are inherent in the TRIPS Agreement or mark the relationship between the latter and other international conventions, such as the CBD, have had a strong impact on the negotiations in the TRIPS Council. At the Ministerial Conference of the WTO in Doha in 2001, the Council was given the task, "besides other issues", of "examining" the relationship between the CBD and the TRIPS Agreement as well as the problem of traditional knowledge. This extended the mandate of the Council and for the first time a connection between these issues and the revision of Article 27.3(b) of the TRIPS Agreement was made on the part of the WTO. At the Ministerial Conference in Hong Kong, which took place in December 2005, governments acknowledged the need to continue discussions on the CBD–TRIPS relationship. Furthermore, the TRIPS Council was urged "to intensify" the consultation process. Negotiations will include "the possible requirement for the disclosure of origin, a mandated review of Article 27.3(b) on the patenting of plants and animals, and the protection of traditional knowledge" (CBD 2006). Thus, one can observe a shift in the perception of problems in the conflicts over genetic resources: besides the legal security of firms from the agro-business and the life sciences sectors, increasingly, developmental issues are symbolically represented. Actors such as NGOs, indigenous organisations and governments of the megadiverse countries have questioned the definitions of problems of Northern actors and expanded the range of the politically negotiable issues.

Up to now, this has not resulted in a substantial revision of the Agreements' most critical stipulations. However, neither have the Northern governments reached their declared objectives: to limit the review of Article 27.3(b) to questions of implementation, which would have primarily concerned developing countries, and to bring the process to a quick end. The agenda of the TRIPS Council remains controversial. The debate as to what should in fact be negotiated runs through the review of Article 27.3(b) like a red thread. Years after the beginning of the review process and after the Doha Declaration had mandated the TRIPS Council to examine the CBD–TRIPS relationship it is "clear that the differing levels of political ambition have yet to be resolved, with one official saying that 'some of us want to play soccer while the others want to play rugby'" (Bridges Trade BioRes 2006a).

4.3 Scale jumping: towards national and bilateral solutions of the IPR issue?

The politicisation of the TRIPS Agreement and the resulting polarisation of positions in the TRIPS Council have led the governments of industrial countries to consider how to reach their objective of a stronger protection of intellectual property in different ways. One result of this is a certain strategic shift which could be described as double "scale jumping" (Smith

1995). On the one hand, efforts are made to downscale to the national level proposals which government representatives of Southern countries have made with respect to the TRIPS Agreement. On the other hand, there are attempts to negotiate standards of intellectual property protection which are even higher than those of the TRIPS Agreement ("TRIPS-plus standards") in bilateral or regional trade agreements.

The first form of scale jumping can be observed in connection with the controversial issue of the disclosure of origin of the genetic resources and traditional knowledge used in an invention. From the point of view of indigenous communities and government representatives from many developing countries, a disclosure of origin is a means to prevent biopiracy. It would oblige a patent applicant to provide information on the country of origin and on the compliance with the legal requirements of the latter regarding prior informed consent and benefit-sharing. If the applicant did not comply with the disclosure requirement, the patent-granting authority would have to deny or revoke a patent. A disclosure requirement made in this way would not only enhance the transparency of patent granting, it would also make it superfluous for a government to verify, in every individual case, whether or not patents which are granted in other countries on the basis of its own genetic resources, comply with its national legislation. Such individual verifications and possibly following legal proceedings taken to revoke a "bad patent" require a long and costly process which is beyond the financial and juridical capacities of many developing countries. In recent years, therefore, there have been several proposals from Southern governments to search for an international solution to biopiracy, that is to amend the TRIPS Agreement, for example in Article 27.3(b), to include a disclosure requirement.[11]

However, these attempts have largely been blocked by the dominant actors, who argue that preventing the misappropriation or theft of genetic resources is not an issue to be regulated under patent law. Thus, following the US government, "those acts fall outside the purview of the TRIPS Agreement and are appropriately the domain of a separate regulatory system".[12] Similarly, according to the position of the European Union, a disclosure requirement is neither an additional nor a substantial criterion for patentability. The disregarding of the requirement, therefore, could not be punished under patent law and, consequently, could not lead to the refusal or withdrawal of a patent. Instead, a disclosure requirement should be "self-standing", that is a system of its own, outside the patent law.[13] Another argument refers to the mechanisms which will guarantee the disclosure of origin and the compliance with national regulations on access and benefit-sharing. As seen above, Southern governments have proposed an international solution within the TRIPS Agreement, which would oblige a patent applicant to provide information on the origin of the genetic resource used in an invention. A national patent authority would be obliged to verify this information. For the US government, such a system would be "a legal and administrative nightmare for all involved" (WTO 2000b: 5). From its point of view, the problem is not a "lack of safeguards in the TRIPS context", as stated by the governments of Brazil, India and other countries, but "the lack of clearly defined national systems directly regulating the use of genetic resources, particularly in the context of access and benefit-sharing (ABS) systems" (WTO 2006e: 2). The already cited position of the European Union, in principle, supports this view: a "sound and effective *national legislation* in the countries providing genetic resources" (emphasis in the original) is the "main legal instrument" of benefit-sharing (WTO 2001: 5). The European Union leaves it to the countries to verify compliance with their national regulations as well as the legality of patents individually.

Thus, whereas far-reaching minimum standards for IPRs have been institutionalised internationally and have strengthened the position of knowledge-based economic sectors, the upscaling of stipulations which would enhance the possibility of Southern actors to control what happens to the genetic resources of their countries has been, up to now, successfully prevented by dominant forces from the North. By defining them as matters of national legislation, governments from the industrialised countries try to keep the claims of Southern governments away from the international level and to downscale them to the national terrain of each WTO member. This affects not only the transparency of patent granting and the possibility of preventing or revoking "bad patents", but also the national regulations themselves, insofar as they may be developed in the shadow of bilateral agreements and the power asymmetries inscribed therein. This is the second form of scale jumping with which Northern governments attempt to circumvent the impasse the negotiations on the TRIPS terrain have got into.

Bilateral agreements are increasingly used, especially by the USA and the European Union, in order to force developing countries to do away with the exemptions from patentability allowed by Article 27.3(b) and to implement substantial stipulations for the protection of intellectual property which go beyond those laid down in the TRIPS Agreement. Even more so than in the negotiations on multilateral terrains, they offer the Northern governments the opportunity to exploit bilateral power asymmetries and the structural supply competition of the biodiversity countries. The US government states this quite openly: "Where genetic resources or traditional knowledge can be obtained from a number of sources, of course, the party seeking access likely will seek the resources or knowledge from the territory that provides the most favourable conditions" (WTO 1999b: 5). Bilateral agreements on the protection of intellectual property are often made via the loophole of aid agreements or trade and investment contracts (GRAIN 2001c; cf. CIPR 2002b: 180 f.; Correa 2004; Hepburn 2002; Lasén Díaz 2005). These then include, for example, the obligation not to exempt plants and animals from patentability, to guarantee the "highest international standards" for the protection of intellectual property or to implement the 1991 version of the UPOV, which strengthens the breeders' rights vis-à-vis the farmers', as *sui generis* protection for plant varieties. They also often provide for their own arbitration mechanisms. GRAIN (2001a: 6) therefore speaks of a "tunnel vision toward one global patent standard".

The increasing importance of bilateral agreements seems to be a major trend in international trade politics (WTO 2003: 26ff.). As such, it is a reflection of the resistance which Northern governments and business interests have been confronted with on the WTO terrain. "Having failed to advance their agenda in the post-1995 multilateral system, industrial countries are now seeking to reverse the centre of gravity away from the WTO" (El-Said/El-Said 2005). The failure of the Ministerial Conferences in Seattle 1999 and Cancún 2003, as well as the suspension of the Doha Round negotiations in the summer of 2006, underline this tendency. However, one has to be careful not to see a zero-sum-game between bilateralism and multilateralism at work here (Görg/Wissen 2003). At least two factors contradict this line of reasoning: first, even if it is contested, the TRIPS Agreement has in no way become meaningless. By institutionalising strong minimum standards of intellectual property protection on an international scale, it rather provides a solid basis for negotiating higher standards bilaterally. Second, the conflicts on one multilateral terrain, the TRIPS Agreement, have raised the status of another, the World Intellectual Property Organization, that is there is a certain forum-shifting back to the WIPO, which, however, has also resulted in the politicisation of this rather "technical" organisation. This can be seen in recent developments within the WIPO: the launching of a "Patent Agenda", which aims at harmonising the regulations of the protection of intellectual property internationally, that is internationalising the standards that are valid in the leading industrial countries; the negotiations within the "Intergovernmental Committee on Intellectual Property and Genetic Resources, Traditional Knowledge and Folklore" (IGC), where subaltern actors struggle for an institutionalisation of their rights; and finally, the initiative to establish a "Development Agenda" which was launched by the governments of Argentina and Brazil. The "resurgence" of the WIPO, which is indicated by these developments, is the subject of the following sections.

4.4 Forum-shifting: imposing higher IPR standards through WIPO's Patent Agenda?

The Patent Agenda was announced in August 2001 by the WIPO Secretary General and led, one year later, to a memorandum on the further development of the international patent system (WIPO 2002). Basically, it is concerned with the international harmonisation of the diverging national regulations on the protection of intellectual property. The Patent Agenda is based on three pillars: the Patent Law Treaty, the reform of the Patent Cooperation Treaty and the creation of a Substantive Patent Law Treaty (on the following see Correa/Musungu (2002) and GRAIN (2002b)). The *Patent*

Law Treaty was signed in June 2000. It came into force in April 2005 after it had been ratified by ten states. Its purpose is to harmonise internationally the procedure of applying for, and granting, patents. Accordingly, it contains a number of formal stipulations concerning, for example, the form, the contents or the point of time of a patent application. The applicant is required to provide only "an express or implicit indication to the effect that the elements [received by the patent office] are *intended* to be an application" and "a part which on the face of it *appears* to be a description" (Art. 5(1) (ii) and (iii) of the Patent Law Treaty, quoted and emphasised by Correa/Musungu 2002: 6). This regulation allows, according to Correa and Musungu, that the rights to an invention be secured at a very early stage, for example on the basis of a hypothesis which has not yet been verified.

The *Patent Cooperation Treaty* is an instrument which makes it easier to have an invention protected internationally. It creates the possibility of an international patent application. This is checked, first of all, in an international search for prior art – conducted by larger national or regional patent offices and at the cost of the applicant. The results of the search are documented in an international search report. The applicant can also apply for an international preliminary examination report, which in contrast to the search report contains a preliminary and non-binding appraisal of the patentability of the invention. The final decision on the granting of a patent is taken by the patent offices in those states in which the invention is to be protected. The Patent Cooperation Treaty has advantages for both the applicants and the national and regional patent offices: for the latter, their work is reduced because they can base their decision on the results of the international search or examination. The former can, on the basis of the search or examination results, better estimate how good their chances are of receiving a patent for their invention. But above all, they have gained time over potential competitors: "A patent application becomes 'claimed territory' before filing at the national level" (GRAIN 2002b: 2). The Patent Cooperation Treaty was finalised in 1970, extended in 1979 and amended in 1984. Since 2000, a new reform process has been underway which is intended primarily to simplify the procedure and to adjust the Patent Cooperation Treaty to the new standards of the Patent Law Treaty. The US government and the governments of other industrial countries are pursuing plans that are even farther reaching: they regard the Patent Cooperation Treaty reform and other reform efforts in the framework of the WIPO, primarily from the perspective of creating, in the long term, possibilities for the granting of a global patent.

The negotiations on the *Substantive Patent Law Treaty* (SPLT) are about establishing substantive patentability standards internationally and thereby going beyond the stipulations determined by the TRIPS Agreement. While the latter lays down minimum standards, the former, according to the governments of leading industrial countries, should establish best practice at the international level (Correa/Musungu 2002; Hepburn 2002). Correa and Musungu, therefore, describe the Substantive Patent Law Treaty as potentially the "most troublesome building-block of the proposed international patent system from the perspective of developing and least developed countries" (Correa/Musungu 2002: 16) because it would remove all the presently existing leeway for national regulations on the protection of intellectual property.[14]

The Patent Agenda can be interpreted as an expression of three problem constellations. The first is the "workload crisis" of the national and regional patent offices. Due to the rising importance of knowledge in the process of the valorisation of capital, the number of patent applications for the protection of intellectual property, and thus the workload of patent offices, have increased significantly (see Chapter 1 and Oldham 2004). The development of an international patent system, it is assumed, would make the examination of patent applications more transparent and avoid the duplication of work tasks, which would lead to an easing of the workload of national and regional patent offices.

Second, the developing countries have emphatically articulated their criticism of the existing system for the protection of intellectual property within the review process of Article 27.3(b) of the TRIPS Agreement. As analysed above, concepts such as benefit-sharing have gained in legitimacy. Against this background, the launching of the Patent Agenda in 2001 can be classified as a type of "counteroffensive" in the interest of dominant actors from the North in order to restore the blemished legitimacy of the patent system as a "public policy tool using the creation and exercise of private rights as a means of promoting the public good" (WIPO 2002: Annex I, p. 4). Because of its expertise, its "technical" character and its narrow mandate, which is limited to providing support for the protection of intellectual property, the WIPO appears to be, like no other, in a position wherein it is authorised to make the protection of intellectual property, both materially and symbolically, a priority once again.

Third, the Patent Agenda is an expression of the efforts of transnational corporations to simplify the procedure for the international recognition of patents, in speeding it up and making it cheaper and thus reducing transaction costs as far as possible, but also – in a substantial sense – in removing exemptions from patentability (see ICC 2002). If the Patent Agenda were successful, the national and regional patent offices would move closer together. A system would come into being which spanned different spatial scales and would guarantee an effective patent protection from the point of view of transnational enterprises. The WIPO, in this case, would get a national and regional "foundation" for the implementation of an international patent law, an advantage which could compensate for the lack of an international sanctioning authority. In addition, the SPLT would exceed the minimum standards for intellectual property protection laid down in the TRIPS Agreement, which would also correspond to the interests of enterprises from knowledge-based economic sectors. The latter, therefore, appear to be paying very close attention to the negotiations within WIPO. They articulate themselves not only indirectly, via their governments, but also directly. In Correa and Musungu (2002), the following description can be found of the behaviour of business representatives and patent lawyers in the SPLT negotiations:

> Curiously, despite their "observer capacity", the referred NGOs participated in the debates on the same footing as governments, making proposals or "reservations", supporting the positions of some governments or being opposed to government positions. There were no NGOs representing the views of consumers or developing countries.
>
> (Correa/Musungu 2002: 17)

It is, above all, the orientation of the SPLT negotiations to the interests of transnational corporations and the weak representation of subaltern interests which leads the critics of the Patent Agenda to make gloomy prophecies. For example, in a paper by GRAIN (2002b: 5), it is stated: "We may even see critics turn around and defend TRIPS, as it may suddenly appear a lesser threat compared to what WIPO comes up with."

4.5 Politicising a "technical" terrain: conflicts about intellectual property, genetic resources and development in the WIPO

The efforts of Northern governments and enterprises to internationally harmonise the standards of intellectual property protection according to their interests, reflect, however, only one side of the resurgence of the WIPO. Recent developments and debates in other WIPO forums indicate that governments of developing countries, NGOs and indigenous communities have managed to put their matters on the agenda of WIPO negotiations, too. One example of this is the setting up of the "Intergovernmental Committee on Intellectual Property and Genetic Resources, Traditional Knowledge and Folklore" (IGC) in 2001. The way in which IPR issues have been addressed here contradicts, to a certain degree, the way this has happened within the framework of the Patent Agenda. For example, a document which was prepared by the WIPO secretariat for the first meeting of the IGC, in order to provide an overview of matters concerning genetic resources, traditional knowledge and folklore, gives an account of discussions which challenge the dominant concept of individualised private IPRs and emphasises the social character of knowledge production:

> The equity of intellectual property rights is discussed not only in the balance between the rights of the creator and society as the user of his creation, but also in the balance of rights between the creator and society as the provider of heritage resources which he utilizes in his

creation. This is the case especially where the provider has conserved the common heritage for generations under *in-situ* conditions, i.e. in the surroundings where the resource developed its distinctive properties.

(WIPO 2001: 4)

Conserving and developing local technologies and products, including plant genetic resources for generations, is referred to as an *informal innovation* because it is not formally recognised as an innovative activity and, therefore, it is not protected by IPRs. It is pointed out that informal innovators now claim rights to intellectual property protection and that they criticise the unequal treatment of formal and informal innovative activity with regard to the protection of intellectual property, which is not objectively justifiable: "The creation of new intellectual property rights for formal innovations in a certain subject matter is seen as contingent upon the creation of cognate rights for informal innovations relating to the same or similar subject matter" (WIPO 2001: 5).

In spite of this quite reflexive outline of the "cultural bias" (Dutfield 2002) of the IPR system, which stood at the beginning of the IGC, the latter's work has not yet produced significantly substantive results. The claim for a legally binding international instrument for the protection of traditional knowledge, as raised by the governments of many developing countries, has been rejected by the representatives of developed countries (see Bridges Trade BioRes 2006c). As the South Centre has pointed out, "historically, the areas of interest to developing countries continue to be characterised by high levels of dialogue with no concrete outcomes" (South Bulletin 2002). As far as the IGC is concerned, this may also be due to the fact that many Southern governments, in contrast to the indigenous communities of their own countries, seem to question the significance of the IGC as a negotiation forum. The influence of the IGC on other WIPO discussions is considered to be quite low. Furthermore, there are concerns

> that a debate in the IGC would distract from or pre-empt a decision by the TRIPs Council on a proposal by a group of developing countries, calling for disclosure requirements and evidence of prior informed consent and benefit sharing related to genetic resources and traditional knowledge in patent applications.
>
> (Bridges Trade BioRes 2004)

Thus, the reflexivity of discussions seems to be closely related to the marginalisation of the forum where the discussions take place.

Another and seemingly more powerful attempt to politicise WIPO is the proposal to establish a "Development Agenda" (WIPO 2004). It was submitted to the WIPO in August 2004 by the governments of Argentina and Brazil, but rapidly found the support of the governments of other developing countries (WIPO 2005: Annex, p. 2). Starting from the crucial significance of technological innovation, science and creative activity for social progress and welfare, the proposal complains about a "knowledge gap" between wealthy and poor nations and reflects on the role which IPRs play in this respect. It criticises WIPO's present efforts at raising the patent protection standards and making them mandatory for all countries, irrespective of their levels of development. Instead it emphasises the "need to integrate the 'development dimension' into policy making on intellectual property protection" in order to create a balance between users and producers of knowledge. The paper proposes a "high-level declaration on intellectual property and development" to be adopted, for example, by the General Assembly of WIPO. In the face of "the inability of existing IP agreements and treaties to promote a real transfer of technology to developing countries and LDCs" it calls for a "Treaty on Access to Knowledge and Technology" as well as an inclusion of clear provisions on the transfer of technology in the treaties which are currently under negotiation in WIPO. Not least, it suggests a strengthening of civil society's participation in WIPO's activities.

The WIPO General Assembly welcomed the proposal in autumn 2004 and decided to examine it in "inter-sessional intergovernmental meetings". One year later the General Assembly established a "Provisional Committee" to continue discussions on the Development Agenda. Up to now, the debates have produced only limited results. Powerful forces deny the necessity of a Development Agenda for WIPO at all. "Simply put", a paper of the US government puts it, "WIPO already has had a robust 'development agenda' in all of its work for a long time" (WIPO 2005: Annex, p. 2). The statement of a US delegate goes even further: "We support WIPO. We would not want to change WIPO in a direction that would diminish that support" (IP-Watch 2005: 2). However, the critics of the proposal did not manage to suppress the discussion on it or to pass the development issue on to a subsidiary WIPO body such as the "Permanent Committee on Cooperation for Development Related to Intellectual Property". Southern governments have successfully resisted such attempts and demanded an integration of development aspects into all WIPO activities (ICTSD 2005a).

Within the NGO community, the idea of a Development Agenda has met with strong and positive resonance. In the "Geneva Declaration on the Future of the World Intellectual Property Organization" (TWN 2004), which was launched in September 2004, 25 NGOs welcomed the paper as "the first real opportunity to debate the future of WIPO". According to the signatories of the declaration, the WIPO had, for a long time, been responding primarily to narrow business concerns. Against this background, the proposal of a Development Agenda is seen as "a long overdue and much needed first step toward a new WIPO mission and work program". It seems to have driven the interest of developmental and consumer-oriented NGOs in WIPO and their efforts to engage themselves in pressing for more transparency and participation within the organisation's activities (see, for example de Paranaguá Moniz *et al.* 2005 and ICTSD 2005b).

The strong and controversial reactions may be due to the fundamental character of the proposal, the condensation of criticism of the WIPO it contains and the translation of this criticism into a reasonable demand: the establishment of a Development Agenda. The proposal is not a contribution to ongoing "technical" discussions on intellectual property protection within WIPO, but tries to reframe the entire debate. The term "Development Agenda" alone implies a criticism of the ongoing discussions in WIPO. It refers to and at the same time dissociates itself from the "Patent Agenda". Furthermore, it creates a link to the "Doha Development Agenda", which was adopted by the WTO Ministerial Conference in 2001 and strengthened the notion of development within the WTO, at least symbolically. Until recently, the task and the character of the WIPO had been considered to be primarily "non-political". The organisation itself had "consistently sought to reinforce the perception that it is a highly technical body to keep away most of the political and economic debate about IPRs" (Correa/Musungu 2002: 4). As such, the WIPO gained in importance from the point of view of Northern business and governments as soon as the tensions and contradictions of intellectual property protection became politicised within the WTO by Southern governments, indigenous communities and NGOs. Pursuing the further tightening of IPR standards in WIPO seemed to be a means for Northern actors to escape the impasse the TRIPS process was caught in. For WIPO itself, this forum-shifting offered an opportunity to gain lost ground vis-à-vis its institutional competitor, the TRIPS Agreement. However, the strong reactions which the proposal of a Development Agenda has provoked, both in favour and against, show that the politicisation of the IPR issue has reached the WIPO, too.

4.6 Contested terrains: summary and conclusions

The examination of the WIPO and the TRIPS Agreement illustrates the momentum which characterises the conflicts over intellectual property rights in the appropriation and valorisation of genetic resources. Both institutions are increasingly politicised by Southern governments, indigenous groups, social movements and NGOs, with the result that the positions of those groups have gained "representational strength" (Jenson 1989) in an environment which has traditionally been dominated by the perceptions and interests of Northern governments and business. Where in the past, the latter had been able to ignore questions of traditional knowledge or benefit-sharing, they must now at least take a position on these issues. The time-factor plays an important role here: while the industrial countries at the conclusion of the TRIPS Agreement had already been familiar with the complex subject matter of IP protection for a long time, many developing countries lacked the necessary experience and expertise. A process of position-finding and organising – partly supported by the expertise provided by NGOs – was therefore necessary before the governments of Southern countries began to articulate themselves perceivably. Further factors which support the politicisation process are the outcomes of the negotiations on other international terrains such as the CBD and the FAO, the attempts of Southern governments to strengthen their negotiation position by intensifying their cooperation and the fact that developmental and consumer-interest NGOs emphatically articulate their demands, especially for the prohibition of patents on living materials. Events such as the protests in Seattle at the end of 1999 or in Cancún in 2003 also play an important role: they have placed the developmental, social and environmental consequences of WTO policies in the public light and strengthened the legitimacy of "Southern" concerns. Even if this has not changed anything in the fundamental positions in the TRIPS negotiations, the *negotiation context* has changed: the review process of Article 27.3(b) of the TRIPS Agreement has increasingly been set under legitimation pressure.

Until now, the politicising of the TRIPS Agreement and the WIPO has primarily led to symbolic shifts in the debate on genetic resources: the definitional sovereignty of powerful Northern forces over what is negotiable and what is not has been questioned. In the frame of the TRIPS Agreement, they were not able to restrict the review of Article 27 to mere implementation issues. Instead, they saw themselves confronted with the demand of Southern governments for substantial revisions. As a consequence, the subject of the review process remains continually contested. Similarly, in the WIPO, governments of developing countries are increasingly reluctant to negotiate about an international high-level harmonisation of IPRs. By launching the proposal of a Development Agenda, they have called for a redirection of the entire system of intellectual property protection. Thus, what are at stake in both organisations are not only controversial issues to be negotiated within largely accepted institutional frameworks, but also the shape of the institutional terrains themselves.

In the conflicts over what should actually be negotiated in the review of Article 27.3(b), the ambivalence of the TRIPS Agreement, even from the perspective of the industrial countries is revealed: on the one hand, it has contributed to the establishment of minimum standards for intellectual property protection and has improved their stability. On the other hand, this was only possible by shifting the IPR issue onto the contested terrain of the WTO. The improved protection of intellectual property was thus paid for with the politicising of the IPR issue, which proved increasingly difficult to deal with in the framework of the TRIPS Agreement. In this context, the WIPO, which had been institutionally weakened by the establishment of an agreement on intellectual property protection within the WTO, gained importance again. A forum-shifting took place in the opposite direction to that of the 1980s and 1990s: the establishment of important negotiations on the protection of intellectual property in WIPO, the most obvious expression of which is the Patent Agenda. One can interpret this process as an attempt to "re-technicalise" and, at the same time, further develop the IPR issue in the direction of a substantial international patent law which abolishes the exemptions from patentability still formally allowed by the TRIPS Agreement. Driving forces are the governments and knowledge-based industries from the industrial countries which seek to free themselves from the dilemma in which the review of Article 27.3(b) finds itself. However, as the recent conflicts over a Development Agenda for the WIPO have shown, the forum-shifting did not simply work in the interest of its driving forces. By contrast, Southern governments and NGOs, which have been sensitised to the consequences of a high-level intellectual property protection by the TRIPS Agreement, seem to have succeeded in politicising the "technical" terrain of WIPO, too.

The repeated forum-shifting shows how far away the international IPR regime is from hegemonic forms of conflict regulation. There is no international institution which is accepted to a similar degree by both dominant and subaltern actors as a terrain for the settlement of conflicts. The conflict terrains themselves are the subject of the disputes. The result of this is that, above all, the dominant forces repeatedly attempt to shift the IPR issue onto that terrain on which the chances of institutionalising their interests currently appear to be best.

From a development perspective, a major threat lies in the effort to establish TRIPS-plus standards of intellectual property protection via bilateral trade agreements. The latter have significantly increased in number recently. For those forces which are interested in tightening intellectual property protection internationally, they offer a way out of the impasse which the TRIPS negotiations have got into and which the Patent Agenda of the WIPO seems to get into, too. In contrast to a forum-shifting from one international organisation to the other, bilateral agreements are much less spectacular. They do not offer a stage to (collectively) politicise the contradictions of North–South relations. Instead, they constitute a realm where bilateral power asymmetries can be fully played out. However, it would be too simple to argue for a "disassembly of multilateral economic order" based on the increasing number of bilateral trade agreements, as for example Dieter (2003) does. More probable is an overlapping of multi-lateralism and bilateralism (see Görg/Wissen 2003). This is especially due to two specific elements of the TRIPS Agreement: first, the conceptual uncertainties and the exceptions from patentability in Article 27.3(b), and second, the fact that the TRIPS Agreement formulates minimum standards but provides no upper limits for the protection of intellectual property. The first element involves the necessity of bilateral processes of clarification when conflicts arise as a result of different interpretations of Article 27.3(b) or of different national regulations which, nevertheless, all comply with the TRIPS Agreement. The clarification can take place in bilateral negotiations or within the framework of the WTO's dispute settlement body. In any case, power asymmetries come into play.[15] The second element comprises the possibility of bilaterally negotiating higher IPR standards without violating the regulations of the TRIPS Agreement. "TRIPS standards will be a floor from which further bilateral, regional and multilateral standard-setting exercise will proceed, a floor with no ceiling above" (Drahos 2001: 10).

The politicisation of the TRIPS Agreement and the WIPO are likely to lead to the further gaining in importance of bilateral strategies for the establishment of TRIPS-plus standards. A danger for multilateralism results from this if the latter – as in regime theory – is regarded primarily under the aspect of cooperative conflict solution. However, proceeding from the assumption that power relationships and bilateral power asymmetries are always inscribed in international agreements leads to a different conclusion: multilateralism is not simply a counterpart to bilateralism, which is seen to suffer if and when the latter gains strength. There is no zero-sum-game between the two. By contrast, multilateralism may form a solid foundation on which bilateralism can unfold its influence. This can be learnt from the TRIPS Agreement: by allowing exceptions to patentability but not proscribing them, and by setting minimum standards for intellectual property protection but setting no upper limit to them, it prepares the field for bilateral *power bargaining*. The TRIPS Agreement is not only the result, but also the precondition and medium for the unfolding of bilateral power asymmetries. Multilateralism, in other words, forms a powerful vehicle which helps bilateralism to establish itself.

The question remains to what extent indigenous communities, small farmers and other less powerful social groups can take advantage of the politicisation of the intellectual property issue analysed in this chapter, that is: does the contradictory constellation offer opportunities for local groups to challenge the unequal relationships of power which shape their living conditions and to maintain or recover control over the latter? This is especially important if one takes into account that struggling internationally against the illegitimate appropriation of genetic resources and traditional knowledge for many Southern governments is not necessarily an end in itself but may also be a means of strengthening their bargaining position in areas such as agriculture and services, which are backed by stronger coalitions of social forces domestically. This seems to apply, for example, to Brazil and India and constitutes an important difference between these countries, on the one hand, and many African countries, on the other (Kaiser 2006). For assessing the opportunities of local control over genetic resources, there is a need to not only analyse the unequal relationships between North and South and among Southern countries, but also analyse those that exist within each country.[16] This is what we shall turn to know, when we exemplarily examine the domestic relationships of power with respect to genetic resources in the megadiverse country Mexico.

5 The relevance of the national and the local

The disputes over a valorisation paradigm in Mexico and Chiapas

To what extent do international political processes represent a political and institutional framework for the treatment of biological diversity in specific national and local contexts? Using a case study conducted in Mexico, and within it at the local level in the state of Chiapas, this chapter explores this question, and three implied subquestions. *First*, are international policies translated relatively directly into national regulations or do they encounter specific interests, relationships of forces, political and institutional conditions and socio-economic dynamics at the national level and if so, are they modified by these? The question of implementation is, as we have already seen, of central importance, especially for a framework agreement such as the CBD (Convention on Biological Diversity). The forms of intervention of different levels are manifold. We shall differentiate here between four such forms: (a) legal regulations, which in a certain sense create "corridors" in which certain confrontations take place, (b) the forms of the constitution of problems and proposals for dealing with them, (c) the ability of certain actors to assert their authority and (d) structural conditions.

Second, it must be examined empirically to what extent in Mexico a "coherent" national biodiversity policy is being formulated, as has been demanded repeatedly by national and international actors. If this is not the case, what are the main reasons for this?

Third, what role is played by the specific place, which is bound into spaces in a multitude of ways? There exist competing ideas and strategies on how to deal with the places, that is the natural living conditions and societal relationships to be found there. Here, too, there are specific relationships of forces which cannot simply be "derived" from the national ones.

The choice of Mexico, and Chiapas, for the case study, was arrived at for several reasons. Mexico is, for one thing, a so-called megadiverse country, and it is also geographically and political-institutionally closely tied to the major "demand country", the USA, namely within the North American Free Trade Agreement (NAFTA). Moreover, questions concerning the appropriation of biological diversity have enjoyed a high level of importance in both expert and public discussion since the end of the 1990s. For the purposes of research this latter fact means that the perspectives and interests of individual actors and also the lines of conflict have been clearly articulated. Mexico is also interesting with regard to the question of the "democratic formation of biodiversity policy". The "question of democracy" has been emphatically discussed since the 1994 uprising of the Zapatista liberation army (*Ejército Zapatista de Liberación Nacional*; EZLN) and its social basis. Particularly in the state of Chiapas in the south-east of Mexico, which is a hot spot as far as biodiversity is concerned and at the same time one of the country's poorest regions, the relationship of forces has shifted as a result of the uprising. How does this change the conditions of democratic politics and thus also of the appropriation of nature? Finally, Mexico was also chosen because the project group already had good contacts there, which meant better access to the subject of the research.[1]

From the outset, this case study was chosen not as a representative model but rather, due to its particularities compared to other countries. In other countries the conditions look partially quite different. In addition, it is only recently that experience with the formulation of a national biodiversity policy has been gained, that is with the development of a political-institutional framework for the appropriation and conservation of biological diversity, and this process has mainly been initiated by international politics. The study also represents a very topical extract from an extremely dynamic political field in which as yet no clear structures have formed, either in Mexico or in other countries and regions. Even if its results can therefore hardly be generalised, the case study nevertheless imparts central insights into post-Fordist relationships with nature and the internationalisation of the state.

First, the most recent development in Mexico and Chiapas will be outlined briefly. Second, different positions will be identified which play a role in the formulation and implementation of a Mexican biodiversity policy. This is a snapshot, since the problems, interests, alliances and political proposals shift continually. Finally, the controversial development of a Mexican biodiversity policy will be analysed and "concretised" for the state of Chiapas.

5.1 A megadiverse country in the process of transformation into a competition state

Mexico is a so-called megadiverse country with ten vegetation zones and two centres of biological diversity: one in the arid North and one in the neotropical South. Of the 250,000 known plant species worldwide, 22,000 to 26,000 are to be found in Mexico of which 40 per cent are endemic, that is they only exist in Mexico (Mittermeier/Goettsch Mittermeier 1992: 69; Delgadillo Macías 1994). Therefore Mexico, following Brazil, Colombia and China, lays claim to the fourth largest share worldwide. Mexico also belongs to the group of countries with the greatest number of animals worldwide (amphibians, reptiles and mammals). The number of known plants only gives an initial indication of Mexico's "natural" *genetic* diversity. The latter has, as yet, been only marginally researched (CONABIO 1997: 6). In addition, in Mexico there is a great diversity of cultivated plants. There are, for example, 41 types of maize with several thousand varieties (Taba 1995 according to Wullweber 2004: 107). This is connected with the fact that in Mexico, as in most of the megadiverse countries, there is great *cultural diversity.* Roughly 230 different languages and dialects are spoken (Toledo Ocampo 1998). About 10–12 per cent of the population describe themselves as indigenous, are largely engaged in agriculture and have developed their own medical systems. The latter play a major role, for in bioprospecting this knowledge serves as a type of "filter" for finding potentially economically valuable substances. With regard to agro-biological diversity, the circumstance is important that the culturally diverse areas are at the same time the socio-economically most "marginalised". The modernisation of the agricultural sector within the framework of the Green Revolution hardly took place here, which is why a high degree of agro-biological diversity has been conserved. In the regions with a large and diverse indigenous population a great plurality of relationships with nature have continued to exist up to the present day.

However, the peripheral Fordist development model (cf. the overall analysis of Aboites 1989) has led to a great erosion of biological diversity, both in agriculture and also with regard to non-domesticated diversity. Driving this erosion are: deforestation, the degradation of the soil, the industrialisation of agriculture, urbanisation, the externalisation of ecological costs in economic processes, population growth, poverty and inequality, water pollution, the lack of incentives for the protection and sustainable use of nature and inadequate state policies. One example of the latter is the existence of a state authority in the 1970s (*Comisión Nacional de Desmontes*) which was responsible for deforestation for the settlement of farmers. The erosion has increased further in the last 20 years (CONABIO 1998; SEMARNAT 2002b). A recent study of the Economic Commission for Latin American (ECLA/CEPAL 2004: 166) underlines the high environmental costs of the currently dominant development model in Latin America with its export-orientation and environmentally unregulated features.

5.1.1 *Democratisation, neoliberal politics and NAFTA*

The context of the current conflicts over the treatment of biological diversity is the present peripheral post-Fordist transformation of society. This context is, first, not intransigent but its production and stabilisation are the subjects of permanent social confrontations. Second, it does not "influence" biodiversity policy "from the outside". The specific forms of the appropriation of nature are – as we shall show – themselves an integral part of the neoliberal post-Fordist transformation of society. The 1990s in Mexico were characterised by two contrary processes: first, neoliberal strategies were established, and second, a complex struggle over the democratisation of the political system took place. Both processes have, as we shall see, affected the societal relationships with nature.

Many observers place the year 1985 as marking the clearest turning-point in the history of the struggles for more democracy, when the system based on the rule of the state party PRI (*Partido Revolucionario Institucional*) showed itself to be incapable of reacting more or less efficiently in the dramatic situation caused by a devastating earthquake in Mexico City. In the presidential elections in 1988 the leader of the opposition and later first non-PRI mayor of Mexico City, Cauthémoc Cárdenas, only lost, in the opinion of many, because of irregularities in the counting of the votes (Laurell 1992). During the 1990s there was a struggle over democracy in Mexico (particularly aimed at the question of the reform of voting rights), which was conducted by many social movements and organisations such as the PRD (*Partido de la Revolución Democrática*).[2] Democratisation was "the" subject of that period. The PRI took up the challenge and presented its candidate in 1994, Ernesto Zedillo, with a victory in "clean" elections. This could not stop the erosion of the PRI, however, which is why in 1997 it lost the first direct elections for the mayor of Mexico City and the parliamentary elections. The change of government at the end of 2000 represents the preliminary end of the democratisation process in Mexico. Due to the confrontations of the 1990s, the state party PRI, which had ruled for over 70 years, was pushed out of the highest executive and continually lost parliamentary elections and elections of governors. Authoritative corporatism was thus clearly weakened and made room for a more formally democratic constellation. This development resulted in more business-friendly politics. The new President Fox Quesada (Popular Action Party) was not only the general manager of Coca-Cola Mexico, but half of his cabinet were businessmen. Never before in Mexican history have so many businessmen been appointed to the heads of government ministries (Camp 2003: 125; Teichman 2002: 505). However, at the beginning of his presidency Fox tried to establish broader social welfare and health policies as well as a tax on wealth, but under economic pressures and resistance from the private sector he soon withdrew his projects (ibid.). In the presidential elections of 2006 – after a probable election fraud and heavy conflicts – again the candidate for the Popular Action Party became president. Felipe Calderón comes, in contrast to Fox, from the political establishment and is much more experienced in combating political opponents. However, he started with much less legitimacy than Fox and has the options of creating it through political and economic compromises with his opponents and their social base and/or increasing repression of them.

Parallel to the struggles over the democratisation of the political system, neoliberal strategies were enforced. Since the 1980s state policies have been directed centrally towards international competition and the allied societal interest groups (Olivier Costilla 2005; Morton 2003; Heigl 2006). For a country such as Mexico this means an increased (subordinate) integration into the international division of labour. A central role is played here by low labour costs, the industrialisation of the agricultural sector, the opening up of the economy to foreign trade and investment, access to and the valorisation of resources, and security for investments and planning. The establishment of neoliberal policies began in the 1980s when the debt crisis became obvious. In 1982 Mexico was the first country which issued a moratorium, which in the ensuing period led to hectic activity on the part of creditors and debtors in the management of the debts (Imbusch 1988: 103–156; Boris 1996: 20–29). The "creditor-driven event" (Rainer Falk, a German NGO intellectual) strengthened the position of the banks and Northern governments, and not only with regard to the maintenance of the flow of payments. The governments of the debtor countries, which were dependent on loans, had to carry out so-called structural adjustment measures: state budgetary discipline, the opening up of the economy to foreign goods and investments, the liberalisation of the financial markets, the privatisation of public enterprises, the deregulation of certain sectors and fiscal reform (Guillén Romo 1997: 97ff.; Morton 2003: 641–646).

However, the shift towards a neoliberal economic and social policy cannot simply be attributed to external constraints. It started as a domestic strategy with an *apertura unilateral* (unilateral opening) from 1985 to 1993, especially through the accession of the GATT Agreement in 1986. Sectors such as mining, transport, real estate, telephones and parts of the oil industry were opened up to foreign capital. Other sectors such as petrochemicals, banks and agriculture had already been opened up step by step within the framework of the debt negotiations in the 1980s. A ministerial order limited foreign investment to 49 per cent and allowed the purchase of Mexican companies by foreign investors without official permit (Teichman 1995: 92). In 1993, the national treatment of foreign investment was legally codified (Ornelas Bernal 1994: 259–266). Privatisation policies – between 1983 and 2002 the number of (predominantly) state-owned enterprises was reduced from 1155 to 202, MacLeod 2004: 71) – also served internal economic groups. However, the currency crisis of late 1994 showed that macroeconomic stabilisation was not assured through the existence of NAFTA. During this time, and especially during the negotiations of NAFTA, Mexico became a major destiny for foreign direct investment (Luna Martínez/González Nolasco 2004: 37; on the recent development of NAFTA, cf. Aguilar/Graizbord 2006). At the same time, the Salinas government tried to create social consensus for neoliberal politics in the 1980s, especially through the introduction of the National Solidarity Programme (*Programa Nacional de Solidaridad,* PRONASOL) which comprised welfare policies and the promotion of productive projects and regional development (Morton 2003: 643–644).

The "interiorising" of external constraints (Nicos Poulantzas) in Mexico encountered a political system which was largely dominated by a complex socio-political structure where the state and the ruling party were decisive for access to political influence and wealth. Within that party, in view of the crisis of the old model of development, the forces oriented towards the world market and the USA asserted themselves. This had already begun under President Miguel de la Madrid (1982–1988) and was intensified under his successors Carlos Salinas de Gortari (1988–1994), Ernesto Zedillo (1994–2000), the first non-PRI president, Vicente Fox (2000–2006), and his successor Felipe Calderón (since 2006), who maintained a high degree of continuity in economic and social policies. The political earthquake – the defeat of PRI – led to a "modernization of neoliberalism" (Morton 2003: 647). The market reform policy process

> was a highly concentrated activity, invariably resting in the hands of a small policy elite from whom highly personalised policy networks spanned outward, incorporating domestic actors who closely collabo- rated in the market reform project – invariably powerful members of the private sector.
>
> (Teichman 2002: 501, also on the conflicts among different capital groups)

Market liberalism led to a concentration of assets in a small number of conglomerates who gained enormous political power, leading to corruption and cronyism (ibid.).

A further step was the creation of the North American free trade zone. The North American Free Trade Agreement NAFTA, which had been negotiated from the end of the 1980s, was concluded in 1992 and came into force in 1994, provides a central institutional framework for the safe- guarding of the neoliberal model. Through it, Mexico became a particularly prominent "partner" of the USA. The Agreement reflects the economic policy paradigm of supply-side orientation and comparative cost advantages: it is above all about rules for investment (as the highest aim and including the securing of intellectual property rights), but also about financing, pro- duction and distribution. By contrast, regulations concerning demand or questions of the distribution of social wealth are not mentioned. The regional bloc-building in North America, as elsewhere, is intended to safe- guard and advance the processes of economic integration in a certain region by means of a political-institutional regulative system. NAFTA represents a process of the "locking in" of neoliberal strategies which cannot simply be reversed by nation-state policies after joining the Agreement; and especially not by a clearly weaker member such as Mexico (Shaiken 1994). According to David Gordon (1994: 295) its purpose is to secure "institutional harbors promising the greatest protection" for capital.

NAFTA was also the model for a much more ambitious project. Starting in 1998 a Free Trade Agreement for the Americas (FTAA, *Acuerdo de Libre Comercio para las Américas*, ALCA) was negotiated in order to create a free trade zone for goods and services and investment security, and secure "modern" intellectual property rights until 2005 (the NAFTA chapter 11 on investment security was to be copied verbatim). Originally, the project was proposed by George Bush Senior in 1990 with his "Enterprise for the Americas Initiative". In November 2005 at the fourth "Summit of the Americas" in Mar del Plata (Argentina), it became clear that the project had failed because of the resistance of many of Latin America's presidents. The reasons are the enormous popular mobilisations against the FTAA since the year 2000 and the split in the Latin American bourgeoisie between those favouring capital oriented towards the US market, especially agro-business, and those preferring capital oriented towards the internal market, that is parts of the industry. A third reason is the victory of leftist governments in many countries such as Venezuela, Brazil, Argentina and later in Bolivia, Chile and Ecuador, all of which were under growing pressure to respond much more to popular demands than the former liberal and conservative governments had done (García 2006; on the resistance movement, see CLACSO 2004). Additionally, discontent had been brewing due to the fact that the US negotiators had taken advantage of the lack of experience of their Latin American counterparts which led to a de-legitimation of the process (Ruiz Caro 2005: 304). A central aspect of the critique of FTAA was the question of unrestricted access to natural resources for transnational corporations as the distribution of benefits is considered to be highly unequal, an overexploitation of resources is an integral part of free trade and the consequences for the environment are usually negative (Ruiz Caro 2005: 300–301). However, the US Government has continued to push for free trade agreements on a bilateral level with quite some success, especially in Central America, which implies even more favourable conditions for transnational capital from the USA and Canada. With respect to biodiversity issues, the free trade agreements promote intellectual property rights in the sense of the TRIPS Agreement and do not include any provisions on regulated access and benefit-sharing (ibid.: 301–305).

The importance of the USA for Mexican economic policy has in fact grown considerably in the 1990s, not least as a result of NAFTA. Exports more than tripled between 1994 and 2001, and imports more than doubled.[3] Half of the exports are however simply re-imports from the Maquiladora industry, which concentrates more than one million industrial jobs, but the value-added in Mexico remains low (Boris/Sterr 2002: 197; Oxfam 2003: 17; Casares/Sobarzo 2004).[4] This growth is above all due to the low wage costs in Mexico, which is why the Maquiladoras became increasingly important. Foreign direct investment, which is also strongly increasing, takes place, in addition to investment in the Maquiladora industry, in the form of the buying out of Mexican enterprises by international capital in the course of privatisations. In recent years there have been increased efforts to spread the Maquiladora model to other parts of the country, for example the south-east of Mexico.

As with other international agreements, the specific effect of NAFTA depends on its specific implementation. An agreement does not simply "have an effect" because there is a treaty text which only has to be implemented. The way in which the real implementation of an agreement takes place depends, rather, on the structural conditions and relationships of forces. However, "corridors" and terrains for future developments are laid down with the fundamental formulation. Therefore, we can also speak, in the case of Mexico, of a "disciplinary neoliberalism" (Gill 2003). It has been shown in recent years that the USA has repeatedly been able to assert itself in controversial questions. Environmental issues do not play any role in the NAFTA. However, US President Clinton had to stick to his promise following his election in 1992 to conclude so-called side agreements on work and the environment.[5]

Finally, it is important that the conflicts over democratisation and neoliberalism are characterised by increasing, overt state and societal violence. The state resorts ever more extensively to overtly repressive means in order to enforce specific policies. Particularly in rural areas, the interests of the agricultural oligarchy are defended in many cases by paramilitary groups (see www.ciepac.org, Ceceña 2006).

5.1.2 Resource and environmental policies in Mexico

In Mexico, in the transition from the colonial to the neocolonial order during the nineteenth century, the exploitation of natural resources remained central. An important turning-point was the Mexican Revolution (1910–1917), at the end of which national sovereignty over natural resources was postulated and in the 1930s was put into effect in important sectors such as oil production and processing. During the peripheral Fordist phase of development the valorisation of natural resources was intensified and extended to other sectors. In Mexico these were the sectors which had already been important in the colonial period: mineral deposits and agricultural products such as maize, wheat, coffee, cocoa and tropical fruit. Following the Second World War, scientific plant breeding, that is primarily the development of hybrid varieties, was advanced with the support of the Rockefeller Foundation.[6] Since the 1950s cattle-ranching and logging have played a growing role, as has oil since the 1970s, large quantities of which were found in Veracruz and southern Mexico and which was produced on a large scale due to the high prices (Morton 2002: 33).[7] As a strategic resource, oil – which still exists in large quantities – and increasingly natural gas, is important not only for Mexico but also for the USA. In 2002 almost half of the oil produced was exported, the larger part of it to the USA (EIA 2003: 9). In the 1980s the production of vegetables intended for export was added to the list.

There have been repeated conflicts over the exploitation of resources, particularly in the form of conflicts over the disposition and cultivation of land (see the classic by García de León 1985). However, a belief in progress was dominant in which the growing exploitation of natural resources was hardly ever questioned due to the existing relationships of forces. State resource policy in the sense of the efficient valorisation of natural resources was central for the peripheral Fordist development model. The protection of resources was of virtually no importance.

Environmental problems came onto the political agenda in Mexico in the 1970s, however, primarily as a problem resulting from the peripheral Fordist development model. Important in the 1970s was the dreadful air pollution in Mexico City,[8] the precarious water supply of the capital and, later on, the toxic waste of the Maquiladoras located at the northern border with the USA. Less attention was paid, throughout the country, to the destruction of the environment by the massive extension of oil production or other regional conflicts such as the planned erection of an atomic power station in the state of Veracruz.

The first comprehensive environmental legislation was passed in 1971, which was intended to regulate air and water pollution, and waste and sanitary issues (Russell 1994: 231). The reasons for this were internal pressure because of the increasing air pollution in Mexico City, mentioned above, the environmental laws which had been passed in the USA and a growing international environmental consciousness, which was expressed in the *UN Conference on Human Environment* in Stockholm. The environmental law was closely based on that of the USA. In addition, national parks were established (see below). Particularly under the government of Miguel de la Madrid (1982–1988) there were attempts to take some of the edge off possible protests and criticism by the symbolic upgrading of environmental policy. Environmental aspects were taken up for the first time in the national development plan which was developed at the beginning of his presidency. In 1988 a Ministry for Urban Development and Ecology (SEDUE) was set up, thereby institutionalising environmental questions at a high level for the first time. As a whole, state environmental policy remained largely symbolic until the beginning of the 1990s, the financial endowment of the Ministry was modest and the control of the legal requirements weak. In 1988 the General Law on Environmental Equilibrium and Protection (*Ley General para el Equilibrio y la Protección del Medio Ambiente*; LEGEEPA) was passed (the version of 1988 with changes in January 2000 and 2005 is valid): public works and polluting industries were obliged to submit a proof of environmental tolerance, pesticides and the transport of toxic substances were regulated. At the present time there is no perceivable environmental movement to speak of.[9]

For a long time, genetic resources, with the exception of seed banks, did not play any role as a political problem or as a subject of state regulation. It was regarded as normal that the area under agricultural cultivation grew from year to year. It was only as a result of the Green Revolution that in the 1970s the erosion of agro-biological diversity was discussed, and the international discussion played an important role in this. Not only was the political-economic side of the appropriation of nature discussed (who profits from its valorisation?) but, as a part of international discussions, the ecological side also attained a voice. The dramatic erosion of agro-biological diversity in the course of the Green Revolution was politicised by epistemic communities close to the FAO. The Mexican government played an important role in the 1980s when the issue was to question gratuitous access to plant genetic resources. This led internationally to the setting up of the CGRFA (*Commission on Genetic Resources for Food and Agriculture*) within the framework of the FAO and in Mexico, with international financial support, to the upgrading of the International Maize and Wheat Research Institute (CIMMYT). This discussion remained limited to small groups of experts, however, and only took place in an international framework (cf. Chapter 3 on this).

During the administration under Salinas (1988–1994), SEDUE was incorporated into the newly established Social Development Ministry (*Secretaría de Desarrollo Social*; SEDESOL), and at the same time in 1992, around the Rio Conference, the norm-setting National Institute of Ecology (*Instituto Nacional de Ecología*; INE), the executive Federal Attorney for Environmental Protection (*Procuraduría Federal de Protección al Ambiente*; PROFEPA) and the National Commission for the Knowledge and Use of Biodiversity (*Comisión Nacional para el Conocimiento y el Uso de la Biodiversidad*; CONABIO) were established. This was the direct result of the more intensive international discussions on environmental policy since the beginning of the 1990s. Since 1994 there has been an independent Ministry of the Environment (today *Secretaría de Medio Ambiente y Recursos Naturales*, SEMARNAT). In 1996 as a part of the implementation of the CBD, the General Environmental Law was revised and utilisation aspects were added to those of protection. In 1996, in addition, a law on plant varieties was passed which is subject to the Agricultural Ministry and regulates the rights of plant breeders (CONABIO 1997: 30). One important regulation in it is that the property-holding of plants existing in nature is prohibited.

The NAFTA Agreement provides a unique regulation of natural resources, that is a special treatment of oil, electricity and petrochemicals which in fact means that US companies have privileged access to Mexico's natural resources. Since the year 2000, the US government formulated explicitly and integrated into its National Security Strategy that Latin American Natural resources are part of US American national security and therefore of geo-strategic considerations. This is a main reason for the strong orientation towards free trade agreements. Among other things, they should guarantee unrestricted access to natural resources for foreign companies through "national treatment", market access and investment security (Ruiz Caro 2005).

The deregulation of the agricultural sector

The neoliberal transformation of society which began in the 1980s comprised, among other things, the deregulation of sectors which had previously been

subject to relatively strong state regulation and were at least partially protected from international competition by tariffs. For the purposes of our
discussion, the Mexican agricultural sector is particularly important. Following the debt crisis of 1982, the Mexican economy was "opened up"
within the framework of the so-called adjustment programmes. "In hardly
any other sector did the elements of neoliberal policies have such an effect as
in Mexican agriculture" (Boris/Sterr 2002: 183, our translation). Mexican
agriculture with its small farmers had, first, to compete increasingly with
the highly productive and highly subsidised US American agriculture.[10]
Reforms in agriculture took place before the coming into force of NAFTA,
especially between 1990 and 1992. For nine out of eleven basic agricultural
goods (except corn and beans) import controls and guaranteed prices were
resigned and the central agricultural institution, CONASUPO, weakened
and then closed (Yúnez-Naude/Barceinas 2004). The previously food-
exporting country of Mexico became, on balance, a food importer (Calderón
Salazar 1992: 80). In addition, cultivation in Mexico itself was increasingly
directed towards cash crops for export.

The reform of Article 27 of the Constitution in 1992 and the NAFTA
Agreement, which came into force on 1 January 1994, are two major insti-
tutionalisations of the transformation to a competition state which had been
taking place since the 1980s. It was a central achievement of the Mexican
revolution that land was given to those who needed it and cultivated it.
With this *Ejido* system a form of collective ownership of the land was
established which was laid down in Article 27 of the Mexican Constitution
of 1917 but which was not applied comprehensively until the 1930s under
President Lázaro Cárdenas. Although the norm had been undermined in a
masked form since the 1950s by the local *caciquismo*[11] and clientelism – that
is, processes of land concentration did take place – nevertheless, the norm
represented an important point of reference in the land question (Calderón
1992: 79ff.; Boris/Sterr 2002: 185). With the amendment of Article 27, the
agricultural reform which had been laid down in 1917 was ended. This
created a legal framework for the permeating of the Mexican agricultural
sector by transnational capital. The amended article of the Constitution is
not the cause of neoliberal agricultural policy, but an important part of a
process which began ten years earlier, which was not clear-cut from the
beginning and which was frequently controversial. Victor Toledo (2000)
estimates, however, that by the end of the 1990s half of the agriculturally
cultivated area in Mexico was still Ejidos or communal land (over 100
million hectares), in which three million families live in 30,000 Ejidos or
communes.[12] In addition, about 80 per cent of the natural and managed
forests are to be found on Ejidos, as well as most of the biosphere reserves.
A large part of the *in situ* biological diversity is also to be found in arable land
and forests. And finally, many reserves of drinking water exist on this land.

The restructuring of the agricultural sector must be seen in close connection with the NAFTA negotiations, for the opening of the agricultural

sector was a central demand of the US representative there (Calderón 1992: 87). Due to the currency crisis in 1994 and the following economic crisis, ongoing governmental subsidies and the high percentage of small farmers in Mexico, profound took place changes in the Mexican agricultural sector. In particular, economic concentration in the agricultural sector, a collapse of corn production and more imports from the US took place (Yúnez-Naude/Barceinas 2004: 93–95).

The establishment of nature protection areas

Mexico's first nature reserve was established as a result of the Constitution of 1917 (the León desert in the north), but in the following decades one cannot speak of a clear policy of nature protection. Although many national parks were established, above all in the 1970s and 1980s, they existed largely on paper (CONANP 2007: 2). The concept was still largely propagated, however, that the protection of nature should take place without human intervention. This did not change until the 1990s.

The General Law on the Environment of 1988, in its version of 2000, lays down in Article 3 that the nation, that is the government, has sovereignty and jurisdiction over the nature reserves. By 2006 the reserves comprised more than 22 million hectares, that is more than 11 per cent of the national territory (CONANP 2007). A large number of the nature reserves have not been withdrawn from human use but is part of so-called regional sustainability development programmes; others are priority reserves and are subject to strict regulations. It is emphasised, however, that the protection of nature must be conducted together with the people who live there, which represents a change compared to the 1970s.

The main reason for the protection policies was and remains the enthusiasm of scientists, and moreover, it is an internationally attractive subject and in this field financial resources were and are available. The first National Report by Mexico to the CBD (CONABIO 1997: 14f.) illustrates that a large part of the money for the administration of the nature reserves comes from international institutions, particularly from the Global Environmental Facility (GEF), which is based at the World Bank, or from the state development agency of the USA, USAID. The GEF participates in the financing of ten nature reserves, mainly biosphere reserves (among others Montes Azules in Chiapas). The second Plan for a *Sistema Nacional de Áreas Protegidas* (SINAP II, National System of Protected Areas) got donations from the World Bank, that is the GEF, of more than 60 million USD. Conservation NGOs in particular, and some private companies, are part of it (Delgado Ramos 2004: 70–80; for a detailed study on the role of the World Bank and its "green programmes" in Mexico see Saxe-Fernández/Delgado 2005: 61–87).

Access by private actors to nature reserves is necessary because of the precarious financial situation of state authorities. According to CONANP (2001: 5) the financial backing is about 20 to 25 per cent of the international standard, a fact which illustrates the problems facing the national park administration rather than effectively helping to solve them. The second five-year plan for a *Sistema Nacional de Áreas Protegidas* therefore develops a strategy to win NGO assistance in the administration of the parks (ibid.: 16) and in view of the difficult financial situation to earn funds via the provision of services and from fees for use (ibid.: 9). This corresponds to the strategies of the financially strong nature protection NGOs, such as the *Worldwide Fund for Nature* (WWF), which favours the setting up of 233 so-called bioregions worldwide, or *Conservation International* (CI) which promotes the protection of 12 so-called megadiverse centres (something similar happened with the Mesoamerican Corridor, see below).[13]

López Ramírez (2005a: 232–234) sees the creation of parallel environmental policy institutions here which are, to a lesser extent, subject to state control but which secure access to the reserves for international actors such as the World Bank or USAID. However, the state remains responsible for the granting of prior informed consent and the negotiation of mutually agreed terms. One NGO representative said, "Mexico protects that which can be sold, which possibly has value abroad" (Mx/17, our translation).

Nature protection policy has experienced a particular change since the 1994 Zapatista uprising. Nature protection policy was enlisted here as a mechanism to pursue a state policy of combating the uprising (Mx/9; Mx/10). From this moment on, nature protection policy became a public problem. This is illustrated further below using the example of the biosphere reserve Montes Azules (*Reserva Integral de la Biósfera Montes Azules*; RIBMA) in the Lacandon Jungle in the state of Chiapas.

Development projects: Puebla-Panamá Plan *and* Mexican Mesoamerican Biological Corridor

Two development projects represent an important element in terms of our ability to appraise the transformation of Mexico under competition state conditions and the importance of biodiversity policy. Both projects were already planned in the 1990s, but were only launched after Fox had become president in 2000. The *Plan Puebla Panamá* (PPP) is a central project of the new government for the south-east of Mexico. It was presented in April 2001 by Alfonso Romo Garza, a friend of the president and chief of the Mexican transnational corporation Pulsar (which does not exist any longer), and was signed by the governments of the Central American countries and Mexico on 15 June 2001. Its purpose is primarily to attract foreign investments to tax-privileged Maquiladoras, and to support the valorisation of natural resources (wood, water, oil, uranium and biodiversity) as well as telecommunications, cattle-ranching, export-oriented and technically intensive agriculture and tourism in the relatively economically poor regions which are, however, rich in natural resources and cheap labour, between the Province of Puebla near Mexico City and the country of Panama. This is to be achieved by using comparative cost advantages. The core of the plan therefore consists of "making strategic investments in infrastructure so that the region is more accessible and can use the potential benefits of Mexico's free trade agreements" (Report of the President according to López Ramírez 2005a: 216, and the outline and appraisal of the plan to be found there, our translation; cf. Barreda 2001). These public investments are to be made, in addition to private investments, in road construction, ports, railways and airports. The Inter-American Development Bank (IDB), a subsidiary of the World Bank, is financing 75 per cent of the 4 billion USD project, and the Mexican Government has contributed the rest.[14]

One special aspect of the PPP is the *centros de integración rural* (rural integration centres), by means of which rural populations are to be organised in a centralised manner in order to provide them with access to infrastructure and basic services and thus to prevent emigration. In reality – according to López Ramírez – their purpose is to more effectively control the population under the guise of social policy and also to push for the release of land for extensive projects. The Maquiladoras have a similar effect. Although the plans always mention the improvement of the living conditions of the rural population (education, housing, health), this is hardly reflected in their actual implementation. Rather, trickle-down socio-economic development effects are expected.

The second project, the *Corredor Biológico Mesoamericano* (CBM; Mesoamerican Biological Corridor) from Mexico to Panama and, as a part of that, the *Corredor Biológico Mesoamericano México* (CBM-M), was designed by the national governments, international financial and development agencies such as the World Bank and USAID and conservation NGOs. It has a time span from 2003 to 2010 (the original plan was from 2001 to 2008). The 90 million USD planned for this project are mainly funded by the GEF and the Mexican government and coordinated by the CONABIO.[15] "The global objective of the project is the conservation and sustainable use of globally significant biodiversity in five biological corridors in south-east Mexico, through mainstreaming of biodiversity criteria in public expenditure, and in selected local planning and development practices" (World Bank 2000: 2). The project consists of research into biological diversity and the causes of its erosion in five zones in the four south-eastern states (two zones are in Chiapas), in order to be able to manage the environment and resources more appropriately and as a result to be able to achieve development and the fight against poverty without environmental damage (ibid.: 3). After seven years in "focal areas", which cover 15 per cent of the corridor area, verifiable objectives should be reached (Soberón 2001: 4). The local population is to be involved in the process and will be the main beneficiary (ibid.: 13). Almost 80 per cent of the budget is earmarked for integrating the corridor region into development programmes. "This component will promote removal of institutional, technical and informational barriers that prevent the adoption, in regular rural development programs, of win–win natural resources and biodiversity management options" (World Bank 2000: 9). Another part of the programme is the development of pilot projects to support the sustainable development of biological diversity through capacity building. The concrete projects are being conducted in Chiapas with Lacandon peoples (not with Mayas), who tended to be neutral in the Zapatista uprising and – in contrast to the Mayas, who migrated there at a later point in time – have lived there since the eighteenth century and know the natural resources best (see the overview in Delgado Ramos 2004: 80–89).

López Ramírez (2005a: 230–231) highlights three major but hidden objectives of the Mesoamerican Biological Corridor: the appropriation of biodiversity, counter-insurgency, especially in Chiapas against the Zapatistas, and the interest in the enormous oil reserves in the region. The fact that Chiapas is part of the Corridor means a "preventive occupation of a strategic space for the energetic needs of the United States" because Mexico becomes more and more important for its Northern neighbour (ibid.: 242).

The difference between the PPP and the CBM-M is that the former is more of a traditional development project, which only takes up social or ecological issues in passing, while the corridor places sustainability and the fight against poverty at the centre of attention. It is explicitly directed towards biological diversity and its protection and valorisation. The corridor project certainly claims to have the potential to support regional development and therefore at first glance finds itself in tension vis-à-vis the PPP. Alfonso López Ramírez nevertheless judges the two development plans to be complementary and sees the geo-strategic interests of the US government behind them because it has declared the strategic resources oil, electricity, drinking water and biological diversity to be essential for the "national security" of the USA (López Ramírez 2005a: 223–234; see also Delgado Ramos 2002). Mexico is the second largest supplier of oil from Latin America after Venezuela and in view of its close ties to the USA, it is politically "more reliable" than the South American country. In addition to large economic projects, which do not push for domestic development but rather impel production in enclaves and an outflow of resources (particularly into the USA), the corridor project is also about an increased control of the migration of people – for this purpose the militarisation of the Mexican–Guatemalan border has been taking place for some years now – as well as being concerned with measures to combat uprisings. In view of the general conditions it is therefore likely that the CBM-M will fit into the general valorisation policies.

In recent years a strong opposition has formed in the region, particularly to the PPP (www.ciepac.org; López Ramírez 2005a: 229, 2005b: 178–179; Delgado Ramos 2004: 183–218 on the alternative proposal of an indigenous biological corridor). In July 2002 representatives of over 350 organisations met in Managua to coordinate their activities and to point out the existing and possible alternatives to the export-oriented development model based on forced valorisation in the context of the PPP, NAFTA and the planned FTAA (Declaración Foro Mesoamericano 2002). Moreover, the reorientation of US international politics and its allies such as the World Bank after the attacks of September 11, 2001 slowed the PPP project down remarkably. Some Maquiladora plants were constructed but the huge infrastructure projects such as highways, harbours and airports were not realised. This is also due to the broad criticism of and resistance against the overall and particular projects (López Ramírez 2005a: 228–229). By contrast, the establishment of a Mesoamerican Biological Corridor continues to take place. In the near future and under the recently elected president Calderón new dynamics might emerge regarding the PPP. As a "condition for success" of the projects it should not be underestimated, however, that the restructuring of the agricultural sector outlined above is accompanied by a deep crisis of the rural population. The current formulation of national development projects such as the PPP, at first sight, offer many people a sort of straw at which they can clutch in their often desperate socio-economic situation.

Preliminary summary

In the outlined fields of politics it is obvious that there is a clear tendency in Mexican resource and environmental policies to increasingly valorise natural resources. This is connected with the gradual transformation to a competition state, with subordinate integration into the world market and with the increasing pressure to earn export profits for servicing foreign debt. In addition to its cheap labour, Mexico's natural resources are perceived as a decisive comparative advantage. This is also a complex process of "primitive accumulation", that is the permeation of social relationships with capitalist patterns of socialisation. Oil plays a central role today and will continue to do so in the future. Particularly due to its close ties to the USA and its formulated "national interest" in strategic resources, Mexico has become a preferred site for capital valorisation. The amendment of Article 27 of the Mexican Constitution as a decisive part of the deregulation of the agrarian sector makes possible the privatisation of land and thus access to natural resources.

NAFTA represents a central institutionalisation of free trade policies and security for foreign investors (for example via the strict securing of intellectual property rights) and has profound effects on societal relationships with nature. The same is true of the debt crisis, following which neoliberal strategies and the accelerated valorisation of nature were established. The definition of nature reserves can, in addition to the intended protection of nature, also be interpreted as a strategy to give the Mexican state responsibility and to take it away from the population living there. This could in particular gain in importance if, within the framework of bioprospecting, prior informed consent and mutually agreed terms are to be granted and benefit-sharing is to be negotiated. The national parks are also part of the privatisation strategies. At the same time there was an increased setting up of environmental policy institutions. This cannot only be understood as part of the tendency towards valorisation but is also connected with the perception on the part of the state that it must effectively deal with the erosion of biological diversity. International agreements, particularly the CBD, play an important role here.

The development plans, already discussed, are decisive because they create central preconditions for the valorisation of labour and nature. However, it is the PPP which is a conventional programme as it is intended to enable economic "development" via investments from abroad and the valorisation of labour and cheap resources. It falls back on rather traditional ideas of progress. They become particularly important in view of the fact that they are also heralded as instruments for repressing uprisings. Finally, it is obvious that all the projects (constitutional amendment, NAFTA, protection of nature policies, development projects) are developed and established largely without the participation of the population involved.

Before we discuss these projects in detail, we shall briefly show how different valorisation strategies compete with one another in the south-eastern state of Chiapas.

5.1.3 The federal state of Chiapas: competing valorisation strategies

Today, Chiapas is a "strategic area" for the restructuring of Mexican society. Immense resources are to be found there, including its cultural diversity which is important for specific sectors of production such as tourism, and a large and cheap "industrial reserve army" which reproduces itself largely at subsistence level. This south-eastern state is "the clearest synthesis of that which is to be expected for the whole of Mexico both in the new international division of labour and in the use of its territory and its productive resources in the context of the worldwide restructuring of capital, the redefinition of hegemonic relationships and geo-economic integration" (Ceceña 2000: 262, our translation; Morton 2002: 30–41).

The natural riches of Chiapas had already been made into money some time ago. Directly following the Spanish Conquest, cocoa, vanilla and fine woods became important; rubber and coffee were added later, followed by extensive cattle-ranching and, since the 1970s, oil and natural gas.[16] The state was a central actor in these processes during the colonial period – in the form of the Spanish administration – and following political independence at the beginning of the nineteenth century it secured extraction by private enterprises in the "neo-colonial order" (Halperin Donghi 1991). Its role changed in Chiapas following the Mexican revolution, when the state itself became more economically active. Excellent examples are the extraction of oil and forestry. Besides state activities of resource use in the fields of agriculture, minerals and water or the legal securing of use by private enterprise, in Chiapas the declaration of nature reserves was for a long time the only environmental policy strategy of the federal and the state government. The declaration was essentially conducted by the *Instituto de Historia Natural y Ecología* (Institute of Natural History and Ecology), an institute which had existed since 1942, which has had juridical functions since the change of government in 2000 and which is a type of environmental ministry in Chiapas. The state has proportionally the largest number of reserves in the whole of Mexico, all of which have been declared in the last 15 to 20 years. There are problems with the communities living around the protected areas. Conflicts arise here partly because the population was not allowed to participate in the process (Mx/14).

Of the 7.5 million hectares of land used today, about 40 per cent is used for forestry activities, about one-third for cattle-ranching and about 20 per cent for agriculture (Pólito Barrios Morfín 2000: 62). Within Mexico, Chiapas is the top coffee producer, takes second place for beef production and third for maize. Two-thirds of the population live from a generally precarious subsistence economy and obtain wages from harvesting or transfer payments from emigrant family members. The most important strategic resources in Chiapas are oil and hydroelectric energy. There are large oil deposits in the highlands and in the Lacandon Jungle, for example in Montes Azules. Today, Chiapas produces more than 20 per cent of Mexico's oil and almost half of its natural gas. Furthermore, large, yet to be tapped deposits are also believed to exist there. Thirty per cent of the country's hydrological resources are to be found in Chiapas, and at the present time, a large proportion of Mexico's hydroelectric energy is produced there. The state's biological diversity – as part of a larger region in the south-east of Mexico and Guatemala which is called *Selva Maya* (Mayan Jungle) – is regarded as a further strategic resource, as is stated in the National Biodiversity Strategy (CONABIO 2000: 21). In particular the Lacandon Jungle is a centre of biological diversity with a high share of endemic plants and animals. On one per cent of the national territory there are 4300 plant species, which represent between 15 and 20 per cent of those known in Mexico. The indigenous peoples use 1800 plants medicinally (Ceceña/Giménez 2002; see in detail Barreda 1999). The biosphere reserve Montes Azules is today the hot-spot of biodiversity while the former hot-spot around Montes Azules – Las Cañadas, also a centre of the Zapatista uprising – was heavily damaged by logging in the 1970s and 1980s.

Since the Mexican revolution affected Chiapas only in a very partial manner and considering that the peripheral Fordist development model was not conclusively able to establish itself there, social relationships such as a large share of subsistence production and reproduction and corresponding "traditional" relationships with nature were maintained which in other regions of the country had been heavily modified in the course of the twentieth century (on the complementary relationship of the peripheral Fordist development model and subsistence production see Aboites 1989). This is connected to a large extent with the high share of indigenous people in the population, most of whom have resisted outside attempts to push them towards "modernity" with all its socio-economic trappings. Instead, they have sought to reproduce and expand upon their own multifarious value systems and lifestyles (see for example Kuppe 2002). The old state party PRI articulated itself in areas that comprised a large indigenous population with the "traditional" forms of rule dominant there, particularly the so-called *caciquismo*. The Chiapan oligarchy is strongly oriented towards the primary sector of the economy and the neofeudal relationships of rule and work are secured by a quasi institutionalised racism. Nevertheless, even in Chiapas some changes have taken place due to the complex and dynamic processes of political democratisation, the neoliberal transformation of society and the emerging post-Fordist relationships with nature. With regard to political democratisation, Chiapas can be seen as being of central importance. Democratisation in Mexico, which found its preliminary zenith in the voting of the PRI out of the federal government in 2000, would be unthinkable without the Zapatista uprising. Even in Chiapas the PRI lost the post of governor for the first time in 2000. However, the victorious candidate of the PAN (*Partido Acción Nacional*) and PRD (*Partido de la Revolución Democrática*) alliance, Pablo Salazar Mendiguchía, is hardly any different from the previous governors. Particularly in the question of indigenous rights and the position of the government towards the Zapatista uprising, nothing has changed. Against this sociocultural and natural background there exist different, partly competing and partly complementary valorisation strategies in the individual areas of Chiapas.

The Chiapan oligarchy lives from large real estate holdings which are based on both agriculture and cattle-ranching. Alejandro Toledo Ocampo (1998) names the process which has been taking place since the middle of the twentieth century – which was accompanied by the expulsion of indigenous and other peoples and the destruction of the vegetation – as the transformation of Chiapas into "a gigantic cattle pen". As we have seen, that led in recent decades to massive conflicts due to the increasing land requirements. Chiapas continues to be an important producer of coffee, cocoa, bananas and citrus fruits, all of which are largely cultivated for export (Pólito Barrios Morfín 2000).

In the future the increased extraction of the large deposits of oil and natural gas is planned, which is not being carried out by the Chiapan oligarchy but by private and state firms.[17] The state-owned company, *Petróleos Mexicanos* (Pemex), with revenues of more than 50 billion USD in 2002 and – because of the growth of the oil price – 83 billion USD in 2005, is the seventh largest oil company in the world and produced, with taxes of over 30 billion USD, more than one-third of the state's revenue. More than 9 per cent of the Mexican GDP and 40 (!) per cent of the budget of the Mexican state comes from Pemex and the exploitation and sales of oil and gas (*El Universal*, 1 September 2006). Interests in oil production are therefore directly connected with the state because Pemex is still the "government's cash cow" (*Business Week*, 13 December 2004). Although the states of Campeche, Veracruz and Tabasco have so far been more important for oil production, in Chiapas there are considerable deposits. The potential conflict especially rests on the fact that most of the oil and natural gas is to be found in the east of Chiapas, where over 90 per cent of the population is indigenous (Ceceña 2000: 269).

"External" interests also exist in land for forest plantations for the cultivation of fast-growing, commercially utilisable forests (the interest in fine woods also continues to exist). Mexican companies and international ones, above all International Papers, have direct interests here. The land question is aggravated by the fact that in the last 15 to 20 years in proportion to other states, the largest numbers of natural reserves in the whole of Mexico have been declared in Chiapas. This led, for example, to conflicts in the Lacandon Jungle because the local population was not involved. In addition Elisabeth Pólito Barrios Morfín (2000: 65) estimates that the control over and availability of drinking water will become one of the central conflicts of the twenty-first century. The availability of drinking water is incompatible in particular with oil production in the same place. The industrialisation plans of the outlined development projects do not affect the east of Chiapas but do impact upon the Chimalapas on the straits of Tehuantepec, one of the last undivided tropical natural forests in North America. The effects on Chiapas are difficult to calculate. A further economically important interest, which is however less politically articulated, is tourism, which represents an important source of income especially in the south. And finally, there is interest in the appropriation of genetic resources.

A clear line cannot be drawn between practices of the use of nature which are "protective" (indigenous life-styles, nature reserves etc.), extractive (wood, oil and natural gas) and extensive (cattle-ranching, agriculture). Nevertheless, this illustrates the potential conflicts because the different practices encroach on each other's preserve. These valorisation strategies also conflict – to differing degrees – with the fact that the state of Chiapas and particularly its resource-rich eastern part is populated mainly by indigenous people. The commodification strategies of dominant forces do not meet per se with rejection or resistance by the population, however. On the contrary, these processes and the accompanying promises of improved living conditions ("development") were seen positively by large numbers of the people living in Chiapas. At the same time it is clear particularly in Chiapas that historically and currently a large part of the confrontations between dominant forces aiming at valorisation and subordinate (i.e. indigenous and local farmers) forces is about the commodification of the living conditions of the latter: their integration as wage workers into private capitalist market processes and the changing of their specific relationships with nature.

5.2 The formation of a Mexican biodiversity policy

In the following section the question will be examined, using decisive points of conflict, of what form Mexican biodiversity policy has taken in recent times. This is understood as a conflictive terrain of the constitution, articulation and confrontation of interests, problem interpretations and proposals for dealing with problems, and of their political institutionalisation. In a first step different positions are identified before their relationship to one another is determined more precisely, in order then to analyse in more detail important conflicts over the strategic and institutional formation of the valorisation paradigm.

5.2.1 *Positions in Mexican biodiversity policy: actors, problem interpretations and interests*

As a result of the studies in Mexico, five typical positions can be identified. They are intended to illustrate different interpretations with regard to the problems which must be politically regulated, different constellations of interest and alliances, and diverging concepts of what constitutes an adequate biodiversity policy. The identification of the different types helps to structure the field of Mexican biodiversity policy.

The "neoliberal" position

The neoliberal position is supported by the transnational biotechnology enterprises which have their seats in other countries. One important actor is AgroBio, an association of five transnational corporations with massive interests in promoting/gaining stronger support for the development of transgenetic plants in Mexico. AgroBio cooperates closely with the US American Biotechnological Industry Association, which is devoted in particular to the international recognition of patents. The essential power of definition of the problems lies with the actors who hold this position: they claim to represent the general interest of the country, namely the desire for progress. The new technologies are the core of development. Technology, which comes mainly from the North, benefits all. The main problem is the lack of a social consensus, which is expressed particularly in the lack of acceptance on the part of consumers. The biotechnology enterprises criticise their own failings here, as not enough information has been provided. For the new developments clearer and simpler state regulations are required, that is regulations with few transaction costs. They should correspond to "the needs of the market". The securing of intellectual property rights takes first priority here. The patenting of living material is the primary objective and imitations should be prevented. Questions of the regulation of access and above all, general stipulations with regard to benefit-sharing have a much lower priority, and should serve merely to improve the conditions of the further valorisation of biodiversity. Protection considerations are hardly to be found in their statements.

The neoliberal position and the forces supporting it are very self-confident. The generalisation of their interests is not without foundation, for in the last 20 years this position has generally been largely accepted in Mexico. It determines the basic direction, has the most direct access to the state apparatus and by far the greatest resources of power and finance. At the same time the protagonists of this position are aware of the highly conflictive nature of its subject-matter. The neoliberal position, as well as the "technocratic-nationalist" position, which will be outlined next, have been coming under pressure from the more recent public debates. Voices of dissent have complained that, "The environmental groups lie a lot, but they work well" (Mx/7).

The "technocratic-nationalist" position

This position is supported by the Environmental Ministry and National Biodiversity Commission (CONABIO), consultants close to them and consultants from research institutes, and a minority in the Ministry of Agriculture. At the international level they are the promoters of the Like-minded Group of Megadiverse Countries (cf. Chapter 2). They too applaud the biotechnological valorisation of genetic resources. The main problem, in their opinion, is the efficient appropriation and further processing of the genetic resources via the development of research and industrial capacity in Mexico. Therefore, a relevant Mexican biotechnological industry must be created. An alliance with research is the necessary precondition for the appropriation of genetic resources. Interest exists particularly in international technology transfer in that the transfer of modern knowledge to Mexico is regarded as being of central importance (Mx/1; Mx/3). That is the best form of benefit-sharing. With adequate development a win–win situation can ensue. They also see themselves as being in a position to formulate Mexico's general interest.

In line with this, the most important cause of the present problems for this position is the blatantly capital-oriented state policy with regard to genetic resources (CONABIO 2000; Mx/1; Mx/3). The dominant tendencies are often criticised. The Ministry of the Economy has an "absolutely commercial attitude" and allows no criticism of the NAFTA or the WTO (Mx/1), and it is downright "religious" in its defence of the economic agreements. The business sector is regarded critically, since it has no interest in a legal framework or in national development. As far as intellectual property rights are concerned, it is stated that TRIPS and NAFTA are very effective and that powerful interests are behind them. However, the basically TRIPS compatible, rigid rights to intellectual property have led, in view of the fact that there is no effective national policy and corresponding institutions, to the situation that the genetic resources end up abroad, where they become valorised without any great benefit to Mexico. The diverse access agreements, despite or even because of their errors, are described as a necessary and important experience (Mx/3).

Conflicts over distribution and questions of participation and decision-making power are given a much lower priority. Benefit-sharing should be "pragmatically defined" (Mx/1). It is regarded as a "social construction" (Mx/3); through a dialogue between indigenous and farming communities and the state (administration and public research institutions) the advantages of the utilisation of biodiversity and procedures for benefit-sharing should be specified. The local communities must understand that in Mexico the institutional and technical capacities have to be set up for the utilisation of genetic resources (Mx/1). Of decisive importance is *capacitación* (capacity building) at the local level (communities and research institutes) and the integration of the use of genetic resources into programmes for rural development (Mx/3).

The international norms of the Food and Agricultural Organization of the United Nations (FAO) and the CBD are regarded as important, although – in the case of indigenous rights – realisable only in 10 to 15 years (Mx/1). Nuances exist, however: some consider the emerging norms to be of more "philosophical value" (Mx/3), which needs to be adjusted to the specific conditions in the individual countries, although no great hopes can be placed on this in the near future. Others consider the drawing-up and implementation of specific legislation to be unavoidable in order to guarantee prior informed consent and benefit-sharing.

As far as the existing relationships of power and rule are concerned, the "technocratic-nationalist" position can be described as pragmatic. It accepts the powerful interests of the dominant actors (businesses and Northern governments) and acts in a "tactically cooperative" manner towards the neoliberal (and the conservationist) position. By contrast, representatives of the democratic and left-wing nationalist positions are described as "extremists" and their positions as "obscurantist" and "medieval" (Mx/1). The concrete criticism of biopiracy in the framework of the bioprospecting agreements is rejected, even if it is not denied that biopiracy exists in Mexico today (Mx/1). There is no attempt on the side of the "technocratic-nationalist" position to strengthen the weaker actors, because otherwise the actors potentially cooperating with Mexican institutions would be scared off and could possibly turn to other countries.

The "conservationist" position

This is a position propagated particularly by NGOs, of which the "Big Three" – the *World Wide Fund for Nature*, *The Nature Conservancy* and *Conservation International* – are the most important (on their policies in Mexico, see Delgado Ramos 2004: 33–42). Historically, they have supported the position that parts of nature should be territorially removed from human influence. This position has a long tradition in the USA where nature protection was often conceptualised on the basis of the exclusion of humans for the conservation of nature. However, this is not possible without severe conflicts in a country like Mexico where many people live directly in the designated protection areas and in a direct relationship with nature. Therefore, in recent years, the conservationist position has been guided, increasingly, by the World Bank models of *grassroots participation* and *listening to the poor*, which have been positively received by the public. They wish to have "a social component" included in legislation and its implementation as well as supporting forms of sustainable use. One example is the "bioregions" supported by the WWF and others. Conservation International Mexico also wishes to create alternative and sustainable sources of income for the local population via economic projects. This type of NGO understands itself strongly as being in the position of an interlocutor between the indigenous communities and the outside world (Mx/12; Mx/16). In addition, they are important for the generation of knowledge concerning the erosion of biological diversity and for the drawing up of inventories. Many NGOs of the conservationist position cooperate closely with enterprises. Many of them have a positive attitude to the privatisation of nature reserves, or at least do not reject it, and involve themselves in their administration ("There are NGOs which believe that privatisation is the solution"; Mx/16, our translation).

The "grassroots democracy" position

Fundamentally critical positions towards current developments are only to be heard from social organisations and some academics: for example from the *Centro de Estudios para el Cambio en el campo Mexicano* (Ceccam; Study Centre for Changes in Mexico's Countryside), which was set up by independent farmers' organisations as a think-tank and lobby group, or from the internationally reputed NGO RAFI (now the ETC Group) with its office in Mexico City, or from the NGOs *Centro de Investigaciones Económicas y Políticas de Acción Communitaria* (CIEPAC; Centre for Economic and Political Investigations of Communitarian Action) and *Global Exchange* which are based in Chiapas.

According to this position, the problem lies in the dominant trend which drives forth neoliberal relationships, transforms life into a commodity and only accords worth to market values (Mx/9; Mx/10; Mx/13). The central accusation in the disputes is that of "biopiracy". The main conflict continues to be rooted in the land question (Mx/10; Mx/9). In addition, it is emphasised that the danger stems from the present trend of forcing communities to recognise property rights with regard to knowledge and nature, which impels continual community fragmentation.

The opponents of this position are, predominantly, the "power groups" (Mx/2), ruthless enterprises which want to appropriate genetic resources and the knowledge connected with them, but also natural scientists who have no sensitivity to social problems. The Ministry of the Environment is accused of using progressive language, for example by speaking of the integration of indigenous people, without putting this into practice. The law is seen as a mechanism to legitimate and indeed ensure that the interests of the dominant economic actors are upheld, irrespective of the social consequences. "The enterprises simply want the legal guarantee so that they can invest" (Mx/10). Nevertheless, there is selective reference to the room for manoeuvre which has been opened up: this is true, in particular, of the regulations on prior informed consent, benefit-sharing and Article 8(j) of the CBD, for example, in order to lend more legitimacy to the Agreement of San Andrés (also Mx/9; Mx/10; see below). The international level is also important because issues are given a political push by international partner organisations (Mx/9).

Altogether, for the "democratic" position, the most important strategy is to create awareness of current developments in the first place. Many farmers did not recognise, for example, the context of the decisive changes in the 1990s and supported the privatisation of land. The definite conviction is that enlightenment is the correct way. The most important current proposal is a moratorium on all forms of bioprospecting. However, the moratorium is not intended to be used to achieve a better position in the "sales negotiations" of Mexican biodiversity. Strategically, the point is to connect questions of human rights with those of environmental justice (*justicia ambiental*) on the basis of *poder local e indígena* (local and indigenous power) and autonomy. The grassroots democracy position has a conflictive understanding of politics. It does not trust in the good will of state actors or research institutes. Questions of self-organisation are important. Therefore, forums on specific issues are repeatedly organised at which activists exchange experience, develop common strategies and place political self-organisation on a broader base.

The "left-wing nationalist" position

The left-wing nationalist position, which is propagated in particular by a number of academics in Mexico City, is closely connected with the grassroots democracy position. The problem interpretations, lines of conflict and political concepts are similar. One major difference is that this position argues in the name of the interest "of the country". It can be interpreted as an attempt to place the particular interests of the indigenous communities and small farmers in a national context and to represent them as capable of generalisation. This position plays an important role in the public debate.

5.2.2 Hierarchy of the positions: dominance of the valorisation interests

The different positions and the social forces propagating them have a hierarchical relationship to one another. The neoliberal position is dominant, the technocratic-nationalist one is highly relevant and the conservationist position is relevant to a certain degree. The public is aware of the left-wing nationalist and grassroots democracy positions, but they hardly flow into the formulation of state strategies. (There was, by the way, a surprising level of agreement in the interviews between the different protagonists in regard to their appraisal of their own position and that of others.)

One pattern of argument which is common to the technocratic-nationalist and the neoliberal positions is that the "already moving train" of the highly technical appropriation of nature must not be allowed to pass without being boarded.[18] Mechanisms for benefit-sharing should above all improve the conditions for further valorisation (particularly via the establishment of corresponding capacities in the communities and research institutes). At the same time there are considerable tensions between the two positions. In view of the increasing pressure on the neoliberal position on decisive questions, not least due to international political processes within the framework of the CBD and the FAO, the technocratic-nationalist position is more than capable of presenting alternatives to the neoliberal position. Most recently, these concern the question of necessary legislation on access. Even the non-Mexican biotechnological enterprises and research institutes, which have a considerable interest in planning and investment security, appear increasingly to speak out in favour of regulation due to the criticism of the non-regulation of access.

The technocratic-nationalist position weakens itself by its own pragmatism, because in view of the desire to have some of the technology cake it largely accepts the stipulations of the neoliberal position. Interestingly, both positions always speak of the "development of the country", and even Monsanto representatives speak of "our Mexico". Both positions wrestle to define the general interest of society in the sphere of biodiversity policy. The current conditions for a development in the technocratic-nationalist sense are realistically estimated to be unfavourable, but nevertheless, its protagonists believe that with good arguments and clever strategies they will be able to achieve at least some of their objectives. All the same, the technocratic-nationalist position is, possibly in contradiction to its intention, closer to the neoliberal position than it thinks, due to a false appraisal of the relationships of forces and the potential for change. Its strategy, which is aimed at cooperation, plays into the hands of the neoliberal position.

The conservationist perspective is propagated above all by national and international NGOs which attempt to make their protection perspective compatible with the dominant tendencies. This refers in particular to the economisation of nature protection policies. NGOs such as Conservation International or The Nature Conservancy are close, even officially, to private corporations and foundations such as the Ford Foundation (cf. 4.1). Conservation International has been accused in Chiapas of working with the military in order to expel local communities and indigenous peoples and of bioprospecting for transnational corporations (Chapin 2004: 29).[19] They also consciously accelerate the privatisation of nature reserves. Other conservation NGOs such as the WWF follow these strategies perhaps less for reasons of conducting biotechnology business than because of the necessity of funding themselves and due to their acceptance of the fundamental relationships of forces. The idea is that if financially strong actors have an interest in the concerns of nature protection, then why should they be refused? In contradiction to an often formulated claim, the conservationist position is in danger of becoming compatible with the dominant forms of the appropriation of biodiversity. Moreover, financial pressures make the needed cooperation with other NGOs and local actors difficult, that is cooperation "has lost ground over the past decade, only to be replaced by often intense competition, largely over money" (Chapin 2004: 30). The conservation NGOs therefore exaggerate their successes and hide a self-critical perspective as well as working with governments and private companies which are often responsible for the environmental problems NGOs aim to solve. In the last years, it became clear that the strict conservationist position is against the involvement and participation of local people and indigenous communities. However, the consequences of this growing awareness are yet not clear.

The left-wing nationalist and the grassroots democracy positions argue more historically and take the experiences of subordinate groups into account, particularly those of indigenous peoples, in order to criticise the win–win perspective of the other positions. They have had hardly any success, however, in the broad public sphere and have lost influence within the state apparatus. Due to the confrontations of the 1990s, above all those over the recognition of indigenous rights and culture in the course of the Zapatista uprising, shifts have taken place and the concerns of the indigenous peoples have gained in legitimacy. But the dominant state and private capitalist forces and the conservation NGOs take up these issues either highly selectively, namely through the symbolic, but not necessarily legal and material, recognition of certain demands, or they reject them. On the question of the documentary proof of property ownership there is a central difference between the first three and the last two positions. The latter reject it or at least call for precaution, while the former regard it as necessary. The dominance of the valorisation interests and the connected paradigms are illustrated most clearly here.

Yet the technocratic-nationalist, left-wing nationalist and the grassroots democracy positions coincide on four points: first, in their criticism of the appropriation of genetic resources by enterprises and research institutes, although there are considerable differences on how and by whom this should be changed. This fact has been politicised for a number of years under the accusation of biopiracy, of which the technocratic-nationalist position has a rather formal understanding and demands that prior informed consent and benefit-sharing be fulfilled. Through the perspective of the entire country and its necessary participation in biotechnological development, tensions between state authorities, research institutes and the local population are regarded as less important. The democratic and left-wing nationalist positions, by contrast, ask more precisely about the specific contents of prior informed consent and benefit-sharing for the local population. They describe biopiracy in general as the attempt to privatise nature and the knowledge related to its treatment.

Second, all three positions see themselves as confronted by powerful interests. The technocratic-nationalist position is present in the Mexican state apparatuses but in the weaker ones where the actors pursue valorisation strategies as well. This takes place in a more politicised manner than in apparatuses like the Ministry of the Economy. The other two positions face-off with representatives of the technocratic-nationalist position as well as with the antagonistic Northern actors.

Third, they all regard a broad public debate as essential for the creation of awareness and to make suitable policies possible. All three positions trust in the fact that they have the better arguments, while by contrast, the neo-liberal and conservationist positions shy away from a public debate on the questions of the concrete appropriation of biological diversity.

Fourth, the problem of supply competition is recognised by all three positions. The technocratic-nationalist position attempts to deal with this by making concessionary offers of cooperation to the neoliberal position, because the latter can confer legitimacy and legal security. A second strategy is to strengthen cooperation with other *providers*, such as can be seen in the constitution of the *Like-Minded Group of Megadiverse Countries* (see Chapter 2). The grassroots democracy and the left-wing nationalist positions also regard international cooperation as important in order to obtain a picture of relationships in other countries and to be able to act together (Mx/10). At the end of 2000 the NGO CIEPAC organised a forum with representatives from six Latin American countries. "And there we discovered that the situation is similar everywhere." For Mexico, a moratorium on bioprospecting is demanded which should be as comprehensive as possible. This is diametrically opposed to the interests of the technocratic-nationalist position.

International regulations at first offer all actors the possibility of referring to them. Thus the neoliberal position emphasises the importance of TRIPS and the CBD access regulations, the technocratic-nationalist position insists on national sovereignty over biological resources and benefit-sharing, the conservationist position emphasises the stipulations concerning conservation, and the grassroots democracy and left-wing nationalist positions also emphasise benefit-sharing, as well as prior informed consent, mutually agreed terms and indigenous rights. That these regulations themselves have a hierarchical relationship to one another has already been described in detail. Important is one other fact: since the actors of the neoliberal and technocratic-nationalist positions played a major role in the formulation of the international systems of regulation, their interpretations of the problems and political strategies are most capable of relating to them.

To summarise, the neoliberal and technocratic-nationalist positions dominate. They are the protagonists of the valorisation paradigm and have by far the greatest financial and legal resources at their disposal. Furthermore, they are backed by the most powerful international agreements. The perspective that the valorisation of genetic resources is desirable and necessary in order to contribute to socio-economic progress establishes itself as by far the dominant view.

5.2.3 Conflicts over the strategic and institutional formation of the valorisation paradigm

In section 5.1.2 central tendencies were shown which led to the formation of a valorisation paradigm in Mexico. The next section focuses on the appropriation of genetic resources, in particular, in reference to the question: in which state strategies is the valorisation paradigm materialised? To avoid misunderstandings it must be understood that the appropriation of biological diversity not only takes place with the aid of state policies; indeed, in many cases it occurs precisely without them. However, from the theoretical perspective already outlined, the state is the form within bourgeois society in which conflicts of interest are primarily fought out and in which the different societal groups struggle for the generalisation and institutionalisation of their interests. The valorisation paradigm does not directly, or necessarily, establish itself, but its concrete form is moulded via social confrontations which are asymmetric with regard to the available resources and access to the state apparatus. In the final section, the preliminary results of this formation are outlined and to lesser extent the confrontations themselves are described. Here we shall no longer deal separately with the policy of nature protection and the project of the Mesoamerican Corridor (cf. 5.1.2).

Competencies and hierarchy of state apparatuses

The Ministry of the Economy is the most important apparatus and acts – almost all of the interviewees and the analysed texts were in agreement on this – in accordance with the wishes of the dominant interest groups. The responsibility for intellectual property, within the framework of both NAFTA and the TRIPS Agreement, is in the hands of the Ministry of the Economy. "They defend it semi-religiously" (Mx/3, our translation). The National Institute for Intellectual Property (INPI) is responsible for implementation. Here, the Mexican biodiversity policy of the 1990s functioned with the least friction in accordance with the wishes of the dominant neoliberal position. The NAFTA treaty, with very strict intellectual property rights, was ratified in 1993 and has been in force since 1 January 1994. As a result, the Law on Intellectual Property Rights was amended in 1994. The same thing happened with the TRIPS Agreement, which came into force in 1995, to which the Mexican legislation was adjusted in 1997. At that time, there was no opposition worthy of mention to the ratification of the two international treaties.[20] The Ministry of the Economy must also examine all laws, including laws on the environment. The Environmental Ministry suggested, for example, that a condition for the granting of licenses to collect should include room for significant Mexican civilian participation. This was rejected by the Ministry of the Economy with a reference to NAFTA; everyone should be able to collect without restriction, which is the rule which won the day (Mx/1). The Biosafety Protocol, which was developed with high international priority, was also negotiated under the leadership of the Ministry of the Economy.

Responsibility for the CBD is in the hands of the Environmental Ministry (SEMARNAT). The Ministry, which was founded in 1994, has the task of introducing a sustainable development model in Mexico. In the unanimous view of those interviewed, this Ministry has had little political weight ever since it was established and under President Fox it has had even less. Issue areas such as forests and fisheries were handed over to the Ministry of Agriculture (which will have considerable consequences in view of the neo-liberal position that exists there; Mx/17). There is no continuity of environmental legislation and its implementation to speak of. During the Zedillo government, SEMARNAT acted "more like an intermediary or facilitator for researchers and private corporations than as guardian of the relevant laws" (Harvey, N. 2001: 1051). The implementation of the CBD is sluggish, not only because there is too little interest on the part of articulate actors such as, for example, a Mexican biotechnology industry, but also because this apparatus has little weight. In the Environmental Ministry, only those active NGOs and experts who basically support the dominant tendencies but would like to give them a technocratic-nationalist touch are listened to (see also the national strategy, which was developed by the Environmental Ministry, CONABIO 2000). Via the National Institute of Ecology (INE), the Environmental Ministry is responsible for granting permission for the bioprospecting of "wild" flora and fauna.

Another important apparatus for biodiversity policy is the Agricultural Ministry (SAGARPA), which is responsible for agro-biological diversity. The head of the last ministry, who has been in office since 2000, is a successful agricultural exporter. One critic sees the Ministry as now being essentially closer to industry and more biotechnology-friendly (Mx/9). In January 2001, only a few weeks after the Fox Government came to power, the "First National Forum for Biotechnology and Biological Security" took place in the Mexican industrialists' club. The organiser was the inter-ministerial Commission on Biological Safety and Genetically Modified Organisms (CIBIOGEM), which had been founded a few years previously, and which has close ties to the Agricultural Ministry. The founder and chairperson of the association is Victor Villalobos, a consultant to the former transnational enterprise Pulsar, and previously a consultant to the company International Papers, who, under the newly inaugurated President Fox, was appointed to the position of Deputy Minister of Agriculture. The Forum took place in cooperation with AgroBio. The Monsanto representative spoke on the environmental risks of genetic technology, and representatives of CONABIO and CIMMYT were not even invited to contribute. A lot of rhetoric was used in reference to "the country" and about the need for "necessary social consensus" and "development", but the programme was very one-sided and provoked the protest of critical NGOs such as RAFI and Greenpeace. In the final declaration, it was stated that under the present government, it was not the Environmental Ministry but rather the Agricultural Ministry which would be responsible for ensuring sustainable development. This illustrates clearly that immediately following the change of government struggles over responsibilities broke out and the CIBIOGEM reclaimed responsibility for biotechnologies and genetically modified organisms (GMOs). The representative of the Agricultural Ministry said, in the context of the biotechnology forum, that it hardly interested anyone whether or not a forum was conducted on access or benefit-sharing (Mx/6).

On the whole, both of the houses of the parliament of the Mexican federation, the Senate and the Chamber of Deputies, play a subordinate role. They are important, however, for juridical initiatives, for example with regard to access legislation.

The National Biodiversity Strategy

Mexico ratified the CBD on 11 March 1993. In Article 6 the parties to the agreement undertake to formulate a national plan, that is a type of inventory and problem synopsis, a national strategy and a plan of action. This process was very protracted in Mexico, which can be interpreted as meaning that the dominant forces are more than happy to live with the existing state of things. The national strategy which was formulated at the end of the 1990s is nevertheless an important document, because here in an extensive process a "national interest" has been outlined, which is not uniform but which nevertheless sets out a dominant perspective with regard to the problems and their treatment. Until now, a country study has been conducted under the leadership of the National Biodiversity Commission (CONABIO 1998) and a national strategy has been formulated as a compromise among different forces (CONABIO 2000). The national plan of action is still on the waiting list. The national strategy is the explicit attempt to formulate a "national interest" in the treatment of biodiversity. Experts have been involved in its formulation, but the process is also said to have been participative (CONABIO 2000: 7), a statement which, however, has been denied by critics. The state document formulates a consistent "we" throughout and thus construes a uniform interest of all Mexicans or even a "we as a country" with regard to a changed treatment of biodiversity. Following the ascertainment of the great importance of biological diversity, it is stated that, "because of its current value, its enormous economic potential, its inestimable services for the environment [*servicios ambientales*] which it provides for all Mexicans, and for ethical and moral reasons, biodiversity must be regarded as a strategic resource for Mexico" (ibid.: 21, our translation).

The main reason for the protection of biodiversity lies in its potential exchange value. The erosion is estimated to be dramatic and a great multitude of strategies are derived from that. The four central sections deal with protection and conservation, the estimation of the value of biodiversity, knowledge and the treatment of information, and the diversification of use. Interestingly, biotechnological utilisation and the regulation of access appear in the first section on "protection and conservation", in the subsection on biological safety (ibid.: 35). That subsection deals with the development of a national biotechnology programme which is to estimate economic value, support genetic technology research in connection with domestic diversity, draw up criteria for safety and "has the objective of appraising and reviving popular knowledge in order to use biodiversity selectively" (our translation). In addition, knowledge and the regulation of access to genetic resources and their utilisation are to be improved, as is the granting of patents, registers or descriptions of origin of those genetic resources which have been developed through domestication, selection or traditional manipulation by Mexican groups (indigenous groups, farmers or others) (ibid.).

Altogether, economically critical remarks, which appear in two places, are insignificant in relation to the general tenor of the strategy: primarily, a stronger awareness of problems and actions is required, particularly a greater "institutional vigilance" and environmental education, a higher evaluation of biodiversity, a legal framework and an "authentic strategy" and "coherent policies". A legal framework is regarded as necessary which defines and protects the intellectual property rights of the indigenous communities and farmers' groups. Tensions are not addressed; instead, they disappear in face of the assumed win–win strategy.

The importance of the strategy is difficult to estimate. As an important discursive element, it certainly expresses a compromise between the neo-liberal and the technocratic-nationalist positions. Some references to the problems and interests of other positions are included in several passages. The long-standing director of CONABIO was surprisingly reticent with regard to these central processes and documents (Mx/1). The official strategy is, furthermore, embedded in a multitude of programmes which were formulated in the sphere of influence of the Environmental Ministry. In particular, the change of government such as that at the end of 2000 has led, in Mexico, to the formulation of a National Plan which covers various areas. Remarkable in this context is a document which is concerned with the protection and the increase of natural capital, in particular via or within the indigenous communities (SEMARNAT/INE 2002; official documents never speak of indigenous peoples). Here, it is suggested that the natural resources and in particular biodiversity should be supported by payments to the communities because this would lead to an appropriate estimation of its value, and that biological diversity should be valorised in order to encourage its sustainable use (ibid.: 13f.)

The failed initiative for access legislation

The existing legal framework for the access agreements, the General Environmental Law LEGEEPA, requires, for scientific (Art. 87) and commercial (Art. 87 extended) collections of wild flora and fauna, the prior informed consent of the Environmental Ministry and of the owners of the land. The results of scientific collections must be published. In the case of commercial collections, the owners or more appropriately, the legitimate owners have the right to a fair benefit-sharing agreement. The competence for consent is clearly regulated for nature reserves: it lies with the Mexican state. Legal uncertainties exist if consent has to be given by indigenous communities, since they, as a rule, do not have clear, individual property relationships. It was clear to the experts who formulated the extension of Article 87 to prior informed consent and benefit-sharing in the mid-1990s that a specification was necessary, either in the form of a separate law or via an ordinance (Mx/8). The Environmental Law is regarded by many of those involved as very imprecise and far removed from reality, as well as being too complex. From the perspective of the local application in Chiapas, the criticism is that it has been formulated by people at the central level with little experience and without a great deal of consultation.

The Environmental Ministry, CONABIO and the Senate therefore convened a National Forum in 1997, from which the legislation process was to begin. A group of experts was formed (*Biodiversidad y Desarrollo en México*; Biodem) which was to be the driving force of the process. This group was charged by the Senate with formulating a draft for an access law. In view of the political situation there was to be no wide consultation. One of the participants of the process said that the "political situation in view of the problems in Chiapas, Guerrero and Oaxaca did not allow discussion" (Mx/8). Nevertheless, different actors were consulted. The Ministry of the Economy was not a driving force but referred to its other international obligations in the question of intellectual property, which could not be ignored. Corporations also took part in the consultations, and particularly the biotechnology firms were interested in IPR. The access legislation was only a subordinate concern for them, however, while they attempted to accelerate legislation on biological safety. At the same time, within the Agricultural Ministry – which was responsible for agro-biological diversity and which was critical of the initiative for a law – discussion began concerning a law on rural development (*Ley de Desarrollo Rural*), for which access regulations were also outlined during the discussions. These were not included in the law which was finally passed, however.

The group handed over the project to the Senate in December 1999. In the end it was laid down that the resources in the nature reserves are in the possession of the nation, independent of whether indigenous knowledge (and thus also the bearers of that knowledge) is to be found there or not. In the Senate, at the beginning of the 2000 election year, the law project was not further pursued. Officially, this was due to a lack of time, but a Mexican access law obviously was not seen as being of high priority. The protagonists of the neoliberal position had no interest in binding Mexican legislation on questions of access. From their point of view, Mexico had already fulfilled the obligation to create appropriate access legislation, which it had entered into with the ratification of the CBD.

The technocratic-nationalist position saw the necessity of filling out the Environmental Law. The state should have a more important role in benefit-sharing than is the case in the General Environmental Law. This poses the question of why these actors, who were quite capable of articulation, did not drive forward the legislation more strongly. One explanation lies in the fact that foreign companies or research institutes with which coalitions were intended should not be scared off. This position has a strong wish to participate in the current biotechnological developments. Its perception of the problem is that there is too little valorisation of resources in the country. Apparently, bilateral negotiations appear more likely to be successful than a law. Of apparent impact is the criticism by enterprises and research institutes of the legislative processes in other countries that the laws there tended to "over-regulate". The low importance of access legislation can therefore be explained by the politicisation of the subject and the sparse interest it provoked, or the other priorities of industry. The interest in planning security was apparently not accommodated by the initiative for an access law. The existing framework, in particular the reformulated environmental law, appears to be regarded as adequate. A non-decision, that is abandoning the original initiative for legislation that provided access, was the best manner of corresponding to the existing power relationship of social and political forces.

Failed prescription of indigenous rights and culture

The struggle of indigenous peoples for their rights and culture is not part of biodiversity politics in a narrow sense but sheds light on the actual power constellations in Mexico which affect the conflict field of biodiversity politics. One of the most important Mexican-wide initiatives of the Zapatista rebels and the National Indigenous Congress (*Congreso Nacional Indígena*) – the autonomous association of the indigenous population which was founded throughout the country at the end of 1996 – was the attempt to prescribe indigenous rights and culture in the constitution (Hernández Navarro 1999, 2000). The "Agreement of San Andrés" was negotiated from 1994 to 1996 between the Mexican government and the Zapatistas as well as indigenous peoples in order to strengthen and constitutionally codify the rights of indigenous peoples in Mexico. A compromise was formed in March 1996 which was accepted by the indigenous population, the implementation of which was, however, refused by the government (see Higgins 2001: 886ff.). Therefore, since the end of 1996, an all-party commission (*Comisión de Concordia y Pacificación*; COCOPA) has been attempting to moderate the conflict. In order to lend emphasis to this initiative, in February/March 2001 the Commander of the Zapatistas left the area under their control for the first time and travelled through Mexico to the capital city in order to move parliament to accept the change in the Constitution. Finally, however, only a considerably weaker version of the law was passed, which in turn was rejected by the *Congreso Nacional Indígena* and the Zapatistas as being unacceptable. The changed version maintains the centralist and paternalistic role of the state towards the indigenous population, which leads Harvey to speak of a "corporatist citizenship" which has existed since the Mexican Revolution (Harvey, N. 2001: 1058), and which is actualised in the law by the greater consideration of the interests of private firms in access to resources on indigenous territory.

> In this way, the future model of citizenship proposed by the Mexican government resembles a hybrid of corporatist and market citizenship, in which the state continues to secure political order ... , while the market seeks to incorporate those who are willing and able to work, produce and consume at globally competitive rates.
>
> (ibid.)

When President Fox, in 2001, pushed for a constitutional recognition of indigenous rights, the Senate presented a very different version which was approved against the will of the representatives of indigenous peoples. The weakened version was anchored in the constitution, ratified by the necessary number of individual states and came into force in August 2001. The law was not ratified, however, by the states with the largest shares of indigenous population: Chiapas, Oaxaca and Guerrero (Harvey, N. 2001: 1049f.). Behind the rejection is a widespread unease, which does not only affect Mexico's political class.

> In the same way in which the search for national unity was tied for years to the idea of "de-Indianizing", today the fear of cultural diversity is behind the universalism of the opponents of indigenous rights. Behind the decade-long dominating idea of the inevitability of *Mestizaje* (Mestization) is both the aversion to the Other and the inability to understand the indigenous question not as a "race issue" but as a question of cultural difference ... The Agreement of San Andrés on indigenous rights and culture demonstrate that the indigenous communities exist, that they are alive and prepared to fight. Neither the old nor the new ideology of integration, whether disguised as nationalism or as universalism, could eliminate them. The agreements

show that they are not "living relics" but political actors with a project for the future, and that in spite of their persecuted cultures they are endowed with an enormous vitality.

(Hernández Navarro 2000: 179f., our translation)

After the defeat of the legal struggle of the indigenous peoples in Mexico for a constitutional recognition of their rights in spring 2001, the Zapatistas decided to stop their public activities and kept silent for more then two years.[21] In the meantime they concentrated on the reinforcement of their own political and socio-economic structures in the almost 600 Zapatista communities in Chiapas. They established *Juntas del Buen Gobierno* (Councils of Good Government) in five *caracoles* (snail-shells) as central expressions of their autonomy and self-government (Bartra 2003).

One success of the Zapatista uprising was that it reopened the discussion on the indigenous people of Mexico. It is not only a question of legal recognition but of a profound change in societal concepts of value and institutional practices. The prescription of indigenous rights and culture in the Constitution, which the indigenous population regards as central and which would have had a great symbolic meaning, could not be enforced, however. That former President Fox supported the initiative on the side of the Zapatistas can be interpreted either as a tactical ploy, or that he hoped in this way to attain more room for manoeuvre for his diverse development and valorisation projects in the South of Mexico. It is too early to say what the strategy of the current president (Calderón) is going to be.

5.3 Local conflicts over the valorisation paradigm in Chiapas

In this section we shall deal with the specific strategies for the appropriation of biological diversity. At the same time, other processes – such as the interests in oil or fine woods – must be understood as "the general framework", because the competing concepts and practices with regard to the formation of societal relationships with nature are important for the different strategies for the appropriation of biological diversity. To put it more pointedly: the massive interest in Chiapas's oil superimposes itself on the dispute with regard to the competing ways of dealing with biological diversity. It does not determine the latter, however; in addition, the specific interests in the appropriation of biological diversity are partly just beginning to form.

In two disputes in recent years, the conflicts and their momentum, as well as the role of the state, are concentrated like rays of light by a magnifying glass: in the dispute over the bioprospecting agreement ICBG-Maya and over the biosphere reserve Montes Azules. The ICBG-Maya project does not stand paradigmatically for the practice of bioprospecting agreements but has its own specific characteristics. It is illustrated particularly clearly here that the general strategies – ICBG projects are conducted worldwide

(Fogarty International Center 2007) – must be connected to the specific national and local conditions. The confrontations over Montes Azules can, by contrast, be taken as an example for other cases. The dominant strategies in Montes Azules show how nature protection interests and valorisation interests can be related to one another in a problematical way. Altogether – and in this the conditions in Chiapas are a special case – the conflict cannot be understood without a strong politicisation and organisation of the population. Chiapas becomes a strategic space in which very different actors operate. Central actors and their interests and strategies with regard to the appropriation of biological diversity will therefore be outlined briefly.

5.3.1 Central actors and their strategies

The decisive difference between the nation-state level of politics and the local, that is that of Chiapas, is the different constellation of forces in this south-eastern Mexican state. The intensive confrontations over the establishment of the valorisation paradigm in Chiapas are due to the strong presence of actors with a grassroots democracy position. This is true in the field of biological diversity/genetic resources, but also of the appropriation of other natural resources, the valorisation of labour and the control of the population. An important point of reference is without doubt the uprising of the indigenous communities organised in the Zapatista liberation army EZLN. These were not so much guerrillas in the traditional sense as a militia which had emerged from a large number of communities and was supported by those communities (*communidades de base*). The Zapatistas not only accelerated the Mexican-wide self-organisation of the indigenous peoples through the founding of the *Congreso Nacional Indígena*, which understands itself as a counterweight to the state-corporatist indigenous association, but also gave impetus to the independent farmers' movements (Hernández Navarro 2000).

The Zapatista rebels, the communities supporting them as well as organisations in other parts of Mexico were sensitised during the conflict as to the meaning of genetic resources and traditional knowledge. Until then, the question of the natural resources and their exploitation was orientated towards the "classical" themes of water, oil and natural gas, timber and agricultural production. In February 2001 the *Congreso Nacional Indígena* at its third nation-wide meeting stated its position for the first time on the question of bioprospecting (Harvey, N. 2001: 1054). For this sensitising, the *Consejo de Organizaciones de Médicos y Parteras Indígenas Tradicionales de Chiapas* (COMPITCH, the umbrella organisation of the indigenous doctors and midwives of Chiapas, www.laneta.apc.org/compitch; Wullweber 2004: 113ff.) played an important role. The Zapatistas with their demands for self-organisation and diversity were apparently able to open a space in which new issues and lines of conflict were outlined and in which other actors could constitute themselves and gain self-confidence. COMPITCH was already in existence, but it was only through the uprising that it broke out of its previously defensive shell (Mx/21).

In local forums facts are discussed, strategies are developed and networks are created. Political demands were summarised, for example, in the declaration of San Gregorio, the final document of a forum planned by the umbrella organisation ARIC-I, Independent Rural Association of Collective Interest (*Asociación Rural de Interés Colectivo Independiente*) in the Montes Azules biosphere in May 2000 (Declaración de San Gregorio 2000). Here the accusation is repudiated that the erosion of biodiversity is due to the agricultural practices of the indigenous farmers. A moratorium on the patenting of living organisms is demanded, as is the defence of traditional knowledge, the protection of biological resources from intellectual property rights and a prohibition of the sale of GMOs by national and international enterprises. Different social groups should cooperate to formulate a law in the sense of Article 8(j) of the CBD and Article 169 of the ILO. Further-more, land rights, health services and education, and the protection of the natural resources in the Lacandon Jungle are demanded. In November 2000, in Amador Hernández, a "forum on demilitarization, indigenous peoples, development and biological diversity", organised by the Zapatistas, took place at which similar demands were discussed, as were the planned large projects and expulsions. The "week for biological and cultural diversity" has already taken place several times, the first time in 2001 in Chiapas, with 171 participating organisations from 16 countries (Declaración de la Semana por la Diversidad 2001). Demands are raised, for example, for the prohibi-tion of the private appropriation of biological diversity and patents on life, for the development of alternative economic projects instead of the Maqui-ladoras and agro-chemical agriculture, for the revision of the international instruments concerning intellectual property rights and for the recognition of the indigenous people and their autonomy.

One good example of the way in which the rebellion was connected with the confrontations over the appropriation of biological diversity is the NGO CIEPAC, mentioned above. It emerged from the National Mediation Com-mission CONAI (*Comisión Nacional de Intermediación*), which had been headed by Bishop Samuel Ruíz, who had been in office since 1959, in order to mediate between the government and the Zapatista rebels. In view of the intransigent stance of the government, the bishop withdrew and the com-mission was dissolved in June 1998. Some office workers founded CIEPAC in July 1998. Beyond questions of peace they are concerned with the com-plex political, economic, strategic and military processes and with the pro-cesses of expulsion and migration in Chiapas. They cooperate with COMPITCH, organise larger forums and smaller workshops in indigenous communities, and produce studies and bulletins translated into various Maya languages. CIEPAC made an essential contribution to making the issues known in the communities and to the position-finding of the com-munities, and is a major actor which contributed to the politicisation of the

ICBG-Maya project. This was connected not least with the great trust which the former CONAI workers enjoyed, and still enjoy today, in the communities. The international NGO Global Exchange, with its seat in San Francisco, also strongly concerned itself in the beginning with questions of human rights and has extended its work to include, among other things, the subject of bioprospecting.

In Chiapas itself, the actors with a left-wing nationalist position do not play any role. This is apparently connected with the fact that the conflict concerning the appropriation of biological diversity "at home" is much clearer and positions, which have the room for manoeuvre of weaker actors in view, cannot proceed here from within a "national interest", no matter how it may be construed. The direct confrontations of the protagonists of the grassroots democracy position take place with key state apparatuses (government, police, military) and with the local oligarchy which has close ties to them and to the paramilitary groups which are financed by them, but also with those who have a direct interest in the appropriation of genetic resources.

A central political and economic actor was for a long time the transnationally operating Mexican corporation Pulsar, which arose like many company groups in Latin American countries in the course of the privatisations of the 1980s and 1990s. Pulsar (or Savia, which was its name in Mexico) was founded in 1991 by Alfonso Romo Garza, who was one of the closest consultants of former President Fox, as well as being a consultant to the World Bank and a member of the board of Conservation International (CI). At the same time, he plays a central role in the Chiapas Fund (*Fondo Chiapas*), founded in 1994, in which Nestlé, the maize giant Maseca, the bank group Serfin and others are organised.[22] The most prominent enterprise of the Pulsar Group was the agro-biotechnology corporation Seminis, the worldwide leader in the production of fruit and vegetable seeds (22 per cent market share), with R&D establishments in 36 countries, and in Mexico in Chiapas, Las Margaritas and Taniperla. Seminis was sold in 2005 to Monsanto, which made Monsanto the largest seed company in the world and gave this US-based company access to many Mexican natural reserves.

The station in Taniperla primarily conducts genetic technological research on plants. In another field of activity, the former Pulsar and now Monsanto subsidiary, *Desarrollo Forestal* has begun to plant 300,000 hectares of eucalyptus for the production of cellulose and simple timbers in three Southern states.

The enterprise supports, together with the Ministry of the Environment and CI, three research stations in the nature reserve Montes Azules in the Lacandon Jungle. Already in 1996 Pulsar raised 10 million USD for the work of CI in the Montes Azules biosphere reserve (Harvey, N. 2001: 1054). It is suspected that bioprospecting is conducted there, which is not necessarily illegal since, jurisdictionally, Pulsar was a Mexican firm and sometimes called the "gene monopolist" (on the firms and their interests see Pólito Barrios Morfín 2000: 67–76).

Conservation International, which as mentioned above takes up a conservationist position, is a further central actor.[23] The branch of CI in Mexico was founded in 1990 and began its work in Chiapas in 1991, among other things with so-called *debt-for-nature swaps* (Harvey, N. 2001: 1054). CI-Mexico attempts in the projects to "couple" the indigenous population to the planned conservation measures. In this way, detailed studies on biological diversity and the knowledge of its treatment are conducted (Delgado Ramos 2004). Neil Harvey (2001: 1055) sees the attractiveness of the CI and Pulsar projects for the local population in the fact that the latter lacks an alternative. The interest in access to biological diversity remains dominant. However, "As in the highlands [a Zapatista stronghold, the authors] the biggest obstacle facing CIMEX and Pulsar are those communities that participate in the area's indigenous organizations." The WWF also plays a role, because it operates in Chiapas with the international project of the so-called bioregions.

The political institutions in Chiapas have little room in which to manoeuvre. Almost all of the legislative competence in the areas of the protection of natural resources and biodiversity are in the hands of the nation-state. The work of CONABIO is very centralised and there are no local consultations. The subject of intellectual property has never been discussed in Chiapas at the level of the state (Mx/14). Responsible for the implementation in Chiapas is the state government, the Institute of Natural History (*Instituto de Historia Natural*) (which has its own collections but does not conduct bioprospecting) and the Ministry for Agricultural Development (*Secretaria de Desarrollo Rural*). In view of the strong centralisation in Mexico, the other apparatuses of the state executive in Chiapas also tend to have the function of transmitting federal policies downwards.

This brief outline of the most important actors and their strategies illustrates that there are enormous differences in resources between the protagonists of the individual positions. Pulsar first, and now Monsanto and CI invest considerable sums of money in conservation activities in Chiapas, have research stations at their disposal and have access to many areas and communities. They have direct access to the government and have an excellent international network. In view of the financial problems of the Mexican government in administering the nature reserves effectively, it is dependent on personnel and financial cooperation and has formulated this explicitly as its strategy.

The most important assets of the grassroots actors are their own public education, politicisation and organisation. Few financial resources are available. Furthermore, they operate under the conditions of a strong police and military presence, which was markedly increased following the beginning of the Zapatista rebellion, and against a reactionary local oligarchy. International politics plays a role in the specific confrontations which refers to the regulations concerning the rights of indigenous peoples or prior informed consent. There is very little access to the formulation of national policies.

The bioprospecting agreement, ICBG-Maya, which will be described in the following section, is an interesting case study.

5.3.2 *The bioprospecting agreement ICBG-Maya*

In the summer of 1992 the research programme *International Cooperative Biodiversity Groups* (ICBG) was founded by the US Health Department, the Ministry of Agriculture and the National Science Foundation, among others. This group was intended to support bioprospecting in Southern countries which was financed by the US government. A first round began in 1993 with five projects, and a second in 1998. For the latter's six projects in ten Southern countries over a period of five years, altogether 500,000–600,000 USD per annum were provided. In 2005, a third period started with an overall funding of 6 million USD. The objective is to find therapeutic substances for cancer, HIV-AIDS, tuberculosis, malaria, heart and lung disease and other illnesses. These should, according to the third call for tenders, take place via innovative approaches with regard to access and benefit-sharing. Biodiversity should be protected through the discovery of bioactive substances, that is an extremely close connection is created between the discovery of natural substances with medicinal value, protection and economic impulses (FIC 2007; NIH 2003; Delgado Ramos 2004: 75–77).[24]

Other preconditions are that prospecting in Southern countries needs to be conducted in close cooperation with research institutes based there, the project management is in the hands of a US institution and that a person named by the US government participates. Participation by a private firm is seen as desirable, in particular with regard to further utilisation and benefit-sharing (see the current call for tenders in the FIC 2002). The CBD is named as a part of a rapidly developing international framework, which is why access, prior informed consent, benefit-sharing and IPR agreements should be carefully formulated. This is connected with the uncertainties with regard to benefit-sharing and intellectual property rights in the first two rounds (see FIC 2007, Final Report). A recently founded *Centre for the Management of IP in Health R&D* is to provide guidance to the applying groups with regard to formulation (www.mihr.org). Critical voices contend that the ICBG project is less a strategy for supporting economic development in the providing countries, and more a strategy related to the US government's wishes to secure access to the genetic resources in Southern countries and to give the rights to this above all to US research institutes and firms (Ceceña/Giménez 2002). In relation to this argument, even on its own, the focus on the complex development of medication for certain diseases leaves hardly any room for manoeuvre for local developments beyond direct work for the projects. According to Delgado Ramos (2001: 491) that is precisely the function of *Bio-Maquiladoras*, that is less skilled and cheap production for export.

In Chiapas the research institute ECOSUR already participated in the tender in the first round in 1992, but was not awarded the contract. In the second tender in 1997 it was successful. The central figure in the application and in the later project was a US American anthropologist from the University of Georgia who had been operating in Chiapas since 1992. He was also a guest researcher at the US *National Institutes of Health* (NIH), which essentially coordinated and funded the ICBG projects. The implementing organisation in Chiapas was ECOSUR, an institute seated in San Cristóbal (and which was also present in three other locations). ECOSUR, like the US anthropologist, had had contact with the indigenous communities in many other projects. For the second round of applications the NIH demanded the integration of a commercial pharmaceutical enterprise. ECOSUR did not desire the participation of a large corporation and therefore chose *Molecular Nature* from Wales which had, at the time, 14 employees. One important difference to the other ICBG projects worldwide, according to a representative of ECOSUR, is that the Maya project was intended to be transparent from the beginning (Mx/11). The protocol was published, for example, and the idea that the research should be useful to the indigenous communities was also novel. The indigenous population was not included in the development of the project, however, and prior informed consent was not provided. The indigenous people's participation was to take place in the course of the project, particularly via an NGO with the name of *Promaya*, which at that time was still to be founded and which was to be involved primarily in the decision on benefit-sharing. The subsequent invitation to participate in Promaya was, however, rejected by the indigenous population.

The interest of ECOSUR was that with the ICBG-Maya project, work could be financed for five years which otherwise would not have been able to take place, particularly taxonomic work, the training of workers and the improvement of the research base, above all in terms of infrastructure, with the building of laboratories. At the beginning, it was not intended that ECOSUR should receive technical equipment for their activites, but it was successful in overcoming such restrictions in later negotiations. ECOSUR was to receive about one-third of the *premio total* (total premium) particularly for wages for over 20 *técnicos indígenas* (indigenous technicians). The equipment was bought by Georgia University and sent to Chiapas in return for a credit note. Certain research, of which ECOSUR was not capable, could have been conducted in the biochemical laboratories of this very US University. The interest of Molecular Nature was to develop potentially commercial substances and then to patent them. In a preliminary form, ECOSUR had the idea that all participants, including the indigenous organisations, should share in the intellectual property of developed products. But finally no co-patents or anything similar with ECOSUR or the indigenous communities were planned. Technology transfer was also not to take place in the form of the transfer of technology from Molecular Nature or

Georgia University to Chiapas. It would have been about "something simpler" than patents (Mx/11).

The ICBG-Maya project was granted permission in 1997, but due to the Zapatista uprising, it did not begin until May 1999 and was conducted only until October 2000. Up to that point, according to the ECOSUR representative, there was no transfer of resources to Molecular Nature. In the first year, furthermore, the concern was based on the two types of permission for the collections: "scientific" and "biotechnological". The application to SEMARNAT for bioprospecting was not approved because the prior informed consent had not been realised. Therefore, up until the end of 1999 there had only been scientific collections, and afterwards even that permit expired. Since it was not renewed, in the course of 2000 no further collections took place. Instead, more than 20 people from different communities were trained, all of whom were to serve as "contacts" between the communities and the prospectors. Among other things a play was developed in order to present the project to the communities and to inform them. This was to serve as a basis for obtaining prior informed consent. One group went into the communities and spoke to the traditional authorities. Some of these indigenous leaders then came to ECOSUR, saw the play and returned to their communities. If the community agreed, the play was presented there also. The communities – each member or the authorities – agreed in 50 cases. However, this was not yet about benefit-sharing. Although by the beginning of 2001 (between the moratorium and the end of ICBG-Maya) a proposal for benefit-sharing had been submitted, a definitive answer had yet to be given. ECOSUR's position at that point was that the indigenous communities should organise themselves, and conduct their own negotiations with the enterprises in which they would be able to say no. In September 1999, criticism of the project by NGOs, indigenous communities and critical media began. A major role was played by the association of indigenous medical practitioners, COMPITCH (Mx/14). They were considered to be the guarantee for access to indigenous communities in a legitimised manner – and turned out to be the major obstacle after they rejected it. In October 2000 the project was suspended by the announcement of a moratorium by ECOSUR. Georgia University and Molecular Nature had no other choice but to accept the moratorium because ECOSUR was the implementing organisation. The NIH paid nothing for a year. The project, such was the situation at that time, could only have been continued if an indigenous group had formed to negotiate benefit-sharing. But that did not happen. One year later, in October 2001, the project was abandoned. It is not the first ICBG project to be prematurely disbanded.

The ECOSUR representative is of the opinion that the conflict escalated because of the existence of non-indigenous advisors who had an interest in its failure and because of biased press which did not want to hear the ECOSUR arguments. Critical NGOs participated, which were sometimes right but occasionally "hit out without seeing the implications" (Mx/11).

The indigenous communities had cooperated well, which was not surprising considering the deplorable living conditions under which many of them existed. "They welcome every initiative." Therefore the criticism concerning prior informed consent was unjustified. However, ECOSUR admits that the lack of participation of the indigenous population was a mistake and names this as a central criterion for future projects. Nonetheless, this position was not heard so clearly from state actors in Mexico City. At the same time ECOSUR was criticised due to the lack of clear concepts as to how prior informed consent could in fact be achieved. The ECOSUR representative is sceptical with regard to whether, in the case of concrete prior informed consent regulations, these could do justice at all, in light of the particular cultural notion of participation held by indigenous people.

For the protagonists of the grassroots democracy position, the ending of the ICBG-Maya project is a significant milestone in the struggle against the illegitimate appropriation of biological diversity. The project was criticised because the negotiation of the agreement took place without the participation of the indigenous population, there was no prior informed consent and the collected samples were to be taken to the USA, out of the reach of indigenous people. In addition, the inherent tendency in the ICBG-Maya agreement, to turn resources and knowledge which were collective goods into private property, was also rejected. Another matter to be criticised was that it remained completely unclear as to how patents on knowledge and resources would affect the living conditions of the providers (COMPITCH 2000 according to Wullweber 2004: 117ff.). The communities would first have to understand prior informed consent. NGOs have an important educational task here. In addition to the lack of information, a methodology with which the communities could define what their benefits should be was also missing; they must define these themselves, and for the long term, independently of NGOs. The firm must listen to the community, not the community to the firm, by, for example, letting the latter define the type of *beneficios* (benefits) (Mx/16). Bioprospecting must take place in a very controlled way and be slowed down as long as these controls and clear legal relationships do not exist. Therefore, the moratorium and the abandonment of the project were regarded as positive outcomes (Mx/14).

ECOSUR's approach of placing value on transparency, at least in certain questions, displays an obvious difference in comparison to other, mostly secret, agreements. It is to be suspected that ECOSUR and the Environmental Ministry wanted to proceed more cautiously than in the case of other agreements in view of the high degree of politicisation in Chiapas. ECOSUR claims to have had good intentions and sees itself as the victim of a slander campaign. It becomes clear that bioprospecting depends decisively on the (non-)information of the population which shares knowledge and resources as well as on the legitimacy of the collectors. A lack of information in the communities was, and is, a favourable condition for the appropriation of genetic resources. If the potential providers are more informed, this increases their chances of self-determination. Although information, international and national political processes, and in particular the work of critical NGOs certainly play a role, it is also evident that they require local conditions in which this information can be spread and judged to be politically relevant. This is where the political character of the often technically understood concept of *capacity building* lies. The relationships in Chiapas, both the requirements of the access agreement and the criticisms of it, are a good example of how international processes are conveyed through local ones. The practical criticism of ICBG-Maya would have taken place anyway, according to the activists (Mx/10; Mx/13). However, the specific constellation in Chiapas, characterised by the Zapatista uprising, not only postponed the beginning of the bioprospecting project, but also "simplified" the politicisation of its subject-matter, because the social organisations were themselves politicised. NGOs which were originally active in work on human rights and peace concerned themselves with it, and the Agreement of San Andrés was a major milestone (Mx/10). In this understanding, the uprising served, in a sense, as a catalyst (Mx/13).

Bioprospecting continues to take place in Chiapas despite the abandonment of the ICBG-Maya project. Collecting very probably takes place in the research stations supported by former Pulsar and CI-Mex. So-called and self-designated "intermediaries" go into the communities and collect plants without permission. Nevertheless, the dispute over the project is very important because an organised and articulate population questioned the dominant forms of appropriation. They did not do so with the argument that knowledge should not be shared. Rather, they criticised the fact that they were not allowed to participate and that the entire context of the bioprospecting was clearly dominated by interests pushing for the privatisation of nature. Thus, future and better formulated bioprospecting agreements which take prior informed consent and benefit-sharing into account remain trapped in the dilemma that highly unequal relationships of power exist and that the dominant valorisation paradigm is rarely questioned, apart from its criticism by the grassroots democracy position. The objectively existing supply competition and the time-pressure created by dominant actors apparently leave little room for the opening-up of learning processes.

5.3.3 *The disputes over the biosphere reserve Montes Azules*

The disputes over the nature reserve Montes Azules (*Reserva Integral de la Biósfera Montes Azules*; RIBMA) in the Lacandon Jungle in Chiapas represent an example of how developments are interpreted and what interests form alliances in the process. Although RIBMA, which covers more than 330,000 ha, was declared a nature reserve in 1978, at first, none of the measures connected with the declaration were implemented. In the course of the 1980s the protection of tropical forests gained in importance and large nature protection NGOs identified the so-called "hot spots" in tropical regions which were to be protected. Since the 1990s the World Bank-based Global Environmental Facility (GEF) co-finances the administration of the RIBMA.

As is the case anywhere else, around the RIBMA, different actors follow different interests (see also Ceceña 2000: 270 and section 2.3). The area is a tropical forest in which timber companies are interested in obtaining licenses to operate. Following logging, rapidly growing eucalyptus trees are to be planted in order to produce cellulose for the production of paper. In addition there are large oil deposits in the area. Despite this fact, the partially privatised petroleum company *Petróleos Mexicanos* (PEMEX) temporarily withdrew from the area in 1994. Furthermore, the Lacandon Jungle is a centre of biological diversity, for it is believed that in 0.16 per cent of the area of the state, 20 per cent of its biological diversity is to be found. And finally, this area is located in the heartland of the Zapatista rebels. This has led, particularly since 1999, to a sharpening and politicisation of the conflict. In the region a road was to be constructed from the community Amador Hernández to one of the largest military bases. After one year of daily protests President Fox stopped the project in December 2000 and soon afterwards the military base was withdrawn.

In April 2000 there was further politicisation when the WWF alarmed the public by stating that the local indigenous farmers had caused dozens of forest fires. This was based on satellite photos which identified various fires. (It was discovered later that the fires had not been observed in the named area but rather had taken place quite some distance away.) The public dispute was about the extent to which it was necessary to resettle 12 indigenous communities in order to prevent the fire-induced destruction of the RIBMA. This was also legitimised with the argument that the reserve was not only ecologically valuable but was also the basis for the Mesoamerican Corridor (cf. 2.2) in which tourism played a significant role. Through the intervention of the Environmental Ministry it was agreed with ARIC-Independiente, an association representing the pro-Zapatista communities, to negotiate over the distribution of land and resources in the region. At first, the national government offered one hectare of land to the families who were prepared to resettle; ARIC-I responded by demanding five hectares as well as guaranteed land titles. When the government then offered the equivalent of 2000 USD per individual in the case of resettlement, ARIC-I refused the offer. They stated that they were not begging for money but wanted to see their rights accepted and suspected that the main reason for the resettlement was the attempt to weaken the Zapatistas (Harvey, N. 2001: 1055f.).

A recent development sheds light on a specific strategy: the European Union funded in 2003, with 31 million USD, a project called *Programa de*

Desarrollo Integral de la Selva Lacandona (Programme for Integrated Development in the Lacandon Jungle) which intended to contribute to the restoration of the destroyed parts of the Lacandon Jungle and, among other things, to educate local people to provide ecosystem services such as eco-tourism or reforestation. After the ICBG-Maya experiences the concept "bioprospecting" was taboo. For many local observers it was a hidden part of the programme, even so. For example, in order to register for an eco-tourist activity local people had to deliver information about biological resources and knowledge to state authorities. However, when the company Sanofi approached COMPITCH in 2005 in order to get consent for access to resources and knowledge about dealing with female diseases in the indigenous communities (and offered for this generics for many local diseases), this was rejected by the organised indigenous communities. Chiapas remains a highly politicised terrain for the disputes over genetic resources. But local actors are aware that the US-oriented strategy of coercive appropriation of genetic resources prevails.

Through the forced resettlements, a (supposedly) empty area would be created in which state authorities would be responsible for permitting bioprospecting and prior informed consent, thereby conveniently bypassing the need for the consent of the local population. Decisive for the issue is the fact that people can be displaced with the argument that they are destroying biological diversity. Here, Montes Azules could be seen as a further example of a specific combination of protection and utilisation strategies (for the Brazilian Amazon region see for example Acselrad 2002).

In Mexico it has now become particularly clear that protection and utilisation are conveyed in a specific way, in the context of the valorisation paradigm, at the cost of the local population. Roughly, two variants can be differentiated, both of which refer highly selectively to the CBD:

a) The "hard" variant is followed if there is interest only in resources and not in knowledge. Then protected areas can be declared, which means that the rights of disposal over the genetic resources are transferred to the state. Prior informed consent from the local population is no longer necessary and benefit-sharing is negotiated with the state. The connection between protection and the "hard" form of bioprospecting functions as follows. The Mexican state is responsible for land and resources. In a way this is a legal form of dispossession of the people who live there. This could be the reason behind the forced displacements in Montes Azules. If a dominant strategy for the protection of biological diversity is to make it economically attractive, then the declaration of nature reserves and bioprospecting are compatible. In this way the participating state actors (government bodies and research institutes) and private actors (firms, NGOs) rid themselves of the hitherto diffuse and politically vulnerable necessity of obtaining prior informed consent and of setting up benefit-sharing mechanisms. Bioprospectors such as Pulsar, or institutes financed by them, are also subject to national legislation such as the General Environmental Law.[25] The strategy also plays a role here of involving private actors to a greater extent in the administration of nature reserves. In the case of international prospectors, the Environmental Ministry would be responsible for "wild" biodiversity and the Agricultural Ministry for agricultural diversity.

b) The "soft" variant of the "reconciliation" between economy and ecology is applied when traditional knowledge is needed as a filter for the bioprospecting. In this case, prior informed consent must be obtained from the local population and a benefit-sharing mechanism must be negotiated with them. Nevertheless, the prospectors can continue to count on some systematic disadvantages for the communities. In particular, the division of the communities can be exploited, that is they are placed in a position of competition with one another. As we have shown in the example of ICBG-Maya, however, organisational processes for demanding prior informed consent are achievable. A possible bioprospecting strategy for the future could be to circumvent the legal requirements of access agreements, for example by involving "only" Mexican actors in bioprospecting. Criticism of biopiracy and bioimperialism could also become more difficult because of this. It seems that this "soft" strategy is more favoured by the European Union whereas the "hard" version, via the military and police, is the stance taken by the US government.

5.4 Summary

Although the use of "Fordist" resources, such as oil or timber, has not been systematically examined, the increased interest in their valorisation is also central to post-Fordism. Their valorisation is becoming more important in view of Mexico's foreign debt, economic integration with the USA and its increasing export orientation. Until now biological diversity and genetic resources have played a rather subordinate role. Nonetheless, even in view of the obvious conflicts, uncertain developments and high expectations in this field, biological diversity has been paid some attention by enterprises, state actors and social organisations. The first issue concerns the controversial possibilities and forms of valorisation and their importance for the socio-economic development of Mexico and in particular for the places in which biodiversity is to be found *in situ*. Second, specific natural geographical conditions, the erosion of biological diversity and the accompanying attempts at protection play an important role. The question is whether and if so how specific living conditions in specific places such as Chiapas become the terrain for a further round of primitive accumulation.

We can speak of a valorisation paradigm because the most important actors – those of the neoliberal and technocratic-nationalist positions together with the conservationist position – do not, in substance, question that the issue is one of valorisation and that this, furthermore, is the most effective form of protection. They are therefore able to strengthen specific perspectives and institutional practices with regard to the treatment of biological diversity in the process of the post-Fordist transformation of society.

It can be stated that at the core of the disputes is the crucial question of control over social processes. The firms attempt to control seed and pharmaceutical markets for the valorisation of capital, for which property rights are a decisive precondition; the Southern governments aim for control over their territories in order to be able to practise valorisation and protection strategies as effectively as possible; the organised local population, in turn, struggles for control over its own social relationships.

5.4.1 Non-simultaneous valorisation: Mexico and Chiapas

In spite of considerable differences, a broadly shared understanding of the problems concerning the valorisation of biological diversity has developed at the *federal level*. Prominent actors accept each other as the legitimate representatives of their interests, and in spite of all differences, largely shared perspectives emerge and those actors with fundamentally different perspectives and interests are kept "outside". The national sovereignty of the state over the natural resources to be found on its territory is just as uncontroversial as the necessity of securing access to genetic resources. The protection and utilisation of biological diversity are seen from within an economic perspective. The main conflict within the valorisation paradigm is over the ranking of "Mexican" interests and the role that is to be played by general, and in particular intellectual, property rights. The possibilities of valorisation have become part of a discourse among experts, and knowledge concerning existing and possible alternatives is suppressed. The grassroots democracy and left-wing nationalist positions are only able to articulate themselves to a limited degree and they are not included in the processes through which state policies are formulated.

Although we can speak of a broadly shared understanding of the problems and mutual recognition of interests on the part of the three dominant positions, it still remains controversial and unsettled as to what forms the political institutionalisation should take. This is expressed in considerable tensions between the apparatuses. In the Ministry of the Economy a valorisation strategy dominates, or is condensed, in which alternative forms of the appropriation of nature do not play any role. Genetic resources are seen as a further resource in international competition. In the Agricultural Ministry those interests are felt more strongly which take the material problem of the erosion of plant-genetic diversity into consideration. Finally, in the Environmental Ministry, the technocratic-nationalist perspective takes priority, but weaker interests also appear to play a role. Here, if anywhere, there is an attempt to combine protection with sustainable use. It emerges, however, that here, too, the valorisation paradigm remains decisive (e.g. in the case of the Mesoamerican Corridor). In addition, the responsibilities for the implementation of international agreements are allocated correspondingly. The Ministry of the Economy is responsible for the WTO and the TRIPS Agreement, and the Environmental Ministry for the CBD. The dominance of the Ministry of the Economy is ensured, among other things, by the fact that it has a right of veto in all legislative processes. In addition, it would fall short of the mark to understand the apparatuses as the expression of competing interests. Even the Environmental Ministry contributes to the establishment of the valorisation paradigm, although in a more fractured way and taking other interests into account than the Ministry of the Economy.

The specific contents of regulations depend not only on what meaning certain actors attach to the regulations but also which actors have a privileged access to the regulating state apparatuses. This cannot simply be operationalised, however, in the sense that it can be examined whose voice is most heard. Biotechnological industry without doubt has far greater access than critical NGOs or marginalised actors. In the state apparatuses themselves, however, selectivities are embedded. A national competition state has emerged even in Mexico: state strategies are guided primarily by the production of competitiveness; attained via attracting foreign investment, pushing for privatisations and the dissolution of the material content of corporatist structures (on paper and as a clientelistic structure, they continue to exist). In contrast to the states of the capitalist metropolis, foreign debt and the accompanying "structural adjustment programmes" are a central condition of internal policies in order to establish interests. This is also true for juridical questions. In the case of regulations there are "corridors" within which certain, but not all, disputes take place. It has been shown that these regulations set a certain political emphasis and thus strengthen certain processes and interests. Furthermore, it becomes clear that the concrete shaping of policies depends on the opportunities for *power bargaining* by more powerful actors. In this context "the lack of a legal culture" was something that was continually criticised throughout the conducted interviews. The difficulties in creating political coherence are, however, not only to be understood as tensions between different state apparatuses, but these tensions are themselves expressions, or rather condensations, of contradictory societal relationships in the apparatuses. The technocratic-nationalist position recognises the neoliberal position but has a different perspective with regard to valorisation and the role of Mexican institutions. According to this position, it is the role of the state to provide a terrain on which at least the dominant interests can wrestle for, and eventually find, compromises; this does not eliminate the contradictory interests but they are made pliable. Furthermore, against completely opposing interests – such as those of the grassroots democracy position – the compromises can if necessary be enforced using violence. This is illustrated particularly clearly in the question of intellectual property: here, in future, compromises between the first three positions are conceivable. At the same time, the interest in the patentability of genetic resources continues to be diametrically opposed to collective use by small farmers and indigenous peoples. Behind the difficult to achieve compromises are also very weighty material problems, which are reflected within the different positions. A forced valorisation of nature and genetic resources is not at all compatible per se with the necessity, which has been articulated politically by various sides, of stopping the erosion of biological diversity. Mexican biodiversity policy is therefore to be interpreted as an attempt to stabilise societal relationships and the opposing interests involved in them in a specific field of conflict. This takes place in a rule-forming way such that certain interests are either not taken into account (declaration of nature reserves, formulation of the draft for an access law, ICBG-Maya formulation) or are violently suppressed (Montes Azules, the repression of the Zapatista uprising as a whole).

The social relationships of forces at the *local level*, for example in the state of Chiapas, must be differentiated from the nation-state level. The strategies for the valorisation of biological diversity compete here in concrete places *on the one hand* much more clearly with other strategies and powerful actors, who for example are more interested in the production of oil, in hydro-electric plants or in cattle-ranching and forest plantations. These follow more traditional concepts of progress. In particular, the catastrophic socio-economic situation of a large part of the rural population strengthens the legitimacy of "traditional" concepts of progress, namely the fundamental alteration of social structures by modernisation processes induced from outside. In the discussions and processes of the formulation of policies at the national level this hardly plays any role. *On the other hand*, the grassroots democracy position is relevant here. Some of the indigenous peoples and small farmers attempt to evade the valorisation paradigm by putting the question of rights and self-determination at the centre of the disputes. One could expect an alliance between the biotechnological interests and the local population against the traditional valorisation paradigm (cattle-ranching, oil etc.). But the population, in the process of becoming politicised, attempts, due to its own historical experiences, to question the entire logic of the valorisation paradigm. This takes place through the concrete refusal of access to resources – not only genetic ones – and knowledge, but also in legal categories (indigenous and local rights). At the centre of oppositional discourses is the viewpoint that the political and social rights of the previous users of biological diversity (particularly the indigenous peoples in the biodiversity regions) are incompatible with the presently dominating perspective of valorisation. This is related primarily to local conditions, namely the high degree of politicisation and organisation of the population. Although these developments are also dependent on support from outside, for example on the provision of specific knowledge or the "translation" of demands to the national and international level, and critical NGOs play an important role here, the political "sustainability" of the grassroot's position is based on the fact that in Chiapas itself actors are organised differently.

At the end of the 1990s the question of bioprospecting gained in public importance. Against the background of the increasing criticism of the ICBG-Maya project this issue was politicised under the label of "biopiracy". This can be regarded as an important condition due to the fact that weaker actors became aware of their interests, organised themselves and developed political positions and strategies. After the threatened expulsion of the indigenous population from the nature reserve Montes Azules, in the Chiapan Lacandon Jungle in August 1999 had been broadly discussed in public, the nature protection policy came under criticism. Connections were increasingly made between bioprospecting, nature protection and indigenous rights, but also militarisation and the repression of uprisings.

The examples presented of the ICBG-Maya project and the disputes in the RIBMA are prominent, because here it was fought out in an exemplary way, what positions the indigenous communities as the bearers of knowledge and also as acting subjects have in this process. For them, in particular, the abandonment of the ICBG-Maya project is a symbolic success, because it illustrated that a "no" to unwanted bioprospecting is enforceable. For this, the organisation and politicisation, which had increased, particularly in the course of the Zapatista uprising since 1994, were important. It has already been emphasised several times that the constellation of forces in Chiapas has shifted as a result of the uprising. The representative of the Chiapan quasi-environmental ministry (Mx/14) expresses it thus: the indigenous population was quite willing to share its knowledge but with the uprising of 1994 it obtained an awareness of its marginalisation and poverty and now demands respect for its culture, its knowledge and its resources. The political and negotiating position of the indigenous population has eminently strengthened since 1994. The Zapatista uprising and – beyond the Zapatista spectrum – the negotiations of San Andrés on indigenous culture, decision-making power and autonomy worked as a sort of catalyst.

The processes outlined did not lead, however, to the grassroots democracy position being able to have its demands accepted. On the contrary: the associated movements are subject to severe repression, and bioprospecting appears to be taking place in spite of the abandonment of the ICBG-Maya project. One still unclear development in Chiapas could prove to be very important both domestically, for Mexico, and more broadly, in the international sphere: in view of the increasing criticism of bioprospecting and the possibilities of exercising criticism legitimately via the regulations of the CBD and the FAO, room could be created for the adoption of a "re-nationalisation" of collection strategies. The alliance of the neoliberal and technocratic-nationalist positions will probably end in the creation of Bio-Maquiladoras in Mexico, that is wage processing plants in which bio-workers process Mexican plant samples for a certain sum (see Delgado Ramos 2001: 491).

One further thing became clear during the study: the constitution of interests as a political process. The specific interests in the appropriation of genetic resources have developed in the light of historical possibilities as well as in disputes. In general, the interests in the valorisation of genetic resources become stronger with the biotechnological potentials for their valorisation. The historical overview of resource and environmental policies in Mexico has shown that already by the 1980s the erosion of biological diversity was the subject of state regulation. However, nature protection policy was understood as severely restricting human residence in the declared areas. However, for example in the disputes over Montes Azules, discursive use is also made of the earlier concept ("the indigenous people destroy nature").

In one further area, the thesis of the constitution of interests as a political process is substantiated. The access legislation – as a necessary part of the implementation of the CBD – apparently receives a higher ranking because in view of the increasing international, but also national and local, politicisation of the subject (in particular through the Southern governments with their developed interest in the marketing of "their" diversity), it is about legal and planning security. One difference became clear, however, between the neoliberal position, which has not been a driving force for access legislation, and the technocratic-nationalist position, which expects an explicit sharing of the "cake" of valorisation from such legislation.

5.4.2 The importance of international politics

A central characteristic of the global multilevel system of biodiversity policy is the highly selective interaction of international regulation processes with those of nation-states and – fractured still further – their national and local effects. A central role is played here by the selectivities of national state apparatuses, dominant interpretations of the problems, interests and socio-economic relationships and structural conditions. The nation-state thus remains an important level of regulation in spite of all the tendencies towards internationalisation. The assimilation of intellectual property rights and the rapid process of the regulation of biological safety show that international policies have a high ranking if they are in the interest of dominant international and national actors. This is less the case with regard to the rights of indigenous peoples or benefit-sharing rules. The great importance of the valorisation paradigm has already been pointed out.

In Mexican biodiversity policy, international regulations play a role primarily in the initiation of national processes. This is also the explicit goal of framework agreements such as the CBD, which is not primarily concerned with individual projects but with the provision of an international framework for national legislation and policies. It was illustrated that the political-institutional securing of the neoliberal model – particularly through NAFTA – plays a central role. In addition there is the "interiorising" of neoliberal strategies through structural adjustment measures. Political processes remain embedded in socio-economic ones, and here the international economic interests in oil and in biological diversity in particular, play a role in Mexico. The fact that economic and political interests are closely interlinked can be seen particularly in Mexico where the US government has declared the resources there to be a part of its "national security".

These regulations are embedded in more comprehensive processes of the constitution of problems. Here, too, it is important to what extent specific perspectives can be brought to bear at different levels. In recent years a valorisation paradigm has gained priority. At the international level, perspectives of non-valorisation play a subordinate role. Other societal relationships with nature – such as those of the indigenous peoples in Mexico and Chiapas – are above all consulted in a functional manner in terms of what they can contribute to the utilisation of biological diversity. At the national level in Mexico, indigenous peoples play hardly any role in the formulation of policies. In a very specific constellation in the last ten years, the relationships of forces in Chiapas have shifted.

The "transference" of the interests in valorisation, that is the neoliberal and technocratic-nationalist positions, into legal forms is easier than for interests which are sceptical or disapproving of the dominant forms of valorisation. At the national level, the interpretations of the problems and the political strategies of those actors which were essentially involved in the formulation of the international systems of regulations, that is, again, the neoliberal and technocratic-nationalist positions, are of course the easiest to integrate. This confronts the democratic position with a dilemma: it must accept a form of dispute for the representation of its own interests which is concerned with state regulation and law (the question of property rights is absolutely central). This form of dispute is, however, itself not a neutral process but to a high degree determined by the formation of power. The indigenous people of Mexico and in particular the rebel communities in Chiapas have partially entered into these disputes (among other things with the COCOPA initiative on indigenous rights and culture), but so far they have been unsuccessful. Even if societal relationships change through daily practice in Chiapas, this does not necessarily have repercussions at the national level.

Internationally, provisions which aim to strengthen weaker actors (farmers' rights, Art. 8(j), we could also include ILO 169) have not been able to be generally accepted in recent years. Rather, a *symbolic* reference to international regulations can be observed, in order to strengthen the legitimacy of one's own position. A one-dimensional perspective would be short of the mark here, however. Very disparate processes, which have been conducted in many countries, have contributed to the development of international legal norms in accordance with the wishes of weaker actors. The international discussion on the rights of indigenous peoples was a long struggle by the peoples themselves and was not put on the international agenda by clever lawyers. In both "directions", that is the transmission from the local level to the international and vice versa, NGOs played a major role.

It was also clearly shown that the national and international levels play a very ambivalent role in Chiapas, as legally regulating but also as levels at which interests are formulated "from outside". The great importance of the local level is shown when the concrete activities concerning protection and valorisation are concerned, but precisely through this the concrete place is tied into national and international developments. In particular, supply competition plays a role here, which leads the technocratic-nationalist position to lean towards the adoption of authoritarian measures. Governments are concerned with achieving as efficient a valorisation as possible, while participative or democratic processes are regarded as a competitive disadvantage. Concrete places also remain tied to developments at a higher level because the forms in which conflicts are fought out – state and law – are in a way already given. The international level plays an important role here, because it privileges the nation-state and legal mechanisms. This is shown in that the different strategies for the legalising of appropriation and the more or less strong upgrading of weak actors can hardly avoid a fundamental tendency: the different forms of appropriation – and protection – are under pressure to identify property.

Finally, the role of international NGOs is of great importance, particularly those with a grassroots democracy position. They contribute to the clarification and politicisation of the interests of actors and their strategies with regard to local resources and to the understanding of complicated regulation questions and the meaning of international processes. They not only have an informative function in this but contribute decisively to the interpretation of specific facts through local grassroots democracy actors, which in turn influences their strategies (see in detail Görg/Brand 2001a).

5.4.3 Dominance and hegemony

In spite of the dominance of a valorisation paradigm we cannot claim, either for the federal level or for Chiapas, that a clear hegemony has formed in biodiversity policy. This is connected at the national level with the continuing and considerable tensions among the dominant positions, which until now could not be brought together to form a stable compromise. At the same time, it is at this level that there exists the strongest possibility of achieving compromises based on the formulation and establishment of corresponding policies. Actors who are fundamentally critical of the developments of valorisation are more weakly represented here and can more easily be ostracised.

The valorisation paradigm is also not hegemonic to the extent that it is not accepted by some relevant local actors. This is seen particularly in Chiapas, but not in the same way as in other states such as Oaxaca or in the North of Mexico. The question of hegemony and thus of the articulation of different levels must be answered in a differentiated fashion: in certain questions – such as the valorisation of biological diversity – it can exist both internationally and nationally. But this must not be the case in all individual places and on all spatial scales. This results in a political dilemma for local actors in the form of a structural supply competition which enables international and national actors to become involved in socio-cultural and natural-geographical places in a relatively flexible – and often violent – manner. This flexibility, in turn, may allow them to appropriate genetic resources where the climate is not politicised.

6 Contested terrains

Towards a neo-Poulantzian approach to International Political Economy

Scientific approaches such as regime theory and most environmental governance approaches see in the emergence of international environmental policy institutions a reaction to transboundary problems, which can only be dealt with multilaterally and in consultation with non-state actors. Due to this, the assessment of global regulation is primarily, if not exclusively, a question of whether and to what extent the institutions are appropriate in view of the given problems – such as, for example, the thinning of the ozone layer, climate change or the erosion of biological diversity. To the extent, however, that only the more or less direct effects of environmental policy institutions are studied and assessed, this understanding of the problems represents too narrow a perspective on the functioning and effects of international environmental politics. There are quite a number of reasons for this. First of all, environmental problems are not given but constituted. More recently, many approaches in political science and environmental sociology take into consideration the question of how that which is to be regarded as an "environmental problem" – or generally as a part of the "ecological crisis" – is scientifically, politically and culturally constructed. It is less often recognised, however, that in this problem constitution the interests of the participating actors play a decisive role. Many analyses only examine whether and if so how a more or less uniform understanding of the problem is reached and institutionalised in the disputes among scientific and political experts. Less attention is paid to the question of whether the results may have been achieved by neglecting or even deliberately disregarding the viewpoints of weaker societal actors. The consequence of this might be that the treatment of global problems is not linked to the (changing) capitalist mode of production and associated gender and ethnic relations, as well as societal relationships with nature and the reproduction of unequal power relations and social domination.

Therefore, a *critical* social science analysis should tread carefully when dealing with such problems and remain critical in the face of pure *problem solving theories* (Cox 1998: 39). With this study we wish to open up a perspective which avoids the usual dichotomisation between ecological and societal problems, on the one hand, and social relations of domination, on the other. Ecological problems and the institutions dealing with them affect the reproduction and re-formation of global domination, just as the treatment of them cannot be understood without taking into consideration societal interests and power relations. That both levels are closely interlinked can be illustrated by the emergence of post-Fordist "globalised" relationships with nature. In the reaction to a global "environmental problem" – the loss of biological diversity – new interests in genetic resources articulate themselves and completely new patterns of the formation of compromises and the regulation of societal contradictions emerge. In this final chapter, we summarise and discuss our arguments and emphasise theoretical consequences. Moreover, we focus on some questions which seem important to us for further research.

6.1 The material dimensions of globalisation and the importance of the local

The field of conflict around genetic resources shows clear evidence that even the production processes based on the latest technological innovations (as captured in the concept of a knowledge society; see Chapter 1) are dependent on a material input and in a certain manner on access to "nature". Thus, nothing is further from the truth than the belief that in the knowledge society humanity has finally emancipated itself from the material conditions of its existence. By contrast, significant changes in the relationships with nature in both their material and their symbolic dimensions are an integral part of the emerging post-Fordist mode of development. Economic interests in genetic resources, however, are not simply given, but depend on scientific-technological development strategies, which are in turn partly determined by social power relations and conflicts. At the same time, contrary views of nature are expressed in these development strategies. On the one hand there is the view that the artificial design of molecules is certainly the faster and more efficient way to the development of new products because "there is nothing special about natural products", as a representative of a biotechnology company is quoted as saying in *Nature* (Macilwain 1998). This is in contrast to the position of the representatives of other firms, who emphasise the evolutionary advantage of nature. Regarding the potentials of combinative chemistry, for example, a representative of Monsanto stated: "Nature has been trying this experiment for two billion years" (ibid.). Particularly in the context of the debates on biological diversity, "Nature's Cornucopia" (Tuxill 1999) is praised. This applauding of nature, nevertheless, often occurs not in contrast, but complementary to the use of genetic technology. "Although we have achieved unprecedented skill in moving genes around, only nature can manufacture them" (ibid.: 6). Nature as a "factory" of basic materials is the notion which most characterises the logic of the *valorisation of biodiversity*.

Nature is in fact being socialised in a new form. Whether these techno-economic strategies will be successful depends not primarily on scientific concepts and the accompanying views of nature, however, but on which strategies find the most favourable conditions on the world market. And these conditions, as shown in this study, are created and enforced politically, essentially by nation-states. Thus, whether in the future the life sciences industries will in fact be able to use the "cornucopia of nature" depends on the organisation of the "global management" of genetic resources, that is on the development of the conflicts over the internationalisation of the state.

This has important theoretical and empirical implications. Our study has demonstrated the necessity of undertaking a critical analysis of the broader process of the societalisation of nature when confronting the issue of biodiversity's preservation – that is the character of post-Fordist relationships with nature and the interests behind them, but also the accompanying conflicts and power relations. As our examination of various international treaties has shown, the process of regulating biodiversity has to be conceptualised as a struggle over the generalisation of certain interpretations of the problem (up to a broadly accepted valorisation paradigm) and their materialisation in international institutions. The result of this struggle depends largely on the power resources the different actors can mobilise, but also on the ability of powerful actors to either integrate or successfully marginalise subordinate actors. The Agreement on Trade-Related Aspects of Intellectual Property Agreement (TRIPS), especially, has to be understood as an institutionalisation of the interests of large multinationals of the life sciences industries whose economic performance is more and more dependent on an international legal framework securing them a strong protection of intellectual property rights. But also "softer" agreements such as the Convention on Biological Diversity (CBD) and the United Nations Food and Agriculture Organization (FAO) seed treaty either favour the commercialisation of genetic resources or remain rather unspecific or instrumental when they deal with the rights of small farmers and indigenous communities. Thus, in the course of and through the internalisation of the state, it is exactly those cultural interpretations, knowledge systems and agricultural practices which stand for less destructive societal relations with nature which tend to be marginalised. It is not intended here to reproduce the myth of peoples "close to nature" who live in harmony with nature. This view overlooks the fact that ecological degradation can also take place there. What is more, a further and greater danger in adopting such a perspective stems from the construction of an absolute otherness of these cultures, which often goes hand in hand with the obligation that they continue in their role as the preservers of biodiversity – which means, to functionalise them. To assume an absolute antithesis between the capitalist commercialisation of nature (valorisation) and the mythical forms of a unity with nature (represented by indigenous people), thus, reproduces the antithesis of economy and ecology. In order to reject these dichotomies, it is important to differentiate among the specific individual forms of the societalisation of nature and to analyse their ecological and socio-economic consequences. As we have seen, non-capitalist forms of treating biodiversity have been closely examined because they play an important role in the conservation of potentially valuable resources or even, as in bioprospecting, they have a particular meaning for the facilitated access to genetic resources. Rights relating to these practices are formally recognised, although within the framework of the CBD (Art. 8(j)) only in an instrumental form, in so far as they are useful for the conservation of biodiversity. Apart from that, both in the CBD and in the International Treaty of the FAO (and there in the concept of Farmers' Rights; see Chapter 3) they are subordinated to the sovereignty of the nation-states. As we could see in the example of biodiversity politics in Mexico, the decisive problem is to what extent nationally based actors have the potential at all to stand up against the interests of stronger actors on different spatial levels.

The development of post-Fordist relationships with nature, however, does not make environmental politics impossible. To some degree, the reduction of emissions, the protection of resources and the improvement of living conditions are rational even under capitalist conditions. But the way the problems are dealt with and the rationality of political regulation are shaped by the new phase of capitalist development. Therefore, environmental measures are influenced by the struggles connected with the rise of this new phase and a neoliberal concept of nature (McCarthy/Prudham 2004). In reverse, it has become clear that societal developments are imparted in a specific way through the treatment of socio-ecological problems. Thus, the individual chapters reveal that, depending on the interests and power relations involved, a highly *selective treatment* of environmental problems – such as the erosion of biological diversity – takes place.

For the *formation of post-Fordist relationships with nature* this means that it is not only a question of whether biological diversity can be conserved at all; indeed, a dramatic erosion of biological diversity has been taking place for a long time and whether this can be stopped remains extremely dubious. The really important question is *why and for whom* this diversity should be conserved. At stake is whether, in the future, only some nature reserve areas will be left, in which the remains of biological diversity are conserved, for example for aesthetic reasons or solvent ecotourism. Perhaps such nature protection areas will be inhabited by "primitive peoples" and will therefore be considered as nature-culture-reservations. They might also be used for the search for natural materials (if this increases the economic impetus for their conservation). Beside these more horrific scenarios, a more specific question is whether the *in situ* conservation of plant genetic resources for food and agriculture is indeed still necessary or whether the already existing *ex situ* collections of industry make enough material available – and under more favourable conditions – for the development of new varieties.

One central aspect in the development of post-Fordist relationships with nature refers to the possibility locally based actors have in shaping their relationships with nature. Are they able to determine their own future, or will they be functionalised by global regulation strategies, their way of life thus transformed and they themselves marginalised? This question affects not only the relationships among different levels of the formulation and implementation of politics ("scale") but also refers to the meaning of the "local" of the specific location ("place"): the extent to which the specific natural environmental conditions are taken into account in the regulation of access to genetic resources. Locally based actors are therefore not only the farming communities and the indigenous peoples but, in a strategic sense, they include all those who wish to emphasise the importance of the specific locality and the practices connected with it in the regulation of societal relationships with nature (i.e. possibly also NGOs or scientists). The decisive question here is at which levels the decision competences are institutionally anchored and whether locally based actors have competences or whether these are taken from them – perhaps with a reference to the ecological importance of the locality. The latter can be observed in the attempt to restore common goods, whereby these common goods in many cases are placed at the disposal of "global resource managers" – representatives of international organisations (such as the World Bank) and NGOs – as Michael Goldman (1998, 2005) has shown. If the question is put in this way, then it quickly becomes clear that the local place, in the sense of self-prescribed practices that help to shape societal relationships with nature, can only be strengthened against the forced tendency of valorisation at all levels jointly. Even on a local scale it is highly doubtful whether those actors who take the specific natural environmental conditions into account can in fact prevail or whether the strategies aimed at exports and the most efficient valorisation of resources will dominate (as for example in the case of the local oligarchy in Chiapas). Not all actors on the local *scale* are interested in the particular *place*. Something similar is true for the national, supranational and international scales.

6.2 North–South relations and the reconfiguration of scale

How scales are constituted, how they differentiate themselves from one another and in what relationship they stand to one another, is essentially determined by power relations and their institutionalisation. The process of globalisation does not at all mean the disappearance of regional, national or local scales, but their *reconfiguration*. The problem connected with this is not limited only to the more or less good cooperation between actors and institutions on different scales, which are presumed to exist. It also relates to the conflicts over their importance to each other. This has been shown in the example of the growing pressure on local actors in Chiapas. The national scale and its importance in international politics is also subjected to a permanent re-interpretation in which the strategies of the actors are very differently accentuated. The states of the South aim, particularly with regard to the disposition of genetic resources, for the strengthening of the national scale. Here, one aspect is crucial: the countries and regions which are rich in biodiversity find themselves in the situation of a *supply competition*. This means that the dominant social forces in those countries, such as the governments, have become interested in the valorisation of biodiversity and especially of genetic resources. Therefore, we consider a valorisation paradigm as hegemonic at the international level around which concrete conflicts take place, but this is also the case in other regions. The initiative of the Like-Minded Group of Megadiverse Countries is a new attempt to lend more weight to national sovereignty in the face of the supply competition between the biodiversity-rich countries. In contrast to this, the leading countries of the North would like to leave open the precise negotiation of the conditions of access (and aim here, in contrast to the countries of the South, for *voluntary* rules) but at the same time attempt to enforce internationally *binding* standards for intellectual property rights (IPRs). The reason is clear: in precisely this point the international scale is clearly moulded by the interests of the metropolitan *user countries*. Multilateralism is to remain valid here at least until more effective bilateral negotiations promise further success. Since the relationship of the scales to one another is itself characterised by power relations, the strategies of the various actors are aimed at strengthening or weakening the corresponding scales according to their own interests. There is a further aspect which complicates the problem of scale considerably. Every scale must itself be understood as a *field of forces* which is characterised by often overlapping constellations of interests and power. This is expressed, for example, in the fact that there is no simple North–South pattern. Thus, "Northern positions", for example the interest of the large or small life sciences companies, research institutes or international nature conservation organisations, can also be found in the South, and there in some cases even on a local scale. Our example showed, at least in Chiapas, that the interests of the nature conservation NGOs ally themselves with those concerned with the valorisation of genetic resources; and on a national scale the interests of the life sciences industry are also present and exercise considerable influence. And by contrast, in Northern countries certain NGOs and social movements take up the interests of the global South (if with less success than industry in the Southern countries). Each scale thus represents a field of forces in which the interests of the different actors are specifically concentrated. Certain configurations repeat themselves here – for example, the conflicts between the interests of local actors and the transnational companies (TNCs) are fought out on international, supranational, national and local scales – only with different power relations and thus with different results.

This does not make the use of the concepts North and South meaningless; rather, it makes a case for being cautious before any overly hasty generalisations are made. The case of Mexico/Chiapas cannot be generalised because of the local, national and regional peculiarities with regard to the specific processes. Certainly, the international and the regional scales play a central role concerning the opportunities of influence which can be exerted on a national and local scale. The relations between the different scales must therefore be examined in detail. But that also means that individual cases are influenced in very different ways due to their specific conditions. When the "effects" of international policies are being examined, in Mexico the natural conditions – in addition to biological diversity also the relatively easy accessibility – the relative political stability of the region, the regional differences, NAFTA and the close connection to the USA, and finally, the particular tradition of the nation-state and the national power relations, must be taken into account. In addition to the simple schematic categories of provider and user, the particular local situation must also be accorded due importance: to what extent is existing biodiversity in fact exploitable and do suitable conditions exist for this? In Mexico, for example, the long-lasting lack of recognition of indigenous cultures in the context of the state ideology of *mestizaje* (mestisation) and the recent processes of democratisation should be pointed out here. Moreover, we saw remarkable differences between Chiapas, where a strong indigenous movement and the Zapatista uprising has re-shaped power relations, and the national level. There is room here for variable and sometimes surprising coalitions and compromises – and not only between a corrupt national elite and foreign capital, as is frequently claimed, but also between locally based and global actors (social movements, NGOs, scientists).

6.3 International institutions as condensations of power relations

The present study focused primarily on political-institutional aspects of the internationalisation of the state. Nevertheless, the more complex creation of international hegemony as well as non-state international actors also played an important role in the reconfiguration of politics. The interests of the individual actors are not inflexibly predetermined or "derivable" from objective situations. That is revealed by the fact that in specific questions such as the regulating of access, benefit-sharing or intellectual property rights political positions emerge or change through politicisation and conflicts. Interest in secure and legalised access is growing, however, due to the politicising of the expropriation of genetic resources via international processes and via national and local criticism. Many Southern countries, to give another example, were not fully aware of the consequences of the TRIPS Agreement at the time when this was negotiated. Their interest in, for example, national control over genetic resources grew when they were confronted with the need to implement the Agreement and with the consequences the implementation would have. The formation of "Southern" interests was influenced by the demands of NGOs to prohibit the patenting of life and by the opportunities offered by the review process of Article 27.3 (b). The argument of the constellation-dependent constitution of *specific* interests should not divert our attention, however, from the fact that some *fundamental* interests do in fact remain stable, such as the interest of firms and research institutes in the appropriation of biological diversity for the purpose of its valorisation. In addition, for these actors legal and planning certainty is of central importance in an economic field which is developing in a highly dynamic fashion; although it is not always absolutely clear what this specifically means and when planning certainty is regarded as adequate. In any case, decisions continue to be made under conditions of uncertainty. For the actual degree of the valorisation of biodiversity, the political and economic framework – including the legal and cultural dimensions – is of central importance.

That brings us to the international political level and to the cooperation of different international institutions as a part of multi-level politics. One result of the study is that doubts are indeed appropriate with respect to whether the apparently attractive picture of "synergy effects" or "coherence" between the various regimes is an apposite one. In the relationship between the CBD, the WTO and the International Treaty of the FAO it is not to be expected that it will be possible to reach consensual solutions, never mind mutually supporting ones, on the really important, controversial issues. On the international scale, due to the dominance of one particular institution, the WTO, we are dealing with *"negotiations in the shadows of hierarchy"* (Scharpf 1993). By contrast to the nation-state framework, on the international scale the "hierarchy" – we prefer the concept of asymmetry in order to avoid the notion of a unilinear top-down relationship – is not anchored within the framework of the state monopoly of legitimate force at the national level. Rather, a hard power bargaining prevails. This has ambivalent effects. On the one hand power relations often have a much more direct effect on the international scale because they are less cushioned by a national legal system or by complex institutional decision-making procedures and majority decisions. On the other hand, these processes are therefore also easier to block and even dominant actors do not necessarily have the means to secure the respecting of certain regulations due to the lack of sanctioning authorities.

At all events, the asymmetry of the negotiation processes plays an important role not only for the ultimate relevance of the individual agreements but also for their formulation during the negotiation process. Above all the compatibility with the TRIPS Agreement is a central criterion for all international agreements with which certain actors – the industrial countries in general and particularly the USA – attempt to influence current negotiations. And as could be seen in the formulation of the International Treaty of the FAO, simply the threat of calling the dispute settlement body of the WTO can be decisive in disputes over certain regulations (cf. Chapter 3). However, the politicisation of certain agreements can make their usefulness for the establishment of dominant interests more difficult or even impossible. Particularly, the politicisation of the TRIPS Agreement in the revision process of Art 27.3(b) is an example of the fact that the new interests, which have now to a certain extent been accepted as legitimate, must be dealt with, for example by relegating them to other forums or, conversely, by upgrading forums such as the World Intellectual Property Organization (WIPO) for the establishment of the dominant interests. This *forum shifting* (cf. Chapter 4) is also an indication of the fact that even in view of international relations, a sanctioning authority corresponding to the nation-state is lacking and the asymmetric relationship of the agreements develops its effectiveness only indirectly and ambivalently.

The influence of international institutions and their relationships to one another cannot be examined from the perspective of a more or less successful coordination. They are themselves the condensation of antagonistic interests in global power relations. What is more, non-coordination has to be seen as the specific "rationality" of existing power relations. On the international scale struggles between highly heterogeneous actors can be observed, among them national governments as central actors. Since the strategies of these state actors are in the final analysis the result of the condensation of differ-ent power relations in the individual state apparatuses, we are dealing here with a *second order condensation of social power relations*. This is not to deny the formation of transnational alliances of social forces, from business organisa-tions up to trans-local coalitions of indigenous people, which try to influ-ence international institutions not only via their respective national representatives but also directly. Furthermore, as we have seen in more detail in the previous chapters, the notion of a "second order" should not be misunderstood as being a hierarchy of control. Rather, it means that the process of the condensation of particular interests to a supposedly higher general interest takes place here in an intensified form. The conflicts on the national scale precede the formulation of a national strategy and thus they also precede the opposition of interests on the international scale and accompany them in the further political process. This occurs even when international processes, as in many cases, provide the impetus for national processes. The priority of the national is thus not meant chronologically, but in the sense that national governments, in order to be able to act on the international stage, have to acquire clarity as to their national interests. In the Multilateral System of the International Treaty the impetus came, for example, from the international level, which was followed by the formula-tion of national interests, for example, in bilateral negotiations. Thus, the concept *second order condensation of social power relations* refers to the produc-tion of "new state spaces" (Brenner 2004) by re-scaling elements of state power and thereby creating new and more complex relationships between different scales of state politics. This is a contested process which is driven by intergovernmental negotiations as well as by the formation of transna-tional alliances of societal actors and by the emergence of networks between state and non-state actors on various scales (see Bieling 2006: 235f.).

The claim of a "general interest" must therefore at least be formulated in order to be useful for the analysis of the international scale. Because this general interest – which is articulated internationally as "national interest", as the condensation of particular (and antagonistic) interests – is in fact fictional, it represents an essential element of the "state fetish" (Hirsch 1994). In international processes this fiction, that is this element of the state fetish, appears to be weaker, for the contradictions between the agreements (here, conflicts over trade and IPRs; there, over environment and nutrition) are much too obvious. But this does not at all mean that the contradictions between the various agreements could in fact be used by other actors with diverging interests, for even here, in the final analysis, the fiction is upheld that a global "general interest", in the sense of a solution to global problems, must be established.

In any case, different interests can be combined to a "general interest" only to a limited extent. This is the reason why the "general interest" always remains fictional, even if the necessity of its formulation for the establishment of social compromises is real. As we have shown in this study, the issue concerns, above all, the stabilisation and thus also the reproduction of the basic structures of social relations. However, within this contentious process the way in which compromises are formed is certainly important. And it is exactly here that the asymmetry of the international systems of regulation plays a decisive role, because it is precisely the WTO-grounded TRIPS Agreement which aims at securing modern capitalist property relations. This agreement is not only dominant in the subsequent testing of existing agreements, but its dominance enters into the negotiating process (as shown in the case of the International Treaty on Plant Genetic Resources, ITPGR) and the additional shaping of international agreements and their national implementation.

A global multi-level system thus includes the condensation of power relations on different scales. These scales are not independent of one another; instead, they exert a mutual influence on each other. But they are also not directly derivable from each other; the combination of the levels is complex. Sometimes it is easier at the local scale to bring the interests of the actors based there to bear. This is not the result of a natural law, however, for local conflicts can be reshaped by the entrance of powerful external actors. Examples of the subjugation of the local scale to global or national strategies of valorisation can be found aplenty, for example in the Amazon basin, where on the Brazilian side local actors have until now hardly had a chance to exert an independent influence (see Acselrad 2002). A change presupposes the shifting of societal power relations at the national scale, which manifest themselves in state policies, among other things. This is also true of the importance of international politics for local relationships: without corresponding national laws and nationally organised capacity building, the local scale can expect to gain nothing from the Bonn Guidelines, for example (see on the problems in the case of Costa Rica: Rodríguez 2002).

A systematic implication for the process of the internationalisation of the state is that although the international scale plays an increasingly important role, the relations of the scales to one another is neither per se complementary, nor is it a type of zero-sum game in which the international scale becomes more important "at the cost" of the national scale. The very meaning of the international scale is ambivalent. Even if the CBD Article 8 (j) on the rights of local communities and indigenous peoples and the FAO concept of Farmers' Rights bring little juridical certainty, they have had great effect as an impetus for the politicisation of the problem. Also, the model law of the African Union was able to increase awareness of the problems of a national access and benefit-sharing legislation on the regional scale and beyond, and precisely the fear of this has caused the harsh reactions of the International Union for the Protection of New Varieties of Plants (UPOV) and WIPO. The international regulations thus do not make the national legislation processes less important, but confront them with a role which is partly new. And in addition, nation-states or their governments play a central role as actors, even if this role is no longer without competition on the international scale. This is meant when we speak of a *second order condensation* in the case of international institutions and the internationalised state in general. The interests and relationships of power which are already condensed in national institutions and strategies are condensed on a further scale in another form, partly with other conflicts and contents and thus with perhaps deviating results – and in this form they have an effect in turn on other scales. This inter-linkage is not really new but in the internationalisation of the state it gains particular weight.

In our research we examined the question of whether any role is played, and if so which one, by the *coherence* of national politics. In political science and in the political process itself the expectation is repeatedly expressed that a coherent state and/or inter-state politics should play a decisive role for a strategy which is appropriate to the problems and which takes into account the side-effects of political measures. In contrast to this, our example can show that because of the highly divergent and partly contradictory interests which play a role in the field of conflict, this coherence tends to be unlikely. Basically, if coherence with regard to the treatment of problems is hardly to be expected, this question nevertheless plays a decisive role in the re-formation of global domination. Furthermore, the problem of coherence shows clearly that power relations in the internationalisation of the state continue to be based at the level of the nation-state. This paradox – a *nationally shaped global domination* – can be understood using Poulantzas's concept of the state as it was introduced in the first chapter. This does not deny the actions and effects of international actors but it does argue against the assumption of a sort of "autonomising" of international apparatuses and the disputes in their "civil society environment" (Görg/Wissen 2003).

State politics can never really be "coherent" in the sense that it is no longer permeated by tensions and contradictory in itself. Understanding the state as a "strategic terrain and strategic process" (Poulantzas 1978/2002: 167) means to conceptualise state politics as a "result of a conflicting coordination of explicit and diverging micro-politics, rather than a rational formulation of a global and coherent project" (ibid.: 168, our translation). If institutionalisation takes place through the formation of compromises, this does not at all mean that a real general interest embodied by the state, in the sense of a reconciliation of opposing interests, has been established. It is precisely in the field of agro-biodiversity and the case study of Mexico that it has been shown that because of the complexity of the problems and the multitude of strategies and actors a real compensation of interests within the framework of the nation-state or even simply a consistent national strategy cannot be formulated. A study on behalf of the World Bank underlines this with surprising clarity (Petit *et al.* 2000). We must therefore differentiate between the real differences of specific interests and the nevertheless more than fictional general interest. This general interest is not simply fictional because at least the interests of the most important actors must be included in a hegemonic compromise. Dominant actors do not only comprise dominant social forces like the most powerful fractions of capital, but also refer to subaltern actors whose interests have to be taken into account, up to a certain extent, in order to prevent these actors from challenging the social power relations. Alternatively, dominant actors must be able to exclude relevant subalterns effectively. Generalised, that is hegemonic interests must also be capable of claiming that their interests correspond not only to the dominant actors but also to the dominant interpretation of the problem and that they present a central contribution to the solution of the problem (as it is understood in the hegemonic interpretation of it). If it fulfils these requirements a general interest, safeguarded by the state, can correspond to the interest of capital in the establishment and safeguarding of capitalist production and property relations.

All these points were easily recognisable in the particular case of the negotiations of the ITPGR. In spite, or even because, of opposing interests it proved possible in this field to establish a compromise in the form of a multilateral agreement which nevertheless has certain similarities to nation-state regulations and continues to require the authority of the nation-state. This was possible due to the fact that the interpretation of the problem "loss of the diversity of plant genetic resources" was strongly established, as were certain basic convictions with regard to the relevance of these resources (economic importance and nutritional security). Thus, a supposedly "global general interest" – the conservation of genetic diversity – was proposed and addressed by the establishment of an international agreement, that is by a multilateral exchange system for particularly important genetic material. In addition, precisely through this multilateral system a compromise between the conflicting interests was established which does justice both to the interest of the governments of the Southern countries in the marketing of "their" biodiversity and to the interest of the life sciences industry in the unreduced protection of its property claims and the establishment of global markets. Interests opposing these dominant interests were, however, not really respected by the compromise which was reached but (like the Farmers' Rights) were subordinated to national interests. The conflict between locally based actors and the interest in valorisation and global marketing was thus not solved in the international agreement, but was referred back to the national level. Here, the structural selectivity of the global regulation system becomes obvious.

However, multilateralism is not merely an inadequate substitute for the regulatory function of the nation-state; it does not preclude the bilateral appropriation of biodiversity either. Rather, the very construction of a public sphere and a general interest in plant genetic resources plays an important role in the commercialisation and privatisation of these resources. This can be recognised in the entire problem of intellectual property rights.[1] Both at the level of the nation-state and at the interstate level, the *structural privileging* of certain interests is obvious, namely of those which aim for the use of biodiversity within the framework of the existing social order – whether by directly propagating capitalist valorisation or alternatively, striving for the mitigating conservation of nature. It must not be forgotten, however, that this process continues to be highly controversial and a firmly established hegemony cannot be assumed. The resistance to the privatisation of plant genetic resources has not at all diminished with the passing of the International Treaty on Plant Genetic Resources, even if this agreement could be judged as being a disappointing compromise.

The lack of hegemony is even stronger in the case of the TRIPS Agreement. Here, important actors such as the governments of Brazil or India were not included in a formally established politico-legal compromise. Rather, their original resistance to the Agreement was broken by economic pressure or sanctions. Only in that way could an agreement be established which is highly structurally selective, that is strongly favouring the interests of economically powerful actors while almost completely neglecting different interests. The latent contradictions of this constellation became manifest when the crucial Article 27.3(b) was to be reviewed. In this situation those interests which were hitherto oppressed by force successfully challenged the dominant interpretation of the problem. However, they did not achieve a substantial revision of the Agreement. Rather, one can speak of a stalemate which gives rise to new strategies of the dominant actors, such as forum shifting in the direction of the WIPO or bilateral power bargaining. The latter has especially gained in importance. This is due to the fact that the strategy of establishing tighter and more substantial IPRs via the WIPO has met with the resistance of influential Southern governments such as those of Brazil and Argentina, which managed to politicise the supposedly "technical" terrain of WIPO by launching the proposal of a development agenda in 2004.

The difficulties of successfully pursuing their interests even on those international terrains which are a material condensation of Northern dominated power relations, that is the WIPO and the TRIPS Agreement, seem to have brought Northern actors to increasingly rely on bilateral bargaining. However, this does not mean that multilateralism is simply superceded by bilateralism. Just as the multilateral agreements of the 1990s cannot be understood without bilateral power asymmetries, the recent rise of bilateralism has to be seen precisely against the background of the possibilities offered by multilateral agreements. As our analysis has shown, multilateral rules like the TRIPS Agreement can provide the ground floor on which bilateral power asymmetries unfold. Far from solving "global problems" in a cooperative manner, they institutionalise international power relations and thereby enhance the opportunities to stabilise and reproduce these relations. On a symbolic level, they are the product as well as the medium of the constitution or reframing of certain issues. The TRIPS Agreement cannot be understood without taking into account the redefinition of the IPR issue against the background of technological developments in the life sciences industry, agro-business and the IT sector. In turn, it is an institutionalisation of the changed problem perception. As such it also defines the claims of what is and is not possible or even discussible in bilateral negotiations. Additionally, by establishing minimum standards of intellectual property protection without defining an upper limit, it creates the possibility for powerful Northern actors to pressure for higher standards in bilateral negotiations without violating the Agreement. Thus, rather than conceptualising bi- and multilateralism as opposed political modes, they have to be understood in their complex interrelationship.

6.4 The question of democracy

Nevertheless, the recent rise of bilateralism indicates a lack of hegemony on the international scale. It reflects the fact that different interests are not only articulated *within* the negotiations on multilateral terrains like the TRIPS Agreement or the WTO in general, but, more fundamentally, that the *multilateral institutions themselves* are the object of struggles. Their acceptance as legitimate terrains where conflicts are fought out and compromises are searched for is increasingly challenged by Southern governments, social movements and developmental and environmental NGOs. This constellation is largely the result of a process of interest formation on the part of the societies and governments of Southern countries, driven by the need to implement the TRIPS Agreement and to develop a position in the review of the controversial Article 27.3(b), and often supported by the expertise of NGOs. It remains an open question whether the "scale jumping" of dominant actors between multilateral and bilateral negotiations and the forum shifting between different multilateral terrains will be able to establish a precarious balance between multi- and bilateralism. Our analysis suggests a rather open situation which implies different possibilities among which such a balance is only one. Another one would be the emergence and strengthening of the scale of South–South cooperation which would limit the power of bilateral strategies of Northern governments and could contribute to further challenging multilateral terrains which are largely shaped according to Northern interests.

But even in the case of strengthening the cooperation between Southern governments, the rights of local communities to their environment would be far from guaranteed. These rights are a question of *democratic biodiversity politics*. A fundamental precondition of these politics is that the affected actors recognise the extent of the problem in order to be able to articulate their interests. In addition, *rights* to participate effectively (rights which can be established by law are further reaching than the usually vague rights of participation) and the realistic possibility of being able, de facto, to claim these rights or to reject undesirable developments must be taken seriously. The right to participate in the democratic shaping of societal developments thus refers not only to the formal decision-making mechanisms with which certain regulations are established. It also refers to the actual chances different interest groups have of their case being heard in the political process and of being able to take part to an adequate degree in deciding by which regulations their own living conditions will be structured. The fact that the process of neoliberal globalisation has decisively weakened the chances for the democratic influencing of social living conditions and of societal relationships with nature is becoming more and more clear, although there is no consensus over the reasons for, and the extent of, this. Some of the developments which are continually discussed in this context – the non-democratically controlled power of international organisations such as the World Bank and of regimes such as the WTO, and the political growth of barely controllable TNCs – are also reflected in the field of biodiversity politics.

With regard to these real possibilities of a democratic shaping of societal relationships with nature the answers vary from reservation to scepticism. While the relevance of the local is recognised on the international scale, this recognition has not been reflected in such a way that legally binding and justifiable rights have developed from it. Neither Article 8(j) of the CBD nor the principle of Farmers' Rights were shaped in such a way (the same is true for recognition within the International Labour Organization, ILO). And as far as the IGC – the Intergovernmental Committee on Intellectual Property and Genetic Resources, Traditional Knowledge and Folklore – within the WIPO is concerned, it is doubtful if a result will be produced which strengthens the position of indigenous peoples. What the rules and forums concerning indigenous and Farmers' Rights have in common is that they, mostly, do not constitute integral parts of their respective treaties and organisations. Instead, they seem to be added, and their compliance is often voluntary or subject to national regulations. Thus, they fulfil the purpose of preventing the negotiations about so-called "hard issues" such as IPR or access rules from being disturbed by subordinate interests. Of course, they are at the same time the result of social struggles and can contribute to strengthening the positions of weaker actors, at least symbolically. On the supranational scale, in our example, the picture is even bleaker, because the North American Free Trade Agreement (NAFTA) is based on neoliberal strategies and institutionalises the interests of globally operating industry. The side agreement on the environment within the framework of NAFTA tends to be of a cosmetic nature, not least because it, too, does not strengthen the interests of the locally based actors. The nature of the supranational level does not necessarily have to be so, however. The orientation of NAFTA is connected with the extreme inequalities of power between the participating states. As the example of the Organization of African Unity (OAU) model law shows, other regions are attempting to set quite different accents in their treatment of genetic resources and the local level — even if with little success so far. It was also shown that Mexico vociferously represents the interests of the indigenous peoples at the international level, but within the country itself the law for indigenous rights was finally passed only in an inappropriate form.

However, the shelving of the planned Free Trade Area for the Americas (FTAA, in Spanish ALCA) in November 2005 due to strong mobilisations and some responsive Latin American governments shows that a re-politicisation is taking place and makes further neoliberalisation at least difficult for dominant actors. A question remains how the *existing* forms of political institutionalisation can be fundamentally challenged and thereafter reformulated.

The decisive level in the process of the internationalisation of the state remains that of the nation-state. What can, in the face of the specific power relations, be implemented here in national laws or in other state measures is also decisive for developments on the local scale. This is confirmed not only by the upgrading of national sovereignty in the context of the CBD but also by similar developments in the framework of the FAO and the ITPGR. Even the advancement of bilateral instruments on the fringe of the WTO is an indication that nation-state regulations ultimately play a decisive role. This does not exclude the further development of multilateral regulating mechanisms; rather, the two instruments complement each other.

Unequal power relations not only result in the ability to establish certain rules in or through political institutions. They are also expressed in a much more comprehensive sense: in the definition of the problems, in the structuring of the terrain, in the concrete formulation of policies and in the potential of certain interests and positions to prevail. Hegemonic interests are also expressed in the fact that they bind other interest groups to a certain view of the problem and the corresponding solutions, and at the same time make concessions to them, to a certain degree. The actual inequalities of power become clear, however, when actors decide in favour of fundamentally different options (indigenous peoples, e.g., for the right to say no to the access of genetic resources) or decide principally against certain measures (e.g. in the rejection of patents on life).

The chances of locally based actors being able to shape their relationships with nature in opposition to the valorisation and the establishment of global markets for genetic resources are therefore doubtful (an analysis that Gramsci taught us) – despite the important case of Chiapas. One of the essential tendencies of post-Fordist relationships with nature is the tendency to destroy other relationships or to functionalise them. In this sense it is a continuation of primitive accumulation: the use of non-capitalist forms, which are transformed in the service of valorisation and subsumed under capitalist forms of socialisation. Our analysis in this point is in line with David Harvey's argument of an "accumulation by dispossession" (Harvey 2003; see also Swyngedouw 2005). However, it also indicates the necessity of modifying and developing further Harvey's argument as far as the role of the state is concerned. In his approach, the driving force of the continued primitive accumulation or the accumulation by dispossession is the "spatial fix", that is "capitalism's insatiable drive to resolve its inner crisis tendencies by geographical expansion and geographical restructuring" (Harvey, D. 2001: 24). Although Harvey repeatedly emphasises the role of the state in this process, his conceptualisation of the latter remains under-complex. The state in Harvey's approach appears mainly as an actor who enforces and safeguards the economic tendencies of spatial restructuring, which result from the inner contradictions of capitalism. Thus, Harvey's approach lacks a concept of the state as a terrain of conflict where economic tendencies are not simply enforced, but where disparate and particular strategies for the resolution of the crisis of over-accumulation struggle for their general-isation, some strategies being structurally and strategically privileged over others. As our analysis has shown, taking these conflicts into account, on various terrains and geographical scales of the state, is crucial in order to understand the establishment of the valorisation paradigm, its character and the contradictions it implies as well as the chances to challenge it in favour of democratising the control over natural resources.

The valorisation paradigm constitutes the overall framework for specific institutional developments in order to deal with the environmental crisis in general and the erosion of biodiversity in particular. This tendency is cru-cially supported by legal rights, primarily by rights to "intellectual prop-erty". In the establishment of these rights nation-states, as the proprietors of the "monopoly of legitimate physical force" and with their material as well as knowledge resources and their experiences, play a central role. The pro-cess of primitive accumulation presents itself at this level as the conflict between different forms of rights: "modern" IPR such as patents versus Farmers' Rights or collective rights. But these rights do not stand alone. They must be seen in connection with certain societal practices and they cannot simply be located in the assumed contradiction of economy versus ecology. The protection of nature is also rational within the framework of the life sciences industry as long as it does not cause disproportional costs and above all as long as access (and thus transaction costs) are not bureaucratically over-regulated. The conservation of biological diversity to a certain degree would therefore be possible if it were not made difficult by other interests which are also oriented towards capitalist utilisation: the extractive industry in Chiapas and elsewhere, but above all the increasing use of land both in the South – meadows, the felling of trees and so on – and in the North – settlements, roads and so on.

Opportunities for democratic influence at the international level – as a precondition for the future shaping of democratic societal relations – arise above all where the contradictions between institutions such as the CBD and the TRIPS Agreement of the WTO have become obvious and can be exploited. That is why the resistance to the patenting of genetic resources correctly stands at the centre of many campaigns. But beyond that a more comprehensive understanding of the contradictions and conflicts is necessary. It is fatal if problems of regulation are misunderstood as disputes purely between experts and the problems referred to are technocratically foreshortened. Behind the apparently neutral questions of fact are far-reaching conflicts of interest and complex power relations, which must be taken into account if the treatment of the problem is to be appropriately judged. A critical theory of the internationalisation of the state must examine the emerging forms of global domination and power relations without appearing to be disinterested in the multitude of details of socio-ecological conflicts and alternative strategies. These are often of decisive importance precisely with regard to the shaping of post-Fordist relationships with nature – for the chances of emancipative action as well as for the material dimensions of societal reproduction. In this sense there is still a great deal of material for further empirical research in the restructuring of societal relationships with nature and the internationalisation of the state.

Notes

Introduction: genetic resources and the internationalisation of the state

1 The aim of our study is not to contribute to the debate concerning whether or not post-Fordism as a new stable mode of development has emerged and how regulation theory can analyse that with its theoretical concepts (see Albritton *et al.* 2001; Brand/Raza 2003; Candeias 2004; Jessop 2002). We use the concept of post-Fordism in a heuristic manner, that is to shed theoretical and empirical light on the societal background of the conflicts about genetic resources.

1 The regulation of nature in post-Fordism

1 This aspect of the specific materiality of nature is neglected by Smith (1984), when he criticises the notion of the "domination of nature" as being based on a dualistic conception of nature and society and instead introduces the notion of the "production of nature", rendering the difference between first and second nature obsolete.

2 Nevertheless, even in Germany there exist different approaches which make use of the concept; some of them start with a constructivist perspective (see Weingarten 1998; Demirovic 1997), while others do not (see Becker/Jahn 2006).

3 We use the concepts in a heuristic way and on an abstract level. We do not intend to capture all the developments in real life but want to figure out general trends.

4 RAFI stands for Rural Advancement Foundation International, ETC for Erosion, Technology and Concentration, naming the three most important problems in the field of agriculture and nutrition (cf. ETC Group 2005a).

5 The consequences of the patents were that Indian famers could no longer export the Neem seed or any associated Neem products and that those who traditionally bought the seeds could not afford to do so any longer because the market price rose tenfold.

6 For a survey of the latter aspect cf. Kütting 2000; Paterson 2000; Lipschutz 2004; Axelrod *et al.* 2005; Betsill *et al.* 2006; on the role of the state in environmental politics Barry/Eckersley 2005.

7 Cf. Smith 1995; Delaney/Leitner 1997; Swyngedouw 1997; Marston 2000; Brenner 2001, 2004; Brenner *et al.* 2003; Novy 2003; Wissen 2007; on the inadequate conceptualising of the term "global" in many contributions cf. also Shaw 2000, Chapter 1.

2 On the value of nature: the Convention on Biological Diversity and the commercialisation of genetic resources

1 Cf. for example the enormous list of participating non-state actors at the eighth COP in March 2006 in Brazil (Secretariat of the CBD 2006b: 5–10); but this was also due to an intense mobilisation of Brazilian farmers and organisations against the introduction of genetically modified seeds.

2 Methodologically, it is a reconstruction of positions which we have extracted from numerous interviews and documents.

3 On ambiguities in the concept of megadiversity cf. Caillaux/Ruíz 2002, footnote 1.

4 Interestingly enough, the Nigerian government, which has introduced a benefit-sharing model in the country, in a top-down process without participation, hardly makes an appearance at the negotiations.

5 Another major issue for the biotechnological industry is, aside from access and intellectual property rights, the so-called genetic use restriction technologies (GURTs) or, as a politicised concept, Terminator Technology. Officially, there is an accepted moratorium which was questioned by the governments of New Zealand, Australia and Switzerland in the beginning of 2006, following an initiative by Canada, allowing a "case-by-case assessment". But this proposal was rejected and the moratorium renewed at COP 8 (ENB 2006a: 15–16).

6 Cf. Görg/Brand 2003; Brand 2000: 203ff. with a classification of six types of NGO. On empirical studies, especially of environmental NGOs, cf. Brunnengräber *et al.* 2001. On a critical socio-theoretical and socio-political placement of NGOs cf. Demirovic 2003; Hirsch 2003.

7 Cf. for example the homepages www.iucn.org, www.panda.org, www.wri.org, www.etcgroup.org, www.grain.org, www.twnside.org.sg.

8 The IIFB is supported by European NGOs which have an important share, both financially and administratively, in the organisation of the forum. On the one hand, this undermines the political self-understanding of the IIFB, but on the other hand, the selection of the participants also does not take place from within a self-organised structure of the IIFB. For this situation, which is regarded by the indigenous peoples as problematic, there exists no solution at present despite an intensive search which is seen as promising future success. By itself, the arduous task of translating the most important documents into the four "major languages" is one which the IIFB can hardly master. In the periods outside the official meetings of the IIFB, the forum, which has no secretariat and has to exist without a permanent representative, is virtually non-existent. From the point of view of the participants, personal contacts are lost between the meetings; new methods of communication are often unavailable due to financial conditions or bad infrastructure in their home regions. Different offices and tasks in the forum are not assigned permanently to particular persons. This creates certain flexibility in the administration – especially if a participant is hindered – but it is accompanied by the additional trouble of a renewed training programme and a possible loss of know-how.

9 Since the 1990s representatives of the San people from Angola, Namibia, Botswana and South Africa have met in order to discuss common problems and promote solutions. In 1996, WIMSA was established to give these efforts continuity, concerning issues such as human rights violations, ownership rights or the documentation of their oral traditions. Moreover, the collaboration was important in raising self-consciousness of the San people (Hoering 2004: 11).

10 They are called Bonn Guidelines because in October 2001 the Open-Ended Ad Hoc Working Group on Access and Benefit-sharing gathered in Bonn and adopted the Guidelines.

11 Quantitative aspects could play a role if, for example, Southern countries agreed to cultivate certain genetically modified products within the framework of the international division of labour. This aspect does not play any role in the negotiations and was mentioned in the interviews only by one NGO activist (CBD/17).

3 Limits to commercialisation? Genetic resources in agriculture and the conflict over a multilateral exchange system

1 In the following section, we concentrate only on plants; but there is a rising awareness that genetic diversity of animals is just as important.

2 Crosby (1986) even sees a causal correlation here: diseases and the European relationships with nature were partly responsible for the conquest of America. For a critical comment see Arnold 1996: 74ff.

3 Although it seems that due to the increasing privatisation of research and development on plant genetic resources some International Research Centres today have changed their strategies and present themselves as being part of the public sector and involved in the production of public goods.

4 The general irritation must have been great, for even the normally rather reticent Earth Negotiations Bulletin speaks not only of an icy atmosphere but even of the preparedness of some delegates to jump into the Lake of Neuchatel (cf. ENB 2000b, 2000d).

5 Binding payments are only required in the case of the commercialisation of the material from the Multilateral Exchange System. IPRs are only mentioned in a general way, with reference to the limitation of access; details must, however, still be regulated by the Governing Body of the International Treaty; cf. ITPGR 2001: Art. 13.2(d).

6 Information given privately to the authors at the sixth extraordinary meeting of the Commission on Genetic Resources for Food and Agriculture, in June 2001, in Rome.

7 Although it must be remembered that these regulations are being violated more and more in practice and that patents on genetic resources are repeatedly registered and granted which are neither new nor an invention. This points to a fundamental problem concerning genetic resources: to what extent can these in fact be invented? More details on this later.

8 In the sense of international law, in the International Treaty the same formulations have been used as were already used in the Biosafety Protocol to regulate its relationship to other agreements. While they were still extremely controversial in the Biosafety Protocol and almost led to the failure of the entire process (Gupta 1999; cf. Görg 2003a: 272ff.), within the framework of the International Treaty they were relatively unproblematic and were taken over with reference to the apparently good solution of the Biosafety Protocol. But the problem with the phraseology taken from the Biosafety Protocol is that these formulations are not really unequivocal, but that the solution consists of listing the different objectives one after the other.

4 Politicising intellectual property rights: the conflicts around the TRIPS Agreement and the World Intellectual Property Organization

1

The previous governance structure for intellectual property had included 135 states as members of the WIPO, although of the eighteen conventions administered, even the Paris convention, with the most signatories, had been ratified by only 108 countries. With the exception of the Bern convention (95 signatories), other agreements overseen by WIPO only had between 20 and 50 signatories.

(May/Sell 2006: 162f.)

2 Cf. the debate on the internationalisation of the protection of intellectual property in the second half of the nineteenth century (May/Sell 2006: 115ff.).

3 See CIPR (2002a: 2), ETC Group (2001: 3f.), Byström/Einarsson (2001), Correa (2000: chapters II and VI), Federal Ministry of Education and Research/OECD (2002), Perelman (2003), Stilwell (2001).

4 Cf. Chapter 2 on this.

5 The following passages are largely based on an analysis of communications from national governments to the WTO concerning the TRIPS Agreement and biodiversity, on the summaries of the positions articulated in these communications which are periodically issued by the WTO and on the newsletter "Bridges Trade BioRes – Trade and Biological Resources News Digest", which is produced by the International Centre for Trade and

Sustainable Development (ICTSD) in collaboration with IUCN – The World Conservation Union. The latter is available at www.ictsd.org/biores/index.htm, the WTO documents under http://docsonline.wto.org. Individual documents are only indicated in the case of citations. For a summary of the positions and the state of negotiations as of spring 2006 see the notes of the Secretariat of the TRIPS Council in WTO (2006b) (concerning the review of Article 27.3(b) of the TRIPS Agreement) and WTO (2006a) (concerning the relationship between the TRIPS Agreement and the Convention on Biological Diversity).

6 The UPOV lays down the criteria for the protection of plant varieties: a plant variety must be new, differentiable, homogeneous and enduring in order to be able to be protected. The UPOV was set up in 1961. Revisions were made in 1972, 1978 and 1991. Until April 1999 non-UPOV members had the opportunity to join the Convention in the version of 1978. Since then it is only possible to join the version of 1991, which, compared to the version of 1978 strengthens the property rights of plant breeders:

> The 1991 revision has brought the Convention more into line with patent law. The 1991 Act requires the authorisation of the right-holder for production or reproduction, conditioning for the purpose of propagation, offering for sale, selling or other marketing, exporting or importing, and stocking for any of these purposes.
>
> (Leskien/Flitner 1997: 61)

7 See a communication from Kenya on behalf of the African Group from 1999 (WTO 1999a: paragraph 21):

> The review process should clarify that plants and animals as well as microorganisms and all other living organisms and their parts cannot be patented, and that natural processes that produce plants, animals and other living organisms should also not be patentable.

8 The prescribed period for industrial countries ended one year after the coming into force of the TRIPS Agreement, that is on 31 December 1995. The least developed countries originally should have implemented the Agreement by 31 December 2005. At the Ministerial Conference of the WTO in December 2005 in Hong Kong, this period was prolonged until the summer of 2012.

9 However, its effects are more symbolic than material. Even if it remains in the framework of the TRIPS Agreement, the international as well as the domestic relationships of power in many African states are likely to prevent the model law from being implemented. This is shown not least in the reactions of WIPO and UPOV. Both organisations saw considerable deficits in the draft with regard to patent protection and the protection of varieties. They rejected the attempt to establish inalienable community rights and to strengthen farmers' rights vis-à-vis the rights of breeders.

10 See for example a communication from Brazil from 2000 (WTO 2000c), in which it is stated, "Traditional knowledge may bring significant benefits for several industrial sectors, in particular the pharmaceutical and agricultural sectors." See also Dutfield (2002: 17), Ribeiro (2002b: 127f.) and Bridges Trade BioRes 2002: "For indigenous groups, TK protection is a rights-based issue, while many governmental representatives regard it as a matter of international equity or national development."

11 For recent initiatives, see the submission of a group of developing countries (WTO 2006c) and of Norway (WTO 2006d) from June 2006, both available under http://docsonline.wto.org. For a summary of both initiatives and the corresponding reactions, see Bridges Trade BioRes 2006b. For a discussion of disclosure requirements as legal instruments to prevent biopiracy and to ensure benefit-sharing, see Chouchena-Rojas *et al.* (2005).

12 Communication from the USA from 2006 (WTO 2006e: 2).

13 See WTO 2001 and WTO 2002b. On this condition, the European Union has declared its willingness to negotiate in the TRIPS Council on a multilateral system for the disclosure

of the origin of genetic resources in patent applications. The disclosure requirement is to be limited to the origin of the resources and should not include a proof of compliance with the regulations on access and benefit-sharing.

14 For a detailed discussion of the SPLT see Tvedt (2005).

15 In the case of a clarification under the WTO's dispute settlement body, the economically stronger countries have an advantage, simply because they can more readily afford the necessary juridical competence than can their weaker country counterparts and because they possess more effective opportunities for retribution. Due to the power asymmetries which can themselves develop to the full in bilateral negotiations, a legalistic argumentation which emphasises the flexibility of the TRIPS Agreement, such as that to be found in Correa (2000) and in Plahe/Nyland (2003), falls short of the mark.

16 Another factor, which however lies beyond the scope of this analysis, is the possibility of the convergence of social movements, that is the chance to establish links between the struggles against the strengthening of intellectual property protection in the area of biodiversity and similar struggles which take place for example in the area of software. See GRAIN (2005b) and Gerstetter/Kaiser (2006) on this issue.

5 The relevance of the national and the local: the disputes over a valorisation paradigm in Mexico and Chiapas

1 Scientific contacts with Mexico existed since the mid-1990s and were intensified between 1998 and 2000 under the EU-financed exchange programme ALFA (*América Latina de Formación Académica*).

2 The PRD is less a centralised, Western European-type party, being more a collection at the level of the provinces of very differing, mostly left-wing groups, which were able to participate in the elections through the PRD.

3 In 2005 imports of goods were worth 232 billion USD and exports 214 billion USD which is far more than the imports and exports of Brazil, for example (WTO 2006f: 11).

4 The Maquiladora industry carries out one particular step in the production process. The inputs can be imported tax-free to Mexico from other countries, for example the USA, and are then exported again tax-free after processing in the Maquiladoras. Important for the producers is cheap labour (and therefore weak trade unions). Laws on this have existed since the 1950s in Mexico; since 1972 the Maquiladora industry has been growing, above all at the border between the USA and Mexico.

> The exploitation of people and nature is the secret of the dynamic Maquiladora industry on the northern border of the country above all since the currency devaluation of 1995, while at the same time in the rest of Mexico crisis and cut-backs in employment – at least since 1997 – were clearly dominant.
>
> (Boris/Sterr 2002: 200, our translation)

The Maquiladora production fell in 2002 for the first time since the 1990s (EIA 2003: 1).

5 We did considerable research on the NAFTA Side Agreement on Environment but it plays hardly any role in the present issue area beside symbolic politics. Therefore, we leave it aside.

6 A representative of the Ministry of Agriculture (Mx/6) points out that this development was not at all uncontroversial, but that, within the Ministry ever since the 1950s, violent disputes over the concentration on high yields and the Green Revolution, as well as the reclaiming of intellectual property, took place.

7 One result is the massive change in the structure of the local economy, particularly because it becomes more attractive for the local population to work in the oil sector instead of in the (to a large extent subsistence-oriented) agricultural sector.

8 Due to the rapid growth of the population from 3 million inhabitants in 1960 to 7 million in 1970 and the extreme growth in the number of cars in the Mexico of the

1970s, which was transforming itself into an oil-producing country, the air pollution in the 2000 metre high capital city surrounded by mountains was the most discussed problem, above all because a large part of manufacturing industry was also based there (Russell 1994: 235ff.) Between 1979 and 1987 emissions of pollutants multiplied by a factor of eight (ibid.: 232).

9 Social groups gained in importance in the 1980s, particularly following the earthquake in Mexico City and the disastrous crisis management by the PRI in 1985. Apart from the main theme of the democratisation of the political system, environmental themes were taken up. The intellectual association "Group of one hundred", centred around Octavio Paz, Carlos Fuentes and Elena Pontiatowska, issued statements on various environmental issues. In the Mexican environmental movement (*Movimiento Mexicano para el Medio Ambiente*) 63 national and regional groups were united in the Alliance of Mexican Ecologists (*Alianza de Ecologistas Mexicanos*), primarily those from the capital city (Russell 1994: 233). The Mexican Green Ecological Party (*Partido Verde Ecológico Mexicano*; PVEM) is unimportant, although it participated in the presidential elections in 2000 together with the PAN (*Partido de Acción Nacional*) and was among the victors (but remained without a ministerial post).

10 John Warnock (1995: 191) quotes a study which illustrates the difference: in the USA 7 tonnes of maize are harvested from one hectare of land, and in Mexico 1.7 tonnes; for the production of a tonne of beans in the USA 4.8 hours of labour are required, and in Mexico 50.6 hours. Oxfam (2003: 9) points to the important fact, however, that the main problem of Mexico's small producers is the immense power of the purchasing concerns and not so much the high productivity of the US farmers.

11 Already in the pre-Columbian world there were intermediaries between the indigenous communities and the centralised political power, whereby the relationships were based on mutual acceptance. During the colonial period this mutual acceptance was lost. In pre-Columbian times the cacique was to all intents and purposes the tribal chief who mediated between his tribe and the imperial power (Incas or Mayas). During and after colonialism, however, the cacique became the *political* chief who mediated between the tribe (village, town) and the nation-state and who aquired power as the political voice of his/her community before the state, thereafter using this power to advance his/her familial and/or groups interests, and thus becoming central for the reproduction of those relationships of power which suppressed the communes. It is today a member of the commune, but does not represent the external power of the state there.

12 In comparison to the beginning of the 1990s, this is not a dramatic shift. Rather, it is an indication not only that the changed legal conditions lead to sales but that the privatisation of the Ejido land is a complex process. The Ejiditarios do not sell immediately and there is generally no direct or huge interest from buyers.

13 Conservation International has a quite different view to the WWF:

> Initiatives led by CI and partners brought peace to the Montes Azules Biosphere Reserve in Chiapas state, site of a long-simmering conflict between government and local communities over indigenous rights. Through sustainable land-use planning, the promotion of alternative livelihoods, and the voluntary relocation of more than 10 squatter groups, previously violent disputes were resolved without a single incident of bloodshed.
>
> (CI 2006: 10)

14 A detailed analysis of the PPP would have to examine to what extent there are competing strategies. In addition to the outlined dominant strategy – which in the final analysis is defined according to the provision of resources – there is, for example, a paper by the Inter-American Development Bank and the CEPAL which proposes several initiatives within the objective of the creation of competitiveness, which emphasise domestic economic connections and sustainable development (see Grupo Técnico Interinstitucional 2001).

15 When the project was announced as comprising over 90 million USD, the GEF share of almost 15 million USD was only small, however, at the beginning of the project the GEF figure remained the same while the rest – particularly the share of the Mexican Government – had shrunk from over 70 million to 2.6 million USD (*La Jornada*, 3 March 2003).

16 Connected with this were specific labour relationships and a constitutive racism (Ceceña 2000).

17 Ana Esther Ceceña (2000: 268) asks the interesting question whether the exploitation of the oil reserves in Chiapas will wait until the privatisation of the Mexican oil industry.

18 Again, at the CBD Conference of the Parties in March 2006, in Curitiba, the positions of the Mexican delegation were very close to that of the US Government, for example concerning weak indications of transgenic food. And as the only government of all mega-diverse countries it tried to promote Genetic Use Restriction Technologies (GURTS, *La Jornada*, 7 April 2006).

19 On important differences between conservationist and indigenous perspectives, see Nigh/ Rodríguez 1995: 177–202.

20 It is paradoxical that from 1991 to 1994 the possibility of being granted patents on living organisms had already existed. This regulation was revoked in the course of the NAFTA implementation under pressure from the Ministry of Agriculture, and today UPOV is in force (Mx/6).

21 On the strategy and effects of the "silencios zapatistas" (Zapatista silences), that is their rejection of any public discourse, see the excellent essay of Rajchenberg/Héau-Lambert (2004).

22 The main objective of the members of the *Fondo* is the economic development of Chiapas through a wide range of investments in labour-intensive agricultural, industrial and tourist sectors, all of which hinge upon, among other things, the creation of industrial parks for Maquiladora industries and support for industries close to agriculture.

23 It may be of interest to note that CI, in the year 2005, raised funds of more than 92 million USD and invested more than 114 million USD (CI 2006: 18–19). The list of the supporters and financiers of CI reads like a "Who's Who" of the international economy. Alfonso Romo of Pulsar, who we have already mentioned, belongs to the Board; among the sponsors are Monsanto, Coca-Cola, McDonald's, Intel Corporation, Ford Motor Company and Starbucks (ibid.: 25–26). Unfortunately, in spite of numerous attempts, it was not possible to interview representatives of Pulsar or Conservation International during our research.

24 The seven programmes which began in 2005 take place in Costa Rica, Panama, Papua New Guinea, Fiji, Madagascar, Laos/Vietnam, Uzbekistan/Kirghizia.

25 It remains unclear whether the fact that the Mexican company Pulsar-Seminis was sold in 2005 to the US-based Monsanto has influenced the possibilities open to action in Mexico.

6 Contested terrains: towards a neo-Poulantzian approach to International Political Economy

1 Of particular relevance is the fate of the existing collections; see Chapter 3.

Bibliography

Aboites, J. (1989) *Industrialización y desarrollo agrícola en México, un análisis del régimen de acumulación en el largo plazo: 1939–1987*, Mexico City: Universidad Autónoma Metropolitana-Xochimilco.

Acselrad, H. (2002) "Die ökologische Herausforderung zwischen Markt, Sicherheit und Gerechtigkeit", in Görg, C. and Brand, U. (eds) *Mythen globalen Umweltmanagements, Rio +10 und die Sackgassen "nachhaltiger Entwicklung"*, Münster: Westfälisches Dampfboot.

Aglietta, M. (1979) *A Theory of Capitalist Regulation, The US-Experience*, London: New Left Books.

Agrawal, A. (1995) "Dismantling the divide between indigenous and scientific knowledge", in *Development and Change*, vol. 26: 413–439, The Hague: Blackwell Publishing.

Aguilar, A.G. and Graizbord, B. (2006) "Latin America: a region of shared loyalties and persistent dependencies", in Geyer, H. S. (ed.) *Global Regionalization, Core Peripheral Trends*, Cheltenham: Edward Elgar Publishing.

Akhter, F. (2001) "Die Nayakrishi-Kampagne: Saatgut in die Hände der Frauen!", in Klaffenböck, G., Lachkovics, E. and Südwind Agnetur (eds) *Biologische Vielfalt. Wer kontrolliert die genetischen Ressourcen*, Frankfurt/M.: Brandes & Apsel.

Albritton, R., Itoh, M., Westra, R. and Zuege, A. (eds) (2001) *Phases of Capitalist Development. Booms, Crises and Globalization*, London: Macmillan.

Alnasseri, S. (2003) "Ursprüngliche Akkumulation, Artikulation und Regulation, Aspekte einer globalen Theorie der Regulation", in Brand, U. and Raza, W. (eds) *Fit für den Postfordismus?*, Münster: Westfälisches Dampfboot.

—— (2004) *Periphere Regulation, Regulationstheoretische Konzepte zur Analyse von Entwicklungsstrategien im arabischen Raum*, Münster: Westfälisches Dampfboot.

Alnasseri, S., Brand, U., Sablowski, T., Winter, J. (2001) "Raum, Regulation und Periodisierung des Kapitalismus", in Albritton, Robert *et al.* (eds) *Phases of Capitalist Development. Booms, Crises and Globalization*, London: Macmillan.

Altvater, E. (1993) *The Future of the Market, An Essay of the Regulation of Money and Nature after the Collapse of "Actually Existing Socialism"*, London: Verso.

Altvater, E. and Mahnkopf, B. (1999) *Grenzen der Globalisierung, Ökonomie, Ökologie und Politik in der Weltgesellschaft*, 4th edn, Münster: Westfälisches Dampfboot.

Anderson, J. and Goodman, J. (1995) "Regions, States and the European Union: Modernist Reaction or Postmodernist Adaptation", in *Review of International Political Economy*, vol. 2, 4: 600–631.

Arnold, D. (1996) *The Problem of Nature*, Oxford: Blackwell Publishing.

Arts, B. (1998) *The Political Influence of Global NGOs, Case Studies on Climate and Biodiversity Conventions*, Utrecht: International Books.

Axelrod, R. S., Downie, D. L. and Vig, N. (eds) (2005) *The Global Environment: Institutions, Law, and Policy*, Washington, DC: C. Q. Press.

Ayales, I., Solís Rivera, V. and Madrigal, P. (2002) "Las mujeres en la conservación de la biodiversidad", in Heineke, C. (ed.) *La Vida en Venta: Transgénicos, Patentes y Biodiversidad*, San Salvador: Ediciones Heinrich Böll.

Bache, I. and Flinders, M. (eds) (2004) *Multi-Level Governance*, Oxford: Oxford University Press.

Baguio Declaration (2004) *Baguio Declaration of the 2nd Asian Indigenous Women's Conference*, 8 March 2004, Baguio City, Philippines, www.tebtebba.org/tebtebba_files/gender/aiwcdec.html

Barreda, A. (1999) *Atlas Geoeconómico y Geopolítico del Estado de Chiapas*, Dissertation: UNAM.

—— (2001) "Los peligros del Plan Puebla Panamá", Manuscript.

Barry, J. and Eckersley, R. (eds) (2005) *The State and Global Environmental Crisis*, Cambridge, MA: MIT Press.

Bartra, A. (2003) "Descifrando la treseava estela", in *Observatorio Social de América Latina*, 12: 279–292, www.observatoriosocial.com.ar/revi12.html

Beck, U. (1992) "Risk Society: towards a New Modernity", London: Sage Publications.

Beck, U., Giddens, A. and Lash, S. (1994) "Reflexive modernization: politics, tradition and aesthetics in the modern social order", Stanford, CT: Stanford University Press.

Becker, E. (2001) "Die postindustrielle Wissensgesellschaft – ein moderner Mythos?", in *Zeitschrift für Kritische Theorie*, vol. 7, 12: 85–106.

Becker, E. and Jahn, T. (1987) "Soziale Ökologie als Krisenwissenschaft", Frankfurt/M.: ISOE.

—— (eds) (2006) "Soziale Ökologie: Grundzüge einer Wissenschaft von den gesellschaftlichen Naturverhältnissen", Frankfurt/M. [u.a.]: Campus-Verlag.

Behrens, M. (ed.) (2005) *Globalisierung als politische Herausforderung: Global Governance zwischen Utopie und Realität*, Wiesbaden: VS Verlag für Sozialwissenschaften.

Bell, D. (1967) "Die nachindustrielle Gesellschaft", Frankfurt/M.: Campus.

Benton, T. (1989) "Marxism and natural limits", in *New Left Review* 178: 51–86.

Berne Declaration (2001) "Keep Crop Seeds Patent-Free in Order to Maintain World Food Security", open letter signed by 255 NGOs, Media Release, 20 January 2001, www.evb.ch/bd/press/20_04_01.htm

Betsill, M. M., Hochstetler, K. and Stevis, D. (eds) (2006) *International Environmental Politics*, Basingstoke: Palgrave.

Bieler, A. and Morton, A. (2004) "A critical theory route to hegemony, world order and historical change: neo-Gramscian perspectives in International Relations", in *Capital & Class*, 82 (Spring): 85–113.

Bieling, H. (2003) "Internationale Politische Ökonomie", in Schieder, S. and Spindler, M. (eds) *Theorien der Internationalen Beziehungen*, Opladen: Leske + Budrich.

—— (2006) "Europäische Staatlichkeit", in Bretthauer, L., Gallas, A., Kannankulam, J. and Stützle, I. (eds) *Poulantzas lesen, Zur Aktualität marxistischer Staatstheorie*, Hamburg: VSA.

BIO – Biotechnology Industry Organization, www.bio.org/ip/

Blank, K. (2002) "Das Internationale Indigene Forum zu Biodiversität im aktuellen Politikprozess der Konvention über biologische Vielfalt", *Forschungsbericht zum VI. Internationalen Indigenen Forum zu Biodiversität*, Manuscript.

BMU – Bundesministerium für Umwelt, Naturschutz und Reaktorsicherheit (ed.) (1992) *CBD, Convention on Biological Diversity, Übereinkommen über die biologische Vielfalt*, Vertragstext, Bonn: BMU.

Bödeker, S., Moldenhauer, O. and Rubbel, B. (2005) "Wissensallmende. Gegen die Privatisierung des Wissens der Welt", *AttacBasisTexte 15*, Hamburg: VSA-Verlag.

Borg, E. (2001) *Projekt Globalisierung, Soziale Kräfte im Konflikt um Hegemonie*, Hannover: Offizin.

Boris, D. (1996) *Mexiko im Umbruch, Modellfall einer gescheiterten Entwicklungsstrategie*, Darmstadt: Wissenschaftliche Buchgesellschaft.

Boris, D. and Sterr, A. (2002) *Foxtrott in Mexiko, Demokratisierung oder Neopopulismus?*, Köln: Neuer ISP-Verlag.

Boyer, R. (1986) *La Theorie de la Régulation: Une Analyse Critique*, Paris: Editions La Découverte.

Braithwaite, J. and Drahos, P. (2000) *Global Business Regulation*, Cambridge: Cambridge University Press.

Brand, U. (2000) *Nichtregierungsorganisationen, Staat und ökologische Krise, Konturen kritischer NRO-Forschung, Das Beispiel der biologischen Vielfalt*, Münster: Westfälisches Dampfboot.

—— (2004) "Hegemonía fragmentada", in Sader, E. and Brie, M. (eds) *Para além do capitalismo neoliberal: concepcões, atores e estratégia*. Sao Paolo: Expressão Popular.

—— (2005) "Order and regulation: Global Governance as a hegemonic discourse of international politics?", in *Review of International Political Economy*, vol. 12, 1: 155–176.

—— (2006) "The Internationalised State and its Functions and Modes in the Global Governance of Biodiversity", paper presented at the conference *Science, Knowledge Communities and Environmental Governance: Global–Local Linkages* at Rutgers University, May 2006.

Brand, U. and Ceceña, A. E. (eds) (2000) *Reflexionen einer Rebellion, "Chiapas" und ein anderes Politikverständnis*, Münster: Westfälisches Dampfboot.

Brand, U. and Görg, C. (2007) "Sustainability and Globalisation: A Theoretical Perspective", in Conca, K., Finger, M.and Park, J. (eds) *Sustainability, Globalization and Governance*, London: Routledge (forthcoming).

Brand, U. and Kalcsics, M. (eds) (2002) *Wem gehört die Natur? Konflikte um genetische Ressourcen in Lateinamerika*. Frankfurt/M.: Brandes & Apsel.

Brand, U. and Raza, W. (eds) (2003) *Fit für den Postfordismus?*, Münster: Westfälisches Dampfboot.

Brand, U., Brunnengräber, A., Schrader, L., Stock, C. and Wahl, P. (2000) *Global Governance, Alternative zur neoliberalen Globalisierung?*, Münster: Westfälisches Dampfboot.

Brenner, N. (2001) "The limits to scale? Methodological reflections on scalar structuration", in *Progress in Human Geography*, vol. 25, 4: 591–614.

—— (2004) "New State Spaces, Urban Governance and the Rescaling of Statehood", Oxford: Oxford University Press.

Brenner, N., Jessop, B., Jones, M. and Macleod, G. (eds) (2003) *State / Space: A reader*, Malden, MA: Blackwell Publishers.

Bridges Trade BioRes (2002) "Misappropriation of Traditional Knowledge Discussed at CBD Working Group", vol. 2, 3, www.ictsd.org/biores/02-02-21/story2.htm

—— (2004) "WIPO Committee Resumes Work on Genetic Resources and TK", vol. 4, 6, www.ictsd.org/biores/04-04-02/story1.htm

—— (2006a) "WTO Disclosure Talks Try to Clarify CBD–Trips Relationship", vol. 6, 5, www.ictsd.org/biores/06-03-17/story4.htm

—— (2006b) "Discussions on CBD–Trips Gain Momentum with New Proposals", vol. 6, 11, www.ictsd.org/biores/06-06-16/story3.htm

—— (2006c) "WIPO Committee Considers Mechanism to Protect TK", vol. 6, 9, www.ictsd.org/biores/06-05-19/story4.htm

Brockway, L. H. (1988) "Plants, Sciences and Colonial Expansion: The Botanical Chess Game", in Kloppenburg, J. R. (ed.) *Seeds and Sovereignty, The Use and Control of Plant Genetic Ressources*, Durham, NC: Duke University Press.

Brühl, T. (2001) "Mehr Raum für unbequeme Mitspieler? Warum Nichtregierungsorganisationen verstärkt in internationalen (Umwelt-)Verhandlungen mitwirken dürfen", in Walk, H., Klein, A. and Brunnengräber, A. (eds) *NGOs als Legitimationsressource*, Opladen: Westdeutscher Verlag.

Brunnengräber, A. and Walk, H.(eds) (2007) *Multi-Level-Governance. Klima-, Umwelt- und Sozialpolitik in einer interdependenten Welt*, Baden Baden: Nomos.

Brunnengräber, A., Klein, A. and Walk, H. (eds) (2001) *NGOs als Legitimationsressource. Zivilgesellschaftliche Partizipationsformen im Globalisierungsprozess*, Opladen: Leske & Buderich.

Brush, S. B. (1993) "Indigenous Knowledge of Biological Resources and Intellectual Property Rights: The Role of Anthropology", in *American Anthropologist*, vol. 95, 3: 653–669.

BSR – Biodiversity Synthesis Report (2005) *Millennium Ecosystem Assessment: Ecosystems and Human Well-being*, Washington, DC.: World Resources Institute.

Buckel, S. (2003) "Global 'Non-State', Überlegungen für eine materialistische Theorie des transnationalen Rechts", in Buckel, S., Dackweiler, R. and Noppe, R. (eds) *Formen und Felder politischer Intervention, Zur Relevanz von Staat und Steuerung*, Festschrift für Josef Esser, Münster: Westfälisches Dampfboot.

BUKO – Kampagne gegen Biopiraterie (2005) *Grüne Beute, Biopiraterie und Widerstand – Argumente, Hintergründe, Aktionen*, Grafenau: Trotzdem-Verlag.

Buntzel-Cano, R. (2000) "Aufruf zu Aktionen", in *Forum Umwelt & Entwicklung*, Rundbrief 3, 24.

Burchardt, H. (2004) *Zeitenwende. Politik nach dem Neoliberalismus*, Stuttgart: Schmetterling.

Burrows, B. (ed.) (2005) *The Catch, Perspectives in Benefit Sharing*, Edmonds: The Edmonds Institute, www.edmonds-institute.org/thecatch.pdf

Buttel, F. H. (1992) "The 'Environmentalization' of Plant Genetic Resources: Possible Benefits, Possible Risks", in *Diversity*, vol. 8, 1: 36–39.

Buttel, F. H., Dickens, P., Dunlap, R. E. and Gijswijt, A. (2002) "Sociological Theory and the environment: An overview and introduction", in Dunlap R. E. *et al.* (eds) *Sociological theory and the environment: classical foundations, contemporary insights*, Lanham, MD: Rowman & Littlefield Publishers.

Byström, M. and Einarsson, P. (2001) *TRIPs, Consequences for developing countries, Implications for Swedish development cooperation, Consultancy Report to the Swedish International Development Cooperation Agency (Sida)*, www.grain.org/docs/sida-trips-2001-en.PDF

Caillaux, J. and Ruíz, M. (2002) "Legislative Experiences on Access to Genetic Resources and Options for Megadiverse Countries", paper presented at the *First Meeting of Like-Minded Megadiverse Countries*, February 2000, Mexico, www.megadiverse.org/armado_ingles/PDF/five/five5.pdf

Calderón Salazar, J. A. (1992) *El TLC y el desarrollo rural*, Mexico City: Ed. CEMO.

Camp, R. A. (2003) *Politics in Mexico, The Democratic Transformation*, 4th edn, New York: Oxford University Press.

Candeias, M. (2004) *Neoliberalismus, Hochtechnologie, Hegemonie, Grundrisse einer transnationalen kapitalistischen Produktions- und Lebensweise*, Hamburg: Argument-Verlag.

Candeias, M. and Deppe, F. (eds) (2001) *Ein neuer Kapitalismus?*, Hamburg: VSA-Verlag.

Casares, E. S. and Sobarzo, H. (eds) (2004) *Diez años del TLCAN en México, Una perspectiva analítica*, Mexico City: Fondo de Cultura Económica.

Castree N. and Braun, B. (1998) "The construction of nature and the nature of construction", in Braun, B. and Castree, N. (eds) *Remaking Reality: nature at the Millennium*, London: Routledge.

Castro Escudero, T. and Oliver Costilla, L. (eds) (2005) *Poder y política en América Latina*, El debate latinoamericano, vol. 3, Mexico City: Siglo XXI/UNAM.

Castro Escudero, T., Mussali Galante, R. and Oliver Costilla, L. (2005) "Revisitando al Estado, Los Estados populistas y desarrollistas: Poner las cosas en su lugar", in Castro Escudero, T. and Oliver Costilla, L. (eds) *Poder y política en América Latina,* El debate latinoamericano, vol. 3, Mexico City: Siglo XXI/UNAM.

Catton, W. R.and Dunlap, R. E. (1978) "Environmental Sociology: A New Paradigm", in *The American Sociologist,* vol. 13: 41–49.

CBD – Convention on Biological Diversity (1992) www.biodiv.org/convention/convention.shtml

—— (2001) *Report of the Ad Hoc Open-Ended Working Group on Access and Benefit-Sharing,* (UNEP/CBD/COP/6/6), www.biodiv.org/doc/meetings/cop/cop-06/official/cop-06-06-en.pdf

—— (2002) "Access and benefit-sharing as related to genetic resources", *Decision VI/6 of the CBD,* www.biodiv.org/decisions/

—— (2006) "International regime on access and benefit-sharing", (UNEP/CBD/WG-ABS/4/CRP.1/Rev.2), 3 February 2006, www.ip-watch.org/weblog/index.php?p = 213&res = 1280_ff&print = 0

CBD-Handbook (2001) *Handbook of the Convention on Biological Diversity,* London: Earthscan.

CEAS (2000) "Study on the relationship between the agreement on TRIPS and biodiversity related issues", *Center for European Agricultural Studies, Final Report for DG TRADE European Commission,* europa.eu.int/comm/trade/miti/intell/ceas.htm

Ceceña, A. E. (2000) "Die Grenzen der Modernität. Kämpfe um strategische Ressourcen", in Brand, U. and Ceceña, A. E. (eds) *Reflexionen einer Rebellion, "Chiapas" und ein anderes Politikverständnis,* Münster: Westfälisches Dampfboot.

—— (ed.) (2006) *Los desafíos de las emancipaciones en un contexto militarizado,* Buenos Aires: CLACSO.

Ceceña, A. E. and Barreda, A. (eds) (1995) *Producción Estratégica y Hegemonía Mundial,* Mexico City: Siglo XXI.

Ceceña, A. E. and Giménez, J. (2002) "Hegemonía y bioprospección, El caso del International Cooperative Biodiversity Group", in Brand, U. and Kalcsics, M. (eds) (2002) *Wem gehört die Natur? Konflikte um genetische Ressourcen in Lateinamerika,* Frankfurt/M.: Brandes & Apsel.

Chambers, W. B. (2004) "Use of Genetic Resources: New Global Rules or a Rocky Path to Nowhere?", in *Environmental Policy and Law,* vol. 34, 2: 61–64.

Chapin, M. (2004) "A Challenge to Conservationists", in *World Watch Magazine,* vol. 17, 6: 17–31.

Chouchena-Rojas, M., Ruiz-Muller, M., Vivas, D. and Winkler, S. (eds) (2005) *Disclosure Requirements: Ensuring mutual supportiveness between the WTO TRIPS Agreement and the CBD,* Gland: IUCN/ICTSD, www.iucn.org/en/news/archive/2005/12/disclosure_requirements_publication.pdf

CI – Conservation International (2006) *Annual Report 2005,* Washington, DC: CI www.conservation.org

CIEL – Center for International Environmental Law and WWF – World Wide Fund for Nature (2001) *Biodiversity and Intellectual Property Rights: Reviewing Intellectual Property Rights in Light of the Objectives of the Convention on Biological Diversity,* Joint Discussion Paper, Gland, Geneva.

CIEPAC – Centro de Investigaciones Económicas y Políticas de Acción Comunitaria, www.ciepac.org

CIPR – Commission on Intellectual Property Rights (2002a) "Integration von geistigen Eigentumsrechten und Entwicklungspolitik", *Bericht der Kommission für geistige Eigentumsrechte (Executive Summary),* London, www.wissensgesellschaft.org/themen/wemgehoert/PropertyRightsCommissiondt.pdf

—— (2002b) "Integrating Intellectual Property Rights and Development Policy", Report of the Commission on Intellectual Property Rights, London, www.iprcommission.org

CLACSO – Consejo Latinoamericano de Ciencias Sociales (ed.) (2004) *Observatorio Social de América Latina*, issue on "movimientos sociales y desafíos políticos" and "resistencias continentales frente al 'libre comercio'", Buenos Aires: CLACSO.

Comor, E. A. (1999) "Governance and the Nation State in a Knowledge-Based Political Economy", in Hewson, M. and Sinclair, T. J. (eds) *Approaches to Global Governance Theory*, Albany: State University of New York Press.

COMPITCH – Consejo de Organizaciones de Médicos y Parteras Indígenas Tradicionales de Chiapas (2000) "Buletín informativo", San Cristóbal de las Casas.

CONABIO – Comisión nacional para el conocimiento y uso de la biodiversidad (1997) "Situación Actual sobre la Gestión, Manejo y Conservación de la Diversidad Bioogica de México", First National Report of the Conference of the Parties of the CBD, Mexico City: Conabio, www.biodiv.org/doc/world/mx/mx-nr-01-es.pdf

—— (1998) "Diversidad Biológica de México: Estudio de País", Mexico City: Conabio.

—— (2000) "Estrategia Nacional sobre Biodiversidad de México", Mexico City: Conabio.

CONANP – Comisión Nacional de Áreas Naturales Protegidas (2007), www.conanp.gob.mx.

Conca, K., Finger, M. and Park, J. (eds) (2007) *Sustainability, Globalization and Governance*, London: Routledge (forthcoming).

Cooper, D., Engels, J. and Frison, E. (1994) "A multilateral system for plant genetic resources: imperatives, achievements and challenges", Issues in Genetic Resources, 2, Rome: IPGRI.

Correa, C. (2000) "Intellectual Property Rights, the WTO and Developing Countries, The TRIPs Agreement and Policy Options", London: Zed Books; Penang (Malaysia): Third World Network.

—— (2001) "Pro-Competitive Measures under the TRIPs Agreement to Promote Technology Diffusion in Developing Countries", paper presented at the *Oxfam International Seminar on Intellectual Property and Development "What Future for the WTO TRIPs Agreement?"*, Brussels, 20 March 2001.

—— (2003) Interview, *Seedling*, January, www.grain.org/seedling/seed-interview-c.cfm

—— (2004) "Bilateral Investment Agreements: Agents of new global standards for the protection of intellectual property rights?", www.grain.org/briefings_files/correa-bits-august-2004.pdf

Correa, C. and Musungu, S. F. (2002) *The WIPO Patent Agenda: The Risks for Developing Countries*, South Centre, www.southcentre.org/publications/wipopatent/toc.htm

Cox, R. W. (1987) *Production, Power and World Order, Social Forces in the Making of History*, New York: Columbia University Press.

—— (1993) "Gramsci, hegemony and international relations: an essay in method", in Gill, S. (ed.) *Gramsci, Historical materialism and international relations*, Cambridge: Cambridge University Press.

—— (1998) *Weltordnung und Hegemonie – Grundlagen der "Internationalen Politischen Ökonomie"*, Marburg: Universität Marburg.

Crosby, A. W. (1972) *The Columbian Exchange*, Westport, CT: Greenwood Press.

—— (1986) *Ecological Imperialism: The Biological Expansion of Europe 900–1900*, Cambridge: Cambridge University Press.

Crucible Group (1994) *People, Plants and Patents*, Ottawa u.a.

Crucible II Group (2000) "Seeding Solutions, Policy Options for genetic resources", vol.1, co-published by IPGRI, Dag Hammarskjöld Foundation and IDRC, Rome: Litopixel.

—— (2001) "Seeding Solutions, Options for national laws governing control over genetic resources", vol. 2, co-published by IPGRI, Dag Hammarskjöld Foundation and IDRC, Rome: Litopixel.

de Boef, W., Amanor, K. S., Wellard, K. and Bebbington, A. (eds) (1993) *Cultivating Knowledge*, London: Intermediate Technology Publications.

Declaración de la Semana por la Diversidad (2001) *Declaración de la Primera Semana por la Diversidad Biológica y Cultural*, www.laneta.apc.org/biodiversidad/semana/declaracion.htm

Declaración de San Gregorio (2000) "Foro por la Defensa de la Vida, la Tierra y los Recursos Naturales", in *Chiapas*, 10: 195–197, www.ezln.org/revistachiapas/No10/ch10gregorio.html

Declaración Foro Mesoamericano (2002) "Frente al Plan Puebla Panamá el Movimiento Mesoamericano pol la Integración Popular", www.foromanagua.com.ni/documentos/declaracion-III-foro-mesoamericano.PDF

Delaney, D. and Leitner, H. (1997) "The Political Construction of Scale", in *Political Geography*, vol. 16: 93–97.

Delgadillo Macías, J. (1994) "Recursos naturales y ecología: bases para un desarrollo sustentable", in *Problemas del Desarrollo*, vol. 25, 96: 125–161.

Delgado Ramos, G. (2001) "Biopir@terie und geistiges Eigentum als Eckpfeiler technologischer Herrschaft: Das Beispiel Mexiko", in *Das Argument*, vol. 242: 481–494.

—— (2002) *La amenaza biológica, Mitos y falsas promesas de la biotecnología*, Barcelona: Plaza y Janés.

—— (2004) *Biodiversidad, desarrollo sustentable y militarización, Esquemas de saqueo en Mesoamérica*, Mexico City: Plaza y Valdéz/UNAM.

Demirovic, A. (1997) *Demokratie und Herrschaft, Aspekte kritischer Gesellschaftstheorie*, Münster: Westfälisches Dampfboot.

—— (2003) "NGOs, the State, and Civil Society: The Transformation of Hegemony", in *Rethinking Marxism*, vol.15, 2: 213–236.

de Paranaguá Moniz, P., Doctorow, C. and Rezende, P. A. D. (2005) "Manifesto for Transparency, Participation, Balance and Access", an open letter to the WIPO, www.cic.unb.br/docentes/pedro/trabs/wipo-en.html

Dieter, H. (2003) "Die Demontage der multilateralen Wirtschaftsordnung durch die Dritte Welle des Regionalismus", in *PROKLA*, vol. 33, 4: 599–624.

Dolata, U. (1999) "Die Bio-Industrie, Märkte, Unternehmen, politische Alternativen", in Emmrich, M. (ed.) *Im Zeitalter der Bio-Macht*, Frankfurt/M.: Mabuse-Verlag.

Drahos, P. (2001) "Negotiating Intellectual Property Rights: Between Coercion and Dialogue", paper presented at the *Oxfam International Seminar on Intellectual Property and Development "What Future for the WTO TRIPs Agreement?"*, Brussels, 20 March 2001.

Drahos, Peter and Braithwaite, John (2003) "Hegemony Based on Knowledge: The Role of Intellectual Property", *Law in Context*, vol. 21: 204–223.

Dutfield, G. (2001) "Biotechnology and Patents: What Can Developing Countries Do About Article 27.3 (b)?", in *Bridges Monthly Review*, vol. 5, 9: 17–18, www.ictsd.org/monthly/bridges/BRIDGES5-9.pdf

—— (2002) "Protecting Traditional Knowledge and Folklore: A review of progress in diplomacy and policy formulation", *UNCTAD/ICTSD Capacity Building Project on Intellectual Property Rights and Sustainable Development*, www.ictsd.org/iprsonline/unctadictsd/docs/Dutfield2002.pdf

ECLA/CEPAL – Comisión Económica para América Latina y el Caribe (2004) *Desarrollo productivo en economías abiertas*, Santiago de Chile: CEPAL.

Egziabher, T. B. G. (2002) "Bedrohte Ernährungssouveränität, internationales Recht und Farmers' Rights in Afrika", in Görg, C. and Brand, U. (eds) *Mythen globalen Umweltmanagements. Rio+10 und die Sackgassen "nachhaltiger Entwicklung"*, Münster: Westfälisches Dampfboot.

—— (2005) "Benefit Sharing", in Burrows, B. (ed.) (2005) *The Catch, Perspectives in Benefit Sharing,* Edmonds: The Edmonds Institute.

EIA – Energy Information Administration (2003) "Mexico", *Country Analysis Briefs*, Washington, DC, www.eia.doe.gov/emeu/cabs/mexico.html

Ekpere, J. A. (2000) *The OAU's Model Law, an Explanatory Booklet*, Lagos, www.grain.org/publications/oau-en.cfm

El-Said, H. and El-Said, M. (2005) "TRIPS, Bilateralism, Multilateralism & Implications for Developing Countries: Jordan's Drug Sector", in *Manchester Journal of International Economic Law*, vol. 2, 1: 59–79, www.electronicpublications.org/stuff.php?id = 106

ENB – Earth Negotiation Bulletin (1997) vol. 9, 68, www.iisd.ca/download/pdf/enb0968e.pdf

—— (2000a) vol. 9, 161, www.iisd.ca/download/pdf/enb09161e.pdf

—— (2000b) vol. 9, 164, www.iisd.ca/download/pdf/enb09164e.pdf

—— (2000c) vol. 9, 165, www.iisd.ca/download/pdf/enb09165e.pdf

—— (2000d) vol. 9, 166, www.iisd.ca/download/pdf/enb09166e.pdf

—— (2000e) vol. 9, 167, www.iisd.ca/download/pdf/enb09167e.pdf

—— (2001) vol. 9, 213, www.iisd.ca/download/pdf/enb09213e.pdf

—— (2002) vol. 9, 235, www.iisd.ca/download/pdf/enb09235e.pdf

—— (2006a) vol. 9, 363, www.iisd.ca/download/pdf/enb09363e.pdf

—— (2006b) vol. 9, 364, www.iisd.ca/download/pdf/enb09364e.pdf

Enquete-Kommission Globalisierung der Weltwirtschaft (2002) "Schlussbericht. Berlin", BT-Drucksache 14/9200, www.bundestag.de/gremien/welt/glob_end/glob.pdf

Escobar, A. (1996) "Constructing Nature. Elements for a poststructural political ecology", in Peet, R. and Watts, M. (eds) *Liberation ecologies. Environment,development, social movements*, London: Routledge.

Esser, J., Görg, C. and Hirsch, J. (eds) (1994) *Politik, Institutionen und Staat, Zur Kritik der Regulationstheorie*, Hamburg: VSA-Verlag.

ETC Group (2001) "New Enclosures: Alternative Mechanisms to Enhance Corporate Monopoly and BioSerfdom in the 21st Century", Communiqué, November/December 2001, www.etcgroup.org

—— (2005a) "Global Seed Industry Concentration – 2005", Communiqué, www.etcgroup.org

—— (2005b) "Oligopoly, Inc. – Concentration in Corporate Power", www.etcgroup.org

Executive Secretary of the CBD (2005) "Annotations to the provisional agenda", UNEP/CBD/COP/8/1/Add.1, www.biodiv.org/doc/meeting.asp?mtg = cop-08

FAO – Food and Agriculture Organization (1989) *International Undertaking on Plant Genetic Resources*, Rome: FAO.

FAO Focus (2006) "Women: users, preservers and managers of agro-biodiversity", www.fao.org/FOCUS/E/Women/Biodiv-e.htm

Federal Ministry of Education and Research/OECD (2002) *Short Summary Report of the Workshop on Genetic Inventions, Intellectual Property Rights and Licensing Practices*, held in Berlin, Germany, 24 and 25 January 2002, www.oecd.org/EN/home/0,EN-home-27-nodirectorate-no-no–27,00.html

Fogarty International Center (FIC) (2002): Announcement for Third Round of Research Grants. http://grants2.nih.gov/grants/guide/rfa-files/RFA-TW-03-004.html

—— (2007) *International Cooperative Biodiversity Groups*, www.fic.nih.gov/programs/research_grants/icbg/index.htm

Finston, S. K. (2005) "Commentary: An American BioIndustry Alliance Perspective on CBD/TRIPS Issues in the Doha Round", in *Global Economy Journal*, vol. 5, 4: 1–8.

Fischer, F. (2000) *Citizens, Experts, and the Environment, The Politics of Local Knowledge*, Durham, NC: Duke University Press.

Flitner, M. (1995a) *Räuber, Sammler und Gelehrte. Die politischen Interessen an pflanzengenetischen Ressourcen*, Frankfurt/M.: Campus.

—— (1995b) "Genetische Ressourcen: Von der Entstehung und den Konjunkturen eines Begriffs", in Mayer, J. (ed.) *Eine Welt – Eine Natur?*, Loccumer Protokolle, Loccum: Evangelische Akademie Loccum.

—— (1999) "Biodiversität oder: Das Öl, das Meer und die 'Tragödie der Gemeingüter'", in Görg, C. *et al.* (eds) *Zugänge zur Biodiversität*, Marburg: Metropolis.

Flitner, M., Görg, C. and Heins, V. (eds) (1998) *Konfliktfeld Natur, Biologische Ressourcen und globale Politik*, Opladen: Leske + Buderich.

Fowler, C. (1995) *Unnatural Selection: Technology, Politics, and Plant Evolution*, Yverdon: Gordon and Breach.

Frankel, O. H. and Bennet, E. (eds) (1970) *Genetic Resources in Plants – their Exploration and Conservation*, International Biological Program Handbook, 11, Oxford: Science Publications.

Frein, M. and Meyer, H. (2005) "The concept of benefit-sharing: A step forward or backward?", in Burrows, B. (ed.) *The Catch, Perspectives in Benefit Sharing,* Edmonds: The Edmonds Institute.

GAIA/GRAIN (2000) *Biodiversity for Sale, Dismantling the Hype about Benefit Sharing*, April 2000, www.grain.org

García, A. (2006) "Es gibt Alternativen zur ALCA, ALBA und warum der ALCA-Prozess gestoppt wurde", in *PROKLA*, vol. 142: 81–94.

García de León, A. (1985) *Resistencia y utopía, Memorial de agravios y crónica de revueltas y profecías acaecidas en la provincia de Chiapas durante los últimos quinientos años de su historia*, 2 volumes, Mexico City: ERA.

Gaskell, G., Allum, N., Stares, S. *et al.* (2003) "Europeans and Biotechnology in 2002", Eurobarometer 58.0, a report to the *EC Directorate General for Research from the project "Life Sciences in European Society"* (QLG7-CT-1999-00286 – 2nd edn: 21 March 2003), http://europa.eu.int/comm/public_opinion/archives/eb/ebs_177_en.pdf

GBF – Global Biodiversity Forum (2002) *Statement of the 16th Session of the Global Biodiversity Forum to the 6th meeting of the Conference of the Parties to the Convention on Biological Diversity*, The Hague, 5–7 April 2002.

Germain, R. D. and Kenny, M. (1998) "Engaging Gramsci: international relations and the new Gramscians", in *Review of International Studies*, vol. 24, 1: 3–21.

Gerstetter, C. and Kaiser, G. (2006) "Gemeinsam die Allmende verteidigen?! Ansätze und Formen des Widerstands gegen die Ausdehnung geistiger Eigentumsrechte in den Bereichen pflanzengenetische Ressourcen und Software", in *Peripherie*, vol. 26, 101/102: 69–98.

Gibbs, D. (2000) "Globalization, the Bioscience Industry and Local Environmental Responses", in *Global Environmental Change*, vol. 10: 245–257.

Giddens, A. (1988) *Die Konstitution der Gesellschaft, Grundzüge einer Theorie der Strukturierung*, Frankfurt/M.: Campus.

Gill, S. (2000) "Theoretische Grundlagen einer Neo-Gramscianischen Analyse der europäischen Integration", in Bieling, H.-J. and Steinhilber, J. (eds) *Die Konfiguration Europas. Dimensionen einer kritischen Integrationstheorie*, Münster: Westfälisches Dampfboot.

—— (2003) "Power and Resistance in the New World Order", New York: Palgrave.

Goldman, M. (ed.) (1998) *Privatizing Nature. Political struggles for the global commons*, London: Routledge.

—— (2001) "Constructing an Environmental State: Eco-governmentality and other Transnational Practices of a 'Green' World Bank", in *Social Problems*, vol. 48, 4: 499–523.

—— (2005) *Imperial Nature, The World Bank and struggles for social justice in the age of globalization*, New Haven, CT: Yale University Press.

Goodwin, M. and Painter, J. (1997) "Concrete Research, Urban Regimes, and Regulation Theory", in Lauria, M. (ed.) *Reconstructing Urban Regime Theory, Regulating Urban Politics in a Global Economy*, Thousand Oaks, CA: Sage Publications.

Gordon, D. M. (1994) "The Global Economy: New Edifice or Crumbling Foundations?", in Kotz, D. M., McDonough, T. and Reich, M. (eds) *Social Structures of Accumulation, The political economy of growth and crisis*, Cambridge: Cambridge University Press.

Görg, C. (1994) "Der Institutionenbegriff in der Theorie der Strukturierung", in Esser, J., Görg, C. and Hirsch, J. (eds) (1994) *Politik, Institutionen und Staat, Zur Kritik der Regulationstheorie*, Hamburg: VSA-Verlag.

—— (1998) "Die Regulation der biologischen Vielfalt", in Flitner, M., Görg, C. and Heins, V. (eds) (1998) *Konfliktfeld Natur, Biologische Ressourcen und globale Politik*, Opladen: Leske + Buderich.

—— (1999a) *Gesellschaftliche Naturverhältnisse*, Münster: Westfälisches Dampfboot.

—— (1999b) "Erhalt der biologischen Vielfalt: zwischen Umweltproblem und Ressourcenkonflikt", in Görg, C., Hertler, C., Schramm, E. and Weingarten, M. (eds) *Zugänge zur Biodiversität*, Marburg: Metropolis.

—— (2003a) *Regulation der Naturverhältnisse, Zu einer kritischen Theorie der ökologischen Krise*, Münster: Westfälisches Dampfboot.

—— (2003b) "Nichtidentität und Kritik, Zum Problem der Gestaltung der Naturverhältnisse", in Böhme, G. and Manzei, A. (eds) *Kritische Theorie der Natur und der Technik*, München: Fink-Verlag.

—— (2004) "Stichwort 'Inwertsetzung'", in *Historisch-kritisches Wörterbuch des Marxismus*, vol. 6, II, Hamburg: Argument-Verlag.

Görg, C and Brand, U. (2001) "Patentierter Kapitalismus, Zur politischen Ökonomie genetischer Ressourcen", in *Das Argument*, vol. 242: 466–480.

—— (2002) "Konflikte um das 'grüne Gold der Gene', Access, geistiges Eigentum und Fragen der Demokratie", in *PROKLA*, vol. 129: 631–652.

—— (eds) (2002) *Mythen globalen Umweltmanagements, Rio+10 und die Sackgassen "nachhaltiger Entwicklung"*, Münster: Westfälisches Dampfboot.

—— (2003) "Post-Fordist Societal Relationships with Nature: The Role of NGOs and the State in Biodiversity Politics", in *Rethinking Marxism*, vol. 15, 2: 263–288.

—— (2006) "Global Regulation of Genetic Resources and the Internationalization of the State", in *Global Environmental Politics*, vol. 6, 4, Cambridge: MIT Press.

Görg, C. and Wissen, M. (2003) "National dominierte globale Herrschaft, Zum Verhältnis von Uni- und Multilateralismus in der 'Neuen Weltordnung'", in *PROKLA*, vol. 133: 625–644.

Görg, C., Hertler, C., Schramm, E. and Weingarten, M. (eds) (1999) *Zugänge zur Biodiversität*, Marburg: Metropolis.

Grahl, J. and Teague, P. (2000) "The Regulation School, the employment relation and the financialization", in *Economy and Society*, vol. 29, 1: 160–178.

GRAIN – Genetic Resources Action International (2000) For a Full Review of TRIPS 27.3 (b) and an update on where developing countries stand with the push to patent life at WTO, www.grain.org/publications/tripsfeb00-en-p.htm

—— (2001a) *IPR agents try to derail OAU process*, www.grain.org/publications

—— (2001b) "A Disappointing Compromise", in *Seedling* December 2001, www.grain.org/publications/seed-01-12-1-en.cfm

—— (2001c) "'TRIPs-plus' through the back door, How bilateral treaties impose much stronger rules for IPRs on life than WTO", GRAIN publications July 2001, www.grain.org/publications/trips-plus-en.cfm

—— (2002a) "Biopiracy by another name? A critique of the FAO-CGIAR trusteeship system", in *Seedling* October 2002, www.grain.org/seedling /seed-02-10-2-en.cfm

—— (2002b) "WIPO moves toward 'world' patent system", GRAIN publications July 2002, www.grain.org/docs/wipo-patent-2002-en.doc

—— (2005) "Convergence Zone?", in *Seedling* October 2005, www.grain.org/seedling_files/seed-05-10.pdf

Gramsci, A. (1991) "Gefängnishefte", edited by Bochmann, K. and Haug, W., Hamburg: Argument-Verlag.

Graz, J. (2006) "Hybrids and Regulation in the Global Political Economy", in *Competition & Change*, vol. 10, 2: 230–245.

Grupo Técnico Interinstitucional para el Plan Puebla–Panamá, BCIE-BID-CEPAL (2001) "Plan Puebla-Panamá, Initiativas mesoamericanas y proyectos", *San Salvador*, 15 June 2001, www.iadb.org/ppp/files/projects/OTRO/OT_PPP_PPP1_ES_PP.doc

GTZ – Deutsche Gesellschaft für Technische Zusammenarbeit (2002) *The Convention on Biological Diversity, Ensuring Gender-Sensitive Implementation*, Eschborn: GTZ.

Guillén Romo, H. (1997) *La contrarevolución neoliberal en México*, Mexico City: Era.

Günther, K. and Randeria, S. (2001) *Recht, Kultur und Gesellschaft im Prozess der Globalisierung*, Bad Homburg: Werner-Reimers-Stiftung.

Gupta, A. (1999) "Framing 'Biosafety' in an International Context: The Biosafety Protocol Negotiations", *ENRP Discussion Paper E-99-10*, Kennedy School of Government, Harvard University.

Gupta, A. and Falkner, R. (2006) "The Influence of the Cartagena Protocol on Biosafety: Comparing Mexico, China and South Africa", in *Global Environmental Politics*, vol. 6, 4: 23–55.

Halperin Donghi, T. (1991) *Geschichte Lateinamerikas von der Unabhängigkeit bis zur Gegenwart*, Frankfurt/M.: Suhrkamp.

Haraway, D. (1991) *Simians, Cyborgs and Women: The Reinvention of Nature*, New York: Routledge.

Harry, D. and Kanehe, L. (2005) "The BS in Access and Benefit Sharing (ABS), Critical questions for Indigenous Peoples", in Burrows, B. (ed.) *The Catch, Perspectives in Benefit Sharing*, Edmonds: The Edmonds Institute.

Harvey, D. (1996) *Justice, Nature & the Geography of Difference*, Malden, MA: Blackwell Publishing.

—— (2001) "Globalization and the 'Spatial Fix'", in *Geographische Revue*, vol. 3, 2: 23–30.

—— (2003) *The New Imperialism*, Oxford: Oxford University Press.

Harvey, N. (2001) "Globalisation and resistance in post-cold war Mexico: difference, citizenship and biodiversity conflicts in Chiapas", in *Third World Quarterly*, vol. 22, 6: 1045–1061.

Haug, W. F. (2001) "Fragen einer Kritik des Biokapitalismus", in *Das Argument*, vol. 242: 449–465.

Hecht, S. B. (1998) "Tropische Biopolitik – Wälder, Mythen, Paradigmen", in Flitner, M., Görg, C. and Heins, V. (eds) (1998) *Konfliktfeld Natur, Biologische Ressourcen und globale Politik*, Opladen: Leske + Buderich.

Heigl, M. (2006) "Private is beautiful? Zu den Auseinandersetzungen um die Eigentumsrechte im mexikanischen Energiesektor", in *Peripherie*, vol. 101/102: 147–165.

—— (2007) "Anfang vom Ende? Zum Zustand des neoliberalen Projekts in Lateinamerika", in *Journal für Entwicklungspolitik*, vol. 22, 1: 125–146.

Heineke, C. and Wolff, F. (2004) "Access to Genetic Resources and the Sharing of Benefits: Private Rights or Shared Use for Biodiversity Conservation?", in *ELNI Review – Environmental Law Network International*, vol. 2: 26–33.

Heins, V. (2001) *Der Neue Transnationalismus*, Frankfurt/M.: Campus.

Heins, V. and Flitner, M. (1998) "Biologische Ressourcen und Life Politics", in Flitner, M., Görg, C. and Heins, V. (eds) (1998) *Konfliktfeld Natur, Biologische Ressourcen und globale Politik*, Opladen: Leske + Buderich.

Held, D. and McGrew, A. (2002) *Governing Globalization, Power, Authority and Global Governance*, Cambridge: Polity.

Hepburn, J. (2002) *Negotiating intellectual property: Mandates and options in the Doha Work Programme*, Quaker United Nations Office, Occasional Paper 10, Geneva.

Hernández Navarro, L. (1999) "El laberinto de los equívicos: San Andrés y la lucha indígena", in *Chiapas*, vol. 7: 71–93.

—— (2000) "Der Kampf um indigene Rechte im Labyrinth der Doppeldeutigkeiten, Die Dialoge und Abkommen von San Andrés", in Brand, U. and Ceceña, A. E. (eds) *Reflexionen einer Rebellion, "Chiapas" und ein anderes Politikverständnis*, Münster: Westfälisches Dampfboot.

Hertler, C. (1999) "Aspekte der historischen Entstehung von Biodiversitätskonzepten in den Biowissenschaften", in Görg, C., Hertler, C., Schramm, E. and Weingarten, M. (eds) *Zugänge zur Biodiversität*, Marburg: Metropolis.

Hewson, M. and Sinclair, T. (eds) (1999) *Approaches to Global Governance Theory*, Albany, NY: SUNY Press.

Higgins, N. P. (2001) "Mexico's stalled peace process: prospects and challenges", in *International Affairs*, vol. 77, 4: 885–903.

Hirsch, J. (1990) *Kapitalismus ohne Alternative?*, Hamburg: VSA-Verlag.

—— (1993) "Internationale Regulation, Bedingungen von Dominanz, Abhängigkeit und Entwicklung im globalen Kapitalismus", in *Das Argument*, vol. 198: 195ff.

—— (1994) "Politische Form, politische Institutionen und Staat", in Esser, J., Görg, C. and Hirsch, J. (eds) *Politik, Institutionen und Staat, Zur Kritik der Regulationstheorie*, Hamburg: VSA-Verlag.

—— (1995) "Der nationale Wettbewerbsstaat, Staat, Demokratie und Politik im globalen Kapitalismus", Berlin: Edition ID-Archiv.

—— (1997) "Globalization of capital, nation-states and democracy", in *Studies in Political Economy*, vol. 54: 39–58.

—— (2001) "Postfordismus: Dimensionen einer neuen kapitalistischen Formation", in Hirsch, J., Jessop, B. and Poulantzas, N. (2001) *Die Zukunft des Staates*, Hamburg: VSA-Verlag.

—— (2002a) *Herrschaft, Hegemonie und politische Alternativen*, Hamburg: VSA-Verlag.

—— (2002b) "Wissen und Nichtwissen, Anmerkungen zur 'Wissensgesellschaft'", in Brüchert, O. and Resch, C. (eds) *Zwischen Herrschaft und Befreiung*, Münster: Westfälisches Dampfboot.

—— (2003) "The State's New Clothes: NGOs and the Internationalisation of States", in *Rethinking Marxism*, vol. 15, 2: 237–262.

—— (2005) "Materialistische Staatstheorie: Transformationsprozesse des kapitalistischen Staatensystems", Hamburg: VSA-Verlag.

Hirsch, J. and Roth, R. (1986) "Das neue Gesicht des Kapitalismus, Vom Fordismus zum Postfordismus", Hamburg: VSA-Verlag.

Hirsch, J., Jessop, B. and Poulantzas, N. (2001) *Die Zukunft des Staates*, Hamburg: VSA-Verlag.

Hoering, U. (2002) "Früchte der Vielfalt, Globale Gerechtigkeit und der Schutz traditionellen Wissens", Bonn: Evangelischen Entwicklungsdienst.

—— (2004) "Biopirates in the Kalahari? How indigenous people are standing up for their rights – the experience of the San in Southern Africa", Bonn: EED/WIMSA.

Hooghe, L. and Marks, G. (1999) "The Making of a Polity: The Struggle over European Integration", in Kitschelt, H. (ed.) *Continuity and Change in Contemporary Capitalism*, Cambridge: Cambridge University Press.

Horkheimer, M. and Adorno, T. W. (1987) "Dialektik der Aufklärung, Philosophische Fragmente", in Horkheimer, M. *Gesammelte Schriften*, vol. 5, Frankfurt/M.: Fischer.

Howard, P. L. (2003) "Preface and Women and the Plant World: An exploration", in Howard, P. L. (ed.) *Women & Plants, gender relations in biodiversity management and conservation*, London: Zed Books.

Hübner, K. (1989) *Theorie der Regulation, Eine kritische Rekonstruktion eines neuen Ansatzes der Politischen Ökonomie*, Berlin: Sigma.

ICBG – International Cooperative Biodiversity Group (2002) "Call for Papers for the 3rd Round", http://grants2.nih.gov/grants/guide/rfa-files/RFA-TW-03-004.html

ICC – International Chamber of Commerce (2002) *Roadmap 2002*, www.iccwbo.org/home/intellectual_property/IP%20roadmap/Roadmap-2002/roadmap2002-REV.doc

ICTSD – International Centre for Trade and Sustainable Development (2005a) "WIPO members create new forum to discuss development agenda", www.grain.org/bio-ipr/index.cfm?id = 451&prints = yes

—— (2005b) "Governments meet in Geneva to discuss WIPO development agenda", in *Bridges Weekly Trade News Digest*, vol. 9, 12, www.ictsd.org/weekly/05-04-13/story1.htm

IFC – International Finance Corporation (2006) *A Guide to Biodiversity for the Private Sector: Why Biodiversity Matters and How It Creates Business Value*, www.ifc.org/ifcext/enviro.nsf/Content/BiodiversityGuide.

IIED – International Institute for Environment and Development (2001) "The Future is Now, For the UN World Summit on Sustainable Development", vol. 1, London: International Institute for Environment and Development, www.iied.org/pubs/pdf/full/9000IIED.pdf

Imbusch, P. (1988) "Mexiko – entwicklungsstrategische Alternativen", Marburg: Verlag Arbeiterbewegung und Gesellschaftswissenschaft.

IPGRI – International Plant Genetic Resources Institute (1996) "Access to plant genetic resources and the equitable sharing of benefits: a contribution to the debate on systems for the exchange of germplasm", in *Issues in Genetic Ressources*, vol. 4, www.bioversityinternational.org/Publications/Pdf/467.pdf

IP-Watch (2005) "Nations clash on future of WIPO Development Agenda", 11 April 2005, www.ip-watch.org/weblog/index.php?p = 42

ITPGR – International Treaty on Plant Genetic Resources (2001), ftp://ftp.fao.org/ag/cgrfa/it/ITPGRe.pdf

IUCN – The World Conservation Union (1989) "Draft articles prepared by IUCN for inclusion in a proposed convention on the conservation of biological diversity and for the establishment of a fund for that purpose", Gland/CH, June 1989.

IWBN – Indigenous Women's Biodiversity Network (2006) *Introduction to the IWBN and History*, www.nciv.net/spaans/iwbn/IWBN.htm

Jacob, M. (2005) "Boundary Work in Contemporary Science Policy: a Review", in *Prometheus*, vol. 23, 2: 195–207.

Jänicke, M. and Jacob, K. (2004) "Lead Markets for Environmental Innovations: A New Role for the Nation State", in *Global Environmental Politics*, vol. 4, 1: 29–46.

Janssen, J. (1999) "Property Rights on Genetic Ressources: Economic Issues", in *Global Environmental Change*, vol. 9, 4: 313–321.

Jasanoff, S. (ed) (2004a) *States of Knowledge: The Co-Production of Science and the Social Order*, London: Routledge.

—— (2004b) "Ordering knowledge, ordering society", in Jasanoff, S. (ed.) *States of Knowledge: The Co-Production of Science and the Social Order*, London: Routledge.

Jasanoff, S., Markle, G. E., Petersen, J. C. and Pinch, T. (eds) (1995) *Handbook of Science and Technology Studies*, Cambridge, MA: Harvard University Press.

Jenson, J. (1989) "'Different' but not 'exceptional': Canada's permeable fordism", in *Canadian Review of Sociology and Anthropology*, vol. 26, 1: 69–94.

Jessop, B. (1990) "Regulation Theories in Restrospect and Prospect", in *Economy and Society*, vol. 19, 2: 153–216.

—— (1997) "Die Zukunft des Nationalstaates – Erosion oder Reorganisation? Grundsätzliche Überlegungen zu Westeuropa", in Becker, S., Sablowski, T. and Schumm, W. (eds) *Jenseits der Nationalökonomie? Weltwirtschaft und Nationalstaat zwischen Globalisierung und Regionalisierung*, Hamburg: Argument-Verlag.

—— (2000) "The State and the Contradictions of the Knowledge-Driven Economy", in Bryson, J. R., Daniels, P. W., Henry, N. and Pollard, J. (eds) *Knowledge, Space, Economy*, London: Routledge.

—— (2002) *The Future of the Capitalist State*, Cambridge: Polity.

—— (2003) "Postfordismus und wissensbasierte Ökonomie, Eine Reinterpretation des Regulationsansatzes", in Brand, U. and Raza, W. (eds) *Fit für den Postfordismus?*, Münster: Westfälisches Dampfboot.

Kaiser, G. (2003) "Wenn Leben zur Ressource wird", in *ila – Zeitschrift der Informationsstelle Lateinamerika, 263*, Bonn: Informationsstelle Lateinamerika e.V..

—— (2006) "Schieflage mit System – die WTO in Hongkong", in links-netz, www.links-netz.de/K_texte/K_kaiser_wto.html

Kay, L. E. (2000) *Who wrote the book of life? A History of the Genetic Code*, Stanford, CT: Stanford University Press.

Keil, R. and Mahon, R. (eds) (2008) *The New Political Economy of Scale*, Vancouver: University of British Columbia.

Keystone Dialogue (1991) *Oslo Plenary Session: Consensus Report*, Keystone: The Keystone Center.

Khor, M. (2001) *Competing Views on Competition Policy in WTO*, www.twnside.org.sg/ title/ views-cn.htm 07.04.01

Klaffenböck, G., Lachkovics, E. and Südwind Agentur (eds) (2001) *Biologische Vielfalt, Wer kontrolliert die genetischen Ressourcen*, Frankfurt/M.: Brandes & Apsel.

Kloppenburg, J. R. (ed.) (1988) *Seeds and Sovereignty, The Use and Control of Plant Genetic Ressources*, Durham, NC: Duke University Press.

Kloppenburg, J. R. and Balick, M. J. (1996) "Property Rights and Genetic Resources: A Framework for Analysis", in Balick, M. J., Elisabetsky, E. and Laird, S. A. (eds) *Medicinal Resources of the Tropical Forest*, New York: Columbia University Press.

Kloppenburg, J. R. and Kleinman, J. L. (1988) "Plant Genetic Resources: The Common Bowl", in Kloppenburg, J. R. (ed.) *Seeds and Sovereignity, The Use and Control of Plant Genetic Ressources*, Durham, NC: Duke University Press.

Kongolo, T. (2001) "New Options for African Countries regarding Protection for New Varieties of Plants", in *The Journal of World Intellectual Property*, vol. 4, 3: 349–371.

Krasner, S. (ed.) (1983) *International Regimes*, Ithaca, NY: Cornell University Press.

Krebs, M., Herkenrath, P. and Meyer, H. (2002) *Biologische Vielfalt zwischen Schutz und Nutzung, 10 Jahre Konvention über Biologische Vielfalt*, Bonn: EED und Forum Umwelt und Entwicklung.

Krohn, W. (2001) "Knowledge Societies", in Smelser, N. J. and Baltes, P. B. (eds) *International Encyclopedia of the Social and Behavioral Sciences*, Amsterdam: Elsevier.

Kuppe, R. (2001) "Der Schutz des traditionellen umweltbezogenen Wissens indigener Völker", in Klaffenböck, G., Lachkovics, E. and Südwind Agentur (eds) (2001) *Biologische Vielfalt, Wer kontrolliert die genetischen Ressourcen*, Frankfurt/M.: Brandes & Apsel.

—— (2002) "Indigene Völker, Ressourcen und traditionelles Wissen", in Brand, U. and Kalcsics, M. (eds) *Wem gehört die Natur? Konflikte um genetische Ressourcen in Lateinamerika*. Frankfurt/M.: Brandes & Apsel.

Kütting, G. (2000) *Environment, Society and International Relations, Towards More Effective International Environmental Agreements*, London: Routledge.

Lander, E. (2006) "La Ciencia Neoliberal", in Ceceña, A. E. (ed.) *Los desafíos de las emancipaciones en un contexto militarizado*, Buenos Aires: CLACSO.

Lasén Díaz, C. (2005) "Intellectual Property Rights and Biological Resources, An Overview of Key Issues and Current Debates", Wuppertal Papers, 151, Wuppertal: Wuppertal Institute for Climate, Environment and Energy.

Latour, B. (1993) *We Have Never Been Modern*, Cambridge, MA: Harvard University Press.

—— (1999) "Is Re-modernization Occurring – And If So, How to Prove It?", in *Theory, Culture & Society*, vol. 20, 2: 35–48.

Laurell, A. C. (1992) "Democracy in Mexico: Will the First be the Last?", in *New Left Review*, vol. 194: 33–54.

Le Buanec, B. (2005) "Plant genetic resources and freedom to operate", in *Euphytica*, vol. 146: 1–8.

Le Prestre, P. G. (2002) "The Operation of the CBD Convention Governance System", in Le Prestre, P. G. (ed.) *Governing Global Biodiversity, The evolution and implementation of the Convention on Biological Diversity*, Aldershot: Ashgate.

Le Prestre, P. G. (ed.) (2002) *Governing Global Biodiversity, The evolution and implementation of the Convention on Biological Diversity*, Aldershot: Ashgate.

Leskien, D. and Flitner, M. (1997) "Intellectual Property Rights and Plant Genetic Resources: Options for a Sui Generis System", in Issues in Genetic Resources, 6, Rome: International Plant Genetic Resource Institute, www.bioversityinternational.org/Publications/Pdf/497.pdf

Liebig, K, Alker, D., Chih, K., Horn, D., Illi, H., Wolf, J. *et al.* (2002) "Governing Biodiversity, Access to Genetic Resources and Approaches to Obtaining Benefits from their Use: the Case of the Philippines", *Reports and Working Papers 5/2002*, Bonn: German Development Institute.

Ling, C. Y. and Khor, M. (2001) "International Environmental Governance, Some Issues from a Developing Country Perspective", *Working Paper by the Third World Network*, www.twnside.org.sg/title/ieg.htm

Lipietz, A. (1985) "Akkumulation, Krisen und Auswege aus der Krise, Einige methodologische Bemerkungen zum Begriff "Regulation"", in *PROKLA*, vol. 58: 109–138.

—— (1987) *Mirages and Miracles, The Crisis of Global Fordism*, London: Verso.

Lipschutz, R. (2004) *Global Environmental Politics, Power, Perspectives, and Practice*, Washington, DC: CQ Press.

López Ramírez, A. (2005a) "Los intereses geoestratégicos de Estados Unidos en el Plan Puebla Panamá y el Corredor Biológico Mesoamericano", in Castro Escudero, T. and Oliver Costilla, L. (eds) *Poder y política en América Latina,* El debate latinoamericano, vol. 3, Mexico City: Siglo XXI/UNAM.

—— (2005b) "La globalización en el sur, La apropiación de los recursos de la biodiversidad en el Corredor Biológico Mesoamericano", in *Estudios Latinoamericanos*, vol. 45: 165–182.

Luna Martínez, S. and González Nolasco, E. (2004) "Libre comercio y convergencia, La macroeconomía del TLCAN", in Casares, E. S. and Sobarzo, H. (eds) *Diez años del TLCAN en México, Una perspectiva analítica*, Mexico City: Fondo de Cultura Económica.

McCarthy, J. and Prudham, S. (2004) "Neoliberal nature and the nature of neoliberalism", in *Geoforum*, vol. 35: 275–283.

McCauley, D. (2006) "Selling out on nature", in *Nature*, vol. 443, 7 September.

McCormick, J. (2005) "The Role of Environmental NGOs in International Regimes", in Axelrod, R. S., Downie, D. L. and Vig, N. (eds) *The Global Environment: Institutions, Law, and Policy*, Washington, DC: C. Q. Press.

McGraw, D. M. (2002) "The Story of the Biodiversity Convention: From Negotiation to Implementation", in Le Prestre, P. G. (ed.) *Governing Global Biodiversity, The evolution and implementation of the Convention on Biological Diversity*, Aldershot: Ashgate.

Macilwain, C. (1998) "When rhetoric hits reality in the debate on bioprospecting", in *Nature*, vol. 392, 6676: 535–540.

MacLeod, D. (2004) *Downsizing the State, Privatization and the Limits of Neoliberal Reform in Mexico*, Pennsylvania: Pennsylvania State University Press.

Malcher, I. (2006) "Private Regulierung der Weltwirtschaft", in *PROKLA*, vol. 142: 127–143.

Marglin, S. A. and Schor, J. B. (eds) (1990) *The Golden Age of Capitalism, Reinterpreting the Postwar Experience*, Oxford: Claredon.

Marston, S. A. (2000) "The Social Construction of Scale", in *Progress in Human Geography*, vol. 24, 2: 219–242.

Marx, K. and Engels, F. (1978) "Die deutsche Ideologie", MEW, 3, Berlin: Dietz.

MASR (2005) *Millennium Ecosystem Assessment Synthesis Report*, Washington, DC: Island Press, www.millenniumassessment.org/

Maus, I. (1991) "Sinn und Bedeutung der Volkssouveränität in der modernen Gesellschaft", in *Kritische Justiz*, vol. 24: 137–150.

May, C. (2000) *A Global Political Economy of Intellectual Property Rights, The New Enclosures?*, London: Routledge.

May, C. and Sell, S. K. (2006) *Intellectual Property Rights, A Critical History*, Boulder, CO: Lynne Rienner Publishers.

Mayntz, R. (2005) "Governance Theory als fortentwickelte Steuerungstheorie?", in Schuppert, G. F. (ed.) *Governance-Forschung, Vergewisserung über Stand und Entwicklungslinien*, Baden-Baden, Nomos.

Mekouar, M. A. (2001) "Treaty Agreed on Agrobiodiversity: The International Treaty on Plant Genetic Resources for Food and Agriculture", in *Environmental Policy and Law*, vol. 32, 1: 20–25.

MIHR – Centre for the Management of Intellectual Property in Health Research and Development, www.mihr.org

Mitsch, F. J. and Mitchell, J. S. (1999) *AG Biotech: Thanks, But No Thanks? Analyse der Deutsche Bank*, 12 July 1999, www.biotech-info.net/Deutsche.html

Mittermeier, R. and Goettsch Mittermeier, C. (1992) "La importancia de le diversidad biológica de México", in Sarukhán, J. and Dirzo, R. (eds) *México ante los retos de le biodiversidad*, Mexico City: Conabio.

Mooney, P. (1981) "Saat-Multis und Welthunger, Wie die Konzerne die Nahrungsschätze der Welt plündern", Reinbek: rororo aktuell.

—— (1998) "The Parts of Life, Agricultural Biodiversity, Indigenous Knowledge, and the Role of the Third System", Special Issue of *Development Dialogue*, Uppsala: Dag Hammerskjöld Foundation.

Morton, A. D. (2002) "'La Resurrección del Maíz': Globalisation, Resistance and the Zapatistas", in *Millennium*, vol. 31, 1: 27–54.

—— (2003) "Structural change and neoliberalism in Mexico: 'passive revolution' in the global political economy", in *Third World Quarterly*, vol. 24, 4: 631–653.

Mulvany, P. and Meienberg, F. (2000) *Seeds for All, Call to Action in the International Undertaking in Plant Genetic Resources*, www.ukabc.org

Mulvany, P. and Redding, I. (2000) "Ours to have and to hold, How world food resources are threatened by seed patents", *Society Guardian*, 6 December.

Murphy, C. (2000) "Global governance: poorly done and poorly understood", in *International Affairs*, vol. 76, 4: 789–803.

New Delhi Ministerial Declaration of Like-Minded Megadiverse Countries on Access and Benefit Sharing (2005) Expert Working Group Session (17–19 January 2005) and Ministerial Session (20–21 January 2005), Delhi, India, www.undp.org/biodiversity/docs/Summary_Report_Dehli_Megadiverse_17_21Jan05.doc

Nigh, R. and Rodríguez, N. J. (1995) "Territorios violados, Indios, medio ambiente y desarrollo an América Latina", Mexico City: Instituto Nacional Indigenista.

NIH – National Institutes of Health (2003) *Third Round Awards are Announced Under Interagency Biodiversity Program*, Press Release, 16 December, www.nih.gov/news/pr/dec2003/fic-16.htm

Novy, A. (2003) "Politik, Raum und Wissen, Zentrale Kategorien eines erneuerten radikalen Reformismus am Beispiel Brasilien", in Brand, U. and Raza, W. (eds) *Fit für den Postfordismus?*, Münster: Westfälisches Dampfboot.

Nuss, S. (2002) "Download ist Diebstahl? Eigentum in einer digitalen Welt", in *PROKLA*, vol. 32, 126: 11–35.

—— (2006) *Copyrights & Copyriot, Aneigungskonflikte im geistiges Eigentum im informationellen Kapitalismus*, Münster: Westfälisches Dampfboot.

O'Connor, J. (1988) "Capitalism, Nature, Socialism, A Theoretical Introduction", in *Capitalism, Nature, Socialism*, vol.1, 1: 11–45.

Oberthür, S. and Gehring, T. (2006) "International Interaction in Global Environmantal Governance, The Case of the Cartagena Protocol and the World Trade Organization", in *Global Environmental Politics*, vol. 6, 2: 1–31.

Oetmann-Mennen, A. (1999) "Biologische Vielfalt in der Landwirtschaft – Luxus oder Notwendigkeit", in Görg, C., Hertler, C., Schramm, E. and Weingarten, M. (eds) *Zugänge zur Biodiversität*, Marburg: Metropolis.

Oh, C. (2000) "The OAU draft law and convention: A model for protecting community rights and access", www.twnside.org.sg/title/co1-cn.htm

Oldham, P. (2004) *Global Status and Trends in Intellectual Property Claims: Genomics, Proteomics and Biotechnology*, www.cesagen.lancs.ac.uk/resources/docs/genomics-final.doc

Olivier Costilla, L. (2005) "Revisitando al Estado, Las especifidades del Estado en América Latina", in Castro Escudero, T. and Oliver Costilla, L. (eds) *Poder y política en América Latina*, El debate latinoamericano, vol. 3, Mexico City: Siglo XXI/UNAM.

Ornelas Bernal, R. (1994) "Nueva Ley de inversiones extranjeras, Cambios y repercusiones de cara al Tratado de Libre Comercio", in *Problemas del Desarrollo*, vol. XXV, 98: 259–266.

Oxfam (2003) "Comercio con Justicia para las Américas, Agricultura, Inversiones y Propiedad Intelectual, tres razones para decir no als ALCA", *Oxfam Briefing Paper*, January, www.oxfam.org/es/files/pp210103_37_FTAA.pdf/download

Palan, R. (2003) *The Offshore World, Sovereign Markets, Virtual Places, and Nomad Millionaires*, Ithaca, NY: Cornell University Press.

Panitch, L. (1994) *Globalisation and the State*, in *Socialist Register*, vol. 30: 60–93, http://socialistregister.com/socialistregister.com/files/SR_1994_Panitch.pdf

Parsons, T. (1975) *Gesellschaften. Evolutionäre und komparative Perspektiven*, Frankfurt/M.: Suhrkamp.

Paterson, M. (2000) *Understanding Global Environmental Politics*, New York: Palgrave.

Pelegrina, W. (2001) "Die Grüne Revolution und ihre Hinterlassenschaft", in Klaffenböck, G., Lachkovics, E. and Südwind Agentur (eds) *Biologische Vielfalt, Wer kontrolliert die genetischen Ressourcen*, Frankfurt/M.: Brandes & Apsel.

Perelman, M. (2003) "Intellectual Property Rights and the Commodity Form: New Dimensions in the Legislated Transfer of Surplus Value", in *Review of Radical Political Economics*, vol. 35, 3: 304–311.

Petit, M., Fowler, C., Collins, W., Correa, C. and Thornström, C. (2000) *Why Governments Can't Make Policy, The Case of Plant Genetic Resources in the International Arena*, www.fao.org/docs/eims/upload/207144/GFAR2003.PDF

Plahe, J. K. and Nyland, C. (2003) "The WTO and patenting of life forms, Options for developing countries", in *Third World Quarterly*, vol. 24, 1: 29–45.

Plehwe, D., Walpen, B. and Neunhöffer, G. (eds) (2006) *Neoliberal Hegemony, A global critique*, London: Routledge.

Pólito Barrios Morfín, E. (2000) "El capital nacional y extranjero en Chiapas", in *Chiapas*, 9: 61–81, www.ezln.org/revistachiapas/No9/ch9polito.html

Posey, D. (ed.) (1999) *Cultural and Spiritual Values of Biodiversity*, London: UNEP and Intermediate Technology Publications.

Potvin, C., Revéret, J., Patenaude, G. and Hutton, J. (2002) "The Role of Indigenous Peoples in Conservation Actions", in Le Prestre, P. G. (ed.) *Governing Global Biodiversity, The evolution and implementation of the Convention on Biological Diversity*, Aldershot: Ashgate.

Poulantzas, N. (1978/2002) *Staatstheorie, Politischer Überbau, Ideologie, Autoritärer Etatismus*, Hamburg: VSA-Verlag; English version (1980) *State, power, socialism*, London: Verso.

—— (1980) *State, power, socialism*, London: Verso.

—— (2001) "Die Internationalisierung der kapitalistischen Verhältnisse und der Nationalstaat", in Hirsch, J., Jessop, B. and Poulantzas, N. (2001) *Die Zukunft des Staates*, Hamburg: VSA-Verlag.

Purcell, M. (2002) "The state, regulation, and global restructuring: reasserting the political in political economy", in *Review of International Political Economy*, vol. 9, 2: 298–332.

RAFI (2000a) *DeCoding the Clinton/Blair Announcement*, www.etcgroup.org

—— (2000b) "Seedy Squabble in Switzerland", *RAFI News Release*, 20 November, www.etcgroup.org

—— (2001a) "Frequently unasked Questions about the International Undertaking on Plant Genetic Resources", RAFI-Communiqué, 18 April 2001, www.etcgroup.org

—— (2001b) "Supporting the Treaty to Share the genetic Commons", *RAFI News*, 19 April 2001, www.etcgroup.org

Rajchenberg, E. and Héau-Lambert, C. (2004) "Los silencios zapatistas", in *Chiapas*, vol. 16: 51–63, www.ezln.org/revistachiapas/No16/ch16rajchenberg.html

Raustiala, K. and Victor, D. G. (2004) "The Regime Complex for Plant Genetic Resources", in *International Organization*, vol. 58, Spring: 277–309.

Reinicke, W. H. (1998) *Global Public Policy, Governing without Government?*, Washington, DC: Brookings Institution.

Ribeiro, S. (2002a) "A Different Perspective", in Heinrich Böll-Stiftung (ed.) *Comments on the Jo'burg Memo*, World Summit Papers of the Heinrich Böll Foundation, 18: 36–41, www.boell.de/downloads/rio+10/wsp18.pdf

—— (2002b) "Biopiraterie und geistiges Eigentum – Zur Privatisierung von gemeinschaftlichen Bereichen", in Görg, C. and Brand, U. (eds) *Mythen globalen Umweltmanagements, Rio+10 und die Sackgassen "nachhaltiger Entwicklung"*, Münster: Westfälisches Dampfboot.

—— (2005) "The traps of 'benefit sharing'", in Burrows, B. (ed.) *The Catch, Perspectives in Benefit Sharing*, Edmonds: The Edmonds Institute.

Ribot, J. C. and Peluso, N. L. (2003) "A Theory of Access", in *Rural Sociology*, vol. 68, 1: 153–181.

Rifkin, J. (2000) *Access, Das Verschwinden des Eigentums*, Frankfurt/M.: Campus.

Risse, T. (2003) "Konstruktivismus, Rationalismus und Theorien Internationaler Beziehungen – warum empirisch nichts so heiß gegessen wird, wie es theoretisch gekocht wurde", in Hellmann, G., Wolf, K. D. and Zürn, M. (eds) *Die neuen Internationalen Beziehungen, Forschungsstand und Perspektiven in Deutschland*, Baden-Baden: Nomos.

Rittberger, V. (ed.) (1993) *Regime Theory and International Relations*, Oxford: Clarendon Press.

Ritter, E. H. (1979) "Der kooperative Staat", in *Archiv des öffentlichen Rechts*, vol. 104, 3: 389–413.

Robinson, W. I. (2001) "Social theory and globalization: The rise of a transnational state", in *Theory and Society*, vol. 30, 2: 157–200.

Robles, A. C. (1994) *French Theories of Regulation and Conceptions of the International Division of Labour*, New York: St Martin's Press.

Rodríguez, S. (2002) "Biodiversitätspolitik und lokale Gegenmacht – Das Beispiel Costa Rica", in Görg, C. and Brand, U. (eds) *Mythen globalen Umweltmanagements, Rio+10 und die Sackgassen "nachhaltiger Entwicklung"*, Münster: Westfälisches Dampfboot.

Rosenau, J. N. (1995) "Governance in the Twenty-First Century", in *Global Governance*, vol. 1, 1: 13–43.

Rosendal, G. Kristin (2001) "Impacts of Overlapping International Regimes: The Case of Biodiversity", in *Global Governance*, vol. 7, 1: 95–117.

Ruggie, J. G. (1982) "International regimes, transactions, and change: embedded liberalism in the postwar economic order", in *International Organization*, vol. 36, 2: 379–415.

Ruiz Caro, A. (2005) "Recursos naturales y aspectos ambientales en los Tratados de Libre Comercio con Estados Unidos", in *Observatorie Social de América Latina*, vol. 17.

Russell, P. L. (1994) *Mexico under Salinas*, Austin, TX: Mexico Resource Center.

Sachs, J. (2000) "A New Map of the World", *Economist*, vol. 24: 81–83.

Sánchez, V. and Juma, C. (eds) (1994) *Biodiplomacy, Genetic Resources and International Relations*, Nairobi: ACT Press.

Saxe-Fernández, E. E. (2005) "La 'gobernabilidad-gobernanza' como ideologema neoliberal globalista", in Castro Escudero, T. and Oliver Costilla, L. (eds) *Poder y política en América Latina,* El debate latinoamericano, vol. 3, Mexico City: Siglo XXI/UNAM.

Saxe-Fernández, J. and Delgado, G. C. (2005) *Imperialismo económico en México, Las operaciones del Banco Mundial en nuestro país*, Mexico City: Random House Mondadori.

Scharpf, F. W. (1993) "Positive und negative Koordination in Verhandlungssystemen", in Héritier, A. (ed.) *Policy-Analyse: Kritik und Neuorientierung*, Opladen: Westdeutscher Verlag.

—— (1999) *Regieren in Europa*, Frankfurt/M.: Campus.

Schedler, A., Diamond, L. and Plattner, M. (eds) (1999) The Self-Restraining State: Power and Accountability in New Democracies, Boulder, CO: Lynne Rienner Publishers.

Scherrer, C. (1998) "Neo-gramscianische Interpretation internationaler Beziehungen. Eine Kritik", in Hirschfeld, U. (ed.) *Gramsci-Perspektiven*, Berlin: Argument-Verlag.

—— (2003) "Internationale Politische Ökonomie als Systemkritik", in Hellmann, G., Wolf, K. D. and Zürn, M. (eds) *Die neuen Internationalen Beziehungen. Forschungsstand und Perspektiven in Deutschland,* Baden-Baden: Nomos-Verlag.

Secretariat of the CBD – Convention on Biological Diversity (2006a) "Global Biodiversity Outlook 2", Montreal, www.biodiv.org/GBO2

—— (2006b) *Report of the 8th Meeting of the Parties to the Convention on Biological Diversity*, Curitiba, Brazil, 20– 31 March 2006, UNEP/CBD/COP/8/31, www.biodiv.org/doc/meetings/cop/cop-08/official/cop-08-31-en.pdf

Secretariat of the CBD – Convention on Biological Diversity / United Nations Environmental Programme (2001) "Global Biodiversity Outlook", Montreal.

Seibert, T. (2003) "Die neue Kriegsordnung, Der globale Kapitalismus und seine barbarisierte Rückseite", in Azzellini, D. and Kanzleiter, B. (eds) *Das Unternehmen Krieg, Paramilitärs, Warlords und Privatarmeen als Akteure der Neuen Kriegsordnung*, Berlin: Assoziation A.

Seiler, A. (1999) "Das TRIPS-Abkommen und die für 1999 vorgesehene Überprüfung von Art. 27.3.(b)", in *Nord-Süd-aktuell*, vol. 2: 312–314.

—— (2000) "Die Bestimmungen des WTO-TRIPs-Abkommens und die Optionen zur Umsetzung des Art. 27.3(b): Patente, Sortenschutz, Sui Generis", *Studie im Auftrag der GTZ*, www2.wto-runde.de/uploads/GTZ-TRIPS-Studie.pdf

—— (2003) "Der Internationale Saatgutvertrag der FAO – ein Ansatz zur Sicherung des nachhaltigen Umgangs mit pflanzengenetischen Ressourcen?", in *BUKO-Agrarinfo*, vol. 120.

Seiler, A. and Dutfield, G. (2001) "Regulating Access and Benefit Sharing, Basic issues, legal instruments, policy proposals", BfN-Skripten, 46, Bonn: Bundesamt für Naturschutz, www.bfn.de/fileadmin/MDB/documents/access.pdf

SEMARNAT (2002a) "Access to Genetic Resources and Fair and Equitable Sharing of Benefits: Building a Common Agenda", paper presented at the *First Meeting of Like-Minded Megadiverse Countries*, February, Mexico, www.megadiverse.org/armado_ingles/PDF/five/five1.pdf

—— (2002b) "Programa estratégico para conservar los ecosistemas y su biodiversidad", Mexico City: Semarnat, www.semarnat.gob.mx/programas/documentos/index.shtml

SEMARNAT/INE (2002) "Programa estratégico para detener y revertir la pérdida del capital natural", Mexico City: Semarnat www.semarnat.gob.mx/programas/documentos/index.shtml

Shaiken, H. (1994) "Advanced Manufacturing and Mexico: A New International Division of Labor?", in *Latin America Research Review*, vol. 29, 2: 39–71.

Sharma, D. (2005) "Selling Biodiversity, Benefit sharing is a dead concept", in Burrows, B. (ed.) *The Catch, Perspectives in Benefit Sharing*, Edmonds: The Edmonds Institute.

Shaw, M. (2000) *Theory of the Global State, Globality as an Unfinished Revolution*, Cambridge: Cambridge University Press.

Shiva, V. (2005) "Bioprospecting as sophisticated biopiracy", in Burrows, B. (ed.) *The Catch, Perspectives in Benefit Sharing*, Edmonds: The Edmonds Institute.

Siebenhüner, B. and Suplie, J. (2005) "Implementing the Access and Benefit Sharing Provisions of the CBD: A Case for Institutional Learning", in *Ecological Economics*, vol. 53: 507–522.

Siebenhüner, B., Dedeurwaerdere, T. and Brousseau, E. (2005) "Introduction and overview to the special issue on biodiversity conservation, access and benefit-sharing and traditional knowledge", in *Ecological Economics*, vol. 53, 4: 439–444.

Smith, N. (1984) *Uneven Development: Nature, Capital and the production of Space*, Oxford: Blackwell Publishing.

—— (1995) "Remaking Scale: Competition and Cooperation in Prenational and Postnational Europe", in Eskelinen, H. and Snickars, F. (eds) *Competetive European Peripheries*, Berlin: Springer.

Soberón, J. (2001) *Corredor Biológico Mesoamericano-México*, Mexico City: Semarnat, www.semarnat.gob.mx/programas/documentos/index.shtml

South Bulletin (2002) *Agendas on Patents*, 48, 15 December, www.southcentre.org/info/southbulletin/bulletin48/bulletin48.pdf

Stehr, N. (1994) *Arbeit, Eigentum und Wissen, Zur Theorie von Wissensgesellschaften*, Frankfurt/M.: Suhrkamp.

Stilwell, M. (2001) "Review of Article 27.3(b)", paper prepared under the *CIEL/South Centre joint project*, Geneva, www.ciel.org/Publications/Article273b_Review.pdf

Stoll, P. (1999) "Werte der Vielfalt aus rechtlicher Sicht", in Görg, C., Hertler, C., Schramm, E. and Weingarten, M. (eds) *Zugänge zur Biodiversität*, Marburg: Metropolis.

Svarstad, H. (1994) "National sovereignty and genetic resources", in Sánchez, V. and Juma, C. (eds) *Biodiplomacy, Genetic Resources and International Relations*, Nairobi: ACT Press.

Swanson, T. (1997) *Global Action for Biodiversity: an international framework for implementing the convention on biological diversity*, London: Earthscan.

Swyngedouw, E. (1997) "Neither Global Nor Local, 'Glocalization' and the Politics of Scale", in Cox, K. (ed.) *Spaces of Globalization, Reasserting the Power of the Local*, New York: Guilford Press.

—— (2004) "Social Power and the Urbanization of Water, Flows of Power", Oxford: Oxford University Press.

—— (2005) "Dispossessing H₂O: The Contested Terrain of Water Privatization", in *Capitalism Nature Socialism*, vol. 16, 1: 1–18.

Taba, S. (ed.) (1995) *Current Activities of CIMMYT Maize Germplasm Bank*, Mexico City: CIMMYT.

Takacs, D. (1996) "The idea of biodiversity. Philosophies of paradise", Baltimore, MD: John Hopkins University Press.

Teichman, J. A. (1995) "Privatization and Political Change in Mexico", Pittsburgh, PA: University of Pittsburgh Press.

—— (2002) "Private sector power and market reform: exploring the domestic origins of Argentina's meltdown and Mexico's policy failures", in *Third World Quarterly*, vol. 23, 3: 491–512.

ten Kate, K. and Laird, S. A. (1999) "The Commercial Use of Biodiversity", London: Earthscan.

Thomas, U. P. (2002) "The CBD, the WTO and the FAO: The Emergence of Phytogenetic Governance", in Le Prestre, P. G. (ed.) *Governing Global Biodiversity, The evolution and implementation of the Convention on Biological Diversity*, Aldershot: Ashgate.

Toke, D. (2001) "Ecological Modernisation: A Reformist Review", in *New Political Economy*, vol. 6, 2: 279–281.

Toledo, V. M. (2000) "La Paz en Chiapas, Ecología, luchas indígenas y modernidad alternativa", Mexico City: Quinto Sol and UNAM.

Toledo Ocampo, A. (1998) "Hacia una economía política de la biodiversidad", in *Chiapas*, vol. 6: 7–40, www.ezln.org/revistachiapas/No6/ch6toledo.html

Touraine, A. (1972) *Die postindustrielle Gesellschaft*, Frankfurt/M.: Suhrkamp.

Trommetter, M. (2005) "Biodiversity and international stakes: A question of access", in *Ecological Economics*, vol. 53, 4: 573–583.

Tuxill, J. (1999) "Nature's Cornucopia: Our Stake in Plant Diversity", *Worldwatch Paper*, 148, Washington DC: Worldwatch Institute.

Tvedt, M. W. (2005) "How Will a Substantive Patent Law Treaty Affect the Public Domain for Genetic Resources and Biological Material?", in *The Journal of World Intellectual Property*, vol. 8, 3: 311–344, www.fni.no/doc&pdf/mwt-JWIP-2005.pdf

TWN – Third World Network (2004) *Launch of Geneva declaration on future of WIPO and joint NGO statement supporting a development agenda in WIPO*, www.twnside.org.sg/title2/twninfo163.htm

Underhill, G. R. D. (2000) "State, market, and global political economy: genealogy of an (inter?)discipline", in *International Affairs*, vol. 76, 4: 805–824.

Van der Pijl, K. (1999) *Transnational Classes and International Relations*, London: Routledge.

Velinga, M. (ed.) (1998) *The Changing Role of the State in Latin America*, Boulder, CO: Westview.

Wade, R. H. (2001) "The Rising Inequality of World Income Distribution", in *Finance and Development*, vol. 38, 4: 37–39.

Warnock, J. (1995) *The Other Mexico, The North American Triangle Completed*, Montréal: Black Rose Books.

WBGU (1999) "Welt im Wandel: Erhaltung und nachhaltige Nutzung der Biosphäre", *Wissenschaftlicher Beirat Globale Umweltveränderungen*, Jahresgutachten 1999, Berlin: Springer.

Weingarten, M. (1998) *Wissenschaftstheorie als Wissenschaftskritik: Beiträge zur kulturalistischen Wende in der Philosophie*, Bonn: Pahl-Rugenstein.

Wendt, A. (1999) *Social Theory of International Politics*, Cambridge: Cambridge University Press.

Wichterich, C. (2000) *The Globalized Woman: Reports from a Future of Inequality*, London: Zed Books.

Wiener, A. (2003) "Konstruktivistische Brückenstationen und ihre Zukunft", in Hellmann, G., Wolf, K. D. and Zürn, M. (eds) *Die neuen Internationalen Beziehungen, Forschungsstand und Perspektiven in Deutschland*, Baden-Baden: Nomos.

Wilson, E. O. (ed.) (1988) *Biodiversity*, Washington, DC: National Academy Press.

—— (1992) *The Diversity of Life*, New York: W.W. Norton.

Wingens, M. (1998) *Wissensgesellschaft und Industrialisierung der Wissenschaft*, Wiesbaden: Deutscher Universitäts-Verlag.

WIPO – World Intellectual Property Organization (2001) *Intergovernmental Committee on Intellectual Property and Genetic Resources, Traditional Knowledge and Folklore*, first session, Geneva, 30 April to 3 May, document prepared by the Secretariat, WIPO/GRTKF/IC/1/3, www.wipo.int/documents/en/meetings/2001/igc/doc/grtkfic1_3.doc

—— (2002) *WIPO Patent Agenda, Options for the Development of the International Patent System*, Memorandum of the Director General, A/37/6, www.wipo.int/eng/document/govbody/wo_gb_ab/doc/a37_6.doc

—— (2004) "Proposal by Argentina and Brazil for the establishment of a development agenda for WIPO", *WIPO general assembly*, 31st (15th Extraordinary) Session, Geneva, 27 September to 5 October, document prepared by the Secretariat, www.wipo.int/documents/en/document/govbody/wo_gb_ga/doc/wo_ga_31_11.doc

—— (2005) "Proposal by the United States of America for the Establishment of a Partnership Program in WIPO", *Inter-sessional Intergovernmental Meeting on a Development Agenda for WIPO*, 1st session, 11–13 April, document prepared by the Secretariat, www.wipo.int/edocs/mdocs/mdocs/en/iim_1/iim_1_2.doc

Wisner, R. N. (2005) "The Economics of Pharmaceutical Crops, Potential Benefits and Risks for Farmers and Rural Communities", *Union of Concerned Scientists*, Cambridge: UCS Publications, www.agmrc.org/NR/rdonlyres/AFC20F70-ADEA-48D8-A367-CCFD72ACBD41/0/economicspharmacrops.pdf

Wissen, M. (2000) "Die Transformation des regionalen Staates. Diskurse und Institutionen regionaler Entwicklung im Wandel", in *Das Argument*, vol. 236: 374–386.

—— (2007) "Politics of Scale, Multi-Level Governance aus der Perspektive kritischer (Raum-)Theorien", in Brunnengräber, A. and Walk, H.(eds) (2007) *Multi-Level-Governance. Klima-, Umwelt- und Sozialpolitik in einer interdependenten Welt*, Baden Baden: Nomos.

World Bank (2000) "Project Appraisal Document on a Proposed Grant from the Global Environmental Facility Trust Fund (...) for a Mexico Mesoamerican Biological Corridor Project", *Project-ID MX-GE-60908*, Washington, DC, www.conabio.gob.mx/institucion/corredor/doctos/PAD-ingles.PDF

WTO (1999a) *Preparations for the 1999 Ministerial Conference, The TRIPS Agreement. Communication from Kenya on behalf of the African Group*, WT/GC/W/302 http://docsonline.wto.org

—— (1999b) "Review of the Provisions of Article 27.3(b), Communication from the United States", IP/C/W/162, http://docsonline.wto.org

—— (2000a) "Review of Article 27.3(b), Communication from Brazil", IP/C/W/228, http://docsonline.wto.org

—— (2000b) "Review of the Provisions of Article 27.3(b), Further Views from the United States", IP/C/W/209, http://docsonline.wto.org

—— (2000c) "Review of Article 27.3(b), Communication from Brazil", IP/C/W/228, http://docsonline.wto.org

—— (2001) "Review of the Provisions of Article 27.3(b) of the TRIPS Agreement, Communication from the European Communities and their member States", IP/C/W/254, http://docsonline.wto.org

—— (2002a) "Review of the Provisions of Article 27.3(b), Summary of Issues and Points Made", Note by the Secretariat, WTO IP/C/W/369, http://docsonline.wto.org

—— (2002b) "Communication from the European Communities and their Member States, The Review of Article 27.3(b) of the TRIPS Agreement, and the Relationship between the TRIPS Agreement and the Convention on Biological Diversity (CBD) and the Protection of Traditional Knowledge and Folklore", A Concept Paper, IP/C/W/383, http://docsonline.wto.org

—— (2003) *Annual Report*, Geneva: WTO.

—— (2006a) *Council for Trade-Related Aspects of Intellectual Property Rights, the Relationship between the TRIPS Agreement and the Convention on Biological Diversity, Summary of Issues Raised and Points Made*, Note by the Secretariat, IP/C/W/368/Rev.1, http://docsonline.wto.org

—— (2006b) *Council for Trade-Related Aspects of Intellectual Property Rights, Review of the Provisions of Article 27.3 (b), Summary of Issues Raised and Points Made*, Note by the Secretariat, IP/C/W/369/Rev.1, http://docsonline.wto.org

—— (2006c) *Council for Trade-Related Aspects of Intellectual Property Rights, Article 27.3 (b), Relationship between the TRIPS Agreement and the CBD, and the Protection of Traditional Knowledge and Folklore*, IP/C/W/469, http://docsonline.wto.org

—— (2006d) *General Council, Trade Negotiations Committee, Doha Work Programme – The Outstanding Implementation issue on the Relationship between the TRIPS Agreemnet and the Convention on Biological Diversity*, WT/GC/W/564/Rev.1, http://docsonline.wto.org

—— (2006e) *General Council, Trade Negotiations Committee, Council for Trade-Related Aspects of Intellectual Property Rights, The Relationship between the TRIPS Agreement, the Convention on Biological Diversity and the Protection of Traditional Knowledge Amending the TRIPS Agreement to Introduce an Obligation to Disclose the Origin of Genetic Resources and Traditional Knowledge in Patent Applications*, WT/GC/W/566, http://docsonline.wto.org

—— (2006f) *World Trade Report 2006*, Geneva: WTO, www.wto.org

Wullweber, J. (2004) *Das grüne Gold der Gene. Globale Konflikte und Biopiraterie*, Münster: Westfälisches Dampfboot.

Young, O. R. (2002) *The Institutional Dimensions of Environmental Change: Fit, Interplay, Scale*, Cambridge, MA: MIT Press.

Yúnez-Naude, A. and Barceinas, F. (2004) "El TLCAN a la agricultura mexicana", in Casares, E. S. and Sobarzo, H. (eds) *Diez años del TLCAN en México, Una perspectiva analítica*, Mexico City: Fondo de Cultura Económica.

Zedan, H. (2005) *Statement by the Executive Secretary of the CBD to the Meeting of the Ad Hoc Open-ended Working Group on the Review of Implementation of the Convention*, Montreal, 5–9 September.

Interviews

Interviews at COP 5 in Nairobi in May 2000

CBD/1:   IPGRI
CBD/2:   SEARICE, Philippine NGO
CBD/3:   IUCN Law Centre
CBD/4:   Swiss Government
CBD/5:   OECD
CBD/6:   PRONATURA, Mexican NGO
CBD/7:   Third World Network, international NGO
CBD/8:   Indigenous Australian Peoples
CBD/9:   Japanese Government
CBD/10: Japanese Biotechnology-association
CBD/11: Kalpavriksh, Indian NGO
CBD/12: member of the Peruvian delegation
CBD/13: private company Novartis
CBD/14: FAO CGIAR
CBD/15: World Resources Institute (WRI)
CBD/16: member of the Malaysian delegation
CBD/17: ECOROPA, European NGO
CBD/18: CBD Secretariat
CBD/19: EU Commission
CBD/20: member of the Ethiopian delegation
CBD/21: RAFI / ETC Group, international NGO
CBD/22: member of the German delegation
CBD/23: member of the Brazil delegation
CBD/24: Indigenous Biodiversity Information Network (IBIN)

Working Group on Access and Benefit Sharing, October 2001, Bonn

CBD/25: Representative of indigenous peoples from Costa Rica
CBD/26: Representative of indigenous peoples from Argentina

Extra

CBD/27   Expert interview German Environment Ministry, Bonn, Mai 2001

Interviews at the 6th Extraordinary Session der CGRFA in June 2001 in Rome

FAO/1   GRAIN, international NGO
FAO/2   ASSINSEL, international plant breeder association (2 persons)
FAO/3   WIPO, World Property Organisation
FAO/4   BIO, international lobby alliance of the biotech-industry
FAO/5   IPGRI/FAO
FAO/6   Greenpeace, international NGO
FAO/7   ITDG, English NGO

Interviews in Mexico

Mexico-City, January 2001:
Mx/1:   Mexican Biodiversity Commission (CONABIO)
Mx/2:   Greenpeace Mexico
Mx/3:   Councelor of CONABIO
Mx/4:   Scientist at the National Ecological Institute
Mx/5:   Councelor of the Commission on Environment and Resources of Mexican House of Representatives
Mx/6:   Ministry of Ariculture
Mx/7:   AgroBio, Association of Mexican Biotechnological Industry
Mx/8:   Lawyer close to Mexican Ministry of Environment
Mx/9:   Think Tank of independent Farmers Organisation CECCAM

San Cristóbal de las Casas, Chiapas, January 2001

Mx/10:   independent NGO CIEPAC, close to Zapatistas
Mx/11:   Research Cenre ECOSUR
Mx/12:   Conservationist NGO PRONATURA
Mx/13:   international NGO Global Exchange
Mx/14:   Instituto de Historia Natural, in fact Ministry of Environment in Chiapas

Different Places in Mexico, February 2001

Mx/15:   International Agricultural Research Centre CIMMYT (near Mexico City)
Mx/16:   WWF Mexico
Mx/17:   NGO DASSUR, Xalapa, Bundesstaat Veracruz
Mx/18:   SEMARNAT, Dept. Of International Relations, Mexico City
Mx/19:   Member of a NAFTA Commission on Environment
Mx/20:   Member of the Group of Biodiversity Experts in Mexico BIODEM, Expert in IPR
Mx/21   RAFI, Office in Mexico City
Mx/22   Member of the Group of Biodiversity Experts in Mexico BIODEM, Expert in access to genetic resources

Index

eBooks – at www.eBookstore.tandf.co.uk

A library at your fingertips!

eBooks are electronic versions of printed books. You can store them on your PC/laptop or browse them online.

They have advantages for anyone needing rapid access to a wide variety of published, copyright information.

eBooks can help your research by enabling you to bookmark chapters, annotate text and use instant searches to find specific words or phrases. Several eBook files would fit on even a small laptop or PDA.

NEW: Save money by eSubscribing: cheap, online access to any eBook for as long as you need it.

Annual subscription packages

We now offer special low-cost bulk subscriptions to packages of eBooks in certain subject areas. These are available to libraries or to individuals.

For more information please contact webmaster.ebooks@tandf.co.uk

We're continually developing the eBook concept, so keep up to date by visiting the website.

www.eBookstore.tandf.co.uk